Self-Regulated Learning and Academic Achievement

Theoretical Perspectives

Self-Regulated Learning and Academic Achievement

Theoretical Perspectives

Second Edition

Edited by

Barry J. Zimmerman

Dale H. Schunk

LEA LAWRENCE ERLBAUM ASSOCIATES, PUBLISHERS
2001 Mahwah, New Jersey   London

Lawrence Erlbaum Associates, Inc., Publishers
10 Industrial Avenue
Mahwah, NJ 07430

Cover design by Kathryn Houghtaling Lacey

Library of Congress Cataloging-in-Publication Data

Self-regulated learning and academic achievement : theoretical perspectives / edited by
Barry J. Zimmerman, Dale H. Schunk.—2nd ed.
    p.   cm.
   Includes bibliographical references and index.
   ISBN 0-8058-3560-1 (alk. paper) — ISBN 0-8058-3561-X (pbk. : alk. paper)
    1. Motivation in education.   2. Academic achievement.   3. Self-control.
 I. Zimmerman, Barry J.   II. Schunk, Dale H.

  LB1065 .S46   2001
  370.15′4—dc21

                                    00-065403

Printed in the United States of America
10 9 8 7 6 5 4 3 2

Contents

Preface

There are nearly 1,000 self-hyphenated words in the English language (English & English, 1958) that describe how individuals react to and seek to control their own physical, behavioral, and psychological qualities. People are clearly fascinated with understanding and regulating themselves—a characteristic that many philosophers, theologians, and psychologists believe most distinguishes humans as a species. Recently, the search for self-understanding and self-regulation has turned to learning and academic achievement processes. As an organizing concept, self-regulated learning describes how learners control their thoughts, feelings, and actions in order to achieve academically.

The label *self-regulated learning* (SRL) may strike some readers as an oxymoron. By definition, doesn't the word *regulation* refer to keeping something regular in the face of changing conditions and doesn't the term *learning* refer to relatively stable changes in performance produced by experience? In fact, SRL seeks to explain how people improve their performance using a systematic or regular method of learning. Instead of focusing on sustaining the status quo, self-regulated learning researchers seek to understand how learners adapt to dynamic contexts by constantly enhancing their skill. We live in societies where changes in human contexts are occurring at the fastest rate in history. Individuals as well as communities must change quickly in the face of rapid technological advances. The viability of even long-standing professions can change dramatically, such as when computers and voice mail began to replace secretaries during the last decade. The half-life of a particular computer program and the skill to use it is now discussed in months rather than years. To avoid obsolescence and unemployment, workers at all levels of society must become effective life-long learners. This volume presents a comprehensive description of the major theoretical perspectives that are guiding research on how students become self-regulated learners. Because of the importance of this topic, researchers from widely divergent theoretical perspectives have been drawn to the issue of how students acquire the capability to self-regulate their learning, and these perspectives are described and compared in the chapters that follow.

This book is organized to facilitate comparisons among these theories. First, we asked the authors to plan their chapters according to a common guideline so their chapters would be integrated series of accounts rather than a collection of disparate accounts. This common format gave cohesiveness to the book, making it appropriate as a text for graduate and advanced undergraduate students in such fields as education, psychology, and child and family development. Second, we wanted each chapter to focus not only on theory and research in self-regulated learning but also on instructional practice. Authors were asked to give specific examples of how teachers or parents might apply the theory to youngsters with self-regulation difficulties. Third, we wanted the text to be of value to a broad spectrum of readers. The contributors represent a diversity of theoretical traditions—operant, phenomenological, social cognitive, information processing, volitional, Vygotskian, and constructivist. By presenting such a range of view points, the common features of self-regulated learning approaches emerged clearly and distinctively.

Finally, we wanted a lively book that would be readable by an audience interested in the field of education but without necessarily having a background in self-regulated learning. The contributors were asked to address their chapters to such an audience, and we were delighted in the success they achieved: Not only were the chapters readily understandable and interesting, but they also laid out important new theoretical ground.

In closing, there are many people who deserve credit for making this book possible. First and foremost, we wish to express our gratitude to our contributors. Their conscientiousness and good spirit made our job as editors personally and professionally rewarding. Second, we would like to thank our wives, Diana and Caryl, for their patience and understanding. Finally, we would like to acknowledge our great debt to Albert Bandura, whose pioneering work in the field of self-regulation was our inspiration.

REFERENCES

English, H. B., & English, A. C. (1958). *A comprehensive dictionary of psychological and psychoanalytic terms*. New York: McKay.

Contributors

Phillip J. Belfiore, Mercyhurst College, Education Division, 501 W. 38th St., Erie, PA 16546. E-mail: belfiore@mercyhurst.edu

James P. Byrnes, College of Education, University of Maryland, College Park, MD 20748.

Lyn Corno, Box 25, Teachers College, Columbia University, New York, NY 10027. E-mail: lcorno@pipeline.com

Daniel T. Hickey, Dept. of Educational Psychology and Special Education, Georgia State University, Atlanta, GA 30303. E-mail: epedth @langate.gsu.edu

Jeffrey M. Hutchinson, G.E.C.A.C. Community Charter School, 641 East 22nd St., Erie, PA 16503.

F. Charles Mace, University of Wales, 43 College Road, Bangor, Gwnedd LL57 2DG, UK. E-mail: f.c.mace@bangor.ac.uk

Barbara L. McCombs, University of Denver Research Institute, 2050 E. Iliff Ave., Denver, CO 80014. E-mail: bmccombs@du.edu

Alison H. Paris, Combined Program in Education and Psychology, 1400 School of Education, University of Michigan, Ann Arbor, MI 48109. E-mail: ahp@umich.edu

Scott G. Paris, Department of Psychology, University of Michigan, Ann Arbor, MI 48109. E-mail: sparis@umich.edu

Mary McCaslin, College of Education, University of Arizona, Tucson, AZ 85721. E-mail: mccaslin@U.Arizona.edu

Dale H. Schunk, 1446 LAB Room 5108, School of Education, Purdue University, West Lafayette, IN 47907-1446. E-mail: dschunk@purdue.edu

Philip H. Winne, faculty of Education, Simon Fraser University, Burnaby, British Columbia V5A 1S6 CANADA. E-mail: winne@sfu.ca

Barry J. Zimmerman, Doctoral Program in Educational Psychology, Graduate School and University Center of the City University of New York, 365 Fifth Ave., New York, NY 10016-4309. E-mail: bzimmerman@gc.cuny.edu

Theories of Self-Regulated Learning and Academic Achievement: An Overview and Analysis

Barry J. Zimmerman
City University of New York

Theory and research on self-regulated academic learning emerged in the mid-1980s to address the question of how students become masters of their own learning processes. Neither a mental ability nor an academic performance skill, self-regulation refers instead to the self-directive *process* through which learners transform their mental abilities into task-related academic skills. This approach views learning as an activity that students do for themselves in a proactive way, rather than as a covert event that happens to them reactively as a result of teaching experiences. Self-regulated learning (SRL) theory and research are not limited to asocial forms of education, such as discovery learning, self-education through reading, studying, programmed instruction, or computer-assisted instruction, but can include social forms of learning such as modeling, guidance, and feedback from peers, coaches, and teachers. The key issue defining learning as self-regulated is not whether it is socially isolated, but rather whether the learner displays personal initiative, perseverance, and adaptive skill in pursuing it. In this initial chapter, I discuss self-regulation theories as a distinctive approach to academic learning and instruction historically and then identify their common features. Finally, I briefly introduce and compare seven prominent theoretical perspectives on self-regulated learning—operant, phenomenological, information processing, social cognitive, volitional, Vygotskian, and cognitive constructivist approaches—in terms of those common features. In the chapters that follow, each theoretical perspective is discussed at length

1

by prominent researchers who have used it to guide their research and instruction.

Contributors to this volume share a belief that students' perceptions of themselves as learners and their use of various processes to regulate their learning are critical factors in analyses of academic achievement (Zimmerman, 1986). This proactive view of learning is not only distinctive from previous models of learning and achievement, but it also has profound instructional implications for the way in which teachers plan their activities with students and for the manner in which schools are organized. A self-regulated learning perspective shifts the focus of educational analyses from student learning abilities and environments at school or home as fixed entities to students' personally initiated strategies designed to improve learning outcomes and environments.

THE EMERGENCE OF THEORIES
OF SELF-REGULATED LEARNING

In order to appreciate the unique qualities of SRL approaches to student achievement, a brief historical overview of several theoretical models that have guided previous efforts to reform American education is presented. Each of these prior efforts to improve American schools was guided by a distinctive view of the origins of students' learning and how instruction should be organized to optimize their achievement. These views grew out of public perceptions of emerging national goals at the time and shortcomings of the existing educational system in meeting those goals.

CHANGING VIEWS OF THE CAUSES OF STUDENT LEARNING
AND ACHIEVEMENT ABILITIES

During the post-World War II period, instruction in American schools was heavily influenced by mental ability conceptions of student functioning. Thurstone's (1938) development of the Primary Mental Abilities Test was widely hailed as providing the definitive factorial description of the full range of student abilities. Once properly tested, students could be classified and placed in optimal instructional settings such as reading groups in elementary school or achievement tracks in secondary schools. Teachers were asked to gear their curriculum to the ability level of each group of students they taught. Cronbach (1957) presented a formal analytic framework for determining the potential benefits of matching the right type of instruction to each student's ability or interest, which he termed an ATI formulation, an acronym for Aptitude (ability or attitude) by instructional Treatment Interaction. The label referred to Cronbach's suggested method for statistically analyzing the results, an analysis of variance model. This formulation prompted educational researchers to investigate scientifically many instructional innovations, such as matching instructional procedures to student ability groups. Although interest in this analysis of instructional effectiveness continues to the present, the research generated by ATI analyses has been generally considered to be disappointing (e.g., Bracht, 1970; Pressley & McCormick, 1995).

Environments

During the early 1960s, social environmental formulations of student learning and achievement rose to prominence. The zeitgeist for reform was fueled by Hunt's (1961) and Bloom's (1964) influential books on the importance of early experience on children's intellectual development and by Lyndon Johnson's War on Poverty. Educational reformers focused their attention on "disadvantages" in the intellectual environment of the home of poor children (e.g., Hess, 1970), and the disparity between this home environment and the curriculum and atmosphere of schools. Given evidence of lower self-esteem by lower class children (e.g., Rosenberg, 1965), humanistic psychologists and educators like Holt (1964), Rogers (1969), and Glasser (1969) proposed a variety of reforms designed to make school more relevant and less threatening to them. They recommended less reliance on grading for promotion, more flexible curricular requirements, more concern about students' social adjustment, and more efforts to involve the parents and families of students in the schools. Head Start was begun as an effort to ameliorate disadvantaged children's lack of exposure to the "hidden curriculum" provided by the home of middle-class youngsters, and the Follow Through Program (U.S. Office of Education, 1973) was developed soon after for children in the primary grades to capitalize on the intellectual gains expected from Head Start experiences. The instructional goal of this reform movement was to compensate for intellectual deficits and differences of disadvantaged children through the use of innovative teaching methods and curricula.

Standards

Declining measures of national achievement and disillusionment with the results of national efforts to eliminate the effects of poverty prompted a new wave of educational reform during the middle 1970s. The decline was widely attributed to declines in educational standards during the 1960s. These standards pertained to the number of courses required in the curricula of both high schools and colleges, the stringency of testing for school entrance, promotion, and graduation, and the qualifications for hiring teachers. A significant marker of this movement to improve the quality was the reestablishment of many basic core curriculum requirements at Harvard University (Fiske, 1976).

Many schools at all levels followed this "Back to Basics" lead and began to limit students' selection of electives. National boards were commissioned by the Carnegie Foundation and by the Secretary of Education to evaluate the quality of instruction in the United States. They published reports such as A Nation at Risk (National Commission on Excellence in Education, 1983) that were generally critical of the quality of teaching, curriculum requirements, and achievement standards. In addition, studies that compared the achievement of American students to those in other countries have revealed lower levels in the United States (Stevenson, Lee, & Stigler, 1986). These reports began a new wave of educational reform aimed at raising standards in all three areas at the state and local level, but concerns have already been raised about the effects of higher standards on increasing the dropout rate in schools, increasing the costs of hiring qualified teachers, and diminishing the vertical mobility of underprivileged youngsters whose language and culture are different from that of the middle class (e.g., Shanker, 1988).

Each of these educational reform movements rested on important assumptions about how students learn. The mental ability movement assumed that student mental functioning was broad in its impact on academic achievement and relatively stable despite changes in grade and age. It was the task of educators to tailor their instructional methods to this important characteristic of students. In contrast, the social environmental view assumed that students' background was relatively unchangeable. Minority children could not and should not be asked to shed their ethnic and cultural identities in order to learn in school. Instead, it was the task of teachers and school officials to make the children's instructional experiences adaptive to their unique needs. The instructional standards approach put the weight of responsibility on teachers and school officials for maintaining standards of quality. These educational reformers assumed that high standards in schools would ensure optimal teaching and student academic achievement.

Each of these reform movements was based on instructional theories that viewed students as playing primarily a reactive rather than a proactive role. That is, students were theorized not to initiate or substantially supplement experiences designed to educate themselves. Instead, emphasis was placed on the role of teachers and other educators to adapt instruction to each student based on his or her mental ability, sociocultural background, or achievement of educational standards. In contrast, SRL theories assume that students (a) can personally improve their ability to learn through selective use of metacognitive and motivational strategies; (b) can proactively select, structure, and even create advantageous learning environments; and (c) can play a significant role in choosing the form and amount of instruction they need. Theories of SRL seek to explain and describe how a particular learner will learn and achieve despite apparent limitations in mental ability (as traditionally assessed), social environmental background, or in quality of schooling. These theories also seek to explain and describe why a learner might fail to learn despite apparent advantages in mental ability, social environmental background, or quality of education.

DEFINING SELF-REGULATED LEARNING

Before turning to these theories, it is important to establish precisely what self-regulated learning is and how self-regulated learners can be identified. Students are self-regulated to the degree that they are metacognitively, motivationally, and behaviorally active participants in their own learning process (Zimmerman, 1986). These students self-generate thoughts, feelings, and actions to attain their learning goals. More precise definitions than these, however, tend to vary on the basis of a researcher's theoretical perspective. Most definitions require the purposive use of specific processes, strategies, or responses by students to improve their academic achievement. Scholars from cognitive orientations, such as constructivists, prefer definitions couched in terms of covert processes, whereas behaviorists prefer definitions in terms of overt responses. In all definitions, students are assumed to be aware of the potential usefulness of self-regulation processes in enhancing their academic achievement.

A second feature of most definitions of self-regulation is a self-oriented feedback loop during learning (Carver & Scheier, 1981; Zimmerman, 1989, 2000a). This loop refers to a cyclical process in which students monitor the effectiveness of their learning methods or strategies and respond to this feedback in a variety of ways ranging from covert changes in self-perception to overt changes in behavior, such as replacing one learning strategy with another. Researchers favoring phenomenological views depict this feedback loop in covert perceptional terms such as self-esteem, self-concepts, and self-actualization. (See McCombs' description in chapter 3, this volume.) In contrast, researchers holding operant views favor overt descriptions in terms of self-recording, self-reinforcement, and self-controlling actions (see discussions by Mace, Belfiore & Hutchinson in chapter 2, this volume.)

The third common feature of all definitions of self-regulated learning is a description of how and why students choose to use a particular self-regulated process, strategy, or response. Theorists differ greatly on this motivational dimension of self-regulated learning. Operant theorists argue that all SRL responses are ultimately under the control of external reward or punishment contingencies. Phenomenologists, on the other hand, view students as motivated primarily by a sense of self-esteem or self-concept. Theorists between these two poles favor such motives as achievement success, goal accomplishment, self-efficacy, and concept assimilation. The ability of self-regulation theories to explain student motivation as well as learning distinguishes them from other formulations and should make them particularly appealing to educators who must deal with many poorly motivated students.

A question of equal importance to viable definitions of self-regulated learning is why students do not self-regulate during all learning experiences. None of the theories of SRL presented in this volume describes self-regulated learning as merely a capacity or stage of development, although several assume that a developmental capacity underlies it. Instead, they assume that SRL involves temporally delimited processes, strategies, or responses that students must initiate and regulate proactively. Therefore, students often may not self-regulate during their learning when they could, and the proposed theories seek to explain this outcome as well as the reverse.

Each of the theories focuses attention on different factors for student failures to self-regulate when learning. Most formulations assume that very young children cannot self-regulate during learning in any formal way. Although both cognitive constructivists and Vygotskians assume that most children develop a capacity to self-regulate during the elementary school years, they differ in their belief about the initial cause of this incapacity (see discussion by Paris, Byrnes, & Paris, chapter 8, and by McCaslin & Hickey, chapter 7, in this volume). Constructivists of a Piagetian orientation assume young children's egocentrism is a critical factor limiting self-regulation, whereas Vygotskians stress the importance of young children's inability to use language covertly to guide functioning. Constructivists who favor Flavell's (1979) view tend to emphasize limitations in young children's metacognitive functioning as the primary factor for their incapacity to self-regulate during learning.

When children reach an age when SRL processes should have emerged developmentally, their failures to use these processes are attributed usually to one or more of three factors: Students may not believe that a known self-regulation process will work, is needed, or is preferable in a particular learning context; they may not believe that they can successfully execute an otherwise effective self-regulation response; or they may not be sufficiently desirous of a particular learning goal or outcome to be motivated to self-regulate.

Cognitively oriented theorists tend to stress the importance of students' perceptions of the usefulness of various strategies as the key factor in their willingness to use them. For example, research by Ghatala, Levin, Pressley, and Lodico (1985) showed that teaching primary school children to recognize the successfulness of using memory strategies (in addition to teaching the strategies themselves) helps to motivate these youngsters to use them.

Social cognitive theorists give special attention to the second explanation for student failures to use known self-regulation processes. They have studied the role of perceptions of self-efficacy in motivating students to use particular SRL strategies (Bandura, 1997; Zimmerman, 2000a). Schunk described evidence (Schunk, Hanson, & Cox, 1987) that even when students observe a self-regulated strategy demonstrated by a model, they may not be motivated to imitate if the model is perceived as dissimilar to them. (Schunk reviews research on self-efficacy in chapter 4, this volume.)

Finally, most theorists assume that student efforts to self-regulate their academic learning often require additional preparation time, vigilance, and effort. Unless the outcomes of these efforts are sufficiently attractive, students may not be motivated to self-regulate. For example, a study strategy of rewriting class lecture notes to emphasize a teacher's main themes and key words can be expected to improve students' understanding of the course material and future test scores. Whether the effort is worthwhile may depend on the importance of the test or perhaps the lateness of the evening! Theorists differ, however, over the type of outcomes they emphasize: Operant researchers tend to prefer extrinsic outcomes, whereas other researchers tend to prefer intrinsic ones such as self-perceived success or mastery. Phenomenological theories as well as some constructivist theories, such as Paris and colleagues (see chapter 8, this volume) emphasize cultivating students' formation of academic identities to enhance their motivation. Students who envision themselves in nonacademic terms, such as pranksters or jocks, often reject academic accomplishment as secondary or even as antithetical to their social reference group and personal goals (Steinberg, Dornbush, & Brown, 1996).

THEORIES OF SELF-REGULATED LEARNING

In seeking to explain what it means to become self-regulated metacognitively, motivationally, and behaviorally as a learner, there are five common underlying issues:

1. What *motivates* students to self-regulate during learning?
2. Through what process or procedure do students become self-reactive or *self-aware?*
3. What are the *key processes* or responses that self-regulated students use to attain their academic goals?
4. How does the *social and physical environment* affect student self-regulated learning?
5. How does a learner *acquire the capacity* to self-regulate when learning?

Each theory of self-regulated learning is discussed in terms of these five common issues next and a summary of this analysis is presented in Table 1.1.

OPERANT VIEWS OF SELF-REGULATED LEARNING

Following the environmentalist principles of B. F. Skinner and adapting his behavioral technology for personal use, operant researchers have produced one of the largest and most influential bodies of research on self-regulation. Their studies of self-recording, which began during the late 1960s, have been extended to a wide variety of areas of human functioning, such as smoking (McFall, 1970) and weight control (e.g., Stuart, 1967), as well as academic performance (e.g., Broden, Hall, & Mitts, 1971). Their preference for the use of single-subject research paradigms and time-series data was particularly suitable for use by individuals seeking greater self-regulation. Instructing people to self-record not only was a reasonable compromise with practicality (because it was often difficult to externally monitor adults across settings), but it also opened covert events to operant investigation and control. Initially termed *covert operants* or *coverants* by Homme (1965), private events were assumed to follow the same behavioral principles as public behavior. In support of these assumptions, operant researchers (e.g., Shapiro, 1984) revealed considerable "reactivity" by subjects who self-recorded and self-reinforced, although the interpretation of these effects remains controversial.

TABLE 1.1

A Comparison of Theoretical Views Regarding Common Issues in Self-Regulation of Learning

Theories	Common Issues in Self-Regulation of Learning				
	Motivation	Self-Awareness	Key Processes	Social and Physical Environment	Acquiring Capacity
Operant	Reinforcing stimuli are emphasized	Not recognized except for self-reactivity	Self-monitoring, Self-instruction, and Self-evaluation	Modeling and Reinforcement	Shaping behavior and fading adjunctive stimuli
Phenomenological	Self-actualization is emphasized	Emphasize role of self-concept	Self-worth and self-identity	Emphasize subjective perceptions of it	Development of the Self-System
Information Processing	Motivation is not emphasized historically	Cognitive self-monitoring	Storage and transformation of information	Not emphasized except when transformed to information	Increases in capacity of system to transform information
Social Cognitive	Self-efficacy, outcome expectations, and goals are emphasized	Self-observation and self-recording	Self-observation, self-judgment and self-reactions	Modeling and enactive mastery experiences	Increases through social learning at four successive levels
Volitional	It is a precondition to volition based on one's expectancy/values	Action controlled rather than state controlled	Strategies to control cognition, motivation, and emotions	Volitional strategies to control distracting environments	An acquired ability to use volitional control strategies
Vygotskian	Not emphasized historically except for social context effects	Consciousness of learning in the ZPD	Egocentric and inner speech	Adult dialogue mediates internalization of children's speech	Children acquire inner use of speech in a series of developmental levels
Constructivist	Resolution of cognitive conflict or a curiosity drive is emphasized	Metacognitive monitoring	Constructing schemas, strategies, or personal theories	Historically social conflict or discovery learning are stressed	Development constrains children's acquisition of self-regulatory processes

Motivation to Self-Regulate

The focus of this controversy is the question of the ultimate source of motivation during self-regulation. Operant theorists contend that a person's self-regulatory responses must be linked methodologically to external reinforcing stimuli. Self-regulation responses are thus viewed as "inter-response control" links (Bijou & Baer, 1961), which are chained together to achieve external reinforcement. Therefore, if self-reinforcement in the form of earned coffee breaks helps a student succeed on an important test, the breaks will be continued. However, should these self-administered coffee rewards fail to improve test performance, operant theorists assume that this form of self-reinforcement will be discontinued or "extinguished." In the view of Mace, Belfiore, and Hutchinson (this volume), self-reinforcers function as discriminative stimuli that guide further responding, rather than as reinforcing ends by themselves. When students self-regulate, they postpone immediate rewards in favor of alternative (and often greater) rewards (Ito & Nakamura, 1998). According to operant theorists, the decision to self-regulate depends on the relative size of the immediate and delayed rewards and the time interval between them.

Self-Awareness

Operant researchers emphasize the importance of self-monitoring or self-recording in becoming self-regulated as learners. These self-recordings can involve narrations, frequency counts, duration measures, time-sampling procedures, behavior ratings, behavioral traces, and archival records. Self-awareness per se is not generally discussed because it cannot be observed directly; however, these researchers are very interested in an important behavioral manifestation of self-awareness, namely, self-reactivity. Thus, it might be said that operant researchers use a behavioral–environmental method for stimulating self-awareness that involves a recording *action* that produces an environmental *stimulus*, a physical record. This process meets formal operant criteria of acceptance because it involves observable events.

Key Self-Regulation Processes

Mace and his colleagues (this volume) describe four major classes of self-regulated learning responses: self-monitoring, self-instruction, self-evaluation, and self-reinforcement. The importance of the self-monitoring has already been discussed. The interest in self-instruction by operant theorists can be traced back to Watson's (1924) hypothesis that thought is actually covert speech. Although few contemporary behaviorists contend that thinking requires laryngeal contractions, they have demonstrated that teaching self-instructions and accompanying nonverbal actions is an effective way of improving functioning in a wide variety of academic areas. Self-instructions can also be introduced as written stimuli for learners to follow.

Unlike other theorists, such as Vygotsky (1962) or Meichenbaum (1977), who viewed self-directed speech as a precursor to thinking, operant theorists view it in stimulus–response terms. Mace et al. (this volume) defines self-instructional statements as "discriminative stimuli that occasion specific behaviors or behavioral sequences that will lead to reinforcement" (p. 48). In their view, self-instructive statements are written or oral stimuli that guide responding in settings or situations where external reinforcers are weak or lacking. Often self-instructive statements explicitly indicate the appropriate responses and resulting consequences. Thus, operant theorists emphasize the stimulus qualities of self-instructive statements, rather than the verbal or covert response qualities.

The third self-regulative process, self-evaluation, requires individuals to compare some dimension of their behavior to that of a standard (Belfiore & Hornyak, 1998). These standards refer to both accuracy (e.g., number of steps completed correctly) and improvement of performance (e.g., rate, percentage, duration). Self-evaluations are expected to influence self-corrective responses such as modifying prior responses to make them more effective or modifying the standards if they are found to be insufficient or unnecessary. Self-evaluations are also the basis for self-administering rewards, which is the fourth and final self-regulative process. *Self-reinforcement* is argued to be a misnomer. Unlike cognitive behaviorists, Mace and his operant colleagues stress the need to externally reward self-reinforcing responses. These responses are not assumed to acquire true "self" sustaining value, but rather are believed to be sustained by immediate and/or delayed external contingencies, such as social surveillance or increased status. Therefore, operant researchers would require that teachers who allow their students to self-reinforce for completion of assignments should have a backup contingency for failures to adhere to stringent reward criteria.

Social and Physical Environment Effects

Of all the theorists about self-regulation, operant researchers are the most explicit about linkages between self-functioning and the immediate environment. Internal processes are defined in terms of their manifestation in overt behavior, and the functional relationship between such behavior and environment are the focus of the operant approach. This environmental linkage is very advantageous in developing effective instructional intervention procedures.

How Does a Learner Acquire a Capacity to Self-Regulate?

Operant theorists have devoted relatively little attention to developmental issues of self-regulation, but instead have emphasized the role of external factors in learning to self-regulate. The key instructional methods they have employed in their training are modeling, verbal tuition, and reinforcement. Initially, external cues and contingencies are imposed, and then self-regulation responses are gradually shaped. Finally, external cues are faded, and short-term reinforcers are thinned gradually. To operant theorists, the key factors leading to a capacity to regulate one's own learning are the presence of effective models of and external contingencies for self-regulative responses.

PHENOMENOLOGICAL VIEWS OF SELF-REGULATIVE LEARNING

Phenomenologists historically have emphasized the great importance of self-perceptions to human psychological functioning. These perceptions were assumed to be organized into a distinctive identity or self-concept that influenced all aspects of behavioral functioning including academic learning and achievement. Human experience was assumed to be filtered through a reactive self-system that could distort the incoming information either positively or negatively in accordance with one's self-concept. Academic errors could be reinterpreted as nascent signs of progress if one's academic self-concept is positive or accepted as signs of failure if one's self-image is negative. Events that diminish students' self-concept were assumed to also diminish their subsequent motivation to learn.

Although phenomenological approaches were quite successful in promoting many educational reforms during the 1960s, such as expanded curricular choices and decreased student testing, the heuristic quality of theory was criticized because of the assumptions of the subjectivity of measures and the monolithic nature of students' self-concepts (e.g., Mischel, 1968; Wylie, 1968). More recent scientific efforts avoided these restrictive assumptions, focusing instead on objective measures of domain-specific self-concepts, and found support for a self-system that is differentiated and hierarchically organized (e.g., Marsh & Shavelson, 1985). This has led to a resurgence of research and theory on self-related measures of academic functioning (e.g., Eccles, Wigfield, Harold, & Blumenthal, 1993; Harter, 1999; Marsh, 1990; and Stipek & Daniels, 1988).

Motivation to Self-Regulate

Phenomenologists assume that the ultimate source of motivation to self-regulate during learning is to enhance or actualize one's self-concept. According to McCombs (this volume), the basic role of the self during learning is to generate motivation to approach and persist in learning activities. This occurs through evaluations of the personal meaningfulness and relevance of learning activities relative to perceptions of one's competencies and goals.

McCombs suggests that self-system structures are divided into global and domain-specific forms. A global self-concept refers to learners' image of themselves as self-regulated learners, which is founded on the belief that they possess the necessary knowledge, skills, and abilities. It is assumed to transcend a single context and may have a futuristic quality of what one might become through learning (e.g., Higgins, 1987; Markus & Nurius, 1987). A domain-specific self-concept is defined as individuals' perceptions of their ability to direct and control their motivation, cognition, affect, and behavior in particular domains, as when learning mathematics, science, or English. These self-perceptions are assumed to determine how students will self-regulate when learning in that domain.

In McCombs's model (this volume), affective reactions play a key role in motivation. If self-perceptions are unfavorable, negative affect such as anxiety results and diminishes motivation. This affect is manifested in helplessness, avoidance, or withdrawal from the learning task and context. In contrast, if self-perceptions are favorable, a student displays not only confidence during learning, but intrinsic motivation. That is, he or she persists in learning even when the external context does not require it.

Self-Awareness

Unlike operant theorists, phenomenologists assume that self-awareness is an omnipresent condition of human psychological functioning. People do not have to be taught to be self-aware or self-reactive; they are so by the nature of their self-concept. However, phenomenologists do see personal defensiveness as a key factor that can inhibit or distort self-perceptions. Students who doubt their ability to learn become anxious and may avoid learning situations or develop elaborate rationalizations for potential failures. In support of this analysis, McCombs (this volume) cites evidence (Davis, Franzoi, & Markwiese, 1987) that high self-consciousness is related to a desire for self-knowledge and low self-consciousness is related to self-defense.

Educators can promote self-awareness by diminishing or possibly eliminating defensiveness. McCombs (this volume) recommends engaging students in self-monitoring and self-evaluation as ways of promoting greater realism, or what is described often as "knowing yourself." Specifically, she suggests that teachers might train students to keep track of what they are "thinking and feeling while learning" in order to increase their subjective awareness of their accomplishments.

Key Self-Regulation Processes

Historically, phenomenologists have stressed the importance of perceptions of self-worth and self-identity as key processes in psychological functioning. In her view of the self-system, McCombs (this volume) categorizes these as self-system structures, which in turn affect an extensive network of more specific self-regulation processes like self-evaluation, planning, goal setting, monitoring, processing, encoding, retrieval, and strategies.

She places particular emphasis on the role of self-evaluation in self-regulated learning. Self-evaluations are made of task requirements against personal needs for competence and control and against self-system structures. These self-evaluations eventually lead to students' use of other self-regulation processes, like planning and goal-setting, that, in reciprocal fashion, affect students' self-system structures and processing.

Social and Physical Environment Effects

Phenomenologists give less emphasis to the objective nature of the social and physical environment than they do to learners' subjective perception of it. McCombs (this volume) suggests a teacher can dispel youngsters' self-doubts by helping them see relevance in learning activities, countering negative self-evaluations of competence and control, and setting realistic learning goals. Similar to Rogers' (1951) client-centered therapy, her suggestions are *student centered* in the sense that teachers must judge the effectiveness of their activities on the basis of students' perceptions rather than external criteria. Also in accordance with phenomenological traditions, McCombs stresses the importance of teachers' encouragement in promoting student self-confidence in learning.

How Does a Learner Acquire a Capacity to Self-Regulate?

McCombs (this volume) views self-regulated learning as dependent on the development of underlying self-system processes. During the primary and middle school years, students' perceptions of academic competence become more differentiated. A global sense of self-esteem or self-worth is assumed to emerge around 8 years of age (Harter, 1987). Before this age, children fail to distinguish mood from interest and have trouble making self-judgments of ability (Nicholls & Miller, 1984). For students who are deficient in self-knowledge and self-regulatory processes, McCombs recommends interventions to strengthen self-system processes. Like other phenomenologists, McCombs takes an activist role in promoting students' self-regulated learning, and her focus is on directly improving self-perceptions as the key to enhancing overt performance.

INFORMATION PROCESSING VIEWS OF SELF-REGULATED LEARNING

Information processing (IP) theory grew out of efforts to develop electronic computers during the 1930s and guidance systems for weapons during World War II (see Winne, chapter 5, this volume). It has been used subsequently to describe and explain general aspects of human cognitive functioning as well as self-regulation across a wide range of endeavors. Cybernetic models sought to explain people's neural limitations as well as their mental adaptations in terms of specific hardware and software components, such as the size of their memory or their use of specific mnemonic strategies. These models sought to close the gap between "mind" and brain descriptions of cognitive functioning, and this enterprise attracted a wide range of scholars, including anthropologists, engineers, linguists, mathematicians, neurologists, philosophers, psychologists, and educators (Johnson-Laird, 1988). These scholars envisioned human mental functioning in terms of two basic types of mental components: memory stores and information processing. The basic unit of human functioning was defined as a symbol, which could be described in terms of bytes of information. This unit of knowledge could be applied to all sources of information, whether it was originally physiologic, semantic, ikonic, acoustic, or numeric in form. Bytes of information were programmed into the memory stores of computers for use during processing.

The basic unit of self-regulation was the recursive feedback loop, which was depicted by Miller, Galanter, and Pribram (1960) as a TOTE sequence (i.e., Test, Operate, Test, Exit). According to this formulation, inputted information is first tested against a predefined standard. If the match is insufficient, the input is operated on (i.e., symbolically transformed) and then is retested. This recursive cycle continues until the information meets the test standard, and at that point, it is exited in the form of output. This TOTE unit could be described as self-regulatory because it enabled the computer or person to adjust to changing input conditions. For example, a thermostat in a home "self"-regulates the heat of the building in terms of a preset level, such as 72°. When the thermometer registers less than 72°, the thermostat begins the heater and continues it until the thermometer reaches the preset level. At that point, the heater is shut off during exiting.

The source of self-regulation during recursive cycles to learn is "negative" feedback, indicating a discrepancy between one's performance and a test standard. This discrepancy is assumed to be noxious and to compel learners to reduce it. If the adaptations are successful (i.e., feedback is no longer negative), efforts to self-regulate cease. Carver and Scheier (1990) suggested that complex forms of self-regulatory functioning, such as writing, reflect the embedding of motoric control loops within more general cognitive control loops. These hierarchical control loops are composed of goals or standards and feedback bearing on those standards. For example, feedback from motoric enactment during writing provides input to a higher level in a hierarchy, such as construction of sentences. These sentence constructions in turn provide feedback to higher control loops, such as writing paragraphs. This hierarchical formulation was termed *control theory* by Powers (1998) and others.

Motivation to Self-Regulate

Historically, the role of motivation to self-regulate learning was given little attention by IP theorists, who focused instead on learners' knowledge states or methods of reasoning. After all, computers need no a priori motivation to perform (just electricity!) This shortcoming increasingly prompted IP theorists to add motivational components to their models. For example, self-efficacy beliefs have been added to control loops in order to deal with self-doubts or anxiety regarding one's capability to perform (Carver & Scheier, 1990). Winne (this volume) expands the list of personal beliefs to include four motivational variables in their model: outcome expectations, judgments of efficacy, attributions, and incentives or values. These "hot" forms of information are combined with "cold" forms to determine the utility of a particular self-regulatory plan or "script." Thus, motivational processes in contemporary IP models are envisioned as affectively laden information, such as personal awards, that is processed like other forms of information within recursive feedback loops.

Self-Awareness

From an IP perspective, cognitive self-monitoring plays a complex but critical role in self-regulation. Self-monitoring provides the window of awareness on one's functioning. Although self-consciousness can assist in making adaptations, it occupies mental capacity, and as a result, must be limited when seeking to attain optimal performance. IP theorists assume that when performances become highly automatized, learners can self-regulate without direct awareness at a motoric level, and this frees them to self-regulate at a higher level in a hierarchy of goals and feedback loops. When motoric subgoals are linked automatically to superordinate cognitive goals (as is consistently reported by experts), more proficient performance can be achieved.

Key Self-Regulation Processes

Three types of memories are utilized during self-regulation. Sensory buffer memories are very brief in duration and are sense-specific in their form (e.g., visual or auditory). Information is stored briefly for a second or two in these memories. Sensory buffer information that is subjected to focal attention shifts to short-term or working memory, which is limited in size but can last up to 20 seconds. Estimates of the size of working memory range from 3 to 7 bytes of information. If information is rehearsed repeatedly, it can be sustained in short-term memory. Information that is encoded or organized is shifted to long-term memory, where it is stored for indefinite periods of time. Failure to remember stored information is attributed to retrieval difficulties by IP theorists. Thus, students can regulate their memory of a fact or event by attending to it and by organizing it into a form that is readily retrievable.

Information in long-term memory is depicted as a network of nodes, chunks, or schemas that are connected by links. Students can increase their recall by *chunking* bits of information into larger units, which frees up their limited short-term memory for other aspects of the learning such as self-monitoring. An example of chunking is recalling of the names of the Great Lakes by using the acronym HOMES as a mnemonic. Students can also create *schemas*, which are generalized slots or categories, such as trees, cars, or birds, for sorting incoming information, such as pine trees, Buicks, and robins. *Strategies* and *tactics* are "if—then" rules for transforming information into more useable forms, such as the reductive memory strategy for converting a list of names into letters of a single word, as was illustrated by HOMES.

According to Winne (this volume), SRL involves a recursive cycle of control and monitoring processes that are used during four phases: perceiving the tasks, setting goals and plans, enacting studying tactics, and adapting the tactics. Control is increased through use of acquired studying tactics. Self-monitoring involves evaluation of outcomes in terms of a person's standards. These cognitive evaluations of matches and mismatches between a student's current outcomes and standards provides the impetus for learning, according to IP theory.

Social and Physical Environment Effects

IP theory historically has given little attention to social and environmental factors in self-regulation. From this perspective, the social and physical environment have little impact during self-regulation unless they are transformed into information that can be processed. If these influences are converted into specific information, they can be self-regulated through control cycles like other sources of information. Winne (this volume) includes social context as a task condition in his model because of evidence that the presence of others affects students' need to self-regulate their learning, such as studying next to a distracting peer. Winne also broke new ground among IP theorists by including self-recording as well as other methods of "off-loading" various aspects of information processing. The value of cognitive off-loading was studied by anthropologists and other situational cognition scholars and was found to occur widely in naturalistic settings, such as during cooking (Brown, Collins, & Duguid, 1989).

How Does a Learner Acquire a Capacity to Self-Regulate?

From an IP perspective, learning entails a permanent increase in the capacity of a person to process information and respond self-regulatively. Siegler and Richards (1983) suggested that students develop increasingly elaborate rule-governed systems for processing information with age and experience, and Winne (this volume) points out that such rule systems form the basis for self-regulation of learning. There are developmental differences in other self-regulatory components involved in IP, such as self-monitoring accuracy, self-evaluation effectiveness, and strategy use.

Winne and Stockley (1998) recommended using a computer-assisted learning system called STUDY to help students to increase or "bootstrap" their level of self-regulation during efforts to study. Specific menus were designed to provide cues, feedback, and supplementary information to students as they learn new instructional content matter. STUDY provides distinctive forms of assistance to students according to their phase of self-regulated learning. Ironically, this use of computers to teach humans to self-regulate their processing of information reverses the historical relationship in which humans initially programmed computers to self-regulate. The cybernetic pupil has now become the teacher!

SOCIAL COGNITIVE VIEWS OF SELF-REGULATED LEARNING

Bandura's social learning theory has guided extensive research on social factors in self-regulation (e.g., Bandura, Grusec, & Menlove, 1967; Bandura & Kupers, 1964). In the most recent version, now labeled as *social cognitive theory*, Bandura (1986) elaborated further his triadic account of human functioning, which focuses on the separate but interdependent contributions of personal, behavioral, and environmental influences. This theory, initially developed to explain modeling influences on human functioning, directs researchers to study bidirectional relationships between social and cognitive events.

In applying a triadic account to self-regulated learning, Schunk (chapter 4, this volume) argues that students' efforts to self-regulate during learning are not determined merely by personal processes, such as cognition or affect; these processes are assumed to be influenced by environmental and behavioral events in reciprocal fashion. For example, self-recording of recollections of dates when preparing for a history test influences both students' environment (i.e., it creates additional study materials) and their intrapersonal processes (i.e., failures may create anxiety). These outcomes are assumed in turn to influence subsequent self-recording and perhaps one's choice of memory strategies.

Motivation to Self-Regulate

In an initial version of his theory, Bandura (1971) emphasized that outcome expectations determined one's motivation. He argued that people are motivated by the consequences that they expect to receive for behaving, rather than by the actual rewards themselves. He distinguished this essentially cognitive position from that of operant theorists who favored treating consequences as environmental events. Although expected outcomes had explanatory advantages over actual outcomes (e.g., Baron, Kaufman, & Stauber, 1969; Kaufman, Baron, & Kopp, 1966), they could not explain easily a student's unwillingness to attempt tasks on which a model could succeed.

In 1977, Bandura postulated the existence of a second expectancy construct, which he termed *self-efficacy*. He reasoned that outcomes a model receives may not be personally sought if one views that model as more able than oneself. Bandura defined self-efficacy as the perceived ability to implement actions necessary to attain designated performance levels, and launched a program of research to establish their predictiveness of motivation, particularly in personally threatening or difficult circumstances. Bandura (1997), Schunk (1984), and Zimmerman (2000b) reviewed extensive research indicating that students' self-efficacy measures were related to their choice of tasks, persistence, effort expenditure, and skill acquisition.

Outcome and self-efficacy expectations provide learners with representations of future consequences, and these presentations help learners to set goals for themselves. Personal goals are not the source of self-motivation themselves, but rather serve as standards against which future performance is evaluated. Once learners make self-satisfaction contingent on goal attainment, they tend to persist until their performances match that standard. Thus, the motivation to self-regulate involves two cognitive sources: self-efficacy and outcome expectations and goals.

Self-Awareness

According to social cognitive theory, self-awareness involves one or more of a number of self-perceptive states, such as self-efficacy, that emerge from specific self-observation responses. Schunk (this volume) suggests that self-observation is most helpful when it focuses on the specific conditions under which learning occurs, like the time, place, and duration of performance.

Students' self-observations can be aided by self-recording using diaries, progress worksheets, or behavioral graphs (e.g., Zimmerman, 1989). Research (e.g., Shapiro, 1984) established that the regularity and proximity of self-recording are critical to the accuracy of self-observational responses. Ultimately, success in SRL is dependent on the accuracy of self-observation because this process provides the necessary information to guide subsequent efforts to self-regulate.

Key Self-Regulation Processes

Bandura (1986) identified three subprocesses in self-regulation: self-observation, self-judgment, and self-reaction. These subprocesses are not assumed to be mutually exclusive, but rather to interact with each other. Self-observations are assumed to prompt learners to self-evaluate, and these cognitive judgments, in turn, are assumed to lead to a variety of personal and behavioral self-reactions.

Self-judgments refer to comparisons of existing performance levels, as self-observed, with one's learning goals. The type of description that social cognitive theorists give to goal setting illustrates the distinctiveness of their triadic approach. Unlike less environmentally oriented cognitive approaches, social cognitive researchers devote particular attention to contextual properties of students' goals, such as their specificity, difficulty level, and proximity in time (Zimmerman, 1983). Unlike operant theorists, Schunk (this volume) gives weight to such personal factors as the importance of goals and performance attributions. Goals that are unimportant or outcomes that are not attributable to one's own ability or effort are unlikely to produce self-reactive effects.

Schunk (this volume) identifies two major classes of self-reactions, one personal and the other environmental. *Evaluative* motivators refer to personal feelings of satisfaction or dissatisfaction. *Tangible* motivators refer to self-administered stimuli or consequences, like work breaks, food, or new clothing, that are made contingent on task completion or success. Self-reactions also include reciprocal adjustments in self-observation or self-judgment. For example, students' success in learning may indicate that systematic record keeping is no longer needed or that achievement goals should be changed.

The interactive nature of self-regulatory processes is depicted according to a three-phase cyclical model involving forethought, performance, and self-reflection. Forethought processes, such as goal setting, set the stage for the performance phase, where strategies designed to attain the goals are deployed. Self-monitoring during performance produces feedback that is evaluated for progress and interpreted for meaning during the self-reflection phase. Self-reflections affect forethought goals regarding subsequent efforts to learn—completing the self-regulatory cycle. This cyclical model not only explains causal links among self-regulatory processes, but also evidence of cumulative effects of efforts to self-regulate, such as increasing self-efficacy and growing skill (Zimmerman & Kitsantas, 1997).

Social and Physical Environment Effects

Social cognitive theorists focused their program of research on relationships between such specific social processes as modeling or verbal persuasion and various self-regulation processes. In addition, environmental factors, such as the nature of the task and setting, were systematically studied. Modeling and enactive mastery experiences were shown to be particularly influential on students' perceptions of self-efficacy achievement. Coping models who overcome adversity to triumph can increase observers' sense of efficacy to the point that they might try it for themselves (Schunk, Hanson, & Cox, 1987). Personal enactive mastery experiences are believed to be most influential in determining self-efficacy perceptions. Schunk and Ertmer (2000) described a wide variety of explicit training procedures for various self-regulation processes, including self-verbalization, self-attributions, and proximal goal-setting.

How Does a Learner Acquire a Capacity to Self-Regulate?

Social cognitive theorists do not assume that self-regulation automatically develops as people get older, nor is it passively acquired during environmental interactions. Although specific learning is assumed to be needed to self-regulate, various subprocesses of SRL are affected by children's development. Schunk (this volume) cites a number of developmental changes that have been shown to affect self-regulation, such as age differences in ability to understand language, knowledge bases, and capacity to make social comparisons and ability attributions. Young children have trouble responding to complex instructions, comparing themselves accurately to others, and making ability attributions. He recommends that training in SRL should take into account developmental limitations of children.

Social cognitive researchers have described the development of self-regulatory competence in terms of four levels. At an *observation* level, students learn to distinguish the major features of a model's skill or strategy. A second or *emulative* level is attained when a learner's performance enactive approximates the general form of a model's skill or strategy. A third or *self-control* level of self-regulation occurs when students can perform a skill or strategy based on mental representations of a model's performance. At a *self-regulation* level, learners can adapt their skills and strategies systematically as personal and contextual conditions change. Thus, from a social cognitive perspective, a learner's acquisition and development of skill or strategy develops initially from social sources and shifts subsequently to self-sources in a series of levels.

VOLITIONAL VIEWS OF SELF-REGULATED LEARNING

Early theological and philosophical conceptions of volition focused on the importance of human will power. For example, St. Augustine viewed the will as the key human faculty: "We are nothing but wills. Will permeates many other psychological activities. Even before sensation, there is an intention, a form of will" (Watson, 1963). Descartes argued that the will played a key role linking thought and action: Will was believed to direct action (Watson, 1963).

Although the will was derived initially from theological assumptions of divinely endowed Free Will, it was envisioned as a distinct faculty by the Wurzburg School in Germany, which was interested in the psychology of human acts. According to this view, people's wills were assumed to be manifested in their intentions to act. Ach, a prominent member of the Wurzburg group, perfected a structured introspection methodology for studying the intentional nature of experience and offered a detailed account of volition that focused the role of selective attention (Misiak & Sexton, 1966).

Ach's theory was challenged subsequently by Lewin (1926), who questioned whether intentions could be distinguished from needs. By equating intentions and needs, Lewin was able to explain volition within a classic motivational theoretical framework without additional assumptions. However, recent research on learned helplessness (Seligman, 1975) convinced Kuhl (1984), a contemporary German theorist, that volition is distinct from motivation. He contended that motivated subjects can become distracted by task-irrelevant thoughts. Volitional processes, which Kuhl discussed primarily in terms of an action orientation, are assumed to guide action under demanding performance circumstances. Corno (chapter 6, this volume) prefers to discuss volition in terms of overt and covert processes of self-control.

Motivation to Self-Regulate

The issue of motivation is a complex one that must be considered at several levels. At the most general level, volition theorists assume the existence of a covert psychological force or forces that control action. At a more specific level, Kuhl (1984) assumed that people's motivation to self-regulate is determined by their value and expectancy for achieving a particular goal. In his view, these motivational processes are distinctive from volitional processes. Corno (this volume) suggests that, motivational processes mediate the formation of decisions and *promote* decisions, whereas volitional processes mediate the enactment of those decisions and *protect* them. Therefore, learners' decisions to use volitional control strategies are prompted by perceptions of such impediments to their learning goals as distractions or competing-action tendencies. However, Corno cautions that although intentions to act are derivative of motivational factors, such as expectancies of success and outcome, volition escalates the intention to learn and steer involvement along. Volition theorists have used Caesar's crossing of the Rubicon River to a life-or-death battle as a metaphor for the distinction between motivation and volition: Once learners are sufficiently motivated to commit themselves to a particular task, volitional processes operate to sustain functioning.

Self-Awareness

Kuhl (1984) assumed that "a sufficiently high degree of awareness is a prerequisite for obtaining access to volitional strategies" and that "access to the full repertoire of volitional strategies is provided only if the current intention is a self-regulated one" (p. 127). Clearly, self-awareness played a key role in his account of volition. However, not all types of self-awareness are conducive to volitional control: Action-oriented cognitions enable the learner to screen out competing-action tendencies and remain focused on the current intention, whereas state-oriented cognitions are preoccupied with emotional states or feelings of doubt. Kuhl assumed that people can be classified on the basis of their dominant cognitive orientation, which he viewed as an ability-like characteristic, and he developed a scale to measure these two orientations.

Kuhl (1984) identified three types of state orientations that can interfere with action control: ruminating, extrinsic focus, and vacillating. *Ruminating* is the inability to screen out thoughts of prior failures; *extrinsic focus* is a preoccupation with future rather than immediate outcomes; *vacillating* results from insecurity when deciding courses of action. These thoughts can intrude between the formation of an intention and its expression in behavior. Corno (this volume) suggests that cognitive monitoring techniques can assist learners to resist these state-oriented cognitions, and Kuhl (1984) described specific attention-control strategies that can shift a learner's focus from self-states to task actions.

Key Self-Regulation Processes

Kuhl (1984) identified six volitional control strategies, which Corno (this volume) places in a larger framework. According to Corno's analysis, three of Kuhl's strategies—attention control, encoding control, and information processing control—can be subsumed under a generic category, control of cognition. Kuhl's incentive escalation strategy is viewed as a subvariety of motivation control. One remaining strategy, emotional control, rounds out Corno's superordinate category, labeled *covert processes of self-control*. Corno subsumes the remaining strategy, environmental control, in her category, overt processes of self-control.

This analysis reveals the highly metacognitive quality of volitional accounts of self-regulation: Only one of Kuhl's six categories was environmental in nature, and it is assumed to be controlled by metaprocesses.

Furthermore, volitional approaches are distinguished by their focus on strategies that affect learners' *intentions* (a cognitive construct) rather than their learning per se. For example, the use of such attention-control strategies as diverting one's eyes from off-task stimuli or tuning out excess noise preserves initial intentions to learn rather than to improve learning directly. Emotional-control strategies such as self-instructions to relax are assumed to sustain intention so that difficult parts of a task can be learned. Motivational control strategies involve boosting one's intent to learn by imagining positive or negative consequences of success or failure.

Social and Physical Environment Effects

In Corno's view (this volume), students' volition to learn can be increased by changes in the task itself or in the setting where the task is completed. These changes may involve such things as asking permission to move away from noisy peers, acquiring the use of aids such as a calculator, or surrounding oneself with hardworking or supportive peers, teachers, or parents.

Although volitional theorists recognize the impact of the environment on emotions and motivation, they view it as secondary to cognitive factors. For example, Kuhl (1984) argued that environmental control can be increased if mediation of action control is improved. In his three-factor model, Kuhl hypothesized that an unexpected failure (the key environmental event) instigates various volitional control processes. Failures are assumed to interrupt automaticity and to trigger self-awareness, a critical condition for volitional processes to occur. However, the environment does not determine the learners' assertiveness or helplessness per se (p. 113). Instead these reactions are assumed to be a product of the learners' volitional orientation (action versus state) and their outcome expectations. In contrast, Corno (this volume) explains these reactions in terms of self-control strategies.

How Does a Learner Acquire a Capacity to Self-Regulate?

Kuhl (1984) regarded a person's action-control or state-control orientation as the "ability to commit oneself to a non-dominant action tendency and to control the execution of this tendency in spite of the strong press of a dominant need" (p. 122). Describing and assessing one's action-control orientation as an "ability" rather than as a "process" implies a relatively low degree of malleability. However, both Kuhl and Corno have taken an activistic stance and have suggested various ways that volition might be increased: They have recommended training subjects to use the six volitional subprocesses involved in self-regulation that were described earlier. In her chapter (this volume), Corno identified students' use of various volitional control strategies in their comments during cooperative learning. Kuhl (1981) asked state-oriented subjects to test explicit hypotheses and concluded that these hypotheses prevented dysfunctional cognitions from impeding performance.

VYGOTSKIAN VIEWS OF SELF-REGULATED LEARNING

Researchers interested in the role of speech during self-regulation were attracted by the work of Vygotsky (see McCaslin & Hickey, chapter 7, present volume). The publication of a translation of his 1934 text *Thought and Speech* in 1962 brought this early Soviet psychologist to the attention of English-speaking developmental psychologists and educators. Their interest centered on two specific features emphasized in Vygotsky's theory: inner speech as a source of knowledge and self-control, and interactive dialogue between adults and children as a vehicle for conveying and internalizing linguistic skill.

A number of prominent psychologists incorporated Vygotsky's ideas in their work. For example, Meichenbaum (1977) developed a procedure for teaching *self-instruction* to children with various learning deficiencies that involved overt imitation of adult speech initially and then covert use of this speech without adult support. Bruner (1984) has used the concept of *ideational scaffolding* to describe an adult's efforts to provide additional structure during the early phases of learning a new concept or skill. Palincsar and Brown (1984) developed a procedure for teaching reading comprehension that was built around a Vygotskian notion of *reciprocal teaching in* which teachers switch roles with students in small groups as they acquire competence. McCaslin and Hickey (this volume) advance the notion of coconstuctivism as the essence of Vygotsky's approach to teaching and learning to capture the process of a mutually formed understanding of a contextually situated task. As these applications suggest, Vygotsky's theory is distinctive from other views of self-regulation presented in this volume by its emphasis on linguistically mediated social agents in children's development and in the functional role of inner speech.

Motivation to Self-Regulate

Vygotsky provided relatively little formal description of the specific processes that motivate learners to self-regulate. Although he distinguished task-involved and self-involved types of inner speech, he cautioned against assuming that each had separate effects on learning and motivation. By self-involved inner speech, he meant motivational and affective statements that are used to improve self-control. Task-involved inner speech referred to problem-solving strategic statements that are used to increase task control. In his view, both task-involved statements and self-involved statements can influence motivation.

Vygotsky was influenced also by the Marxist dialectical notion that the objective environment is a codeterminant of human functioning with human mental processes (see McCaslin & Hickey, present volume). He believed that the functional value of human knowledge acquired from social interactions in naturalistic contexts was self-evident, and this belief contributed to his unwillingness to rule out the effects of task-involved statements on human motivation. Mastery of the environment was viewed as an individual and collective goal, and self-directive speech enabled individuals to achieve this goal.

Self-Awareness

Vygotsky viewed awareness as a subarea of consciousness, which he viewed as the highest state of psychological functioning. He envisioned the basic unit of consciousness as word meaning (Gallimore & Tharp, 1990). Words evoke consciousness when their meaning is internalized, which occurs when children shift control of their performance from the speech of others to covert inner speech. This transition is facilitated by children's use of overt egocentric or self-directed speech to help them perform. According to Vygotsky, as word meaning becomes internalized, children are increasingly able to consciously guide, plan, and monitor their own activities (Diaz, Neal, & Amaya-Williams, 1990). Vygotsky (1978) suggested that once a skill is mastered to the point of automaticity, self-consciousness (i.e., intentional self-regulation) is no longer needed and can be detrimental to the smooth integration of task performance. However, Gallimore and Tharp (1990) cautioned that "for every individual, at any point in time, there will be a mix of other- regulation, self-regulation, and automatized processes" (p. 186), and thus self-awareness must be selectively focused on those aspects of a skill that are emerging in the zone of proximal development.

Key Self-Regulation Processes

A key process in self-regulation is egocentric speech, which Vygotsky (1962) defined in the following way: "The child talks only about himself, takes no interest in his interlocutor, does not try to communicate, expects no answers, and often does not even care whether anyone listens to him" (p. 15). Vygotsky viewed this egocentric speech as a transition from external to inner speech control. Inner speech and external speech were viewed by Vygotsky (1962, p. 131) as opposite ends of a bi-directional sociolinguistic process: External speech involves turning thought into words, whereas inner speech involves turning words into thoughts. When speech becomes internalized, self-direction is possible.

Social and Physical Environment Effects

Like other Marxists, Vygotsky emphasized the role of the social and physical environment on children's development. He believed that children develop within an influential sociohistorical context and that speech plays an essential role in their adaptation to and control of that context. A youngster's internalization of speech stemmed initially from social encounters, especially with adults, but once internalized, inner speech was assumed to have a dynamic of its own. Inner speech was envisioned as a tool that enables the learner to act on the physical and social reality of the immediate environment to produce newly adaptive levels of mental, physical, and social functioning. Thus, inner speech was a self-regulatory tool "for the solution of difficult tasks, to overcome impulsive action, to plan a solution to a problem prior to its execution, and to master their own behavior (Vygotsky, 1978, p. 28).

How Does a Learner Acquire a Capacity to Self-Regulate?

Vygotsky (1962) described the process of development of self-regulation in terms of internalization. He suggested that social interactions between children and adults provide the content for what is being internalized by the youngsters. At birth, human infants are controlled by the physical properties of sounds (a first signal system), but through repeated exposure to the word meanings of other persons, the words acquire meaning independent of their stimulus properties (i.e., a second signal system). Children's first step toward self-directed action occurs when they begin to use the means that adults have used to regulate them (primarily speech) in order to regulate themselves. Thus, self-regulation begins at an interpersonal level through contact with adults, and it is gradually internalized by children. Eventually, through the mediation of inner speech, children can exercise self-direction at an intrapersonal level.

COGNITIVE CONSTRUCTIVIST VIEWS
OF SELF-REGULATED LEARNING

The origins of this view are diverse; however, the work of two individuals is widely cited as seminal: Bartlett and Piaget. His research on adult memory for common stories led Bartlett (1932), a British psychologist, to the conclusion that the key underlying mnemonic process involved reconstructing cohesive accounts from underlying schemas and incoming contextual information—not merely recalling previously stored information. A *schema* refers to a plan, plot, or outline that specifies the relationship between a number of component ideas or concepts (English & English, 1958). Bartlett called attention to nonrandom errors over recall trials, which he felt revealed that learners tended to embellish or "sharpen" information associated with the plot of the stories and leave out or "level" information that was not. His account convinced many people that analyses of human memory needed to focus on learners' formation and use of schemas.

From his research on young children's intellectual development, a Swiss epistemologist, Piaget (1926, 1952), also concluded that children formed schemas during learning, even very young infants who are engaged in repetitive sensorimotor sucking of a rattle. Piaget credited children with forming schemas through twin processes called *assimilation* and *accommodation*. Assimilation refers to children's absorbing information, such as the sensory qualities of rattles, and accommodation refers to changes that were made in existing schemas (e.g., when a rattle of a new color was encountered). These schemas were not assumed to be static, but rather to undergo qualitative improvements in their structure and flexibility during development.

Both Bartlett and Piaget advanced the notion of a cognitive schema as the underlying basis for human learning and recall, and both ascribed a major role to logic and conceptual coherence in the formation of these schemas. In their view, human experience was formed into schemas, often in idiosyncratic fashion, and psychological analyses should focus on those constructions and that constructive process. Paris, Byrnes, and Paris (chapter 8, this volume) adopted the notion of a *theory* as the basis for constructive representation instead of a schema; nevertheless, they assume that students construct personal theories of learning in accordance with principles derived from the work of Bartlett, Piaget, and others. These constructivist views of cognitive functioning presume that learners play an active personal role during learning and recall, a view with a particular implication for self-regulation.

Motivation to Self-Regulate

Cognitive constructivists assume that a human motive to construct meaning from experience is inherently compelling. Paris, Byrnes, and Paris (this volume) assert this belief as a historical principle of constructivism: There is an intrinsic motivation to seek information. Piagetian scholars (e.g., Sigel, 1969) use the notion of *cognitive conflict* to convey their assumption that information that cannot be assimilated readily (because it conflicts with existing schemas) is noxious. Some theorists (e.g., Berlyne, 1960) see curiosity as a closely associated drive. In both cases, an unpleasant state forces learners to make cognitive accommodations in order to regain their cognitive *equilibrium.* However, there is a growing awareness that constructivist researchers may need to incorporate additional motivational constructs to explain SRL in naturalistic contexts. For example, Paris and colleagues (this volume) include a theory of agency and control in their constructivist theory in order to answer questions of motivation to self-regulate (see *Key Self-Regulation Processes* in the next section).

Self-Awareness

Self-awareness plays a central role in children's formation of schemas, according to Piagetian constructivists. Young children are unable to understand the motives and perspectives of others due to their egocentrism, and this limits the accuracy of their cognitive constructions (Piaget, 1932, 1970). Children's thinking does not become fully logical (i.e., operational) until the children can integrate their perceptions of themselves and the world with those of other people. The highest level of self-awareness related to self-regulation cannot occur until the child enters Piaget's ultimate period of development, formal operations. When this occurs, youth are aware of their own thoughts and can treat them as hypotheses to be tested. Flavell (1979) described this level of functioning, using the prefix *meta-* to convey the idea that human cognitive functioning becomes monitored and controlled at a higher cognitive level.

 Paris, Byrnes, and Paris (this volume) describe developmental changes in children's self-awareness in detail. They summarize research indicating that young children's perceptions of academic competence are unrealistically high when they enter school (Benenson & Dweck, 1986; Stipek, 1981), but decline during the late elementary and early junior high school grades (Eccles et al., 1983; Simmons, Blyth, Van Cleave, & Bush, 1979). These self-perceptions also become more domain-specific (Marsh, 1986) and more accurate, according to their teachers (Harter, 1982). Paris and colleagues (this volume) attribute these changes in self-awareness to developmental changes in cognitive functioning, such as an increased ability to differentiate between academic and social competence (Stipek & Tannatt, 1984) and between effort and ability (Nicholls, 1978), and to changes in social context of the school, such as normative feedback, grades, and social comparative information.

Paris and colleagues also emphasize the role of self-identities that students are trying to construct and the self-regulatory practices that exemplify those aspired identities. Self-schemas are constructed creatively and selectively from an individual's past experiences in a domain. Developmental changes in ideal self-representations occur during middle childhood when children shift from motivation by the goals and standards of others toward self-constructed idealized selves. However, the disparity between academic idealized selves and declining actual views of self often lead to students' loss of self-worth and frequent adoption of an alternative nonacademic identity, such as prankster, slacker, or jock. Whatever their form, students' identities gain recognition for them, and these identities motivate students to behave in specific ways that are consistent with them.

Key Self-Regulation Processes

According to Paris, Byrnes, and Paris (this volume), SRL is multifaceted. Students are hypothesized to construct theories to regulate four components of their learning: self-competence, agency and control, schooling and academic tasks, and strategies. The component of strategies is evident in most constructivist accounts of learning. *Strategies* refer to deliberate actions performed to attain particular goals, such as processing information as well as managing time, motivation, and emotions. Students' theory of strategies involves knowledge about what strategies are (i.e., declarative knowledge), how they are used (i.e., procedural knowledge), and when and why they should be used (i.e., conditional knowledge). The latter two forms of knowledge are often labeled as *metacognitive* by other theorists.

In a departure from classical constructivist traditions, which focused mainly on *competence*, Paris, Byrnes, and Paris (this volume) develop their multifaceted account to explain self-regulated *performance* as well. This goal is achieved by including component theories of self-competence, agency and control, and schooling and academic tasks as well as strategies. Students' theory of self-competence was hypothesized to involve perceptions of personal academic ability, and to answer the question, Can I self-regulate? Students' theory of agency and control focused on their interpretations of success and failure as well as their intentions and actions, and was hypothesized to answer the questions, Why should I self-regulate? or *How* much effort should I expend on this task? Finally, students' theory of schooling and academic tasks, which involved students' beliefs about key task properties such as variety, diversity, challenge, control, and meaningfulness, and their influence on the students' goal orientation, lead them to adopt either mastery goals or ego/performance goals and enable them to answer the question, *What* is needed to learn this task?

Social and Physical Environment Effects

Historically, Piagetian constructivists advocated instructional procedures that seek to increase cognitive conflict through use of discovery learning tasks (e.g., Smedslund, 1961) or social conflict learning groups (e.g., Murray, 1972). Discovery learning procedures involve presenting a learner with unexpected outcomes, such as seeing a metal blade bend when heated over a flame and then return to its original position as it cools. Social conflict, such as confronting students with different viewpoints or cognitive levels, was also expected to produce cognitive conflict necessary for constructive growth (Zimmerman & Blom, 1983).

Instead of adopting a cognitive conflict on constructivism, Paris, Byrnes, and Paris (this volume) adopt a situated cognition perspective (e.g., Brown, Collins, & Duguid, 1989) and suggest that students' conceptions of self and use of self-regulatory methods are adaptive to social and historical contexts, including the tools, values, and customs of local communities. Paris and colleagues refer to this as the *second wave of constructivism* because it rejects assumptions that constructivism could be explained at a solitary individualistic level. The constructs of discovery learning, cognitive conflict, and equilibration from "solo cognition" accounts have been largely replaced as mediating constructs with cooperative learning, personal theories, identities, and adaptive actions in Paris and colleagues' formulation.

How Does a Learner Acquire a Capacity to Self-Regulate?

Historically, constructivists emphasized changes in children's stage of cognitive development as essential to their increases in self-regulatory capacity to learn. Paris, Byrnes, and Paris (this volume) assume that there are significant developmental constraints on learning that affect students' theories of competence, agency and control, schooling and academic tasks, and strategy use. As mentioned earlier, there are significant declines in perceived self-competence with age and schooling. In addition, children's global sense of self-competence becomes organized hierarchically as they increasingly differentiate task-related features of competence, such as academics, social, and physical skills. Paris and colleagues also posit developmental changes in children's (a) understanding of the role of ability and effort in academic performance, (b) estimates of the amount of control that they can exert, (c) understanding of the nature of academic tasks, and (d) quality of the strategies they construct. These changes combine to produce developmental changes in children's theories of self. These emerging theories produce distinctive identities, which are hypothesized to greatly influence the direction of learning and use of self-regulatory methods.

CONCLUSION

The ultimate importance of the *individual* student in accounts of learning and achievement has been emphasized by American educators for many years. Unlike previous models that spurred educational reform, theories of self-regulation place their focus on *how* students activate, alter, and sustain specific learning practices in solitary as well as social settings, in informal as well as formal instructional contexts (Zimmerman, 1986). These theorists believe that learning is not something that happens to students; it is something that happens by students. They assume that, for learning to occur, students must become proactively engaged at both a covert and an overt level. Their research has evolved to the point where detailed theoretical accounts of SRL and academic development can now be offered and appreciated. In an era in which student self-regulation often seems alarmingly absent, theories that can offer direction as well as insight to educators into the processes of self-regulated learning may be of particular merit.

REFERENCES

Bandura, A. (1971). *Social learning theory.* New York: General Learning Press.

Bandura, A. (1977). Self-efficacy: Toward a unifying theory of behavioral change. *Psychological Review, 84,* 191–215.

Bandura, A. (1986). *Social foundations of thought and action: A social cognitive theory.* Englewood Cliffs, NJ: Prentice-Hall.

Bandura, A. (1997). *Self-efficacy: The exercise of control.* New York: W. H. Freeman and Company.

Bandura, A., Grusec, J. E., & Menlove, F. L. (1967). Some social determinants of self-monitoring reinforcement systems. *Journal of Personality and Social Psychology, 5,* 449–455.

Bandura, A., & Kupers, C. J. (1964). The transmission of patterns of self-reinforcement through modeling. *Journal of Abnormal and Social Psychology, 69,* 1–9.

Baron, A., Kaufman, A., & Stauber, K. A. (1969). Effects of instructions and reinforcement feedback on human operant behavior maintained by fixed-interval reinforcement. *Journal of Experimental Analysis of Behavior, 12,* 701–712.

Bartlett, F. C. (1932). *Remembering.* London: Cambridge University Press.

Belfiore, P. J., & Hornyak, R. S. (1998). Operant theory and application to self-monitoring in adolescents. In D. H. Schunk & B. J. Zimmerman (Eds.), *Self-regulated learning: From teaching to self-reflective practice* (pp. 184–202). New York: Guilford.

Benenson, J., & Dweck, C. (1986). The development of trait explanations and self-evaluations in the academic and social domains. *Child Development, 57,* 1179–1187.

Berlyne, D. (1960). *Conflict, arousal, and curiosity.* New York: McGraw-Hill.

Bijou, S. W., & Baer, D. M. (1961). *Child development: A systematic theory.* New York: Appleton-Century-Crofts.

Bloom, B. S. (1964). *Stability and change in human characteristics.* New York: Wiley.

Bracht, G. H. (1970). The relationship of treatment tasks, personalogical variables, and dependent variables to aptitude-treatment interaction. *Review of Educational Research, 40,* 627–745.

Broden, M., Hall, R. V., & Mitts, B. (1971). The effect of self-recording on the classroom behavior of two eighth-grade students. *Journal of Applied Behavior Analysis, 4,* 191–199.

Brown, J. S., Collins, A., & Duguid, P. (1989). Situated cognition and the culture of learning. *Educational Researcher, 18,* 32–42.

Carver, C. S., & Scheier, M. F. (1981). *Attention and self-regulation: A control theory approach to human behavior.* New York: Springer-Verlag.

Carver, C. S., & Scheier, M. F. (1990). Origins and functions of positive and negative affect: A control-process view. *Psychological Review, 97,* 19–35.

Cronbach, L. J. (1957). The two disciplines of scientific psychology. *American Psychologist, 12,* 671–684.

Davis, M. H., Franzoi, S. L., & Markwiese, B. (1987, August). *A motivational explanation of private self-consciousness.* Paper presented at the annual meeting of the American Psychological Association, New York.

Diaz, R. M., Neal, C. J., Amaya-Williams, M. (1990). The social origins of self-regulation. In L. C. Moll (Ed.), *Vygotsky and education: Instructional implications and applications of sociohistorical psychology* (pp. 127–154). New York: Cambridge University Press.

Eccles, J., Adler, T. F., Futterman, R., Goff, S. B., Kaczala, C., Meece, J. L., & Midgley, C. (1983). Expectations, values, and academic behaviors. In J. T. Spence (Ed.), *Teacher expectations.* Hillsdale, NJ: Lawrence Erlbaum Associates.

Eccles, J., Wigfield, A., Harold, R. D., & Blumenfeld, P. (1993). Age and gender differences in children's self and task perceptions during elementary school. *Child Development, 64,* 830–847.

English, H. B., & English, A. C. (1958). *A comprehensive dictionary of psychological and psychoanalytical terms.* New York: McKay.

Fiske, E. (1976, November 10). Harvard review drive for major overhaul in liberal arts. *New York Times,* p. B4.

Flavell, J. H. (1979). Metacognition and cognitive monitoring: A new era of cognitive developmental inquiry. *American Psychologist, 34,* 906–911.

Gallimore, R., & Tharp, R. (1990). Teaching mind in society: Teaching, schooling, and literate discourse. In L. C. Moll (Ed.), *Vygotsky and education: Instructional implications and applications of sociohistorical psychology* (pp. 175–205). New York: Cambridge University Press.

Ghatala, E. S., Levin, J. R., Pressley, M., & Lodico, M. G. (1985). Training cognitive strategy monitoring in children. *American Educational Research Journal, 22,* 199–215.

Glasser, W. L. (1969). *Schools without failure.* New York: Harper & Row.

Harter, S. (1982). The perceived competence scale for children. *Child Development, 53,* 87–97.

Harter, S. (1987). The determinants and mediational role of global self-worth in children. In N. Eisenberg (Ed.), *Contemporary topics in developmental psychology.* New York: Wiley.

Harter, S. (1999). *The construction of self: A developmental perspective.* New York: Guilford Press.

Hess, R. D. (1970). Social class and ethnic influences on socialization. In N. P. H. Mussen (Ed.), *Carmichael' manual of child psychology* (3rd ed., Vol. II, pp. 452–558). New York: Wiley.

Higgins, S. (1987). Self-discovery: A theory relating self and affect. *Psychological Review, 94,* 319–340.

Holt, J. (1964). *How children fail.* New York: Pitman.

Homme, L. E. (1965). Perspectives in psychology, XXIV: Control of coverants, operants of the mind. *Psychological Record, 15,* 501–511.

Hunt, J. McV. (1961). *Intelligence and experience.* New York: Ronald Press.

Ito, M., & Nakamura, K. (1998). Humans' choice in a self-control situation: Sensitivity to re-inforcer amount, reinforcer delay, and overall reinforcer density. *Journal of the Experimental Analysis of Behavior, 69,* 87–101.

Johnson-Laird, P. N. (1988). *The computer and the mind.* Cambridge, MA: Harvard University Press.

Kaufman, A., Baron, A., & Kopp, R. E. (1966). Some effects of instructions on human operant behavior. *Psychonomic Monograph Supplements, 1,* 243–250.

Kuhl, J. (1981). Motivational and functional helplessness: The moderating effect of state versus action orientation. *Journal of Personality and Social Psychology, 40,* 155–170.

Kuhl, J. (1984). Volitional aspects of achievement motivation and learned helplessness: Toward a comprehensive theory of action-control. In B. A. Maher (Ed.), *Progress in experimental personality research* (Vol. 13, pp. 99–171). New York: Academic Press.

Lewin, K. (1926). Untersuchungen zur Handlungs-und Affekt-psychologie. II. Vorsatz, Wille und Bedurfnis. [Investigation of action and affect psychology. II. Intention, will, and need]. *Psychologische Forschung, 7,* 330–385.

Markus, H., & Nurius, P. (1987). Possible selves: The interface between motivation and the self-concept. In K. Yardley & T. Honess (Eds.), *Self and identity: Psychosocial perspectives.* New York: Wiley.

Marsh, H. W. (1986). Verbal and math self-concepts: An internal external frame of reference model. *American Educational Research Journal, 23,* 129–149.

Marsh, H. W. (1990). The structure of academic self-concept: The Marsh/Shavelson model. *Journal of Educational Psychology, 82,* 623–636.

Marsh, H. W., & Shavelson, R. (1985). Self-concept: Its multifaceted, hierarchical structure. *Educational Psychologist, 20,* 107–123.

McFall, R. M. (1970). The effects of self-monitoring on normal smoking behavior. *Journal of Consulting and Clinical Psychology, 37,* 80–86.

Meichenbaum, D. H. (1977). *Cognitive behavior modification.* New York: Plenum.

Mischel, W. (1968). *Personality and its assessment.* New York: Wiley.

Miller, G. A., Galanter, E., & Pribram, K. (1960). *Plans and the structure of behavior.* New York: Holt, Rinehart and Winston.

Misiak, H., & Sexton, V. S. (1966). *History of psychology.* New York: Grune & Stratton.

Murray, F. B. (1972). The acquisition of conservation through social interaction. *Developmental Psychology, 6,* 1–6.

National Commission on Excellence in Education (1983). *A nation at risk: The imperative for educational reform.* Washington, DC: U.S. Government Printing Office.

Nicholls, J. G. (1978). The development of the concepts of effort and ability, perceptions of own attainment, and the understanding that difficult tasks require more ability. *Child Development, 49,* 800–814.

Nicholls, J. G., & Miller, A. I. (1984). The development of the concepts of effort and ability: The differentiation of the concept of ability. In J. G. Nicholls (Ed.), *The development of achievement motivation* (pp. 185–218). Greenwich, CT: JAI Press.

Palincsar, A. S., & Brown, A. (1984). Reciprocal teaching of comprehension-fostering and comprehension-monitoring activities. *Cognition and Instruction, 1,* 117–175.

Piaget, J. (1926). *Language and thought of the child.* London: Routledge & Kegan Paul.

Piaget, J. (1932). *The moral judgment of the child.* New York: Harcourt.

Piaget, J. (1952). *The origins of intelligence in children.* New York: International Universities Press.

Piaget, J. (1970). Piaget's theory. In P. H. Mussen (Ed.), *Carmichael's manual of child psychology* (3rd ed., Vol. 1, pp. 703–732). New York: Wiley.

Powers, W. T. (1998). *Making sense of behavior: The means of control.* New York: Benchmark Press.

Pressley, M. J. , & McCormick, C. (1995). *Advanced educational psychology for educators, researchers, and policymakers.* New York: Harper/Collins.

Rogers, C. R. (1951). *Client-centered therapy: Its current practice, implications, and theory.* Boston: Houghton Mifflin.

Rogers, C. R. (1969). *Freedom to learn.* Columbus, OH: Merrill.

Rosenberg, M. (1965). *Society and the adolescent self-image.* Princeton, NJ: Princeton University Press.

Schunk, D. H. (1984). The self-efficacy perspective on achievement behavior. *Educational Psychologist, 19,* 199–218.

Schunk, D. H., & Ertmer, P. A. (2000). Self-regulation and academic learning: Self-efficacy enhancing interventions. In M. Boekaerts, P. R. Printrich, & M. Zeidner (Eds.), *Handbook of self-regulation* (pp. 631–649). San Diego: Academic Press.

Schunk, D. H., Hanson, A. R., & Cox, P. D. (1987). Peer-model attributes and children's achievement behaviors. *Journal of Educational Psychology, 79,* 54–61.

Seligman, M. E. P. (1975). *Helplessness: On depression, development, and death.* San Francisco, CA: Freeman.

Shanker, A. (1988, March 6). The same old fashion "cures". . . They produce the same old results. *New York Times,* p. B7.

Shapiro, E. S. (1984). Self-monitoring procedures. In T. H. Ollendick & M. Hersen (Eds.), *Child behavior assessment: Principles and procedures* (pp. 148–165). New York: Pergamon.

Sigel, I. E. (1969). On becoming a thinker: A psycho-educational model. *Educational Psychologist, 14,* 70–78.

Siegler, R. S., & Richards, D. D. (1983). The development of two concepts. In C. J. Brainerd (Ed.), *Recent advances in cognitive-developmental theory: Progress in cognitive development research* (pp. 51–121). New York: Springer-Verlag.

Simmons, R. G., Blyth, D. A., Van Cleave, E. F., & Bush, D. M. (1979). Entry into early adolescence: The impact of school structure, puberty, and early dating on self-esteem. *American Sociological Review, 44,* 948–967.

Smedslund, J. (1961). The acquisition of conservation of substance and weight in children. V. Practice in conflict situations without external reinforcement. *Scandinavian Journal of Psychology, 12,* 156–160.

Steinberg, L., Dornbush, R., & Brown, B. (1996). *Beyond the classroom.* New York: Simon & Shuster.

Stevenson, H. W., Lee, S., & Stigler, J. W. (1986). Mathematics achievement of Chinese, Japanese, and American children. *Science, 231,* 693–699.

Stipek, D. J. (1981). Children's perception of their own and their classmates ability. *Journal of Educational Psychology, 73,* 404–410.

Stipek, D. J., & Daniels, D. H. (1988). Declining perceptions of competence: A consequence of changes in the child or the educational environment? *Journal of Educational Psychology, 80,* 352–356.

Stipek, D. J., & Tannatt, L. (1984). Children's judgments of their own and their peers' academic competence. *Journal of Educational Psychology, 49,* 800–814.

Stuart, R. B. (1967). Behavioral control over eating. *Behavior Research and Therapy, 5,* 357–365.

Thurstone, L. L. (1938). Primary mental abilities. *Psychometric Monographs, No. 1.* Chicago: University of Chicago Press.

U.S. Office of Education. (1973). *A guide to Followthrough.* Washington, DC: U.S. Government Printing Office.

Vygotsky, L. S. (1962). *Thought and language* (E. Hanfman & G. Vakar, Eds.). Cambridge, MA: MIT Press.

Vygotsky, L. S. (1978). *Mind in society: The development of higher psychological processes.* Cambridge, MA: Harvard University Press.

Watson, J. B. (1924). *Behaviorism.* New York: Norton.

Watson, R. I. (1963). *The Great Psychologists.* New York: Lippincott.

Winne, P. H., & Stockley, D. B. (1998). Computing technologies as sites for developing self-regulated learning. In D. H. Schunk & B. J. Zimmerman (Eds.), *Self-Regulated Learning: From teaching to self-reflective practice* (pp. 106–136). New York: Guilford Press.

Wylie, R. (1968). The present status of self-theory. In E. Borgotta & W. Lambert (Eds.), *Handbook of personality theory and research* (pp. 728–787). Chicago: Rand McNally.

Zimmerman, B. J. (1983). Social learning theory: A contextualist account of cognitive functioning. In C. J. Brainerd (Ed.), *Recent advances in cognitive developmental theory* (*pp.* 1–49). New York: Springer.

Zimmerman, B. J. (1986). Development of self-regulated learning: Which are the key subprocesses? *Contemporary Educational Psychology, 16,* 307–313.

Zimmerman, B. J. (1989). A social cognitive view of self-regulated academic learning. *Journal of Educational Psychology, 81,* 329–339.

Zimmerman, B. J. (2000a). Attainment of self-regulation: A social cognitive perspective. In M. Boekaerts, P. Pintrich, & M. Zeidner (Eds.), *Self-regulation: Theory, research, and applications* (pp. 13–39). Orlando, FL: Academic Press.

Zimmerman, B. J. (2000b). Self-efficacy: An essential motive to learn. *Contemporary Educational Psychology, 24,* 82–91.

Zimmerman, B. J., & Blom, D. E. (1983). Toward an empirical test of the role of cognitive conflict in learning. *Developmental Review, 3,* 18–38.

Zimmerman, B. J., & Kitsantas, A. (1997). Developmental phases in self-regulation: Shifting from process to outcome goals. *Journal of Educational Psychology, 89,* 29–36.

Chapter 2

Operant Theory and Research on Self-Regulation

F. Charles Mace
University of Wales, Bangor

Phillip J. Belfiore
Jeffrey M. Hutchinson
Mercyhurst College

Most theories of self-regulation advance a view of human behavior that is to one degree or another self-determined. In this view, the "self" performs operations from within to direct or control behavior. Beginning with this assumption obligates these theorists to describe, speculate, or otherwise account for the operations performed by the self, by their cognitions or exercises of free will, of which self-regulated behavior is believed to be a function.

The starting point for operant psychology is somewhat different. When operant theorists speak of self-regulation, they are generally referring to (a) an attempt to provide a natural science account of phenomena our common experience refers to as commitment, self-control, or impulsivity, or (b) a systematic application of behavior change strategies that result in the desired alteration of one's own behavior (Cooper, Heron, & Heward, 1987). In the first, through controlled experimentation (e.g., Boehme, Blakely, & Poling, 1986; Ito & Nakamura, 1998; Logue, Pena-Correal, Rodriguez, & Kabela, 1986; Rachlin & Green, 1972), functional relationships between observable environmental events and behaviors are demonstrated and assigned such descriptors as stated earlier (i.e., commitment, impulsivity, or self-control). Alternatively, theoretical accounts of these behaviors have been derived through logical extensions of the methods and products of a natural science of behavior (e.g., Skinner, 1953). In either case, the objective is to understand, in terms amenable to scientific inquiry, certain ways of behaving that traditionally attracted mentalistic explanations.

The second meaning that operant theorists assign to self-regulation is actions of individuals that alter the environment at one point in time and that make more or less probable certain actions of theirs at a later point in time (Zimmerman, 1989). Behaviors such as setting an alarm, counting calories, and taking a limited supply of cash on shopping trips illustrate means by which individuals play a role in controlling their behavior through environmental consequences. The important point here is that a person's behavior, as part of the environment, can alter the environment and, as a result, the probability of his or her own behavior. Thus, operant psychologists consider self-regulation behaviors to be like most other behavior, ultimately controlled by the environment.

Our goals in this chapter are to (a) provide a brief overview of general operant theory from which the operant view of self-regulation is directly derived, (b) provide an overview of self-regulated behaviors from the view of operant psychology, (c) review and describe research on key sub-processes in operant self-regulation, and (d) examine the recent litera-ture on self-regulation of social and academic behaviors in educational settings.

GENERAL OPERANT THEORY

Skinner (1979) sought simply to apply the methods of natural science to the study of behavior. This required direct measure of the subject matter and the variables of which it could be a function under well controlled conditions. Decades of laboratory research resulted in the discovery of orderly relationships between the behavior of organisms and specific environmental variables (Ferster & Skinner, 1957; Skinner, 1938). The principles of behavior derived from animal research were found to be general across species, including humans, although the complexity of behavior varied widely with phylogeny (Catania, 1992).

Skinner's subject matter was *operant behavior*. Operant behavior is be-havior whose occurrence depends on the environmental consequences it produces. A behavior becomes more likely to occur through positive reinforcement, that is, if that behavior results in sustenance, physical comfort or arousal, or events that historically have been paired with these (e.g., social stimuli, money, material good, etc.). For example, teacher at-tention provided contingent on the improved test scores of a student may increase the likelihood of continued good academic performance in the future. Similarly, a behavior becomes more probable through negative reinforcement, that is, when that behavior discontinues or averts both physical discomfort and associated events, and withdrawal of sustenance or other positive reinforcers. For example, a student who discontinues disruptive behavior and resumes the in-seat assignment in response to a teacher's stare may be more likely to engage in seatwork during subsequent class periods, thereby avoiding the teacher's stare. Thus it can be seen that the primary goal of an operant analysis of behavior is to identify the consequences that a given behavior produces (i.e., those necessary for the acquisition and maintenance of a particular behavior and/or those maintaining behaviors that may compete with more socially desirable responses).

Events antecedent to behavior may also influence the probability that a given behavior will occur. Antecedent stimuli that are predictive of reinforcement for behavior are referred to as *discriminative stimuli.* These stimuli acquire their control of behavior as a result of their presence being associated with a comparatively higher rate of reinforcement and their absence with a comparatively lower rate of reinforcement. As a result, individuals are much more likely to emit a particular response or responses when one or more discriminative stimuli are presented because of the increased likelihood of reinforcement. For example, when a teacher asks the class to complete the reading assignment quietly at their seats, the probability is much greater that in-seat reading will result in teacher praise than if the students work on mathematics, read out loud, or talk to their friend. Students, with this classroom history, learn to emit behaviors at specific times (i.e., when reading silently at their seats is likely to result in teacher approval) and not others.

The known principles of behavior are many and far too complex to present here (see Catania, 1992). What is important for the further discussion of self-regulation is the designation of two classes of controlling stimuli, those that occur antecedent to behavior and those that occur as a consequence of behavior. Key subprocesses of self-regulation from an operant perspective center around how individuals alter antecedent and consequent stimuli to regulate their own behavior. The following section provides an overview of self-regulation, with important elements of the operant view of self-regulation identified, and a discussion on the major subprocesses of self-regulation that are currently receiving the most attention from operant theorists and researchers.

THE OPERANT VIEW OF SELF-REGULATION

When students, teachers, and others engage in self-control, impulsivity, or commitment, they are choosing among alternative courses of action. The majority of research on self-regulation in humans has focused on procedures in which both reinforcer amounts and time delays to rein-forcement differ among choice alternatives (Ito & Nakamura, 1998). When describing self-control, the choice response involves foregoing or postponing an immediate reward and, instead, behaving in a man-ner that will result in an alternative (and often greater) reward at a later point in time (Brigham, 1982; Rachlin & Green, 1972). When de-scribing commitment, the choice response guarantees a larger delayed reinforcement by making the alternative choice between the small im-mediate or larger delayed unavailable (Catania, 1992; Rachlin & Green, 1972). For example, Rachlin and Green (1972) demonstrated that as time increased, choice responding shifted to a single option, more de-layed, greater alternative, thereby eliminating the alternative, two-choice option of either a small immediate or delayed larger choice. This pref-erence for the larger delayed alternative only could be described as an instance of advanced commitment to a given course of action (Rachlin & Green, 1972). Impulsivity involves selecting an immediate, often smaller, reward at the exclusion of the more delayed, greater alternative (Catania, 1992). Examples of self-control might include the student who studies for the geometry exam rather than go to the movies with friends, the teacher who completes a lesson plan the night before in order to avoid a chaotic lecture the next day, or the first-grade student who persists in a mathematics assignment despite temptations from his or her peers to converse and giggle. Examples of commitment might include payroll de-ductions for a savings account, where a person prefers saving a portion of his or her paycheck (Rachlin & Green, 1972) with the understanding that the saving account provides a fixed return on the investment, or the student who studies alone rather than with the study group, knowing that at times the study group opts to go to the bar rather than follow the study agenda. An example of impulsivity might be the student who opts to go to the party with friends, even though not preparing for the next-day exam may result in a failure in the course, requiring retaking the course.

The critical features of self-regulation from an operant perspective involve (a) choosing among alternative actions, (b) the relative rein-forcing value of the consequences for the response alternatives, and (c) the temporal locus of control for the alternatives (i.e., immediate vs. delayed consequences; Brigham; 1982; Rachlin & Green, 1972). The im-portance of (a) is common to all theories of self-regulation (self-control, commitment, and impulsivity), for without multiple options from which to choose, the description of self-regulation does not apply. The combi-nation of (a) and (b) alone, however, does not represent self-regulation, but rather reflects the individual's preference for one consequence over another. It is the addition of (c), the temporal locus of control, that causes us to invoke the term self-regulation. The behavior emitted as an outcome of (a), (b), and (c) distinguishes self-control, commitment, and impulsivity.

KEY SUBPROCESSES OF SELF-REGULATION

Although hallmarks of self-regulation usually include either selecting a delayed consequence over an immediate alternative (i.e., self-control), or selecting a guaranteed delayed consequence over the choice of delayed or immediate alternatives (i.e., commitment), there are many things an individual can do to increase the probability of emitting self-regulated behavior. These actions leading to self-controlled or commitment behavior are part of the self-regulation process. Operant researchers have analyzed the self-regulation process into subprocesses that include self-monitoring (SM), self-instruction (SI), self-evaluation (SE), self-correction (SC), and self-reinforcement (SR). Much of this research focused on developing and implementing procedures that promote self-regulation, and analyzing variables that make various procedures effective. Procedures are often combined to create a self-regulation program that can be taught to students in the general and special education curriculum in order to reduce the students' dependence on teacher-directed educational programs (Belfiore & Hornyak, 1998).

Self-Monitoring

The initial, and at times the only, component of a self-regulation program is *self-monitoring*. Self-monitoring (SM) can be described as a multistage process involving the observation and recording of one's own behavior (Mace & Kratochwill, 1988). In general, self-monitoring involves two steps. First, self-monitoring requires the individual to discriminate the occurrence of the target response that is to be controlled. As with all events, the reliability of this discrimination depends, in part, on the saliency and consistency of the stimuli being observed, as well as the experience one has in making the discrimination. Second, the individual records (i.e., self-recording) some dimension of the target response (e.g., frequency, duration, or latency).

Observations and recordings of one's own behavior are usually structured by the use of a data sheet or a mechanical recording device (e.g., golf counter). Students are generally trained to use standard behavioral-assessment methods to accurately self-monitor their behavior. Among the more common SM methods are (a) narrations, (b) frequency counts, (c) duration measures, (d) time-sampling procedures, (e) behavior ratings, and (f) behavioral traces and archival records. In general, (a) through (d) are considered direct assessment methods (i.e., they assess behavior as it occurs), whereas (e) and (f) are indirect methods that record information at a point in time distant from the occurrence of the behavior (Mace & Kratochwill, 1988). The selection of an SM method is usually determined by factors such as compatibility with the target response, functioning or developmental level of the student, the degree of reactivity desired, and practical considerations.

Narrations and self-reports are written descriptions of the individual's behavior and perhaps the context in which it occurs. These accounts vary in their degree of structure from completely open-ended to very specific requests for descriptions of antecedents, behaviors, and consequence. Self-reports may be useful for a student to directly record his or her activities during study periods. Reporting on the efficacy of self-reports, Finney, Putnam, and Boyd (1998) found that when report accuracy was prioritized and prompted, adherence to the reporting schedule and accuracy in the self-report increased. *Frequency counts* are useful to record the number of times one or more discrete responses occur during a given time period. The technique is commonly used because of its simplicity; however, it provides no information about when during the SM period each behavior occurred. Lee and Tindal (1994) required students, at 2-minute equal interval tones, to mark above mathematics responses just completed, count the cumulative number of responses completed, and record the number beside a mark on the worksheet. Other examples of SM using frequency counts include spelling words practiced (Reid & Harris, 1993) and story writing (Martin & Manno, 1995). *Duration measures* record the amount of time a behavior or chain of behaviors occur (e.g., study time), which may be important information for behaviors that vary considerably on this dimension. *Time-sampling methods* divide observation periods into smaller time intervals (e.g., 10s, 30s, or 60s) and record (a) the number of times a behavior occurred during each interval, (b) the occurrence/nonoccurrence of the behavior during each interval, or (c) the occurrence/nonoccurrence of the behavior at the end of each interval (i.e., momentary time sampling). Time-sampling is useful to record behaviors such as time on-task during academic activities and in-seat assignments (e.g., Maag, Reid, & DiGangi, 1993).

As an indirect SM method, *behavior ratings* call for estimations of the degree to which one or more dimensions of behavior occurred during a given time period. Rating categories vary in their specificity and length of observation interval (e.g., never, seldom, sometimes, or often during the day, vs. < 2, 3-5, 6-8, or > times during each class period). This method has been used to estimate the occurrence of such behaviors as out-of-seat, cooperative play, and accuracy of manuscript letter strokes. Although behavior ratings are convenient to use, SM accuracy and reactivity diminish as specificity decreases and the observation interval increases (Nelson, 1977). Finally, *behavioral traces* and *archival records* are permanent products or byproducts of behavior that exist independent of their formal assessment, which an individual may observe and self-record. For example, worksheet scores may be an indirect measure of on-task behavior or home study, nurse records as a measure of stomach complaints (Miller & Kratochwill, 1979), and fingernail length as an indicator of nail-biting (McNamara, 1972). Although potentially accurate measures of behavior, traces and archival records generally have a limited effect on the reactivity of SM because these measures are usually temporally distant from the target behavior (see following section on reactivity).

Reactivity of Self-Monitoring. The SM methods just described have been used widely in educational settings to transfer responsibility of behavior assessment from the teacher to the student. Beyond their value as an assessment strategy, however, SM methods have been employed because of their potential as a behavior-change agent. Self-observation and self-recording introduce stimulus conditions into the environment that can change how persons respond to existing reinforcement contingencies. This tendency for behavior to change as a result of self-observation and self-recording is referred to as the *reactivity of self-monitoring*. Some studies found reactive effects for SM to exceed those achieved by obtrusive teacher assessment of behavior (e.g., Hallahan, Lloyd, Kneedler, & Marshall, 1982), suggesting that the mechanism may be similar but more powerful than the reactivity that accompanies direct observation (cf. Kazdin, 1979).

The reactive effects of SM were extensively documented in numerous studies beginning in the 1960s. SM reactivity was shown to generalize across a wide variety of academic, social, vocational, and clinically aberrant behaviors with non-handicapped and handicapped children and adults, and across virtually all clinically relevant settings (Mace & Kratochwill, 1988). In academic settings, for example, SM increased adaptive behaviors such as time on-task (DiGagni, Maag, & Rutherford, 1991; Reid & Harris, 1993), rate of assignment completion (Morrow, Burke, & Buel, 1985), accuracy of manuscript letter-writing strokes (Jones, Trap, & Cooper, 1977), appropriate play (Stahmer & Schriebman, 1992), and mathematics performance (DiGagni, Maag, Rutherford, 1991; Kirby, Fowler, & Baer, 1991). Similarly, SM proved effective in reducing maladaptive behaviors such as out-of-seat (Sugai & Rowe, 1984), and inattentive/disruptive behaviors (Christie, Hill, & Lozanoff, 1984). A further therapeutic advantage of SM is its potential contribution to maintenance and generalization of the effects of other interventions. For example, Fowler (1986) found peer monitoring of students' behavior was effective in reducing classroom disruption and nonparticipation. Effects were maintained after peer monitoring was discontinued by having students self-monitor their compliance with classroom rules.

Variables Affecting the Reactivity of Self-Monitoring. Although reactive effects of SM have been widely documented, several investigators reported mixed results or a lack of reactivity altogether (e.g., Shapiro & Ackerman, 1983; Shapiro, Browder, & D'Huyvetters, 1984). Such inconsistent findings stimulated considerable research into the variables affecting the reactivity of SM. Subjects in most of these studies self-monitored one or more behaviors under multiple SM conditions to determine which variations of SM resulted in the greatest reactivity. Some specific variables shown to affect the reactivity of self-monitoring include motivation, valence, experimenter instruction or experimenter surveillance, the nature of the target behavior and timing, the recording device, goals, feedback, and reinforcement.

Motivation to alter the self-monitored response appears to affect the degree to which SM is reactive. In studies with smokers, only those subjects who volunteered for the habit-reduction study or indicated motivation to stop smoking were successful in decreasing smoking with SM (Lipinski, Black, Nelson, & Ciminero, 1974; McFall & Hammen, 1971). Valence of the target behavior often determines the direction and extent of behavior change. Several studies showed that negatively valenced behaviors decrease and positively valenced behaviors increase when self-monitored (e.g.,. Nelson, Hay, & Carstens, 1977; Willis & Nelson, 1982). Further, some researchers found reactivity to be greater for positively valenced behaviors than for behaviors with a neutral or negative valence (Litrownik & Freitas, 1980). Experimenter instructions or surveillance provided prior to and during SM can, in certain cases, influence the magnitude of reactivity. Belfiore, Mace, and Browder (1989) demonstrated that reactive effects of SM were increased substantially by the experimenter's surveillance of adults with developmental disabilities during a vocational task. Timing of self-recording in relation to the occurrence of the target behavior can affect the degree to which SM is reactive. For example, Frederickson, Epstein, and Kosevsky (1975) found continuous and immediate SM to produce greater reactivity than intermittent self-recording (e.g., at the end of the day). Reactivity may also depend on the nature of the target behavior and recording device. In general, self-recording discrete, overt, nonverbal behaviors results in greater reactivity than monitoring verbal behaviors or private events (Harmon, Nelson, & Hayes, 1980; Hayes & Cavior, 1977). In addition, monitoring actual academic productivity produces greater change than self-recording attentional or on-task behavior (Harris, 1986). Several studies also demonstrated that reactivity is greatest when SM occurs using an obtrusive SM device such as wrist-worn or hand-held counters (Maletzsky, 1974; Nelson, Lipinski, & Boykin, 1978), visible data sheets (Kirby, Fowler, & Baer, 1991; Piersel, 1985), and audible cues to self-record behavior (Hems, Lloyd, & Hallahan, 1986). Finally, goals, feedback, and reinforcement were shown to facilitate the reactive effects of SM. For example, Kazdin (1974) reported that providing subjects with a performance standard when self-monitoring as well as frequent performance feedback resulted in the largest increase in the use of target pronouns. Likewise, observable reinforcement for the self-monitored response appears to be critical to reactive SM (Mace & Kratochwill, 1985; Mace, Shapiro, West, Campbell, & Altman, 1986).

Operant View of Self-Monitoring Reactivity. The operant explanation for reactive SM was shaped by operant theory's general view of self-regulated behavior as well as the large literature on the variables responsible for the reactivity of SM. The question for operant theorists is, "How does SM affect the relationship between behavior and its controlling consequences?" The answer to this question rests on analyzing the functional relationships among variables in the SM process, the target behavior, and the consequences that ultimately control the target behavior. SM variables antecedent to the target behavior may serve as discriminative stimuli, setting events, or rules that set the occasion for more or lesser performances of the target response (cf. Nelson & Hayes, 1981). Examples of discriminative stimuli are obtrusive recording devices, audible prompts to self-record, and feedback on prior responses. These discriminative stimuli may evoke behavior at levels sufficient to yield reinforcement (e.g., 20 out of 25 math problems completed). Setting events, on the other hand, such as teacher surveillance during self-monitored study periods, may alter the probability of the target response because of the increased likelihood of "good" behavior being reinforced under these conditions. Setting events are stimuli that do not occasion behavior by themselves but, rather, establish other events as discriminative stimuli or reinforcers for particular behaviors (Michael, 1982; Wahler & Fox, 1981). Finally, variables such as instructions and performance standards may function as rules describing the delayed contingencies of which the target behavior is subject (Malott, 1984). Rules can occasion behavior by indicating the response to perform and its likely outcome. Self-recording responses, on the other hand, occur as a consequence of performance of the target behavior. The literature cited here indicates that reactive effects are greatest when continuous and immediate records are made of the target behavior (Frederickson et al., 1975). Several theorists believe that the act of recording one's own behavior provides an immediate consequence for the target behavior that strengthens or mediates the relationship between the target behavior and the delayed consequences that ultimately control it (Kirby et al., 1991; Mace & West, 1986; Malott, 1984; Nelson & Hayes, 1981; Rachlin, 1974). Baer (1984) described the relationship as follows:

> Formally, they look like stimuli in a chained schedule: They are direct and immediate consequences of a necessary initial performance: they mark the correct completion of that initial performance and set the occasion for a subsequent performance that can now lead to the reinforcers or avoid the punishers in those rearranged contingencies that the self-controlling person is attempting to use. By doing so, they support that initial performance (p. 212).

Self-Instruction

Another major subprocess of self-regulation studied extensively by operant theorists is self-instruction (SI). We should note at the outset that operant self-instruction differs in many respects conceptually and procedurally from cognitive–behavioral self-instruction (e.g., Meichenbaum (1977). From the operant perspective, the SM process can provide discriminative stimuli for regulating the level of one's own behavior in accordance with reinforcement standards, whereas SI provides discriminative stimuli that occasion specific behaviors or behavioral sequences that will lead to reinforcement.

SI statements generally correspond to one of two types of discriminative stimuli. First, the individual may arrange the environment so as to come in contact with one or more discriminative stimuli that set the occasion for desired behavior. These stimuli may be verbal or nonverbal and have the capacity to occasion behavior because performing that behavior in the past has resulted in reinforcement. For example, a girl may place her milk money or a written reminder next to her lunchbox at night to help her remember to take the money to school. The money or the note is likely to occasion taking the money to school because doing so in the past was necessary to have milk during recess. By arranging the environment in this manner, the girl has increased the likelihood of compliance with the school rule. The second type of SI statement takes the form of rules that individuals use to govern their own behavior. Skinner (1969) defined a rule as a set of discriminative stimuli that describe contingencies. An SI statement of this type would specify both the response to perform and the consequence for doing so. For this reason, operant theorists have characterized some forms of self-instructed behavior as rule-governed behavior (Zettle & Hayes, 1982).

The first type of SI statement is illustrated in a study by Grskovic and Belfiore (1996). In a strategy designed to increase spelling performance, students were asked to self-instruct using white erase boards. The verbal self-statements included (a) write the word the teacher said on the board, (b) compare what you wrote to the teacher's model, (c) erase only the errors made, leaving all correct letters on the board, and (d) copy the correct letters from the teacher's model. Other SI strategies include the use of antecedent prompt cards (Cassel & Reid, 1996), and contract worksheets (Seabaugh & Schumaker, 1994). Belfiore and Hornyak (1998) described a homework routine checklist that required students to follow steps for homework completion in an afterschool program. The SI sequence required a checklist of self-statements including:

1. Did I turn in yesterday's homework?
2. Did I write all homework assignments in my notebook?
3. Is all homework in homework folder?
4. Are all my materials to complete homework with me?
5. Begin homework.
6. Are all homework papers completed?
7. Did someone check homework to make sure it was completed?
8. After checking, did I put all homework back in folder?
9. Did I give this paper to teacher? (p. 190)

As with SM, the SI process takes the form of a chained schedule in which each step in the sequence sets the occasion for the succeeding step and, at the same time, performance of the step is reinforced by the opportunity to perform its successor (Baker, 1984; Catania, 1992). Thus, by performing each response in the SI sequence, the student can regulate his or her own behavior to maximize the likelihood of reinforcement for completing the sequence.

The second type of SI incorporates the use of rules to promote self-regulated behavior. For example, Swanson and Scarpati (1985) taught students with mild disabilities a comprehensive SI strategy to improve their reading comprehension and spelling. Students learned to respond to and later generate a sequence of questions, directions, and rules that facilitated performance on exams and assignments. The following samples represent key components of the SI sequence for reading comprehension:

1. How do I understand the passage before I read it? I need to look at the title, identify and circle new words and phrases, and underline persons' names and words that show action.
2. I need to ask myself, Who, What, Where, When, and How before I read the story.
3. Now, from my lesson yesterday, if I forgot these steps, I won't remember what the passage is about. Yesterday I didn't underline words so I could not answer the question about what happened (Swanson & Scarpati, 1985).

While reading the story passage, students used a list of written instructions or symbols to prompt them through the SI sequence. Wood, Frank, and Wacker (1998) required students learning multiplication facts to say to themselves, "If I use the correct strategy, I will get the problem right" (p. 327).

The Swanson and Scarpati (1985) study illustrated how the combination of the two types of discriminative stimulus form an SI procedure. The SI statements in 1 and 2 specify problem-solving responses to perform. By contrast, the SI statements in 3 represent rules for behaving that not only specify what to do, but also indicate the likely consequences for each act. The initial effectiveness of these SI statements is less dependent on the students' direct experience with the consequences for SI compliance. Rather, a history of reinforcement for academic rule compliance is generally sufficient to establish the rule as a discriminative stimulus for problem solving (Skinner, 1969: Zettle & Hayes, 1982).

Self-Evaluation and Self-Correction

Self-evaluation (SE) requires the person to compare some dimension of his or her behavior with that of some set standard or criteria (Belfiore & Hornyak, 1998). The dimension to be evaluated may take the form of (a) accuracy of self-monitoring (e.g., number of steps completed correctly), (b) improvement of performance over time (e.g., rate, percentage, duration), and/or (c) the overall performance for one specific session (Belfiore & Hornyak, 1998). Given these parameters, SE may result in modifying the SM system currently in place (as in a), or self-delivering some consequent based on target behavior performance (as in b and c). For example, students following a nine-step routine for completing and turning in homework may complete the routine and realize that step 3 was not completed. The student, upon evaluation of the SM checklist, may either complete the step or modify the checklist if the step has become obsolete. Once the SM checklist (either the original or modified version) is complete and homework is turned in to the teacher, the student may deliver some reinforcer as a consequent to his behavior. In this example, SE is dependent on student discrimination as determined by the steps of the SM system in place or student discrimination as determined by the outcome of the performance when compared to some preset standard. DiGagni et al. (1991) instructed students to tell themselves that they had done either a "really good job" (8–10 intervals marked out of a possible 10 total intervals) or an "okay" job (4–7 intervals marked out of a possible 10 total intervals) depending on the frequency of tallied marks made while self-recording on-task behavior. Additionally, Sweeney, Salva, Cooper, and Talbert-Johnson (1993) instructed students to self-evaluate their writing performance across such variables as letter size, slant, letter shape, and spacing. In these two instances, on completion of the task, students made some evaluative statement of their performance, in reference to a preset standard of performance.

Self-correction (SC) requires a student to self-evaluate performance, and alter or modify the previous response based on the results of the evaluation. Whereas self-evaluation requires a discrimination to be made between some standard or required performance and a person's performance, self-correction requires a modification of performance to more closely approximate the standard. McGuffin, Martz, and Heron (1997) described spelling self-corrections sessions as requiring the student's to listen to taped spelling words, write each word on a sheet of paper, compare their written words to a correct, prewritten model of the word on the folded section of the paper, and correct errors to their words based on the prewritten model. Similarly, Grskovic and Belfiore (1996) had students self-evaluate by observing the teacher's written model and correcting their errors based on the teacher model. In both of these studies, spelling performance improved when students self-corrected from a prewritten model when compared to training without self-correction.

Self-Reinforcement

Self-reinforcement (SR) describes a process in which a person, often after satisfying a performance standard or criteria, comes in contact with a stimulus following the occurrence of a response that, in turn, results in an increase in the probability of the occurrence of the response subject to the performance standard. We prefer this definition because it is descriptive of the process and avoids labeling (a) stimuli as reinforcer, (b) the relationship between the stimulus and target behavior as contingent, (c) the spatial locus of the reinforcer, and (d) the source controlling the integrity of the SR sequence. These features of the process set apart the operant view of SR from other perspectives.

We can understand SR from the operant viewpoint by first distinguishing it from other theoretical positions. A view held widely among social-cognitivists is that individuals can and do reinforce their own behavior (Bandura, 1976; Schunk, 1989). Cognitive theorists consider the SR process to be one of true reinforcement. Individuals are believed to regulate their own behavior by making access to freely and continuously available reinforcers contingent on responses that meet or exceed self- or externally imposed standards for performance (Bandura & Mahoney, 1974). In addition, the spatial locus of the reinforcer may be private (e.g., thoughts or feelings), or public (e.g., material or social rewards) events. Many social-cognitive theorists consider self-administered verbal or tangible rewards to be functionally equivalent to external contingencies, thus promoting a view that individuals can and do provide much of the reinforcement for their own behavior (Bandura, 1976; Kanfer, 1977; Schunk, 1989; Thoresen & Mahoney, 1974).

Operant View of Self-Reinforcement. Operant theorists have questioned whether SR procedures constitute a true reinforcement process (Catania, 1975; Goldiamond, 1976; Rachlin, 1974; Skinner, 1953). We can illustrate this concern with some practical examples: Consider the student who has been taught the following SR procedure: After completing the workbook exercises in each math unit, the girl sets a performance goal that is at or above her previous math-unit test score. The student takes the math exam and awards herself two points for meeting her goal plus one point for each point of her test score that exceeds her goal. During recess, the student exchanges her points for a variety of back-up reinforcers such as games and reading time. Using this procedure over the course of a semester improved the student's math test scores by 15 percentage points.

Did the student reinforce her superior test performance by awarding herself points for attaining her goals? In order for this example to be a case of true reinforcement, both the points and back-up reinforcers must be freely accessible to the student and be awarded contingent on meeting the performance standard. Furthermore, the contingent relationship between test scores and self-awarded points must increase the probability of high test scores. On the surface, these conditions may appear to hold, thus satisfying the criteria for true reinforcement. Yet, an operant analysis of the case would raise the following questions: Is the student really free to access points and back-up reinforcers noncontingently? What happens if points and back-up reinforcers are claimed without meeting the performance standard? How is the SR sequence learned and maintained? What will happen to the student's test performance if the SR sequence is not monitored and enforced by the teacher?

Such questions are likely to reveal that the teacher maintains the SR sequence by (a) scheduling times for study, testing, and reinforcer access, (b) monitoring the accuracy of the student's self-evaluation and awarding of points and reinforcers, and (c) punishing cheating or violation of the SR rules. In this situation, reinforcement may be self-administered but the conditions for its delivery are controlled by the teacher.

There are other examples in which the contingencies that control maintenance of the SR sequence are less obvious. We may observe a boy reliably do his homework within an hour after arriving home from school. After homework, his next activity may be to prepare a snack, telephone friends, read a book, or watch television, which the student may describe as rewards for completing his homework. Although the SR sequence may be followed consistently, we may question whether the rewards actually reinforce homework completion. In order for us to consider the rewards as reinforcing homework behavior, the baseline level of homework completion must depend on the contingent access to rewarding activities. For most students, however, the contingencies that control homework completion are related to how teachers and parents respond to this behavior as well as the positive relationship between studying and grades.

If the student would continue to do his homework without the rewards, what then accounts for maintenance of the SR sequence? An operant account centers on the consequences for following or failing to follow the SR sequence. For example, the work-then-play sequence may be positively reinforced because (a) the conditions may be more favorable to concentrate on schoolwork immediately after school, and/or (b) the student is able to engage in reinforcing activities in the evening without the encumbrance of homework. Furthermore, the student may have experienced various negative consequences for attempting homework at other times (e.g., late at night or just before a social engagement) that may have initially established the work–play sequence and continue to maintain it.

These examples help to illustrate that SR for operant theorists is a misnomer (Catania, 1975; Goldiamond, 1976; Nelson, Hayes, Spong, Jarrett, & McKnight, 1983; Skinner, 1953). The self-administered stimulus that follows the target response is not considered a reinforcer because its access does not depend on the occurrence of the behavior. In laboratory studies, response-independent reinforcement consistently decreases response rates (Nevin, 1974), reflecting the importance of the dependency between response and reinforcer. The establishment of most SR sequences may be traced to externally imposed contingencies that either do not permit free access to reinforcing stimuli (e.g., teachers are unlikely to permit access to recess without prior engagement in academic work; Catania, 1975) or they promote an efficient path to obtain delayed consequences (Baer, 1984; Malott, 1984; Skinner, 1953). In the latter case, SR effects may be attributed to the provision of immediate consequences for a target response that mediate or strengthen the relationship between behavior and the delayed consequences that control it (Nelson et al., 1983).

Self-Reinforcement Research. Several literature reviews evaluated the empirical evidence to support use of the term *self-reinforcement* (Gross & Wojnilower, 1984; Jones et al., 1977; Mace & West, 1986; Martin, 1980; Sohn & Lamal, 1982). We briefly summarize the findings of these reviews here and refer readers to the sources cited for detailed discussions. First, the immediate reinforcement history of subjects in many SR studies is shaped by their experience with externally managed reinforcement programs. For example, many classroom studies preceded or contrasted SR conditions with formal or informal token or social reinforcement programs that leave unclear whether contrast or sequence effects may have affected student performance during SR (Drabman, Spitalnik, & O'Leary, 1973; Kaufman & O'Leary, 1972; Santogrossi, O'Leary, Romanczyk, & Kaufman, 1973). Bowers, Clement, Fantuzzo, and Sorensen (1985) assessed the attending behavior of 8- to 11-year-old boys with learning disabilities under self- and external-reinforcement conditions. Differences in performance under self-reinforcement and teacher-administered reinforcement conditions were apparent only when self-reinforcement preceded external reinforcement, suggesting the effect may have been due to the contrast between the two reinforcement conditions presented in that order.

Second, performance standards in some SR studies are established by teachers or experimenters (e.g., Humphrey, Karoly, & Kirschenbaum, 1978), whereas in other studies students set their own performance standards (e.g., Wall, 1983). Self-administration of rewards is then determined by the students' performance relative to the standard. This practice is problematic because several studies have shown that performance standards can improve student behavior independent of SR programs (e.g., Kazdin, 1974). Moreover, performance standards imply that reinforcers cannot be accessed without meeting the criterion. Yet, it is essential that subjects understand that they are free to obtain reinforcers regardless of their performance of the target behavior (Bass, 1972; Catania, 1975). Unless these conditions are satisfied, what appears to be SR may actually be self-administered consequences that are controlled by an external event.

Third, students in most SR studies experience surveillance by teachers or other authority figures that may influence their SR practices (e.g.,

Belfiore et al., 1989). For most students, teachers are well-established discriminative stimuli for certain behavior patterns and may discourage unearned consumption of reinforcers.

A fourth type of external confound is instructional sets and external contingencies on the self-reinforcing responses. In many SR studies, students are provided definitions of the target response and informed of the available reinforcers and the rules for self-administration of reinforcers (e.g., Salend & Allen, 1985). Other studies include specific contingencies for accurate SR (e.g., Drabman et al., 1973) or SM (Kaplan, Hemmes, Motz, & Rodriguez, 1996) Such external constraints on the SR process limit inferences regarding the self-determination of behavior.

A final external confound concerns the presence of external contingencies on the target behavior in addition to SR. Most classrooms arrange contingencies for academic work and social behavior that often operate concurrently with SR programs (e.g., Kaufman & O'Leary, 1972). In addition, effects may be supplemented by natural contingencies that accompany improved behavior such as grades, privileges, attention, and avoidance of aversive consequences.

In these examples, the five classes of external events often co-occur with SR interventions. Although extraneous contingencies also hamper clear interpretation of other types of research, as external sources of control in SR research, their effects make it difficult to interpret behavior change as being self-directed.

Operant research on SR investigated two major hypotheses: (a) When access to reinforcers is freely available, will individuals administer them contingent on their own behavior? and (b) Do self-administered consequences function as discriminative stimuli for behavior controlled by delayed environmental contingencies?

With regard to hypothesis (a), Bass (1972) observed that the notion of self-reinforcement runs counter to the Premack principle (Premack, 1959). Bass contended, "There is no reason to believe that individuals will switch from emitting high probability behavior to emitting low probability behavior in order to administer themselves rewards that they already possess and can administer to themselves in any event" (p. 196). Instead, Bass believed that individuals would consume unearned reinforcers if they knew there were no aversive consequences for doing so. He exposed different groups of fifth-grade students to different reinforcement histories for compliance with a nonacademic, laboratory-type task prior to an SR condition. Children with a history of reinforcement for noncompliance with instructions consistently awarded themselves money without meeting their own criteria for reinforcement compared to subjects without this history. In a similar vein, Wall (1983) found that fifth-grade students free to determine their own standards for performance within reinforcement contingencies set for themselves increasingly lenient standards for completing language-arts work units over a 6-week period. Jones and Ollendick (1979) reported that third- and fourth-grade, low SES students' self-rewarded arithmetic performance dropped sharply with low external performance demands. Many other studies similarly reported that children inflated their records of their performance to obtain unearned reinforcers when aversive consequences were not applied for cheating (e.g., Hundert & Batstone, 1978; Speidel & Tharp, 1980).

Several studies tried to assess the discriminative or feedback properties of SR procedures. Nelson et al. (1983) compared a work–reward and a reward–work sequence using standard SR procedures. Both sequences increased the number of workbook questions attempted over a control condition, although the reward–work sequence resulted in more accurate answers. Obtaining similar effects from either sequence suggested that SR may have a discriminative rather than a reinforcement function.

Two studies by Hayes and his associates found SR effects to be dependent on publicly known performance goals. In the first study, Hayes et al. (1985) found that SR produced no effects when subjects' self-determined goals and contingencies were private. However, when subjects wrote their goals on paper and the experimenter read each person's goal aloud, self-administration of rewards produced a sharp increase in correct answers on a reading quiz. The second study similarly found that SR procedures that included goal setting were ineffective without public-performance feedback (Hayes et al., 1986). Public feedback with goal setting and SR likewise failed to improve performance. Together, these findings suggest that social contingencies apart from the SR procedure had ultimate control of behavior. The act of self-administering rewards may have strengthened the relationship between the target behavior and the social contingencies that controlled it. As Hayes et al. (1986) stated, "One possibility is that goal setting works not because it sets a self-standard, but because it sets a *social* standard. . . . Thus, goal setting might establish a socially available standard against which [subjects'] performance can be evaluated" (p. 35). Results consistent with this interpretation have also been reported by Castro, de Perez, de Albanchez, and de Leon (1983) and Mace and Kratochwill (1985).

Viewed collectively, the operant studies on the SR process answer some questions and raise many others. We share the conclusion of several other authors that there is little evidence to support the view that individuals regulate their own behavior by making their access to freely available reinforcers contingent on meeting performance standards. Across several studies, subjects consistently consumed reinforcers noncontingently when they were aware that there were no negative consequences for doing so. In other studies, a consistent temporal relation between behavior and self-administered rewards could be explained by numerous uncontrolled external variables.

Operant theorists, argued that self-administered consequences, especially when coupled with feedback and performance standards, have a mediational, cueing, or discriminative function. Thus, operant theorists say, SR serves to strengthen the relationship between behavior and the delayed consequences of which the behavior is a function. In our view, research findings thus far neither confirm nor contradict the operant explanation. This is not surprising when we consider how slippery terms like *mediation* and *cueing* are. A necessary step in the further development of operant theory on self-regulation is to *specify* the operant processes that link behavior to its delayed consequences. For example, Baer (1984) suggested that the process is similar to a chained schedule. This hypothesis is valuable because it is testable and it corresponds to a known behavioral phenomenon. If the analogy holds, we need to learn which sequences of stimuli produce the most effective chain and why some stimuli, like self-administered consequences and public goal setting, seem to facilitate SR effects more than others.

Although much research is needed to provide a full account of self-regulation from the operant perspective, existing theory and research offer specific direction for the development of self-regulation programs in educational settings. The following section summarizes the major variables that appear to promote self-regulation and illustrates their application with a hypothetical case.

CASE ILLUSTRATION OF OPERANT SELF-REGULATION

Operant theory and research has identified several factors that appear to be central to the development and maintenance of self-regulated behavior. First, the response to be self-regulated should be discriminable. SM methods should be adopted that help an individual notice when and how many target behaviors have occurred. Second, the environment should be arranged to include several salient discriminative stimuli that set the occasion for desirable behavior. Likewise, discriminative stimuli that occasion maladaptive behaviors should be eliminated or reduced in number wherever possible. Third, discriminative stimuli for desirable behavior should be arranged in an effective instructional sequence that makes it clear what behaviors should be performed, when each behavior should be performed, and what should be done if an incorrect response occurs. Fourth, the immediate and delayed consequences for emitting and failing to emit the target behaviors should be explicitly stated. Frequent verbal or nonverbal reminders of these consequences should be provided.

Fifth, each step in the self-regulation process should be followed by an immediate consequence that is likely to strengthen performance of the step and prompt performance of the next step in the sequence.

The following hypothetical case illustrates how these key elements can be combined to create a comprehensive self-regulation program. Our hypothetical student is Art, a fourth-grade boy of average intellectual ability. Art has an experienced teacher who is generally skilled at instruction and classroom management. The teacher uses a variety of instructional methods and materials for most students and attempts to individualize instruction where possible. Since the beginning of the school year, Art's academic performance and conduct have deteriorated steadily. His average grades on homework, seatwork, and tests have dropped from Bs to Ds and Fs in reading and mathematics. Although his overall grades are poor, the pattern of his performance is very inconsistent within and across assignments that cover essentially the same material. Art's academic performance appears to be related to his frequent misconduct in the classroom. Several times throughout the day, Art is observed to be out of his seat without permission, teasing his classmates, talking loudly and calling out during work periods, and generally being off-task during assignments and lectures.

The first step in developing a self-regulation program is for the teacher to solicit Art's cooperation with the program. In addition to describing the program to Art, operational definitions of Art's target behaviors will be provided to Art so that he understands clearly which of his behaviors are to be increased and which are to be decreased. In Art's case, target behaviors to increase are the percentage of assignment and test items answered correctly and the number of class periods per day with good behavior, Target behaviors for Art to decrease included unauthorized out-of-seat behavior, talking out of turn, and teasing his classmates.

The teacher will instruct Art to use a comprehensive self-monitoring procedure. Training will include definition of the target behaviors and repeated practice using the SM device. A list of good behaviors and misbehaviors to be self-monitored will be taped to Art's desk. Designated good behaviors include sit in seat, work on the assignment, raise hand for questions or help, look at and listen to the teacher when the teacher speaks, and answer the teacher's questions. Art's list of misbehaviors include out-of-seat. talking out-of-turn, and teasing or disrupting classmates. During seat assignments and tests, Art will record his completion of each step in the problem-solving sequence (see discussion of self-instruction in the next paragraph) on an SM form. The SM form lists each SI step and has a space to record its completion for each problem attempted. Art will also be able to record his score on each assignment or test at the top of the SM form. A second SM form will be used to record Art's classroom conduct. The form will list the targeted inappropriate behaviors across the top of the sheet and list half-hour blocks of time along the left-hand side of the form. Art will self-record each occurrence of the inappropriate behaviors in the half-hour time blocks. If no inappropriate behaviors occur in a time block, Art will place a cartoon sticker of his choice at the end of the time block indicating a "good behavior" period. The accuracy of Art's SM will be checked randomly by the teacher and points will be deducted for inaccuracies.

Art will also be taught to use a self-instruction procedure when completing assignments and tests. The teacher will specify an ideal problem-solving sequence for Art to follow for each type of reading and math problem. A sample SI sequence for division problems (e.g., 483 divided by 7) might consist of the following steps:

1. Determine the greatest number of times the first two numbers of the dividend are divisible by the divisor and write this number (6) above the second number in the dividend (8).
2. Multiply this number (6) by the divisor (7) and write the product (42) under the first two numbers of the dividend (48).
3. Subtract the product (42) from the first two numbers of the dividend (48).
4. Write the third number of the dividend (3) next to this difference (6).
5. Determine the greatest number of times the number in step 4 (63) is divisible by the divisor (7) and write the number (9) above the third number in the dividend (3).

These steps may be written and/or illustrated by color enhancing each step in the sample problem. Art may read each step aloud or to himself.

The final portion of the self-regulation program would specify the contingencies for improved behavior and would involve Art in the self-administration of consequences. On a weekly basis, Art and his teacher should agree on performance standards for his academic performance, academic improvement, and classroom conduct. Art will grade his own papers (self-evaluation) within 10 minutes after completing the assignment of test (with periodic accuracy checks by the teacher) and award himself 5 points for each assignment and 10 points for each test in which his score meets or exceeds the standard. If he does not meet the standard, but improves from the past score, he will award himself 1 point for each assignment and 2 points for each test. Answers to the problems will be available from the teacher key. Art will also earn 5 points for each half-hour period without inappropriate behavior above his daily goal.

Point totals for the day are self-recorded at the end of each day in a report card that Art takes home and has his parents sign. At the beginning of the week, Art, his parents, and his teacher should agree on a privilege that Art can earn if he meets his overall daily goal four out of five days. To remind Art of his goals, he can make a sign designating his reward for the week and post it in a conspicuous location.

To summarize, Art will observe the following self-instructed learning sequence:

1. Read the problem (aloud or silently).
2. Read each problem solving step.
3. Write the answer to each step in the appropriate location.
4. Record completion of each SI step on the SM form.
5. Write the final solution.
6. Grade the assignment/test using the teacher-made answer key.
7. Record the number correct on the SM form.
8. Award points for meeting or exceeding performance standard.
9. If performance standard is not met, award points if improved from previous score.
10. Self-record daily point total on report card.
11. Exchange points for back-up reinforcers.

In practice, not all of these self-regulation procedures may be necessary to produce satisfactory improvement in Art's behavior. The goal would be to use the minimum number of components necessary initially to achieve the performance goals and maintain performance over time.

SUMMARY

This chapter reviewed the basic tenets of the operant theory of self-regulation. Operant theorists view self-regulated behavior to be like all operant behavior, a function of its consequences. Behavior becomes self-regulated when individuals arrange the environment in a variety of ways to alter the probability of their behavior producing reinforcing or punishing stimuli. Terminology representing self-regulated behavior may be described as commitment impulsivity, and self-control. The arrangement of the environment can be considered subprocesses of operant self-regulation, and include self-monitoring, self-instruction, self-evaluation, self-correction, and self-reinforcement. Using self-monitoring, individuals can learn to better discriminate occurrences of their behavior and its relation to environmental consequences. Techniques of self-instruction provide discriminative stimuli for solving problems and enhancing accuracy in self-monitoring. Self-evaluation and self-correction require discriminations and modifications to be made based on personal performance compared to preset standards or criteria. Self-delivery of reinforcement provides immediate consequences for chains of behaviors that ultimately lead to reinforcing environmental consequences.

There is considerable research that calls into question the view that humans control their behavior by contingently supplying public or private reinforcers. Additionally, the operant view of self-regulation, whereby the techniques of self-control and commitment strengthen the relationship between behavior and its delayed consequences, has been acquiring additional empirical support in the literature. Further progress in an operant formulation of self-control and commitment will depend on more specific theoretical explanations explained through experimental analysis, and continued generalization of theory into applied practice.

REFERENCES

Baer, D. M. (1984). Does research on self-control need more self-control? *Analysis and Intervention in Developmental Disabilities, 4,* 211–218.

Bandura, A. E., (1976). Self-reinforcement: Theoretical and methodological considerations. *Behaviorism, 4,* 135–155.

Bandura, A. E., & Mahoney, M. J. (1974). Maintenance and transfer of self-reinforcement functions. *Behavior Research and Therapy, 12,* 89–97.

Bass, B. A. (1972). Reinforcement history as a determinant of self-reinforcement. *The Journal of Psychology, 81,* 195–203.

Belfiore, P. J., & Hornyak, R. S. (1998). Operant theory and application to self-monitoring in adolescents. In D. H. Schunk & B. J. Zimmerman (Eds.), *Self-regulated learning: From teaching to self-reflective practice* (pp. 184–202). New York: Guilford.

Belfiore, P. J., Mace, F. C., & Browder, D. M. (1989). Effects of experimenter surveillance on reactive self-monitoring. *Research in Developmental Disabilities, 10,* 171–182.

Boehme, R., Blakely, E., & Poling, A. (1986). Runway length as a determinant of self-control in rats. *The Psychological Record, 26,* 285–288.

Bowers, D. S., Clements, P. W., Fantuzzo, J. W., & Sorensen, D. A. (1985). Effects of teacher-administered and self-administered reinforcers on learning disabled children. *Behavior Therapy, 16,* 357–369.

Brigham, T. (1982). Self-management: A radical behavioral perspective. In P. Karoly & F. H. Kanfer (Eds.), *Self-management and behavior change: From theory to practice* (pp. 32–59). New York: Pergamon.

Cassel, J., & Reid, R. (1996). Use of a self-regulated strategy intervention to improve word problem-solving skills of students with mild disabilities. *Journal of Behavioral Education, 6,* 153–172.

Castro, L., de Perez, G. C., de Albanchez, D., & de Leon, E. P. (1983). Feedback properties of "self-reinforcement": Further evidence. *Behavior Therapy, 14,* 672–681.

Catania, A. C. (1975). The myth of self-reinforcement. *Behaviorism, 3,* 192–199.

Catania, A. C. (1992). *Learning.* Englewood Cliffs, NJ: Prentice-Hall.

Christie, D. J., Hill, M., & Lozanoff, B. (1984). Modification of inattentive classroom behavior: Hyperactive children's use of self-recording with teacher guidance. *Behavior Modification, 8,* 391–406.

Cooper, J. O., Heron, T. E., & Heward, W. L. (1987). *Applied Behavior Analysis.* New York: Macmillan.

DiGagni, S. A., Maag. J. W., & Rutherford, R. B. (1991). Self-graphing of on-task behavior: Enhancing the reactive effects of self-monitoring on on-task behavior and academic performance. *Learning Disabilities Quarterly, 14,* 221–229.

Drabman, R. S., Spitalnik, R., & O'Leary, K. D. (1973). Teaching self-control to disruptive children. *Journal of Abnormal Psychology, 82,* 10–16.

Ferster, C. B., & Skinner, B. F. (1957). *Schedules of reinforcement.* New York: Appleton-Century-Crofts.

Finney, J. W., Putnam, D. E., & Boyd, C. M. (1998). Improving the accuracy of self-reports of adherence. *Journal of Applied Behavior Analysis, 31,* 485–488.

Fowler, S. A. (1986). Peer monitoring and self-monitoring: Alternatives to traditional teacher management. *Exceptional Children, 52,* 573–581.

Frederickson, L. W., Epstein, L. H., & Kosevsky, B. P. (1975). Reliability and controlling effects of three procedures for self-monitoring smoking. *Psychological Record, 25,* 255–264.

Goldiamond, I. (1976). Self-reinforcement. *Journal of Applied Behavioral Analysis. 9,* 509–514.

Gross, A. M., & Wojnilower. D. A. (1984). Self-directed behavior change in children: Is it self-directed? *Behavior Therapy, 15,* 501–514.

Grskovic, J. A., & Belfiore, P. J. (1996). Improving the spelling performance of students with disabilities. *Journal of Behavioral Education, 6,* 343–354.

Hallahan, D. P., Lloyd, J. W., Kneedler, R. D., & Marshall, K. J. (1982). A comparison of the effects of self-versus teacher-assessment of on-task behavior. *Behavior Therapy, 13,* 715–723.

Harmon, T. M., Nelson, R. O., & Hayes, S. C. (1980). The differential effects of self-monitoring mood versus activity in depressed patients. *Journal of Consulting and Clinical Psychology, 48,* 30–38.

Harris, K. R. (1986). Self-monitoring of attentional behavior versus self-monitoring of productivity: Effects of on-task behavior and academic response rate among learning disabled children. *Journal of Applied Behavior Analysis, 19,* 417–423.

Hayes, S. C., & Cavior, N. (1977). Multiple tracking and the reactivity of self-monitoring: I. Negative behaviors. *Behavior Therapy, 8,* 819–831.

Hayes. S. C., Munt, E. D., Korn, Z., Wolfert. E., Rosenfarb, I., & Zettle, R. D. (1986). The effect of feedback and self-reinforcement instructions on studying performance. *The Psychological Record, 36,* 27–37.

Hayes, S. C., Rosenfarb, I., Wolfert, E., Munt, E. O., Korn, Z., & Zettle, R. D. (1985). Self-reinforcement effects: An artifact of social standing setting? *Journal of Applied Behavior Analysis. 18,* 201–204.

Hems, E. D., Lloyd, J. N., & Hallahan, D. P. (1986). Cued and noncued self-recording of attention to task. *Behavior Modification, 10,* 235–254.

Humphrey, L. L., Karoly, P, & Kirschenbaum, D. S. (1978). Self-management in the classroom: Self-imposed response versus self-reward. *Behavior Therapy, 9,* 592–601.

Hundert, J., & Batstone, P. (1978). A practical procedure to maintain pupils' accurate self-rating in a classroom token program. *Behavior Modification, 2,* 93–112.

Ito, M., & Nakamura, K. (1998). Humans' choice in a self-control choice situation: Sensitivity to reinforcer amount, reinforcer delay, and overall reinforcer density. *Journal of the Experimental Analysis of Behavior, 69,* 87–101.

Jones, J. C., & Ollendick, T. H., (1979). Self-reinforcement: Assessment of external influences. *Journal of Behavioral Assessment, 1*, 289–302.

Jones, J. C., Trap, J., & Cooper, J. O. (1977). Technical report: Students' self-recording of manuscript letter strokes. *Journal of Applied Behavior Analysis, 10*, 509–514.

Kanfer, F. H. (1977). The many faces of self-control, or behavior modification changes its focus. In R. B. Stuart (Ed.), *Behavioral self-management: Strategies, techniques, and outcomes* (pp. 1–48). New York: Brunner/Mazel.

Kaplan, H., Hemmes, N. S., Motz, P., & Rodriguez, H. (1996). Self-reinforcement and persons with developmental disabilities. *The Psychological Record, 46*, 161–178.

Kaufman. K. E., & O'Leary, K. D. (1972). Reward, cost. and self-evaluation procedures for disruptive adolescents in a psychiatric hospital school. *Journal of Applied Behavior Analysis, 5*, 293–309.

Kazdin, A. E. (1974). Reactive self-monitoring: The effects of response desirability, goal setting, and feedback. *Journal of Consulting and Clinical Psychology, 42*, 704–716.

Kazdin, A. E. (1979). Unobtrusive measures in behavioral assessment. *Journal of Applied Behavior Analysis, 12*, 713–724.

Kirby, K. C., Fowler, S. A., & Baer, D. M. (1991). Reactivity in self-recording: Obtrusiveness of recording procedure and peer comments. *Journal of Applied Behavior Analysis, 24*, 487–498.

Lee, C., & Tindal, G. A. (1994). Self-recording and goal setting: Effects on on-task and math productivity of low-achieving Korean elementary school students. *Journal of Behavioral Education, 4*, 459–479.

Lipinski, D. P., Black, J. L., Nelson, R. O., & Ciminero, A. R. (1974). The reactivity and unreliability of self-recording. *Journal of Consulting and Clinical Psychology, 42*, 118–123.

Litrownik, A. J., & Freitas, J. L. (1980). Self-monitoring in moderately retarded adolescents: Reactivity and accuracy as a function of valence. *Behavior Therapy, 11*, 245–255.

Logue, A. W., Pena-Correal, T. E., Rodriguez, M. L., & Kabela, E. (1986). Self-control in adult humans: Variation in positive reinforcer amount and delay. *Journal of the Experimental Analysis of Behavior, 46*, 159–173.

Maag, J. W., Reid, R., & DiGangi, S. A. (1993). Differential effects of self-monitoring attention, accuracy, and productivity. *Journal of Applied Behavior Analysis, 26*, 329–343.

Mace, F. C., & Kratochwill, T. R. (1985). Theories of reactivity in self-monitoring: A comparison of cognitive behavioral and operant models. *Behavior Modification, 9*, 323–343.

Mace., F. C., & Kratochwill, T. R. (1988). Self-monitoring: Applications and issues. In J. Witt, S. Elliott, & F. Gresham (eds.), *Handbook of behavior therapy in education* (pp. 489–502). New York: Pergamon.

Mace, F. C., Shapiro. E. S., West, B. J., Campbell, C., & Altman, J. (1986). The role of reinforcement in reactive self-monitoring. *Applied Research in Mental Retardation, 7*, 315–327.

Mace, F. C., & West, B. J. (1986). Unresolved theoretical issues in self-management: Implications for research and practice. *Professional School Psychology, 1*, 149–163.

Maletzky, B. (1974). Behavior recording as treatment: A brief note. *Behavior Therapy, 5*, 107–111.

Malott, R. W. (1984). Rule-governed, self-management, and the developmentally disabled: A theoretical analysis. *Analysis and Intervention in Developmental Disabilities, 4*, 199–209.

Martin, J. (1980). External versus self-reinforcement: A review of methodological and theoretical issues. *Canadian Journal of Behavior Science, 12*, 111–125.

Martin, K. F., & Manno, C. (1995). Use of a check-off system to improve middle school students' story compositions. *Journal of Learning Disabilities, 28*, 139–149.

McFall, R. M., & Hammen, C. L. (1971). Motivation, structure, and self-monitoring: Role of nonspecific factors in smoking reduction. *Journal of Consulting and Clinical Psychology, 37*, 80–86.

McGuffin, M. E., Martz, S. A., & Heron, T. E. (1997). The effects of self-correction versus traditional spelling on the spelling performance and maintenance of third grade students. *Journal of Behavioral Education, 7,* 463–475.

McNamara, J. R. (1972). The use of self-monitoring techniques to treat nailbiting. *Behavior Research and Therapy, 10,* 193–I 94.

Meichenbaum, D. (1977). *Cognitive behavior modification.* New York: Plenum Press.

Michael, J. (1982). Discriminating between discriminative and motivational functions of stimuli. *Journal of the Experimental Analysis of Behavior, 37,* 149–155.

Miller, A. J., & Kratochwill, T. R. (1979). Reduction of frequent stomachache complaints by timeout. *Behavior Therapy, 10,* 211–218.

Nelson, R. O. (1977). Methodological issues in assessment via self-monitoring. In M. Hersen, R. M. Eisler, & P. M. Miller (Eds.), *Progress in behavior modification* (Vol. 5, pp. 263–308). New York: Academic Press.

Nelson, R.O., Hay, W. M., & Carstens, C. B. (1977). The reactivity and accuracy of teachers' self-monitoring of positive and negative classroom verbalizations. *Behavior Therapy, 8,* 972–975.

Nelson, R. O., & Hayes, S. C. (1981). Theoretical explanations for reactivity in self-monitoring. *Behavior Modification, 5,* 3–14.

Nelson, R. O., Hayes, S. C., Spong, R. T., Jarrett, R. B., & McKnight, D. L. (1983). Self-reinforcement: Appealing misnomer or effective mechanism? *Behavior Research and Therapy, 21,* 557–566.

Nelson, R. O., Lipinski, D. P., & Boykin, A. R. (1978). The effects of self-recorders' training and the obtrusiveness of the self-recording device on the accuracy and reactivity of self-monitoring. *Behavior Therapy, 9,* 200–208.

Nevin, J. A. (1974). On the form of the relation between response rates in a multiple schedule. *Journal of the Experimental Analysis of Behavior, 21,* 237–248.

Piersel, W. C. (1985). Behavioral Consultation: An Approach to problem solving. In J. R. Bergen (Ed.), *School psychology in contemporary society* (pp. 252–280). Columbus, OH: Merrill.

Premack, D. (1959). Toward empirical behavior laws: 1. Positive reinforcement. *Psychological Review, 66,* 219–233.

Rachlin, H. (1974). Self-control. *Behaviorism, 2,* 219–233.

Rachlin, H., & Green, L. (1972). Commitment, choice, and self-control. *Journal of the Experimental Analysis of Behavior, 17,* 15–22.

Reid, R., & Harris, K. R., (1993). Self-monitoring of attention versus self-monitoring of performance: Effects on attention and academic performance. *Exceptional Children, 60,* 29–40.

Salend, S. J., & Allen, E. M. (1985). Comparative effects of externally managed and self-managed response-cost systems on inappropriate classroom behavior. *Journal of School Psychology, 23,* 59–67.

Santogrossi, D. A., O'Leary, K. D., Romanczyk, R. G., & Kaufman. K. F. (1973). Self-evaluation by adolescents in a psychiatric hospital school token program. *Journal of Applied Behavior Analysis, 6,* 277–287.

Schunk, D. H. (1989). Social cognitive theory and self-regulated learning. In B. J. Zimmerman & D. H. Schunk (Eds.) *Self-regulated learning and academic achievement: Theory, research,* and practice. New York: Springer-Verlag.

Seabaugh, G. O., & Schumaker, J. B. (1994). The effects self-regulation training on the academic productivity of secondary students with learning problems. *Journal of Behavior Education, 4,* 109–133.

Shapiro, E. S., & Ackerman, A. (1983). Increasing productivity rates in adult mentally retarded clients: The failure of self-monitoring. *Applied Research in Mental Retardation, 4,* 163–181.

Shapiro, E. S., Browder, D. M., & D'Huyvetters, K. (1984). Increasing academic productivity of severely multihandicapped children with self-management: Idiosyncratic effects. *Analysis and Intervention in Developmental Disabilities, 4,* 171–188.

Skinner, B. F. (1938). *The behavior of organisms.* New York: Appleton-Century-Crofts.

Skinner, B. F (1953). *Science and human behavior.* New York: Macmillan.

Skinner, B. F. (1969). *Contingencies of reinforcement: A theoretical analysis.* New York: Appleton-Century-Crofts.

Skinner, B. E. (1979). *The shaping of a behaviorist.* New York: Knopf.

Sohn, P., & Lamal, P. A. (1982). Self-reinforcement: Its reinforcing capability and its clinical utility. *Psychological Record, 32,* 179–203.

Speidel, G. E., & Tharp, R. G. (1980). What does self-reinforcement reinforce? An empirical analysis of the contingencies in self-determined reinforcement. *Child Behavior Therapy, 2,* 1–22.

Stahmer, A. C., & Schreibman, L. (1992). Teaching children with autism appropriate play in unsupervised environments using a self-management treatment package. *Journal of Applied Behavior Analysis, 25,* 447–459.

Sugai, G., & Rowe, P. (1984). The effect of self-recording on out-of-seat behavior of an EMR student. *Education and Training of the Mentally Retarded, 19,* 23–28.

Swanson, H. L., & Scarpati, S. (1985). Self-instruction training to increase academic performance of educationally handicapped children. *Child and Family Behavior Therapy, 6,* 23–39.

Sweeney, W. J., Salva, E., Cooper, J. O., & Talbert-Johnson, C., (1993). Using self-evaluation to improve difficult-to-read handwriting of secondary students. *Journal of Behavioral Education, 3,* 427–443.

Thoresen, C. E., & Mahoney, M. J. (1974). *Behavioral self control.* New York: Holt, Rinehart, & Winston.

Wahler, R. G., & Fox, J. J. (1981). Setting events in applied behavior analysis: Towards a conceptual and methodological expansion. *Journal of Applied Behavior Analysis, 14,* 327–338.

Wall, S. M. (1983). Children's self-determination of standards in reinforcement contingencies: A re-examination. *Journal of School Psychology. 21,* 123–131.

Willis, S. E., & Nelson, R. O. (1982). The effects of valence and nature of target behavior on the accuracy and reactivity of self-monitoring. *Behavioral Assessment, 4,* 401–412.

Wood, D. K., Frank, A. R., & Wacker, D. P. (1998). Teaching multiplication facts to students with learning disabilities. *Journal of Applied Behavior Analysis, 31,* 323–337.

Zettle, R. D., & Hayes, S. C. (1982). Rule-governed behavior: A potential theoretical framework for cognitive-behavioral therapy. In K. R. Harris & S. Graham (Eds.), *Advances in cognitive-behavioral research and therapy* (Vol. 1, pp. 73–118). New York: Academic Press.

Zimmerman, B. J. (1989). Models of self-regulated learning and academic achievement. In B. J. Zimmerman & D. H. Schunk (Eds.) *Self-regulated learning and academic achievement: Theory, research, and practice.* Springer-Verlag: NY.

Self-Regulated Learning and Academic Achievement: A Phenomenological View

Barbara L. McCombs
University of Denver Research Institute

When I wrote this chapter more than a decade ago, my purpose was to present recent theoretical and empirical work regarding the contribution of a phenomenological view to our understanding of self-regulated learning (SRL) and how best to enhance students' development of self-regulated learning capacities. In this revision and update, my purpose remains the same; however, I focus attention on what has changed, what has remained the same, and how the phenomenological view is being interpreted and used today in research and practice. I start with what has been said by some of our most distinguished theoreticians about the self—the self as a primary phenomenon, an experience of the experiencing self—that permeates and directs human behavior. I begin with a look historically at the roots of the "scientific"[1] search into self and its associated phenomena. The evolution of these roots to the present time is then explored as the means to understanding current theoretical positions and how they are converging on our increased knowledge of the role of self phenomena in all of human behavior, and particularly human behavior in learning contexts. As I proceed, I explore answers to the following questions: How can properties of the self (including its structure and processes) contribute to our understanding of its role in initiating and regulating the chain of events leading to effective,

---

[1] "Scientific" is in quotes because of the ongoing debate within the scientific community regarding what constitutes science as concept and method.

self-regulated learning? How do the properties of the self further define the nature of the cognitive and affective activities students engage in while in learning situations? Can our understanding of the self-system and its operations help us provide more effective educational environments and practices to maximize student motivation and learning?

THEORETICAL OVERVIEW

When examining what is generally meant by a phenomenological view and how this view can be defined in the context of self-regulated learning, it is necessary to start with the meaning of phenomenology as a construct and concept. *Phenomenology* is defined (Mish, 1988) as the study of the development of human consciousness and self-awareness. That is, it accepts as reality those experiences that are apparent to the senses and can be scientifically described and evaluated, including abstract and nonobservable phenomena such as perceptions of self and others. In its strictest sense, phenomenology is a philosophical position and study of philosophical assumptions about reality and a methodology for validating the "truth" of this position. The methodology is based on the assumption that all knowledge derives from and is grounded in first-person experience and that the "experience" of consciousness and of self are real and can be systematically studied and verified (Werkmeiseter, 1940). Such self phenomena as perceptions, cognitions, and emotions related to the self or external events are considered primary influences on the way information is processed, interpreted, and acted on. In the context of self-regulated learning, a phenomenological perspective is one that accepts the primacy of self phenomena in directing learning behaviors; it favors a person-referenced over a performance-referenced account of SRL processes and activities.

HISTORICAL BACKGROUND

The term *phenomenology* was coined in the middle of the 18th century by European philosophers (Misiak & Sexton, 1973). According to Misiak and Sexton (1973), a phenomenological approach is defined as:

> In the *broadest* sense, any psychology which considers personal experience in its subject matter, and which accepts and uses phenomenological description, explicitly or implicitly, can be called phenomenological psychology. It is contrasted with psychology which admits only objective observation of behavior and excludes introspection and phenomenological description in its methodology. (p. 40)

Although various doctrines have been encompassed within the phenomenological movement, a common core is the method—a systematic and full exploration of consciousness and the objects of consciousness, that is, all that is perceived, imagined, doubted, or loved. Traditionally, consciousness is explored in three phases: intuiting, analyzing, and describing. Fundamental assumptions underlying this exploration are the intentional and directional characteristics of consciousness, the recognition that consciousness is always consciousness of something, and the ontological priority of consciousness in making possible the apprehension of all other forms of being that compose reality (Jennings, 1986; Misiak & Sexton, 1973; Rosenberg, 1986).

In the phenomenological method, introspective observations are given rigorous analysis and careful description (Jennings, 1986; Mays, 1985). "First-hand" subjective accounts are assumed to be valid and are directed at the self as experimental subject or at the external world. Because of the primacy or ontological priority of consciousness in all perception, cognition, and affect, the phenomenological study of consciousness provides the information base both for building theory and for deciding whether various theories give an adequate account of the actual experiences of consciousness, the actual "facts of perception" (Jennings, 1986; Mays, 1985). More recently, Richardson (1999) argued for the use of concepts and methods of phenomenographic research for the study of personal experiences and self phenomena. *Phenomenography* is defined as "... an empirically based approach that aims to identify the qualitatively different ways in which different people experience, conceptualize, perceive, and understand various kinds of phenomena" (Richardson, 1999, p. 53). In addition, Natsoulas (1999) pointed out that the scientific understanding of consciousness and perception has again become a central concern of psychology, with efforts currently being made to combine ecological and phenomenological approaches to study the structure of consciousness. Thus, current directions continue to seek ways to apply scientific rigor to subjective phenomena.

Phenomenology began as a reaction to deterministic and naturalistically oriented theories of human behavior. Edmund Husserl (1859–1938) is credited with advancing phenomenological psychology as a response to prevalent "world view philosophies." He argued that these philosophies ignored the essential nature of reality as being unable to exist apart from the conscious experience of beholding it, and instead contended that psychological phenomena could be reduced to and understood by the laws of physical phenomena (Jennings, 1986). Husserl was convinced that philosophies that "equated" consciousness with physical nature—correlating mental and physical events—could not provide a full understanding of human nature. He recommended that phenomenological analyses *precede* experimental studies as a way to apprehend and delineate the essential acts of consciousness (Jennings, 1986; Misiak & Sexton, 1973). Those currently working within the field of living systems are confirming the value of these methods in identifying— via intuition, analysis, and self-reflection—the self-organizing and inter-dependent nature of all living things, particularly the dynamic principles and processes that account for human behavior based on inherent needs for relationships and meaningful lives (Wheatley, 1995, 1999; Wheatley & Kelner-Rogers, 1996, 1998).

In the historical context of his times, however, Husserl was a catalyst for growing dissatisfaction with the logical positivism base of psycho-logical theorizing and the physical sensation limits this base placed on the conception of experience (Spiegelberg, 1972). With phenomenol-ogy, the self and a range of new phenomena and new interpretations in psychology were "allowable" objects of scientific inquiry. Heidegger also advocated a union between psychology and philosophy during the 1920s by arguing for the necessity of a phenomenological approach to understanding the unique and primary human experience of "being" (McCall, 1983; Spiegelberg, 1972). His "hermeneutic" phenomenology allowed an interpretive approach to defining human existence by our relations not only to other beings, but also to Being itself and its fun-damental characteristics (McCall, 1983; Spiegelberg, 1972). During the 1930s, Husserl's student, Marvin Farber, was credited with bringing phe-nomenology to America by founding the International Phenomenolog-ical Society (Misiak & Sexton, 1973).

Two early indigenous phenomenologists in America were Donald Snygg and his collaborator, Arthur Combs. In the 1940s Snygg pre-sented his view of the "phenomenal self" as the world within an indi-vidual that is maintained and enhanced by a relatively permanent "per-ceived self" (Misiak & Sexton, 1973). Other "self-theorists" (also called "humanists") who appeared around this time included Carl Rogers, Rollo May, Abraham Maslow, and Viktor Frankl (Misiak & Sexton, 1973; Spiegelberg, 1972). A fundamental assumption apparent in Combs' (1962) perceptual view led him to contend that a focus of all organi-zations and individuals involved in human development be on creating the kinds of experiences that will affect changes in perceptions neces-sary to produce truly adequate, healthy people, defined as those who have a positive view of self, identify with others, are open to experience and acceptance, and have a rich and available perceptual field. Combs later spent a considerable part of his career exploring person-centered, perceptual approaches and qualities of effective helpers in the fields of teaching, counseling, social work, pastoral care, and clinical psychology. From 13 studies he found that the common qualities of effective helpers that led to positive self development were "... a direct outcome of the helper's perceptual organization or belief system. It is what the helper believes that makes the difference" (Combs, 1986, p. 55).

Slowed down by the rise of Skinnerian and other behaviorist theories in the 1950s and 1960s, phenomenology was, according to Jennings in 1986, attracting ever-growing attention. Jennings (1986) contended that this reemergence reflected more than an appreciation for subjective self-report data; it included a concern with understanding and experimentally studying the essential character of consciousness. In fact, many current theorists are dealing directly with links between consciousness and self-phenomena in addressing differences between an *I* self and a *Me* self, linking philosophical assumptions with psychological experiences (McCombs & Marzano, in press). There is also a growing literature on the role of self-phenomena, and in particular, the self-concept as one of the most important regulators of behavior (Kanfer & McCombs, 2000; Markus & Wurf, 1987; Marsh, 1994; Marsh & Yeung, 1998).

The next section summarizes the views of those concerned with studying self-phenomena presented more than a decade ago and provides more current views that confirm the increased attention being given this area.

CURRENT VIEWS

In 1987, Nicholls argued that approaches that take a "technical" orientation to human affairs of necessity have to abandon " ... anything of metaphysical comfort and moral significance, (thereby) reducing the value of psychology for answering questions about how we should conduct our lives" (p. 2). In the decade of the 1990s and as advice for the 21st century, many current researchers and educators are arguing for person- and learner-centered models of education that address holistic personal and individual needs that underlie complex behavior, including learning, motivation, and self-regulation (cf. Kanfer & McCombs, 2000; McCombs & Whisler, 1997). In general, person- and learner-centered models focus on the personal rather than the technical or organizational levels of an educational system (McCombs, 1999).

With a focus on the person and needs that must be supported in living systems, researchers are beginning to acknowledge and work within the uncertain and chaotic nature of life and living things. This has led to a heightening interest in phenomenological approaches that focus on understanding the perceptions, assumptions, beliefs, and values of individuals and their congruence because of the infinite possibilities of influence and interaction (Combs, 1991; McCombs, 1999; Wheatley,

1994, 1999). In a personal conversation in March 1997, Combs further emphasized that helping learners at all levels of the system to learn new perspectives related to positive functioning and outcomes is a far simpler process than attacking complex external factors or behavior. He explained that the aim of this internal learning process in any living system—from the individual to organizational level—is to clarify beliefs about what is important in terms of "other" versus "self" orientation, including appropriate levels of freedom and control, for example, how you view yourself and others, and how much freedom—or control—is appropriate for the person or the organization (McCombs, 1999).

Combs and his colleagues further verified that person-centered ideas and their application continue to encounter resistance in the fields of psychology and education (cf. Combs, Miser, & Whitaker, 1999). In our March 1997 dialogue, Combs described how basic principles of learning from perceptual psychology that had been known since the 1940s are being ignored in favor of behavioral and mechanistic models that put the focus on external factors. He expressed frustration at how long it has taken for educators to accept perceptual ideas, but was optimistic about current perspectives—including systems thinking, brain research, constructivism, and social constructivism. These approaches emphasize connections, relationships, and fields of meaning that surround us and promise to transform our thinking and our systems to better serve the needs of all (McCombs, 1999).

In contrast with criticisms levied by Robinson (1987) that current psychological theories of human motivation and behavior discount the importance of self phenomena, particularly the explanatory value of "agency" in motivation and behavior, current views and educational practices are recognizing the importance of individual choice and control in learning and systems change. For example, in line with Robinson's (1987) view that "authentic" agency is the full expression of self as a self-defined and self-disciplined agent that seeks full self-expression under the standards of self-perfection, many current theorists are pursuing the study of higher order self-processes and innate characteristics of the self that predispose individuals to the natural display of self-organizing, self-regulating behaviors under conditions that support basic self-nurturing and positive self-development needs (e.g., Covington, 1992; Mills, 1995; Pransky, 1998). This is in keeping with Robinson's (1987) view that humans are "authentic" to the degree they self-select and define those external influences that appear most nurturing of self, as well as with Giorgi's (1985) view that "a radical shift in perspective [in scientific research] is necessary to do justice to human phenomena" (p. vii). Giorgi (1990) contended that phenomenology clarifies psychology's foundation as a human science and allows greater fidelity to conscious phenomena than traditional science.

Sameroff (1987) criticized both the passive person–active environment models underlying behavior modification and other Skinnerian approaches and the active person–passive environment models of Piaget and Chomsky for the limits they placed on understanding. He contended that what is needed is a transactional model—an active person–active environment model—in which individuals change reality and these changes affect the behavior of individuals, in a dynamic developmental process in time between individuals and their social context. Similarly, Gardner (1987) took a "phenomenal" perspective on human development and expressed dissatisfaction with prevailing modular views of intelligence as separate information-processing systems. He stated, "From a phenomenological perspective, we individuals do not feel like a number of different systems; there is the perception of a unified entity, with a sense of self and with a single consciousness" (p. 6). Gardner's more recent work on multiple intelligences reflects his concern with more integrative conceptions of personal capabilities that encompass a range of preferences and predispositions that derive from complex and dynamic person–environment interactions (Gardner, 1993, 1995a, 1995b).

Howard's (1986) contention—that because humans are continually and actively involved in their own process of "becoming," they can be influenced, positively or negatively, by how the sciences, particularly psychology, view them—is still valid today. He argued for the subjective, personal, and intuitive side of research as a way to understand fully the unique volitional and self-determined nature of human functioning. Thus the science of psychology must *begin* with an analysis of humans and their characteristics and *then* agree on the techniques, procedures, and designs that are most appropriate to understanding their characteristics—not the reverse, as happened with the acceptance of logical positivism as the philosophical base for psychology. Howard further argued for an active agency model of self-creation through meaningful actions in pursuit of the agent's goals, plans, and intentions, a model also advocated by Harre and Secord (1972) and Manicas and Secord (1983). Howard (1986) believed this type of model can give us knowledge regarding human possibilities as causal and interpretive beings.

Human volition is viewed by Howard (1986) as a generative structure that is goal directed, purposeful, or teleological in nature—a structure that gives entities their causal force, with self as the agent who "wields the power of personal agency" (p. 4). This position was developed more recently by McCombs and Marzano (1990, in press), Mills (1995), and Pransky (1998) in a view of self as the agent who orchestrates mind, thought, and consciousness through his or her understanding of personal qualities as inherent and as transcending the physical self. Attempts are also being made by a number of theorists (e.g., Deci & Ryan, 1991; McCombs, 1991; McCombs & Marzano, 1990, in press; Mills, 1991, 1995) to describe the processes and structures that distinguish the *I* and *Me* selves, the higher order, nonlocal nature of "the I behind the me in the mirror" (Harter, 1990, 1992), and role of the *I* self in will and self-regulated learning (cf. Kanfer & McCombs, 2000, McCombs & Marzano, in press; See Corno, chapter 6, this volume for further information about volitional processes.)

With these general trends in current theorizing in mind, I turn next to a look at changes during the past decade in self theorists' views on the nature and purpose of self-phenomena in self-regulation in general and in self-regulation of learning in particular.

THEORIES ABOUT THE SELF

William James was one of the first American psychologists to develop ideas and theories regarding the self (Brownback, 1982). James distinguished between self-feelings, self-love, and self-estimation. To him, *self-feelings* conveyed worth or status and equated to self-esteem; *self-love* referred to will and actions toward self-preservation; *self-estimation* referred to intellectual judgments based on more objective assessments of competency. James also identified a number of *I* processes including personal continuity over time, distinctiveness from others, agency over life events, and volition. Thus, James's notions encompassed the affective, motivational (volitional), and cognitive aspects of self.

Among a number of contemporary theorists, the self is viewed as the active constructor of cognitive representations and understanding of an objective world. For example, Rosenberg (1986) argued that this is possible because the self is both a "self-conscious" subject of experiences and the object of them. That is, the self can "know itself" in two ways: as a position in social space and as a causally potent spatiotemporal natural object. In this sense, the self is a dynamic center, always in a state of becoming, an agent and the product of its own creation (Westphal, 1982). More recently, my colleagues and I (Kanfer & McCombs, 2000; McCombs & Marzano, in press) summarized theory and research on the "self as agent" in the self-regulation of personal learning, motivation, and development—contingent on levels of self-awareness and self-reflection. Similar views were also posited by Ridley (1991) and Ryan (1992). It is interesting to note that with the rising popularity of constructivist and social constructivist views of learning, the focus has been more on the *process* of learning as one of constructing personal meaning, generally aided by the social context and interactions with others, than on the *processor* or the person guiding and directing that process. (See chapter 8, this volume, by Paris, Byrnes, & Paris for current views on constructivist approaches to self-regulated learning.)

Harter (1987, 1998, 1999) theorized about and empirically studied self development and the self-system's role in motivation and achievement from a structural and process-oriented (functional) perspective. Her work was particularly influenced by the theories of James and Cooley— particularly James's (1892) notion that self-esteem is directly related to the ratio of one's successes to one's aspirations in specific domains (domain-specific evaluations of the importance of these domains), and Cooley's (1902) notion that self-worth is based on our perceptions of what significant others think of us. In Harter's (1985, 1987, 1992a) view, self-evaluations are primary determinants of affect, motivation, and achievement. Individuals' evaluations of competence and signifi- cant others' attitudes determine self-worth to the degree they are con- sidered important in specific domains. Harter (1999) recently pointed out that most self- theorists agree that one's own self-view—that is clearly differentiated from the views of others—emerges gradually and becomes fully operative relatively late in human development.

Harter (1992a; 1998; Harter, Whitesell, & Junkin, 1998) contended that global self-concept is not the sum of all the evaluations that are made about the self. Rather, it is a function of how important students view different domains and/or doing well in these domains, as well as the sup- port available from significant others. Domains with the largest discrep- ancies between importance and competence/adequacy judgments for adolescents are cognitive, romantic appeal, and appearance, with impor- tance ratings being particularly predictive of overall self-worth for high school students (Harter et al., 1998). If importance ratings are ignored, interventions can target the wrong dynamics and actually erode versus enhance self-worth. Harter et al. (1998) noted that Marsh (1993, 1995) argued that importance ratings add little to the prediction of self-esteem, but this is based on correlational methods rather than procedures that take importance ratings into account, such as comparing correlations of competence/adequacy scores for domains rated important with corre- lations of scores for domains rated unimportant. The latter procedures do reveal that consideration of importance enhances the predictability of self-worth.

The active, self-initiated nature of children's development of self- knowledge continues to be emphasized in Ruble's (1987; Ruble & Dweck, 1995) work. According to this view, self-development is a self-defined and constructed process of information seeking, motivated by age-related needs and interest. Findings confirm that children are maximally sensitive to certain kinds of information during relatively circumscribed time periods. Ruble (1987) stated, ". . . the kind of information available at the time of heightened interest in or susceptibility to relevant information is important because once a conclusion about the self is formed (e.g., as incompetent in school), subsequent information processing is likely to be selective and behavioral choices restricted" (p. 262). Recent work illustrates not only the important influence self-evaluative processes and existing self-structures have on the way information is processed and acted on, but also demonstrates gender differences in self-constructions of ability that interact to influence self-evaluations (Martin & Ruble, 1997; Pomerantz & Ruble, 1997). Cross and Madson (1997) and Marsh and Yeung (1998) also found differential development of gender differences in self-concept in math and English domains using longitudinal structural equation modeling, with boys not keeping pace with the educational gains experienced by girls.

Eccles' (1983, 1984) earlier work emphasized that a person's interpretations of events are more powerful determinants of actions than the events themselves. Her findings indicated that an individual's self-perceptions, needs, and goals play a major role in the value he or she attaches to a learning task, expectations for success, and achievement behaviors like persistence and performance. Also cited as contributing to the overall value of the task are variables such as the importance of doing well (attainment value), the inherent and immediate enjoyment expected from engaging in the task (intrinsic or interest value), and the perceived importance of the task for some future goal (utility value). These variables mediate students' choices about whether they will engage in the types of activities (e.g., self-regulated learning processes) that promote task mastery. Other important mediators discussed by Eccles (1983) included individuals' sex-role identity and values, and the perceived cost of success or failure, such as the perceived effort required, the perceived loss of valued alternatives, and the perceived psychological cost of failure (e.g., loss of self-esteem). The personal value students attach to a task is thus one variable that influences their motivation and use of SRL.

In the last decade, Eccles continued to explore adolescent self-beliefs and their relationships to academic motivation and achievement (e.g., Eccles & Wigfield, 1995; Eccles, Wigfield, Midgley, Reuman, & Mac Iver, 1993; Wigfield, Eccles, & Pintrich, 1996). More recently, however, her work has focused on the application of her findings to conditions that foster healthy development of self-evaluations and self-esteem in home and school settings (e.g., Eccles, Barber, Jozefowicz, Malenchuk, & Vida, 1999; Eccles, Early, Frasier, Belansky, & McCarthy, 1997; Frome & Eccles, 1998). Among the most important findings are the potentially negative influences of school transitions and changes in family and peer relations and a definition of factors in the school, classroom, and home environments that can offset these influences. For example, parents' perceptions and adolescents' self-perceptions have been compared in a longitudinal investigation (Frome & Eccles, 1998), and these results are being used to clarify gender differences in girls' and boys' achievement strivings and sense of competence across the adolescent years and to identify protective factors. Eccles et al. (1997) also verified three dimensions of school and family contexts for healthy development: connection, regulation, and autonomy. The presence of these dimensions was found to be related to higher grades and more positive adolescent functioning across contexts, including selection of well-functioning peer groups and positive sibling and parent relationships within the home.

Higgins's (1987; Moretti & Higgins, 1999a, 1999b) "self-discrepancy theory" considers the specific kinds of discomfort or emotional problems associated with particular types of belief incompatibility. This theory posits three basic domains of the self: (a) the actual self, or the self-state representations of attributes you or another person believe you actually possess; (b) the ideal self, or the self-state representations of attributes you or others would like you, ideally, to possess; and (c) the ought self, or the self-state representations of attributes that you or others believe you should possess. Crossing these three domains with the "own"/"other" dimensions yields six basic types of self-state representations. Our own and others' beliefs about our "actual self" are said to be the basis of our self-concept; the other combinations (ideal/own, ideal/other, ought/own, ought/other) are "self-guides" that motivate and direct our behavior.

In Higgins's (1997) framework, approach–avoidance motivation is described in terms of *regulatory focus*. This focus can be on promotion (accomplishments and aspirations) or prevention (safety and responsibilities). Regulatory focus is posited as a motivational principle that describes self-regulation toward desired end-states. Depending on the caretaker ideals and aspirations or beliefs about responsibilities and duties, children learn very different ideas about self-regulation. They can learn a focus on advancement, growth, and accomplishment (promotion focus) or a concern with protection, safety, and responsibility (prevention focus). Further, Higgins (1997) reported that motivation and performance are enhanced when strategies used to attain desired goals are compatible with an individual's regulatory focus while working on the task, that is, their expectancies and values within a particular regulatory focus. For example, if students have a promotion focus within a learning goal orientation, positive emotions and motivation occur, whereas if students have a prevention focus within this same learning goal orientation, negative emotions and motivation to protect self-worth would be expected (e.g., Covington, 1985, 1992; Covington & Omelich, 1987; Covington & Teel, 1996).

Highly consistent with the preceding frameworks—while at the same time providing an intuitively appealing integration of both our current and historical understanding of self phenomena—is the theorizing of Markus and her colleagues that emphasized the motivational role of the self-system in basic striving for desired self-conceptions and self-fulfillment (Markus & Nurius, 1987; Markus & Wurf, 1987; Ruvolo & Markus, 1986). This theory suggested that individuals' images of their self in future situations become part of their working self-concepts and, as such, these images provide a specific self-relevant form and direction to motivation. Of particular interest in Markus's work is the notion of "possible selves"—cognitive manifestations of enduring goals, aspirations, fears, and threats that exist within an individual's self-system. *Self-structures* are defined as generalizations derived from prior experience, which can define past, present, and future (possible) selves, and which can help in the integration and explanation of our own behavior. It is the possible selves that provide the plans and strategies for the future—that put the self in action. In this view, individuals will control and regulate their behavior because of investments in future plans by their possible selves. Ruvolo and Markus (1986; Markus & Ruvolo, 1990) contended that possible selves have two functions: an affective function of making one feel good or bad, and a motivational function of creating incentives and guiding actions. The nature of self-concept structures is also seen as continuous and stable, as well as dynamic and capable of change even into older age (Herzog, Franks, Markus, & Holmberg, 1998). Thus, a dynamic trait–state view of self-system development is posited.

Markus and Wurf (1987) emphasized the dynamic and multifaceted nature of self-concept—a schema that is both a structure and a process and that can present the self as both "known" and "knower." Self-concept is seen as domain-specific and global, with different degrees of accessibility. What is termed the "working self-concept" is the accessible self-concept of the moment, a continually active and shifting array of self-conceptions that are tied to the prevailing circumstances. Markus and Wurf (1987) argued that there are direct ties between self-structures (what individuals think, feel, and believe about themselves) and self-regulation. This position is based on the generally accepted view that self-regulated behavior is directed toward some goal. The first step in self-regulation, then, becomes goal selection, which is determined singly or jointly by (a) expectations about self-competencies and task outcomes; (b) affective factors such as needs, motives, and values; and (c) desired self-conceptions that represent general life goals, which have been personalized into particular goals and behaviors. As goals are selected, they give form and direction to the second step in self-regulation, planning, and strategy selection. Finally, in the performance execution and evaluation step, self-monitoring and self-evaluation processes assist in the maintenance of attention, comparison of actual and desired goals, and attempts to reduce performance discrepancies.

In further discussing research on the role of the self-concept in self-regulation, Markus and Wurf (1987) contended that self-concept is seen as a critical variable in how smoothly self-regulatory processes function— their effectiveness, efficiency, consistency, and so forth. The facilitative or debilitative effects of self-focusing, however, are cited as evidence that finer distinctions are needed between the structural and functional aspects of the self. Markus and Wurf (1987) suggested that the resolution may lie in distinguishing the *I* (process-oriented agent, dynamic aspects of self) and the *me* (structural and descriptive content of the self). In their model of the dynamic self-concept, it is the working self-concept— the accessible self-representations—that regulates individuals' ongoing actions and reactions. In turn, the contents of the working self-concept are determined by the individual's self-motives along with social circumstances. In this view, then, self-regulation is more determined by dynamic self-structures than by the *I* or agenic and volitional characteristics of self.

According to Markus and Wurf (1987), the dynamic structural aspects of the working self-concept shape and control both intrapersonal processes (self-relevant information processing, affect regulation, motivational processes) and interpersonal processes (social perception, social comparison, seeking out and shaping interactions with others). Intrapersonal processes involved in the regulation of affect include defending the self against negative emotional states, which may be motivated by goals for self-consistency and self-enhancement. That is, individuals will strive for consistent and positive self views and will regulate negative affect to protect these self views. The interpersonal and cultural aspects of the self were the focus of Markus' (1998; Cross & Markus, 1990, in press; Markus & Kitayama, 1991a, 1991b, 1994, 1998) more recent work. This work provides evidence of cultural self-concept variations, particularly American versus Japanese conceptions of self as independent and interdependent, respectively. The cultural context is shown to play an important role in shaping self-concepts and how they operate in human motivation and behavior. For example, Japanese students show the opposite of the self-serving bias in denying themselves credit for their successes and accepting responsibility for their failures. They are thus less likely to show this fundamental attribution error as compared to American students who define themselves in less contextually constrained ways.

As we have just seen, research on variables such as self-concept, self-esteem, and possible selves (e.g., Markus & Ruvulo, 1990; Markus & Wurf, 1987) indicates that the self is an organizing force in motivation and behavior. Not only is the importance of self-constructions well documented, but it is increasingly clear that learners have the capacity to understand the constructive process and to be aware of the "self-as-agent" (McCombs, 1986; McCombs & Marzano, 1990, in press). One of the most comprehensive discussions of the *I* self is offered by Deci and Ryan (1991). In simplified terms, integration is the most basic of human drives for Deci and Ryan. The drive for integration operates on three basic needs: competence, autonomy, and relatedness. As described by Deci and Ryan (1991), the need for competence encompasses people's strivings to experience control over outcomes and to understand and be able to reliably effect the instrumentalities that lead to desired outcomes. The need for autonomy encompasses the need for people to feel like the origin of their behavior. Finally, the need for relatedness encompasses a person's striving to relate to and care for others and feel related to and cared for by others. In short, for Deci & Ryan, the *I* self is a set of innate processes: "... there is an inherent rudimentary self, a set of processes and potentials... that represent the beginning of a developing self" (Deci & Ryan, 1991, p. 16).

Ryan (1991) noted that conceptualizations of the self historically have given a central role to the organizing and synthetic tendencies of the self—humans naturally conceive of themselves as coherent and consistent whole beings, whether or not they act that way from the perspectives of others. He redefined autonomy and self-determination to incorporate the capacity for mutually reciprocal relatedness such that the true self emerges only in the context of authentic relating with others. In this view, autonomy and relatedness are mutually dependent, rather than mutually exclusive, aspects of the self and allow one to examine and confirm aspects of the self. These two processes assist in self-integration and self-cohesion as well as deepen relationships, thereby speaking to the integration of the other into the psychology of self. Ryan took exception, however, to looking-glass or social-comparative models of the self. His is an organismic view that presumes there is an organizing tendency in human nature that strives for self- and relational cohesion based on basic needs for autonomy and relatedness. Ryan (1991) stated,

"Although humans are quite wide-ranging in what they may 'take in,' regulations and values in conflict with basic needs for autonomy, competence, or relatedness ultimately cannot be fully integrated. The nature of the self is not infinitely malleable. It is perhaps the case that the humanism of a culture or the socializing context can be gauged by the extent to which its structures are capable of being integrated, rather than producing fragmentation and conflict within the individual and within relational aspects of social organizations" (p. 232).

Within a living systems perspective, this is compatible with Wheatley's (1999) view that no behavior can be understood in isolation from the whole of the system and its interdependent dynamics in time. She described a principle from biology that if a system is in trouble, connecting it to more of itself can restore health; thus, to make a system stronger, stronger relationships must be created with *itself.* That means that the nature of humans as living systems is to *learn more about themselves from themselves* through self-discovery and the creation of new relationships. Further, Wheatley maintained that self-reference is the process by which all living things decide what is worth noticing at any one point in time while being surrounded by and existing in fields rich with potential relationships. Choices are made based on self-reference and reality is cocreated through self-reference, but at different levels of consciousness (which helps us create or discover meaning) dependent on whether we use our consciousness to be more aware and reflective about the meaningfulness of information. Ryan (1991), also stated,

> "Once acknowledging that the overall direction of life is toward interdependence and synthesis, we can see that conceptions that overly reify the self run the risk of disembedding it from its nature as a set of organizational *processes* (author's emphasis) within and between persons. These organizing processes are both less integral and stable than the term *I* suggests and perhaps less fully connected than the term *we* might connote" (p. 233).

In understanding how individuals achieve integration in both positive and negative social or cultural contexts, theorists have posited concepts of personal autonomy, agency, self-awareness, and other higher order self processes that Mills (1991, 1995) called a "psychological vantage point." That is, the *I* self can be understood as more than the sum of beliefs about self (*me* self), interactions with the environment, or the actual environmental influences. According to Mills, the *I* self has the natural capacity to step outside the boundaries of conditioned beliefs or habits of thinking and see the self as the originator of thoughts, perceptions, and the experience of the moment. This psychological vantage point is the *I* self at its highest level of awareness and not bounded by physical or psychological "realities" of the past, present, or future. In this view, self-regulation in its natural form can be understood as emanating from the highest level of understanding about psychological functioning, the role of thought in creating experiences, and the degree of choice in any given moment or situation: the choice over what we think.

As argued by self-determination theorists (e.g., Deci & Ryan, 1991), it is the nature of human beings to be intrinsically motivated and actively involved in the learning process when basic needs for autonomy, competence, and relatedness are met. Evidence for this phenomenon is plentiful among young children who eagerly and persistently explore and learn about their world. This natural curiosity and motivation to learn resurfaces as learners pursue topics of strong personal interest in situations where the learner has personal control and autonomy. For example, Mills, Dunham, and Alpert (1988) found that when students were helped to understand their agency or personal control over self processes, such as awareness, reflection, and thinking, they could step outside these processes and move beyond negative self-beliefs and thinking. In turn, they experienced more control and the learning process became positively self-confirming. Turner and Paris (1995) reported similar findings in a study of first graders' motivation for reading. That is, major variables related to motivation included provision for choice and teachers' beliefs that students are able to assume responsibility for their own learning.

Even young children develop their own beliefs and theories about who they are (their abilities, agency, control, or efficacy), and these beliefs are highly susceptible to influence by external variables (e.g., success experiences, support from others). Young children can easily learn to see themselves as "helpless" and thereby abdicate responsibility for their own learning. What children can learn from constructions based on negative self perceptions is that causality lies outside rather than within the self. Just as failure can become a learned schema, it can also be unlearned by appropriate experiences, strategies training, and social support. Paris and Byrnes (1989), for example, described how constructivism operates as the way in which people transform and organize reality based on common intellectual principles that interact with development, the environment, and self. Mills (1991, 1995) extended these ideas and presented evidence that a higher self provides the control and direction to self-construction in the sense that self-schemas can be objectively examined and changed.

For Deci and Ryan (1991), learning is a natural process directed primarily at creating the self, elaborating and integrating one's capacities and interests into a unified structure that is coherent and self-regulating. Ryan (1992) contended that needs for autonomy and competence fuel intrinsic motivation and integration of the individual among and between other persons. Autonomy is "self-rule" or self-determination in which one experiences the self as agent. However, Ryan and Powelson (1991) argued that putting too much emphasis on the natural organization and internalization process runs the risk of ignoring the role of the self in enacting behaviors that can deter or foster this natural process. There is an "agent in the middle of organization" and development depends on both the dynamics of agency and the social context (Ryon & Powelson, 1991). The self is thus seen as lying outside of the learned system of self-beliefs or at a higher level of organization. In addition, Ryan (1995) argued that there are innate integrative or actualizing tendencies underlying self-development that are dynamic but dependent on social–contextual supports for autonomy, competence, and relatedness. Ryan and Deci (1996) emphasized that self- determination theory points to the importance of the psychological meaning of events as derived from self-perceptions and self-evaluations in determining the level and quality of a person's motivation, agency, and self-regulation.

What I suggested in my original chapter as needed to extend the existing theoretical framework to encompass the phenomenological perspective has been taking place to a large degree in the last decade. First, the distinction between the experience of self and its operation suggests that the creative and self-generated aspects of self are separate from what is created—even if what is created is a complex and dynamic hierarchical structure. The concept of "authentic agency" as described by Robinson (1987)—the self-determined and volitional aspects of self–scannot be equated with the structures (the "what" or content of self-knowledge) or with the self-creative and self-defining processes (the "how" or metacognitive[2] means for self-definition) that build these structures, as currently being argued by theorists such as Deci and Ryan (1991) and Mills (1995). As I recently argued (McCombs & Marzano in press), the phenomenological perspective can continue to assist us in understanding the "who" aspects of self as both the knower and the known, the constructor of meaning and what is constructed.

The phenomenological perspective continues to help us understand the "who" aspects of self as well as how best to enhance not only students' development of positive self-concepts, perceptions of self-worth, and competence, but also their beliefs about their locus of responsibility, degree of self-determination, and sense of agency in creating positive possibilities for self-development and self-regulation. A structural cause for the development of these beliefs appears to be insufficient for fully explaining the nature of the self-phenomena as we experience it. Continued exploration and theorizing about the self-system helps us

---

[2] *Metacognition* generally refers to the use of higher order thinking, reasoning, and learning skills during learning, examples of which include goal setting, problem solving, and self-evaluation strategies. A learner or trainee is said to be metacognitive to the degree to which he or she employs these higher order thinking, reasoning, and learning skills. Metacognition can also be defined as thinking about thinking, a higher order process that involves the self in control and self-regulation of emotions, cognitions, learning, and training activities.

understand the role of the *I* and *me* aspects of self in the development of metacognitive processes for the regulation of thought, feelings, and actions. In addition, it helps us define interventions for helping students become self-regulated and self-determined, and for achieving positive self development.

In summary, then, this theoretical overview has led us through the historical background of the phenomenological perspective in psychology. We looked at the philosophical assumptions underlying the validity of self-phenomena and the methodology that is appropriate for systematically studying these phenomena. We also looked at the evolution of phenomenological views about the nature of the self from early to present self theories. We saw in these current theories the recognition of the primacy of self-system structures and processes in self-regulation, and an understanding of the global and domain-specific structural organization of the self-system as well as its dynamic and relatively stable characteristics. Further, we saw a recognition that self-system structures and the processes that support the building of these structures develop over time via individuals' interactions with their social–physical environment. We heard a consensus among current self theorists regarding the self's continual and active role in its own becoming—an active agent model of self-definition. Finally, we explored the role that self-system structures and processes play in self-regulation in general and self-regulated learning in particular, and the importance of self-evaluations of personal agency and learning competence to the development and execution of self-regulated learning behaviors, cognitions, and affect. We turn next to a delineation of specific self-system structures and processes in SRL and how these can be assessed from a phenomenological perspective.

SELF-SYSTEM STRUCTURES AND PROCESSES IN SELF-REGULATED LEARNING

Just as self-development is a generative and active process, so is learning, with the self playing a key role in generating hypotheses, interpretations, predictions, and in the processing and organization of information (Iran-Nejad, 1990; Wittrock, 1987). The self's basic role in the learning process is to generate the motivation to approach and persist in learning activities—as a function of evaluating the personal meaningfulness and relevance of learning activities relative to individual goals and beliefs about one's competencies and abilities. As Wittrock (1987) stated, motivation is a function of one's beliefs and ". . . above all, it is the belief in one's self, as a teacher or as a learner" (p. 13). We know from the preceding section that our beliefs are organized in self-structures and are

formed by a variety of self-processes. Self-structures represent our personalized and self-defined conceptualizations of self-attributes—organized
as a global, relatively stable self-concept and as domain-specific conceptualizations in specific areas relevant to our lives at particular periods
and moments in time. Self-processes include a variety of metacognitive
or higher order processes for "thinking about our thinking and experiences" that include self-awareness, self-evaluation, and self-reflection
(Kanfer & McCombs, 2000). In this section I explore the phenomenological perspective to understanding and assessing self-system structures
and processes relevant to self-regulated learning. To guide the reader
in visualizing the self—and its structures and processes—Fig. 3.1

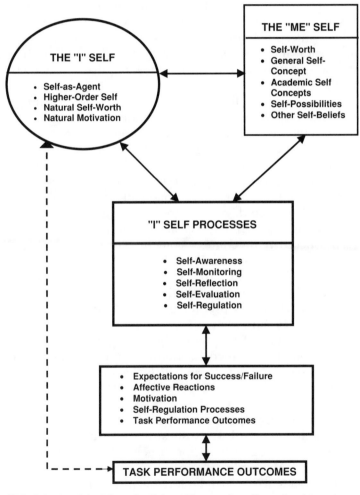

FIG. 3.1. Model of the role of the self-system in self-regulated learning.

presents a graphic representation of the conceptualization presented here.

Self-System Structures

Self-system structures can be classified, then, as either global or domain-specific conceptualizations individuals generate regarding their attributes, including their self-concept, self-image, and self-worth. These structures are formed over time, as individuals develop from infancy into adulthood through interactions with the social and physical environment. Information acquired about the self as a result of interactions with the external context is transformed and modified cognitively to fit unique experiences of self or being, including individual perceptions of needs and goals of self-development. As individuals change and develop, their conceptualizations of themselves change and develop such that more enduring and permanent aspects of self can be thought of structurally as existing separately from the more dynamic and changing aspects of self.

Global self-concept in the context of self-regulated learning can be defined as individuals' beliefs and perceptions of their ability to direct and control their cognition, affect, motivation, and behavior in learning situations in general. In large part, it is both a learner's *belief* that he or she possesses the necessary knowledge, skills, and abilities for the self-regulation of learning and an *image* of himself or herself as a self-regulated learner. For example, one might assess this self-view by asking students to express their degree of agreement with statements such as, "I believe I can work independently to achieve my learning goals." Thus, a global self-concept in this context is one that incorporates self-beliefs as well as self-goals or values regarding self-regulated learning. In the sense discussed by Markus (1998; Cross & Markus, 1990, in press; Markus & Ruvulo, 1990), it may even include the "future possible self" as a self-regulated learner. From the psychological perspective, then, the *me* self is both what one *knows* and what one *believes* about the self in general and in particular domains. Perceptions of competencies, personal characteristics, control, worth, self-goals, and future possibilities have all been identified as part of the self-system beliefs that define the global *me* self (e.g., Harter, 1992b, 1998; Markus & Ruvulo, 1990; Marsh & Shavelson, 1985).

Metacognitive knowledge and awareness of the self as the agent or architect of self-schemas distinguishes the operational importance of the *me* self versus *I* self in behavior in general and SRL in particular (McCombs, 1994; McCombs & Marzano, in press). From the *me* self perspective, motivation to learn and self-regulating learning generate from personal evaluations of what one knows and believes about self in general and in a given learning situation. Research on causal linkages between personal beliefs, affect, motivation, and learning by Harter (1992b) and others (e.g., Dweck, 1986, 1991; Eccles, 1983) confirmed that students *want to learn* to the degree they assess themselves as competent, have high expectations for success, and see the task as personally meaningful and relevant to personal goals and interests. Self-beliefs within the *me* self perspective are the source of motivation in these models. That is, these beliefs give rise to expectations that, in turn, influence feelings; feelings then directly influence motivation to learn and self-regulation of learning. In the *me* self psychological perspective, motivation and self-regulation are *byproducts* of self-beliefs.

Domain-specific self-concept in the context of SRL can be defined as individuals' beliefs and perceptions of their ability to direct and control their cognition, affect, motivation, and behavior in a particular type of learning situation or context (e.g., specific content areas and/or instructional approaches). Items such as "I believe that in performing this mathematics problem I will be able to keep myself from getting discouraged and giving up" could be used to assess domain-specific self-concept. Thus, as individuals approach a learning task, situation, and content domain, critical to their effectiveness are their beliefs and images of themselves as self-regulated learners, able to direct and control their learning processes competently in that domain and context. Again, it is their "working self-concept," which is accessible at any given time, that structures their plans and strategies and puts the self in action. In addition, Harter (1998; Harter et al., 1998) found that individuals demonstrate complex profiles of perceived strengths and weaknesses and that newer, multidimensional instruments provide for an examination of individual profile scores across domains. These methodologies have contributed to a renewed interest in self perceptions and other self-variables related to motivation, learning, and self-regulatory processes such as self-evaluations.

The measurement of self-concept and the validation of general and specific areas in which individuals define themselves have important implications for how we assess individuals' capabilities and competencies in learning situations. In reviews by Byrne (1984, 1996; Byrne & Shavelson, 1986, 1987, 1996), self-concept (SC) was found to be characterized as organized, multidimensional, hierarchical, stable, developmental, evaluative, and differential. These characteristics refer to the fact that (a) people categorize the vast information they have about themselves and relate these categories to one another; (b) people organize information about themselves hierarchically, with perceptions of behavior at the base, moving up to inferences about the self in certain domains (e.g., academic English, science, history, mathematics), and then to inferences about the self in general; (c) one's general self-concept is stable, changing little over time, but as one goes down the hierarchy, self-concept becomes increasingly situation specific and less stable; (d) as people develop from infancy into adulthood, self-concept becomes increasingly multifaceted (organized into domains of relevance to the individual); (e) people both describe and evaluate themselves, as when they say, "I am happy" and "I do well in mathematics"; and (f) people can differentiate their general and domain-specific self-concepts from other constructs such as personal or academic achievement. Byrne (1984) contended that for individuals to maintain an overall positive self-concept, they must balance their poor performance in one domain with good performance in another. Fleming and Courtney (1984), however, took the point further. In addition to distinguishing our measurement of global and domain-specific self-concept, self-awareness (self-consciousness) must be distinguished from self-evaluation (self-esteem). Self-concept is considered to be a more general term that subsumes self-esteem; that is, self-concept is self-descriptive whereas self-esteem is self-evaluative.

More recently, Byrne and her colleagues (1996; Byrne & Gavin, 1996; Byrne & Shavelson, 1996) reconfirmed Shavelson, Hubner, & Stanton's (1976) multidimensional, hierarchical model of self-concept in a number of studies that showed general academic self-concept to be at the apex, with various domains, including a social self-concept, becoming increasingly differentiated and better defined with age. Furthermore, research by Marsh, Byrne, & Shavelson (1988) demonstrated that general academic self-concept was predicted by verbal and math self-concepts, which has now been well documented by Marsh and Yeung (1998). Items measuring verbal (or English) and math self-concepts addressed student reports of how quickly they learned things in each of these classes, whether they considered it one of their best subjects, got good marks in that subject, or did well on tests in that class, as measured by Marsh's (1990, 1994) Self-Description Questionnaire.

The need for both global and domain-specific assessments of self-system structures and processes has thus received wide support from multidimensional and hierarchical self-concept theorists (e.g., Byrne, 1996; Byrne & Shavelson, 1996; Fleming & Courtney, 1984; Harter, 1985, 1998; Marsh, 1986, 1993; Marsh et al., 1988). Harter (1992a, 1998) argued for assessing dimensions of the self-system as well as domains within these dimensions that have meaning in the life of the individual. Within her framework, *dimensions* refer to constructs such as perceived competence, anxiety, and motivational orientation in the classroom; *domains* refer to areas such as scholastic competence, social competence, and athletic competence. In addition to these domain-specific areas of assessment, Harter (1992a) argued for an independent assessment of individuals' global self-worth. She maintained that global self-worth is best assessed by having individuals think about their global self-worth as a person— by tapping these feelings directly rather than inferring them from a sum or average of responses to a large array of items tapping a diverse self-concept content (as is done in the Coopersmith or Pier–Harris self-concept measures).

Overall, Harter (1982, 1998) contended that global self-worth appraisals are somewhat independent of the specific self-evaluations in discrete domains—the whole is more than the sum of its parts. Fleming and Courtney's (1984) and Marsh and Yeung's (1998) research supported this position and suggested that global and domain-specific measures are differentially important depending on the criterion variable of interest. For example, the domain-specific self-concepts tend to be related to grades or other achievement measures, whereas the global measures of self-concept are often related to measures of adjustment (e.g., anxiety, depression) or motivation (e.g., effort, persistence). By assessing both global and domain-specific self-evaluations, then, a much richer picture of self-system variables emerges.

From a developmental perspective, there is general agreement that one's judgments about the self become more differentiated with increasing age. In Harter's (1985, 1998) work, for example, six self-domains were found to be relevant in preadolescent learners: scholastic competence, athletic competence, social competence, social acceptance, physical appearance, and behavior/conduct. In the last decade, Harter's (Harter et al., 1998) work focused on high school students and young adults, and eight competence domains were identified as part of the profile of pathways to self-worth: cognitive, athletic, conduct, romantic appeal, appearance, likeability, job, and friendship. The concept of one's global self-esteem or self-worth emerges about mental age 8 and is operationalized and measured by its own independent set of items that assess how much one likes oneself as a person (e.g., Some teenagers are often disappointed with themselves, but other teenagers are pretty pleased with themselves. Which is most like you?) Self-worth is further predicted by the discrepancy between domain-specific judgments and ratings of the importance of success in each domain, as well as by perceived social support for students at all age ranges.

In research with elementary and middle-school children, Harter (1987) found that the importance one attaches to being competent in a particular domain and the support that one perceives is available from significant others were relatively independent determinants of global self-worth. In addition, she found that although self-worth has some small direct effect on motivation, its influence is primarily mediated through affect, thus supporting the position that self-worth is not epiphenomenal—a secondary phenomenon caused by something else. Developmental changes noted in primary and middle-school children were predominantly in their perceptions of the importance of particular domains and dominant sources of support. She also found that children below the age of 8 do not have a consolidated concept of worth as a person (i.e., general self-worth items did not form a separate factor nor did the items systematically cross-load on other factors) and do not distinguish mood from interest (i.e., items focusing on the degree to which one is happy or sad were not distinguishable from items tapping the degree to which one liked or wanted to engage in specific activities).

I argued the need for state and trait measures of both global and domain-specific self- system constructs in my original chapter and subsequently (McCombs, 1991) in discussing primary motivational processes emanating from the self. There was fairly widespread support from others in the field (Anderson, 1987; Bandura, 1982; Mischel, 1977; Nyquist, 1986; Spielberger, Gorsuch, & Lushene, 1983). For example, Anderson's (1987) work suggested that our processes of self-inference are active and dynamic (states), but can lead to self-concept stability (traits) via self-maintaining cognitive strategies. Bandura's (1982) work also suggested the need for state measures, in that proximal self-perceptions have been shown to bear a closer relationship to action than remote ones. My own work (McCombs, 1991) in the area of designing and validating a battery of primary motivational variables (global and domain-specific, trait and state evaluations of competence and control) shows that trait and state measures have differential relationships to other self-system processes (expectancies, intentions) and somewhat different factor structures, suggesting separate and differential contributions to an understanding of underlying causal relations among self-system variables. More recently, Levy and Dweck (1998) discussed trait versus process (or state) measures of social judgment (e.g., ways in which the self perceives, interprets, and reacts to the same people, groups, events, or outcomes). Evidence is presented that individuals differ in terms of the lens through which they evaluate people or actions, thereby necessitating the use of multiple measures that capture these trait versus state attributes and judgments. This research suggests that not only does the self-system consist of structures and processes, but also that individuals differ in terms of areas where they are most comfortable making judgments about others. In addition, this research helps us understand that beliefs about human attributes influence judgments about self and others.

Self-System Processes

Just as self-system structures are global and domain-specific, so are self-system processes. In earlier reviews (McCombs, 1984, 1986), I found considerable consensus regarding the importance of the following self-system processes in motivation and self-regulated learning: self-awareness, self-evaluation, judgments regarding the importance of specific competencies, expectations for success or failure, self-development goals, and evaluations of the personal significance of the task as assessed against these goals and the outcomes of other self-processes. More recent reviews also highlighted the importance of self-reflection and self-monitoring in generating what Mills (1991, 1995) referred to as a "psychological vantage point" from which the *I* self perceives his or her natural capacity for self-regulation—unbounded by *me* self beliefs (e.g., Kanfer & McCombs, 2000; Lambert & McCombs, 1998; McCombs & Marzano, in press; McCombs & Whisler, 1997).

Widespread agreement continues to exist that a particularly important process in SRL is self-evaluation, particularly as this process relates to judgments of personal control and competence in general and in specific situations (e.g., Baird & White, 1984; Bandura, 1982; Bandura, Pastorelli, Barbaranelli, & Caprara, 1999; Connell & Ryan, 1984; Covington, 1985; Deci & Ryan, 1991; Harter, 1985, 1998; Harter & Connell, 1984; Kanfer & McCombs, 2000; Maehr, 1985; McCombs & Marzano, in press; Paris & Newman, 1990; Ryan, 1995; Schunk, 1984, 1995; Showers & Cantor, 1985; Turner & Paris, 1995; Urdan & Maehr, 1995; Wang, 1983, 1992; Zimmerman, 1985, 1995). From the phenomenological perspective, however, I recently argued that other self-system processes important to self-regulation are those aimed at (a) creating beliefs in one's personal competence and control in learning situations; (b) defining self-relevant learning and self-regulation goals and expectations; (c) attending to and monitoring self-states, expectations, and goals; and (d) regulating and directing affect, motivation, and behavior (cf. McCombs, 1984, 1986, 1999; McCombs & Marzano, 1990, in press; McCombs & Whisler, 1989, 1997).

Carver and Scheier (1991) are among those theorists who recognized the experience of a coherent self, but pointed out that there is a hierarchical organization of three interconnected self-systems that range from an overlearned and unconscious set of processes that organize self-information, to a more sophisticated system and conscious set of processes for making decisions about self-information, to a final system for representing the self that allows for self-awareness and self-reflection. In their model, the self has a dynamic and flexible organization that can continuously process and evaluate data from all levels of functioning. Furthermore, work by Salovey (1992) and his colleagues (DeSteno & Salovey, 1997; Green & Salovey, 1999; Mayer & Salovey, 1993) suggested that "emotional intelligence" is a self-referenced process that is at the core of self-regulation. It is the ability to monitor one's own and others' emotions and then to use information from this process to guide thinking and action. As individuals become aware of positive or negative emotions through the processes of self-monitoring and self-reflection, attention is turned toward the self prior to taking action. According to Salovey (1992), all actions can be thought of as having a self-referenced origin in which the individual evaluates value to self based on emotional feedback.

Those studying self-schema have identified a *metacognitive process* aspect to self-knowledge: an awareness of self-beliefs, or the combination of what is known and believed about oneself. At the process level, the concept of self-as-agent involves thinking about self as independent from self-beliefs (McCombs, 1994). This higher order thinking about self involves a metacognitive awareness or what Ridley (1991) termed reflective self-awareness. Higher levels of reflective awareness are a function of seeing and understanding one's control over thinking and learning processes. As such, it is a self-system process that is related to intentions, performance goals, effort, task perseverance, and performance. Ridley (1991) contended that higher levels of reflective awareness make it possible for learners to metacognitively assess the validity and usefulness of their thoughts, feelings, and actions in a given learning context. His research suggested that higher level awareness and understanding of one's personal agency over lower order cognitive processes, thoughts, and beliefs positively impacts the selection of goals, affect, motivation, and performance in a complex learning situation (Ridley, 1991). To measure this self-regulation process, self-reports of reflective self-awareness as *traits* (assessed as the *frequency* [how often] one agrees with items such as "I think about recent events as they explain my behavior") as well as *states* (assessed as the *intensity* [how much] one reports experiencing specific thoughts, emotions, or actions at this moment on similar items) are frequently used.

Additional clarification of higher order processes associated with the *I* self comes from the work of Mills and his colleagues (Mills, 1991, 1995; Pransky, 1998). This work indicated that as individuals become more aware of the role of their thinking in producing moment-to-moment experiences that are a combination of feelings and specific thoughts, they develop a deeper understanding of their agency or choice over how seriously they take thoughts at different mood levels. Through the process of "thought recognition," individuals can step outside their conditioned thinking and belief systems and recognize that they are the creators of their thoughts (Pransky, 1998). As a result, individuals can have a shift of consciousness as a function of discrete events (e.g., learning new information) that helps them see new things and see them differently. New insights occur in which there is a transformation in perspective or a qualitative change in awareness. As individuals understand that they are free to choose what to think—and are not bound by their beliefs, what their parents or culture told them—they are free to reevaluate their interest in and capabilities for learning particular tasks. They understand the role of thought in producing feelings, how the quality of their thinking changes in different mood states, and that they can choose to do something about dysfunctional thinking that gets in the way of learning and motivation. They can act before rather than after their thinking as in the *Me* self conceptualization (Mills, 1995).

This view is compatible with research linking intrinsic motivation and self-regulated learning. For Deci and Ryan (1985, 1991), motivation, performance, and development are maximized when learners have the opportunity to satisfy basic psychological needs for autonomy, competence, and relatedness. Motivation is enhanced by opportunities to satisfy any one of these needs, but Deci and Ryan (1991) pointed out that for learners to be self-determined rather than controlled, they have to engage in these actions volitionally and see them as of value to their sense of self (i.e., as "endorsed by one's sense of self"). A critical point in this theory is that when an action or behavior is self-determined, the regulatory process is choice rather than compliance, as in the case of controlled behavior. It is the difference in regulatory processes between self-determined and controlled behaviors that is important; both can be motivated or intentional (Deci, Vallerand, Pelletier, & Ryan 1991). Further, Deci et al. (1991) argued for distinguishing between intrinsically motivated behaviors, which involve willingly engaging in activities that are personally interesting without external rewards or constraints, and self-determined behaviors, which are engaged in because they are judged to be personally important for a valued outcome. Both involve autonomous self-regulation, but self-determined forms of motivation lead to important educational outcomes such as staying in school, high academic performance, doing schoolwork, self-esteem, enjoyment of academic work, and satisfaction with school.

Extending this view to a more unconditioned or "authentic" view of the self that is not constrained by the boundaries of *Me* self constructions and beliefs, Mills (1995) presented a non-deterministic perspective. In this view, will is an unnecessary concept when learning is seen as a natural and effortless process that is part of human life, a natural response to being at one with experiences and not controlled by needs, constructed beliefs, or dysfunctional habits of thinking. The process of learning, discovery, and competence building is fun and exciting when learners suspend analytical and conditioned thinking, when they get out of the way of old thoughts and habits of thinking. Suspending the *Me* self gets learners beyond the psychological traps of thinking that operate when they engage in analyzing the products of their thinking. This view helps us move to a recognition that we all have the capacity to engage in new, diffuse thinking that leaves us free or open to the thoughts and experiences of the moment, unhampered by old constructions. In this state of mind, learners get "turned on" to the joy of learning that is not controlled. Assessing *I* self processes in this framework also assumes a *state* measure format—measuring intensity (how much one reports engaging in processes for monitoring and controlling thoughts, emotions, and actions) of reflective self-awareness processes.

Next I look at some of the current literature supporting the structural and functional role of self-phenomena in SRL.

SUPPORTING LITERATURE

This section highlights recent findings that provide substantiation for the importance of self-phenomena—both structure and process—for an increased understanding of self-regulated learning. I begin by taking a look at evidence in support of the role of self-system structures in SRL.

Support for Self-System Structures in Self-Regulation

In defining the structure of self-knowledge, we saw in the preceding section a growing consensus that the self is a complex and dynamic set of multiple, hierarchically organized cognitive structures—influenced by developmental, cultural, and gender differences—that exert a powerful influence on attention, organization and categorization of information, and judgments about others and events. As individuals grow and develop, they begin to define themselves in part by information they receive about their capabilities to manipulate and control objects in their environment (e.g., "If I hit this ball, I can make it roll") as well as information they receive from significant others (e.g., "Johnny's such a tall, strong boy"). Markova (1987) emphasized that self-knowledge is achieved through making decisions and doing, and that knowledge in general is gained through self-knowledge. On the other hand, Connell & Ryan (1984) emphasized that as children develop and grow, information about the self is learned from interactions with physical objects and other people. This information becomes more consolidated as well as more differentiated into areas or domains of self-knowledge. If a girl consistently sees that she can successfully master physical activities, for example, she will come to see herself as physically competent. Similarly, as a boy learns that praise from Mother comes when he consistently behaves according to her rules, he will come to see himself as able to direct and regulate behavior toward external standards.

According to Connell & Ryan (1984), self-regulation develops with the development of the self—with the internalization of selected external standards and the development of self-control and competence. Self-control in this context refers to the internalization of self- regulation knowledge and processes such that the self operates consciously through autonomous (self-controlled) choice. Development of self-control is a gradual process of internalizing self-regulation knowledge and skills through observation, direct teaching, and feedback from others. In this sense, then, as the child accumulates more consistent knowledge about the self as self-controlled and self-directed, his or her concept as being capable of self-regulation develops. In Markus and Nurius' (1987) view, however, the self-concept cannot guide and regulate one's behavior without well-defined views of the self in particular future situations. Research recently reported by Miller and Brickman (1997) confirmed that future goals and self-concepts of ability can directly predict cognitive engagement and achievement. Similarly, Urdan, Pajares, & Lapin (1997) found self-goals and intentions to learn versus to perform are related to higher self-efficacy, lower anxiety, greater effort and persistence, and more confidence in self-regulatory skills.

In a recent literature review by Moretti and Higgins (1999b), research findings supported the view that individuals are motivated to self-regulate emotions, cognitions, and actions in order to reduce the discrepancy between their actual and ideal selves. Self-regulatory styles develop in relation to whom individuals choose as self-guides (e.g., significant others, own self views) that have an impact on self-esteem. Others can become positive guides in supporting self-regulation, which ultimately emerges as a system that represents a fluid and integrated reality about the self that is shared with significant others (Moretti & Higgins, 1999a). Data supporting this theory indicate that discrepancies between one's actual and ideal self are better predictors of self-esteem (feelings of worth) than global self-concept (how we define ourselves). In this view, affective reactions to self-evaluations that yield discrepancies between what we are and want to be are primary determinants of motivation to achieve our self-goals.

Recent research by Wolters (1998) looked not at the regulation of learning with cognitive strategies such as elaboration, rehearsal, or organization, but at the regulation of motivation. The assumption was made that self-regulated learners are generally highly motivated to engage in, provide effort for, and persist in learning tasks. Wolters found that college students regulate their level of effort in academic tasks by a variety of cognitive, volitional, and motivational strategies. In addition to cognitive and metacognitive strategies, students used emotion-control or volitional strategies such as blocking out distractions, focusing attention, improving physical or emotional readiness to learn, or optimizing time on task. Willpower or "just do it" strategies were found to be less effective than volitional strategies in maintaining intentions to persist and complete a task, suggesting that SRL involves active monitoring and regulation of willingness to provide effort and persistence. Students were also found to adapt and modify strategies to fit situational demands. Finally, students who used intrinsic regulation strategies tended to have learning versus performance goal orientation and to engage in more cognitive and metacognitive strategies. These findings fit Mills' (1991, 1995) concept of a "psychological vantage point" in motivation and self-regulation from the *I* self perspective, Renkl's (1997) recent clarification of skill and will strategies in self-regulated learning, and Williams' (1997) findings with college students that perceived control had direct effects on perceived competence and motivation, while indirectly predicting self-regulated learning.

Theory and research on "possible selves" and their structural properties by Markus and her colleagues (Inglehart, Markus, & Moore, Brown, 1987; Inglehart, Wurf, Brown & Moore, 1987) was dominant a decade ago in further explaining aspects of self-variables related to self-regulation. For example, this research revealed that possible selves have a cognitive (structuring) and an energizing (perseverance) influence on behavior. Self-system structures were found to incorporate both goals and enduring representations of goal attainment, and the very process of working toward important and valued self-goals itself enhances well-being and positive affect. Cultural variations in these structures and goals has been and continues to be a dominant area of research, with these differences being noted not only in the work of Markus and her colleagues (e.g., Markus & Kitayama, 1998), but also in the work of other motivational researchers. For example, Stipek (1998a) recently examined differences between American and Chinese college students in self-conceptions evoking self-related emotions and behaviors. She found significant differences in attitudes about expressing pride and circumstances in which shame and guilt would be felt between American and Chinese students— all of which have implications for the role of self-system variables in motivation and SRL. Similarly, Boekaerts and Niemivirta (in press) reported that for effective self-regulation to develop, students need a social context in which they can find a balance between personal learning goals and ego-protective goals.

A decade ago researchers were investigating the central role of self-structures in learning and beginning to look at social context influences on motivation, SRL, and achievement. For example, Srull and Gaelick (1983) argued that the self is a cognitive prototype with a core that can be a fixed reference point to guide the processing of new information. In a study with college students, a feature-matching approach was used in assessing students' self and other similarity judgments. Students were asked how similar others were to themselves or how similar they were to others on pairs of personality-trait adjectives (e.g., intelligent/witty). This method was found to be an effective way to examine both general self-processes and individual differences, as well as to investigate the nature of the self and how it operates in a social context. Similarly, the relative importance of self-reference versus other-reference in motivation and achievement was highlighted also in a study by Reeder, McCormick, and Esselman (1987). In a prose-recall task with undergraduate students, self-reference reading orientation ("As you read this passage, continually ask yourself whether this passage describes you") was compared with other-reference ("As you read this passage, continually ask yourself whether this passage describes Princess Diana"), linguistic ("As you read this passage, continually ask yourself whether there are any misspelled words in this passage"). and control ("Read this passage") orientations. Self-reference produced better recall than other-reference or control when students were working on tasks that were not too difficult. Reeder et al. argued that self-reference tasks are highly motivating, leading to greater involvement and interest, and greater elaboration and deeper processing. Further, they found that the benefits of self-reference are not limited to narrative material that is most easily associated with the self.

Examples of current trends to examine social learning, social goals, social contexts, and their influence on student self- and other-perceptions can also be found in the work of a number of contemporary researchers. For example, Urdan and Maehr (1995) suggested that we move beyond a two-goal theory of motivation and achievement and examine the role of social goals and social relationships across various developmental stages. Research is presented that highlights the importance of social goals to motivation and engagement in learning at different grade levels. These findings are consistent with those of Cassady and Johnson (1997), who found that even young children develop domain-specific academic self-concepts, and findings by Vispoel and Boo (1997) with early adolescents that as domain importance increases (as with social competence), the greater the influence of self-concept on learning-related behaviors.

From this brief review, then, we see that self-system structures play a central role in the organization and processing of information, in the generation of positive affect, and in the regulation of behavior. I turn next to recent work on self-system processes found to be important in self-regulated learning.

Support for Self-System Processes in Self-Regulation

As we saw in the theoretical overview at the beginning of this chapter, self theorists generally assume that behavior is motivated, at least in large part, by inherent self-fulfillment or self-development goals and goals for self-determination or personal control. From a phenomenological perspective, learners strive for these goals in a self-defined and self-disciplined fashion, as active agents molding and creating our self-concepts by the continual engagement of processes that support the accomplishment of these goals. Learners engage in self-monitoring and self-evaluation processes to support our self-awareness, self-definition, and abilities to regulate and control our own self-development process. As learners grow and develop, learning tasks and experiences can provide opportunities for the acquisition and application of self-system processes for directing and controlling learning processes and behaviors. In effect, the development of self-system structures and processes is assumed to be the fundamental phenomenon that explains the development of self-regulation. In the process of self-development, increasing capabilities emerge for regulating and controlling affect, motivation, and behavior—all in support of self-development and self- goals.

Now, what does the research literature have to say in support of these points? We begin with some research by Salovey (1987, 1992; DeSteno & Salovey, 1997; Mayer & Salovey, 1993). Of those self-system processes identified as important to self-regulated learning, Salovey highlighted the centrality of self-evaluation and self-reference processes to attention, memory, affect, and behavior. As I argued in the preceding section, motivation to learn follows from learner's perceptions that they have the natural capacity to be self-regulated under the right internal and external conditions. Important internal conditions are (a) an understanding of the self as agent in orchestrating thinking, feelings, motivation, and self-regulated behaviors; (b) operating from a conscious awareness of inherent self-regulatory capacities, and (c) perceptions that the learning task or experience is personally meaningful and relevant (McCombs & Marzano, in press). External conditions that support these internal conditions include provisions for relevancy, choice, control, challenge, responsibility, competence, personal connection, and support from others in the form of caring, respect, and guidance in skill development. Thus, self-regulation can be conceptualized as a *natural response to learning opportunities* that is the result of: (a) self-evaluations of the meaning and relevance of a particular learning opportunity relative to one's personal interests, needs, and goals; (b) an understanding of one's agency and capacities for self-regulation; and (c) contexts that support perceptions of meaningfulness and self-control.

A complementary line of research on self-process influences on learning follows directly from social cognitive theory (e.g., Schunk, 1995). Schunk (1995), for example, emphasized the role of self-regulation processes as they affect the learning process. Building on theory and research in social cognitive theory (e.g., Bandura, 1982), Schunk noted the importance of three self-regulation processes: self-observation, self-judgment, and self-reactions. These processes are posited to influence a range of cognitive and affective variables, including concentration and attention; organizing, rehearsal of information to be remembered, and effective use of resources; beliefs about self, learning tasks, and outcomes; and the experience of satisfaction and pride in one's work. (See also Schunk's description of the role of self-efficacy in chapter 4, this volume.)

Self-efficacy judgments refer to the learner's judgment of his or her competency for successful task accomplishment (cf. Bandura, 1986, 1991). Having an optimal sense of self-efficacy (not too high or too low) is viewed as necessary for effective self-regulation. Learning is maximized when attributions about the cause of outcomes enhance self-efficacy and motivation to learn. For example, attributing failure to lack of effort (i.e., a cause one can do something about) is regarded as more effective than attributing failure to lack of ability. When students make self-evaluations of their progress that attribute difficulty to effort rather than failure, motivation to improve is strengthened. Bandura presented research evidence that strongly suggested students are aided in acquiring strategic competence during learning when they can self-regulate attributions. Using effective task strategies during self-regulated learning helps students acquire needed skills. In addition, both efficacy beliefs and skill performance are increased when students maintain positive attributional beliefs that stress both ability and effort for success.

Several studies document the positive influence of self-regulatory efficacy in classroom learning. Zimmerman and Bandura (1994), for example, studied the role of self-efficacy beliefs (about both academic attainment and regulation of writing, goals, and self-standards) in writing course achievement. Self-regulatory efficacy for writing had its strongest influence on self-efficacy for academic achievement, which in turn was related to grade goals, self-set evaluative standards, and final grades. Similarly, Menec, Hechter, and Perry (1995) investigated the relationships among self-regulatory strategies, self-efficacy, and individual differences in action orientation (Kuhl, 1985) among 280 introductory psychology students. They found that self- efficacy was associated with the use of self-regulatory strategies, and that high self-efficacy and high expectations of success contributed to high course grades. Interestingly, action orientation was related to the use of particular self-regulatory strategies (integration, comprehension, monitoring, and emotion/motivation control strategies), but had little effect on grades.

The primary importance of self-evaluative processes related to how one judges one's personal competence and control was stressed by Nicholls (1983, 1984, 1987). He argued that students' level of intrinsic motivation is higher when they are mastering tasks they want to do — tasks that they exercise some control in choosing, tasks on which they feel competent to succeed, and tasks consistent with their personal needs and goals. Dweck (1986, 1991) took a similar position, pointing out that motivation can be adaptive or maladaptive as a function of its goal orientation. If students have learning goals, they seek to increase their competence (knowledge and skills); if they have performance goals, they seek to gain favorable judgments of their competence or seek to avoid negative judgments. Thus, goals aimed at self-development rather than approval of others contribute to positive and adaptive motivational patterns that can underlie self-regulated learning. Research by Ames (1987, 1992) and Stipek (1998b) confirmed that the classroom learning environment can directly influence learning goal orientations and student motivation.

Earlier work by Abrahams, Wageman, and Harackiewicz (1987) with high-school students supported the role of perceived importance to self in affect and motivation for academic tasks. Positive feedback was found to raise interest only when a student cared about doing well on the evaluated task. When students were given task-focused feedback (information regarding their scores on the task), interest was raised compared with normative feedback on how they were doing relative to others. With college students, Epstein, Stokes, and Harackiewicz (1987) found task interest to be a function of students' affective states, which, in turn, were a function of students' interpretations of competence cues about how well they would do on academic tasks. These findings suggest that students have to be aroused affectively, which results from valuing competence and engaging in positive self-evaluations, to be optimally motivated. More recently, however, Tauer and Harackiewicz (1999) found that an achievement orientation (goals) moderated the negative effects of competition (performance goals) on intrinsic motivation.

Manderlink and Harackiewicz (1984) suggested that for effective self-regulation, individuals need to direct their behavior at minimizing the discrepancy between their current performance level and their goals. Goal achievement enhances feelings of competence and also positively affects intrinsic motivation for the task. Their evidence indicated that competence feedback benefits existing intrinsic motivation by strengthening beliefs of personal control over goal attainment. These feelings of personal causality are believed to be a more important determinant of continued intrinsic motivation than perceptions of competence. On the other hand, self-efficacy may be more critical than self-determination in initiating task interest. They further suggested that, after competence has been sufficiently developed, feelings of personal control and self-determination may be more relevant to self-motivation and intrinsic interest. It is recognized, however, that students' abilities to capitalize on self-reference strategies depend on self-awareness and self-monitoring processes. Much current work in these self-processes related to SRL has focused on cultural differences (e.g., Purdie & Hattie, 1996) in perceptions of others and social context (e.g., Maden, Jussim, Shelley, Eccles, 1998). This research shows that not only do students from different cultures use different strategies to regulate their own learning processes (e.g., memorization versus elaboration strategies), but cultural beliefs and stereotypes can exert powerful effects on perceptions of learning requirements and performance depending on students' self-awareness.

Figurski (1987a, 1987b) suggested that the development of self-awareness and other-awareness is dependent on the ability to manipulate one's perspective. He argued (1987a) that . . . "if we cannot consider the experience of the other, we can never be objective toward ourselves. The ability to manipulate perspective toward the self is also the ability to manipulate perspective toward others" (p. 200). An egocentric to allocentric developmental sequence is reported, highlighting the value of nonlaboratory, phenomenological approaches to understanding self-awareness (Figurski, 1987b). Findings are also reported that self-awareness is related to affect when the current activity is perceived as voluntary. Self-awareness is seen as antecedent to self-evaluation and affect in the development of self-system processes. In addition, self-awareness is considered to be a state, whereas self-consciousness is considered a trait variable.

Further work on self-awareness processes by Davis, Franzoi, and Markwiese (1987) suggested that for individuals high in self-consciousness (i.e., high self-awareness of their own thoughts and thinking processes), there is a desire for self-knowledge. For individuals low in self-consciousness, however, there is a desire for self-defense. Davis et al. argued that this finding supports the notion of an underlying motivational component in self-awareness, rather than a more automatic model. In fact, such differences in private self-consciousness (i.e., inner thoughts that are not shared with others) may be due to what Rhodewalt (1987) described as self-handicapping behaviors of students with low self-esteem. He reported that students engage in strategic acts to protect

their self-image or self-esteem and that "...attributions play a determining role in motivating self-handicapping; attributing success to ability or failure to lack of effort appear to be the preconditions to self-
handicapping when entering evaluative situations" (p. 7). A frequently
used self-handicapping strategy is for students to discount the importance of academic tasks so that, in the face of failure, they can protect
their self-esteem (Covington, 1992).

In the applied learning environments, Kanfer and McCombs (2000)
described the two-stage motivation process with two potential sources of
motivational difficulty: (a) (un)willingness to engage in learning (e.g.,
to adopt explicitly and extrinsically stated training goals—the "will do"
component), and (b) presence or absence of competencies for sustaining motivation over time and in the face of obstacles to goal attainment
(the "can do" component). In K–12 classrooms, motivational difficulties
often pertain to deficits in the "will do" component. Students may fail to
perceive personal value for mastery of assigned material, or lack commitment to the learning process, particularly when they do not participate in
the development of learning goals and/or use learning methods that are
of no apparent personal value. Self-regulation difficulties, however, may
most often occur due to the "can do" component. "Can do" difficulties
emerge if students encounter obstacles to learning that create self-doubts
about performance capabilities and/or do not provide self-regulatory
support for learning. In this view, motivation involves two related sets of
processes, goal choice (i.e., the "will do" component of motivation) and
goal striving (i.e., the "can do" component of motivation).

Goal choice processes govern the individual's allocation of personal
resources toward goals desired by the teacher or system (Kanfer &
McCombs, 2000). Contemporary theorizing suggests that individuals
make such decisions on the basis of three considerations, perceptions
of competence, the cost of exerting effort, and the attractiveness of goal
accomplishment. Although preferences for effort expenditure may be
largely determined by dispositional factors, educational program components may influence both perceptions of competence and the attractiveness of performance in ways that can facilitate goal choice and
commitment to learning activities. Thus, commitment to learning is a
necessary but not sufficient condition for knowledge and skill development. Goal striving refers to the self-regulatory processes by which individuals implement their intentions. Beginning with the goal, individuals
must self-monitor, self-evaluate, and self-reinforce their actions. These
self-regulatory processes enable corrective action, foster learning, and
sustain effort for development of higher level skills. Self-regulatory skill
deficits may cause frustration and lead to premature withdrawal from
the learning process.

Research by Perry (1998) and her colleagues (Perry, Donohue, & Weinstein, 1999; Perry & Weinstein, 1998) demonstrated qualities of social contexts that support SRL in young children. This research builds on earlier findings that children age 4 to 6 had higher perceptions of their abilities, higher expectations for success on academic tasks, and were more independent and self-regulated in child-centered rather than in teacher-directed classes. In Perry's (1998) study, children in Grades 2 and 3 were compared in classrooms where teachers differed in terms of the choice, challenge, self-evaluation, peer support, and teacher support provided—all conditions related to whether they were likely to promote SRL. Student perceptions of how often these conditions were present differed in high versus low SRL classrooms; as a result, students in high SRL classes adopted skills and attitudes of SRL learners, whereas students in low SRL classes adopted defensive, self-handicapping approaches to learning. Also revealed was that even young children can differentiate classroom types and reliably report their perceptions if measures target issues they value, use language and response formats they understand, and assess their responses in the context of activities that are relevant and meaningful to them. Perry (1998) concluded that assumptions can be questioned that young children (a) cannot reliably differentiate classroom contexts, (b) do not adopt motivational orientations that undermine SRL, or (c) do not have the cognitive capability required for SRL.

Perry and Weinstein (1998) argued that the school adjustment of young children should result in high levels of academic functioning (skill acquisition and motivation, including metacognitive skills and competence-related beliefs), social functioning (positive peer and adult relations, including a sense of belonging and social goals), and behavioral functioning (positive role behaviors and self-regulation of attention and emotion, including delaying gratification and directing attention). Their research found that children can accurately report differential teacher treatment and that child-centered versus teacher-directed classrooms led to positive social and emotional functioning among children—at no academic cost. The importance of supportive positive relationships between teachers and children as well as among peers was stressed, with evidence that these relationships are linked to many social and academic competencies, including better grades, more prosocial behavior, and more positive attitudes toward school.

Furthermore, Perry et al. (1999) studied kindergarten children's adjustment to school by looking at student perceptions of learner-centered (LC) practices. If students perceived LC classrooms, they had higher academic achievement, greater attainment of end-of-year achievement standards, and less likelihood of being named as disliked peers. Similarly, my colleagues and I (Daniels, Kalkman, & McCombs, in press) examined K–3 students' perceptions of teacher practices and learning in LC and non-learner-centered (NLC) classroom contexts and found that young children (a) report good teachers to be caring, helpful, and stimulating regardless of context, (b) are more interested in schoolwork and learning in LC versus NLC classes, and (c) had views of learning that were consistent with their classroom practices such that NLC contexts tended to produce more passive versus active views. Of importance was the finding that children with contemporary, active views of learning who were in NLC classrooms (contexts that had practices inconsistent with the children's views) showed signs of becoming alienated from school (lower motivation, lack of interest). These findings highlight the importance of considering young children's self, other, and context perspectives in identifying how to enhance continuing motivation and self-regulated learning. In addition, in my own research (McCombs, 1998; McCombs & Lauer, 1997, 1998; McCombs & Whisler, 1997), student perceptions of classroom practices—with students in kindergarten through college— were significantly more predictive of their motivation, use of SRL strategies, and achievement than were teacher perceptions of their own practices. This verifies the importance of self views and phenomenological perspectives in the sense that the closer the learning is to the self (i.e., learner views), the stronger the links to self-regulation, motivation, and learning outcomes.

In summary, we see from the foregoing selected review that self-evaluation processes are among the most important in the developing self-system for acquiring self-knowledge and maintaining a sense of self-esteem. In addition, students' processes of self-awareness and self-monitoring contribute significantly to their self-determination and self-development goals. Therefore, students' development of these self-system processes provides a basis for the development of capability for self-regulation. In the final sections of this chapter, I complete our excursion by looking at the implications of what has been learned for enhancing the development of SRL capacities in students.

IMPLICATIONS FOR THE DEVELOPMENT OF SELF-REGULATED LEARNING

Recent work on the self revealed a close link between the development of self-system structures and processes and the development of SRL capacities. For some students, however, it is necessary to facilitate development in both these areas. How can our understanding of self-phenomena—particularly the role of the self in generating will and skill—help us enhance students' development of SRL capacities? To address this question, let us look at what is required in self-regulated learning and the learner-centered practices and contexts that support the role of the self in this process.

Self-Regulated Learning

Self-regulated learning pertains to the self-regulatory and metacognitive processes by which students accomplish learning goals (e.g., Schunk & Zimmerman, 1998). For example, Zimmerman (1990) defined SRL as students' active participation in their own learning processes. In the self-regulated learning perspective, emphasis is placed on metacognitive, motivational, and behavioral processes that facilitate learning, such as planning, setting personal goals, organizing, self-monitoring, self-efficacy, reconstructing and creating ideas, practicing automaticity, and refining personal skills and behaviors. Similarly, Carr (1996) defined SRL as one's ability to learn independently of a teacher. Thus, effective SRL requires some knowledge of the content area, basic skills for learning, and motivation to learn. Carr (1996) emphasized the importance of student self-reflective skills and self-awareness of self as the learner as essential for self-regulated learning.

Butler and Winne (1995) also described SRL as involving deliberate, adaptive, and judgmental processes that involve awareness of self, task, and desired or required actions (knowledge and performance goals). Building on prior research on feedback, Butler and Winne (1995) argued, however, that the inherent catalyst for all self-regulated activities is feedback and noted that the provision of external feedback enhances learning. Internal feedback generated by self-monitoring processes that describe various outcomes (e.g., motivational state, mood, learning progress) facilitates use of external feedback by providing confirmation of or explanation for one's ideas. Based on a research review, Butler and Winne (1995) identified five functions of feedback proposed to be independent of the need to separate internal and external types of feedback: (a) feedback to confirm understanding of instructional objectives, (b) feedback to add information that elaborates and enriches prior knowledge, (c) feedback to replace or overwrite incorrect or inappropriate prior knowledge, (d) feedback to tune or adjust understanding, and (e) feedback to help restructure schemata to accommodate new material and/or replace false or incompatible theories. Adding the phenomenological perspective to this review, however, I would add the need for feedback to confirm agency (operation of the

I self) in overseeing strategy use and effectiveness as well as efficacy in executing appropriate control of emotions, thought, and strategy use, thereby controlling negative thinking that can lesson motivation and will to learn by generating negative affect.

During the past decade, a number of educational researchers integrated the learner- centered perspective to learning with self-regulatory approaches to study what is termed "self-regulated or self-directed" learning as it occurs in classroom contexts (cf. Kanfer & McCombs, 2000). For SRL to develop in students, it is essential that they have choice and responsibility; the individual's role in choosing to learn is viewed as critical for developing an active approach to learning in the school context. As students engage in SRL, they are posited to attribute the consequences of their successes and failures to their own actions, rather than to forces and experiences beyond their control (e.g., school). As such, students involved in self-regulated learning are expected to take greater pride in learning and schooling and to see themselves as owners of their behavior.

Complementary perspectives on SRL in the classroom were also offered by Areglado, Bradley, and Lane (1996), who defined self-regulated learning as a synergistic process—a process of teacher–student interaction in which the teacher provides the student with assistance in developing various strategies and skills for self-directed learning, then gradually gives students increasing responsibility for using and defining these learning strategies for themselves. According to Areglado et al. (1996), the self-regulated learner is characterized by the following: exhibits initiative, independence, and persistence in learning; accepts responsibility for his or her own learning and views problems as challenges, not obstacles; is capable of self-discipline and has a high degree of curiosity; has a strong desire to learn or change and is self-confident; is able to use basic study skills, organize his or her time, set an appropriate pace for learning, and develop a plan for completing work; and enjoys learning and has a tendency to be goal-oriented.

The SRL perspective thus views self-regulatory processes as critical for learner-centered education. In this perspective, student motivation is facilitated through the development and use of practices that promote student self-awareness of their learning process, the use of self-regulatory strategies during learning (such as goal setting, self-monitoring, self- reflection, and self-evaluation), and student initiative in seeking external feedback on learning progress. Characteristics of such environments include explicit student and teacher training in the development and use of self-regulatory strategies and increasing student choice and control over features of training such as what to study and feedback opportunities (McCombs, 1998).

Developing Self-Regulatory Skills

From the phenomenological perspective, theory and research on SRL places emphasis on specific components of the self-regulatory process, and suggests that motivational deficits may be partly addressed by building learner-centered program elements to facilitate SRL. Another approach to the development of self-regulation stems from recent work by Kanfer and Heggestad (1997) that focused on the role of individual differences in self traits and self-regulatory skills in learning. In this person-centered approach, emphasis is placed on distinguishing between dispositional tendencies (traits) that affect goal choice and acquired, integrated patterns of self-regulatory behaviors that take place during goal striving (self-regulatory skills). This approach represents self-regulatory activities as basic skills used during learning. Individual differences in self-regulatory skills are proposed to be influenced by both person and situation factors, but to be distinct from motivational traits in their effects on learning and performance, and to aid in the explanation of how students of similar ability levels and motivation for training may show marked differences in learning outcomes.

As suggested by Kanfer and McCombs (2000), two basic self-regulatory skills are needed in addition to cognitive strategies in the development of self-regulation and the learner's understanding of the role of the self in orchestrating the learning process: motivation control and emotion control. Motivational control skills refer to self-regulatory efficacy in sustaining attentional effort in the absence of external controls. Individuals with strong motivational control skills engage in self-regulatory activities specifically aimed at keeping attention on the task, such as interim goal setting and goal visualization. Kanfer, Ackerman, and Heggestad (1996) indicated that such skills are particularly important during the later phases of skill acquisition, when learners seek to improve performance beyond a minimally acceptable level. During the initial phase of skill learning, learners must typically devote substantial amounts of attentional effort to understanding task requirements due to task demands. As performance improves, however, task demands on attention gradually declines.

In summary, the phenomenological perspective suggests that the best way to enhance our SRL capacities is to understand the importance of our belief in ourselves as self-regulators. The problem is that many of us do not believe it, do not want to be responsible for our own self-regulation, or do not know how. Phenomenology as a method and philosophical system helps us understand the primacy of our own perceptions and thinking about ourselves and the world in being able to direct and regulate our behavior. It helps us understand how to help students know their worth, their competencies, their abilities to choose and be in control, and their responsibilities for generating the will to learn.

APPLICATION OF THE PHENOMENOLOGICAL APPROACH

To understand how phenomenological research on the self and various self-system processes and structures can be applied to educational practice, this section outlines what my own and others' research has demonstrated as sound practices.

Practices That Enhance Self-Regulated Learning by Focusing on Self-System Development

We saw that self-regulation develops naturally with the development of self-concepts and self-processes such as self-awareness, self-monitoring, and self-evaluation. Still relevant in this new decade are the self-regulation steps spelled out by Markus and Wurf (1987); there are clear implications for the role of self-development in students' abilities to execute each step. Let us look at these steps in more detail from a phenomenological perspective.

At the first step in self-regulation, *goal setting*, students must be able not only to select goals, but also to define what is important to them. Defining what is important to them requires that students know themselves and have realistic expectancies for what they can accomplish. They need to have a sense of things they enjoy, their interests, needs, and values; they need some level of self-awareness and self-acceptance. With these self-understandings, they can generate and select personally meaningful and relevant self goals. They are also able to assess possibilities for success or failure, generate outcome expectations, and commit to pursuing their goals. It is their self-knowledge and abilities to think about and evaluate personal relevance and importance that is an essential first step in generating enduring commitments to and positive affect toward goal attainment. Most important, however, is that students also understand their responsibility for defining themselves and taking an active role in their own self-development. They must understand their agency in making choices about how best to direct and regulate cognition, affect, motivation, and behavior. They must be understanding of self-as-agent to generate the psychological vantage point to create an image of themselves as self-regulated learners.

During the second step in self-regulation, *planning and strategy selection*, students have the opportunity to put themselves in action, to make personal plans, and to select the appropriate strategies for accomplishing learning goals expressive of their more general self-development and self-determination goals. In specific learning situations, the personally meaningful and relevant goals students selected for mastery, accomplishment, or growth in knowledge and skills have the purpose of forming and directing the kind and nature of planning activities and strategies selected. At this step, it is critical that students have developed the level of metacognitive knowledge (including self-knowledge) and processes (including self-monitoring, self-reflection, and self-evaluation) for engaging in effective planning and strategy selection.

The final step of self-regulation, *performance execution and evaluation*, further requires the development of self-monitoring, self-reflection, and self-evaluation processes. To put the self in action, students need to direct and maintain their attention appropriately, evaluate their progress relative to desired goals, regulate and control their affect, and execute the actions necessary for reducing the performance discrepancies between actual and desired goals. Again, the development of self-awareness, self-monitoring, and self-evaluation processes is critical to effective performance execution and evaluation in a self-directed and self-regulated sense. For students lacking in self-knowledge and self-regulation processes, interventions help to enhance or supplant existing self-values, capacities, and skills.

Practices That Enhance Self-Regulated Learning by Focusing on Understanding of Inherent Capacities for Motivation and Learning

Another approach to the development of self-regulated behavior is that developed by Mills (1995). This approach suggested that self-regulation is the natural response to learners' understanding of their inherent capacities for motivation and learning—combined with their understanding of the role of their thinking in feelings and motivation as well as their agency in choosing what to think on a moment-to-moment basis. From this perspective, the interventions most needed are those that *educate* learners about their psychological functioning, how to create a different psychological vantage point or shift in perspective regarding themselves, their learning interests, and their capabilities to regulate their own learning and succeed. Interventions are directed at creating insights and helping learners understand their agency over the processes and content of their thinking. It aims at freeing students from dysfunctional thinking that gets in the way of accessing the natural will to learn and to self-regulate learning, thus opening the doors to creativity and new ways of learning that are beyond currently conceived limits.

What is most needed, then, from the phenomenological perspective, are learner-centered interventions that focus on positive self-development and personal responsibility for actively participating in that self-development. Environmental modifications in line with this goal are certainly needed; also needed, however, are interventions that focus on modifying and enhancing student perceptions, self-evaluations, interpretations, affect, motivation, and self-regulated learning processes. Students must be able to see the self-possibilities from learning experiences—possibilities for growth and development of their unique capabilities and skills. They need to understand their relationships and responsibilities to themselves and others as well as to the social and environmental context. Students need to understand that part of being human is to create and discover positive possibilities for their overall growth in intellectual, physical, social, and spiritual realms. They need also to understand that this growth is a function of unique situational, dispositional, and developmental factors, all of which must be taken into consideration in selecting realistic and meaningful goals. Finally, they must understand that commitment to positive and responsible self-goals is a basic key to positive self-development.

From the perspective of a learner, when learning is perceived to be personally meaningful and relevant, and the context supports and encourages personal control, self-regulation of the learning process occurs naturally (McCombs & Whisler, 1989, 1997; McCombs & Marzano, 1990, in press; Ridley, 1991). That is, in situations the learner perceives as related to personal interests and goals that can be pursued in self-determining ways, the learner is usually not even aware that he or she is engaging in self-regulatory processes and behaviors. The learner is caught up in the activity and attention is directed at accomplishing the personal goal. In many ways, when learning is perceived to meet personal needs and goals, the learner is in a state of "flow" or immersion in the enjoyment of the activity (cf. Csikszentmihalyi, 1990). In this state, the process of learning is intrinsically motivating and will to learn is enhanced. Learners then want to regulate their learning and make the decisions necessary to reach personal learning goals or pursue personal interests. From the learner's perspective, then, self-regulation is a natural part of striving to accomplish desired goals. The problem is that students many times do not see current educational content and practices as relevant to their desired goals and personal interests. They also do not see the context as one that supports basic personal and social needs, such as to be self-determining, competent, and connected to others (cf. Deci & Ryan, 1991).

Practices That Enhance Self-Regulated Learning by Focusing on Learner Choice and Control

Zimmerman (1994) argued that self-regulation is, by definition, only possible in contexts that provide for choice and control. If students do not have options to choose among or if they are not allowed to control critical dimensions of their learning (such as what topics to pursue, how and when to study, and the outcomes they want to achieve), regulation of thinking and learning processes by the self is not fully possible. Externally imposed conditions then regulate the content, structure, and process of learning. Zimmerman went on to argue that if students are not allowed choice and control, they are not likely to learn strategies for regulating their own learning and, as a result, do not attach value to self-regulation strategy training or *willingly* self-initiate and control the use of various strategies. Training in setting learning and performance goals, monitoring comprehension while learning, and controlling negative emotions and cognitions enhances school learning and performance (Zimmerman, 1994). However, if the major conditions required for self-regulation (choice and control) are not present, schools will actually work against helping learners *want to learn and self-regulate their learning.*

When looking at interventions for enhancing SRL from a living systems perspective that considers the person and personal needs, a more systemic and holistic approach is needed. For example, Ford (1992) presented an integrative motivational systems theory based on the evolving conceptions of human motivation. This theory is presented within a living systems framework that recognizes human capacity for self-determination, self-regulation, and self-direction. As Ford stated, "People are not simply bodies in a classroom or boxes in an organization chart or information-processing machines—they are thinking, feeling, self-directed human beings with a very personal repertoire of goals, emotions, and self-referent beliefs that *must* [author's emphasis] be treated with respect and care if efforts to facilitate desired motivational patterns and the development of human competence are to succeed" (p. 257). Similarly, Kohn (1996) provided evidence from school-based research and examples that to achieve the goals of self-regulated learners, students must have choice and autonomy; schools must provide both an engaging curriculum and a caring community. He stated, "Community is not enough; we need autonomy, too. In fact, when both of these features are present, there is another way to describe the arrangement that results; it is called democracy" (p. 119).

Turner and Paris (1995) suggested that contexts be created that enhance motivation based on what research says about how learners learn and what motivates them to learn. Many of the suggestions given are those that also can be derived from the *Learner-Centered Psychological Principles* (APA, 1993, 1997). Conditions need to be created such that the learning context provides choice, challenge, control, collaboration, opportunities to construct meaning, and positive consequences. From my own work (McCombs, 1995, 1998; McCombs & Whisler, 1997), additional conditions for addressing learner-centered principles include opportunities to experience personal relevance, responsibility, respect, cooperation, competence, connections to personal interests or talents, and positive relationships with adults and peers.

Practices That Help Learners and Teachers Self-Assess Self-System Structures and Processes

A final area of application is in supporting self-regulation through self-assessment and other measurement tools that can help identify self-beliefs, self-perceptions, and self-processes. In our work with learner-centered practices and self-assessment tools for teachers and students in K–12 and college classrooms, based on the APA *Principles* (1993, 1997), we found that what defines learner-centeredness is not solely a function of particular instructional practices or programs (McCombs & Lauer, 1997, 1998; McCombs & Whisler, 1997). Rather, it is a complex interaction of qualities of the teacher in combination with characteristics of instructional practices, as perceived by individual learners. That is, learner-centeredness is in the eye of the beholder and varies as a function of learner perceptions that, in turn, are the result of each learner's prior experiences, self-beliefs and attitudes, and constructions about schools and learning as well as their current interests, values, and goals.

We found, consistently across kindergarten through college-age students (McCombs, 1998, 1999), that it is student perceptions rather than teacher perceptions and beliefs that predict student motivation and achievement. This confirms that the closer an experience is to the self, the stronger the relationship to self-outcomes. Thus, practices that can help teachers and other educators better improve SRL and motivation outcomes in classroom settings are those that use measures of student perceptions of practices and their perceptions of how self-regulated their learning processes are in terms of active learning, goal setting, and other dimensions addressed in other chapters in this book.

SUMMARY, CONCLUSIONS, AND FUTURE DIRECTIONS

Phenomenologists believe that the development of students' natural tendencies for self-regulation depends on the development of self-system knowledge structures and the processes of self-awareness, self-monitoring, self-reflection, and self-evaluation. Self-regulation also depends on the development of students' self-concepts and self-images as active agents, responsible for the regulation of learning behaviors (cognition, affect, motivation) as well as learning outcomes. This view contributes to our understanding of the development of SRL capacities because of its focus on the primacy of self-phenomena, and particularly the *I* or volitional self, in this development and the recognition that self-regulation develops naturally with self-system development. Many students, however, need interventions specifically aimed at the development of positive self-views of themselves as competent, followed by specific training in self-regulation processes, in order for self-regulation to emerge.

The literature reviewed in this chapter indicates substantial progress during the past decade in identifying key self-system determinants of SRL. Contemporary self theories emphasize the role of personal beliefs about self-as-agent, interests, intrinsic motivation, constructions of meaning, and self-regulatory processes that emphasize the learner as an active agent in the learning process. Learner goals established early in the educational process appear to have substantial impact on subsequent self-regulatory and metacognitive processes involved in learning. Learning/mastery goals appear to facilitate goal striving, whereas performance-oriented goals appear to hinder learning and reduce metacognitive and self-regulatory efficiency.

In my view, the most difficult problem in implementing theory into practice pertains to changes that a learner-centered approach implies for teachers and staff developers. Learner-centered activities that promote learner involvement in the content and process by which knowledge and skills are developed often require trainers and teachers to develop new strategies for classroom management and instruction—that is, to develop new knowledge and skills for accomplishing their work as learning partners, facilitators, and models. Strong organizational support for skill development is necessary for such changes to occur. In K–12 settings, such support implies the provision of training experiences that help teachers to learn how students think, and opportunities to generate their own classroom applications of what is known about learners, learning, and effective instructional strategies, and to develop an understanding of the self-as-agent perspective. They also need to see models of and be mentored by other teachers working effectively with students in facilitating SRL processes.

Finally, what are some promising research and development directions that can support implementation of the interventions suggested? From a basic research perspective, additional work is needed on the self-as-agent and how the *I* self and our human experiences of consciousness can be effectively studied. Research should be directed at understanding not only the "what" (self-structures) and "how" (self-processes) aspects of self, but also the "who" (self-determination, volition, agency) aspects of human consciousness that are active in directing and regulating learning. From the applied research perspective, additional work is needed on defining and evaluating interventions for modifying and challenging negative and erroneous student perceptions, interpretations, expectations, and beliefs that impede their natural progress toward self-development and self-determination goals. Research on the types of strategies that are most effective for students at different ages and stages of development, the unique nature of these strategies from the students' own perspectives, and how these strategies can best interface with classroom practices and teacher and parent training programs is also needed. Furthermore, more research is needed on how best to educate educators (teachers and others involved in the educational process) about the *I* and *me* aspects of the self and their operation in educational settings. These are our challenges as researchers and practitioners for better understanding the role of self-phenomena in SRL and for identifying effective methods for fostering positive possibilities for the growth and development of all learners.

REFERENCES

Abrahams, S., Wageman, R., & Harackiewicz, J. M. (1987, August). *Focus-of-evaluation and intrinsic motivation.* Paper presented at the annual meeting of the American Psychological Association, New York.

Ames, C. (1987, April). *Social context and student cognitions.* Paper presented at the annual meeting of the American Educational Research Association, Washington, DC.

Ames, C. (1992). Achievement goals and the classroom climate. In D. H. Schunk & J. L. Meece (Eds.), *Student perceptions in the classroom* (pp. 327–348). Hillsdale, NJ: Lawrence Erlbaum Associates.

Anderson, S. M. (1987). The role of cultural assumptions in self-concept development. In K. Yardley & T. Honess (Eds.), *Self and identify: Psychosocial perspectives.* New York: Wiley.

APA Task Force on Psychology in Education (1993, January). *Learner-centered psychological principles: Guidelines for school redesign and reform.* Washington, DC: American Psychological Association and Mid-Continent Regional Educational Laboratory.

APA Work Group of the Board of Educational Affairs (1997, November). *Learner-centered psychological principles: A framework for school reform and redesign.* Washington, DC: American Psychological Association.

Areglado, R. J., Bradley, R. C., & Lane, P. S. (1996). *Learning for life: Creating classrooms for self-directed learning.* Thousand Oaks, CA: Corwin Press.

Baird, J. R., & White, R. T. (1984, April). *Improving learning through enhanced metacognition: A classroom study.* Paper presented at the annual meeting of the American Educational Research Association, New Orleans.

Bandura, A. (1982). The self and mechanisms of agency. In J. Suls (Ed.), *Psychological perspectives on the self* (Vol. 1, pp. 3–39). Hillsdale, NJ: Lawrence Erlbaum Associates.

Bandura, A. (1986). Fearful expectations and avoidant actions as coeffects of perceived self-inefficacy. *American Psychologist, 4*, (12), 1389–1391.

Bandura, A. (1991). Self-regulation of motivation through anticipatory and self-regulatory mechanisms. In R. A. Dienstbier (Ed.), *Perspectives on motivation: Nebraska symposium on motivation* (Vol. 38, pp. 69–164). Lincoln, NE: University of Nebraska Press.

Bandura, A., Pastorelli, C., Barbaranelli, C., & Caprara, G. V. (1999). Self-efficacy pathways to childhood depression. *Journal of Personality and Social Psychology, 76*(2), 258–269.

Boekaerts, M., & Niemivirta, M. (in press). Self-regulated learning: Finding a balance between learning goals and ego-protective goals. In M. Boekaerts, P. R. Pintrich, & M. Zeidner (Eds.). *Handbook of self-regulation*. San Diego: Academic Press.

Brownback, P. (1982). *The danger of self love*. Chicago: Moody Press.

Butler, D. L., & Winne, P. H. (1995). Feedback and self-regulated learning: A theoretical synthesis. *Review of Educational Research, 65*(3), 245–281.

Byrne, B. M. (1984). The general/academic self-concept nomological network: A review of construct validation research. *Review of Educational Research, 54*(3), 427–456.

Byrne, B. M. (1996). Academic self-concept: Its structure, measurement, and relation to academic achievement. In B. A. Bracken (Ed.), *Handbook of self-concept* (pp. 287–316). New York: Wiley.

Byrne, B. M., & Gavin, D. A. (1996). The Shavelson Model revisited: Testing for the structure of academic self-concept across pre-, early, and late adolescents. *Journal of Educational Psychology, 88*(2), 215–228.

Byrne, B. M., & Shavelson, R. J. (1986). On the structure of adolescent self-concept. *Journal of Educational Psychology, 78*(6), 474–481.

Byrne, B. M., & Shavelson, R. J. (1987). Adolescent self-concept: Testing the assumption of equivalent structure across gender. *American Educational Research Journal, 24*(3), 365–385.

Byrne, B. M., & Shavelson, R. J. (1996). On the structure of social self-concept for pre-, early, and late adolescents: A test of the Shavelson, Hubner, and Stanton (1976) model. *Journal of Personality and Social Psychology, 70*(3), 599–613.

Carr, M. (1996, Fall). *Teaching children to self-regulate: A resource for teachers*. (Instructional Resource No. 34). University of Georgia and University of Maryland: National Reading Research Center.

Carver, C. S., & Scheier, M. F. (1991). Self-regulation and the self. In J. Strauss & G. R. Goethals (Eds.), *The self: Interdisciplinary approaches* (pp. 168–207). New York: Springer-Verlag.

Cassady, J. C., & Johnson, R. E. (1997, March). *The accuracy and multidimensionality of first and second grade students' academic self-concepts*. Paper presented at the annual meeting of the American Educational Research Association, Chicago.

Combs, A. W. (1962). A perceptual view of the adequate personality. *1962 ASCD Yearbook: Perceiving, behaving, becoming: A new focus for education* (pp. 50–64). Washington, DC: Association for Supervision and Curriculum Development.

Combs, A. W. (1986). What makes a good helper? A person-centered approach. *Person-Centered Review, 1*(1), 51–61.

Combs, A. W. (1991). *The schools we need: New assumptions for educational reform*. Lanham, MD: University Press of America.

Combs, A. W., Miser, A. B., & Whitaker, K. S. (1999). *On becoming a school leader: A person-centered challenge*. Alexandria, VA: Association for Supervision and Curriculum Development.

Connell, J. P., & Ryan, R. M. (1984). A developmental theory of motivation in the classroom. *Teacher Education Quality, 11*(4), 64–77.

Cooley, C. H. (1902). *Human nature and the social order*. NY: Charles Scribner's Sons.

Covington, M.V. (1985). The motive for self-worth. In C. Ames & R. Ames (Eds.), *Research on motivation in education: The classroom milieu (pp.* 77–113). New York: Academic Press.

Covington, M. V. (1992). *Making the grade: A self-worth perspective on motivation and school reform.* New York: Cambridge University Press.

Covington, M.V., & Omelich, C. L. (1987). "1 knew it cold before the exam": A test of the anxiety-blockage hypothesis. *Journal of Educational Psychology, 79*(4), 393–400.

Covington, M. V., & Teel, K. M. (1996). *Overcoming student failure: Changing motives and incentives for learning.* Washington, DC: American Psychological Association.

Cross, S. E., & Madson, L. (1997). Models of the self: Self-construals and gender. *Psychological Bulletin, 122,* 5–37.

Cross, S. E., & Markus, H. R. (1990). The willful self. *Personality and Social Psychology Bulletin, 16*(4), 726–742.

Cross, S. E., & Markus, H. R. (in press). Culture and personality. In L. Pervin & O. John (Eds.), *Handbook on personality research and theory.* New York: Wiley.

Csikszentmihalyi, M. (1990). *Flow: The psychology of optimal experience.* New York: Harper & Row.

Daniels, D. H., Kalkman, D. L., & McCombs, B. L. (in press). Young children's perspectives on learning and teacher practices in different classroom contexts: Implications for motivation. *Early Education and Development.*

Davis, M. H., Franzoi, S. L., & Markwiese, B. (1987, August). *A motivational explanation of private self-consciousness.* Paper presented at the annual meeting of the American Psychological Association, New York.

Deci, E. L., & Ryan, R. M. (1985). *Intrinsic motivation and self-determination in human behavior.* New York: Plenum.

Deci, E. L., & Ryan, R. M. (1991). A motivational approach to self: Integration in personality. In R. Dienstbier (Ed.), *Nebraska symposium on motivation. Vol. 38. Perspectives on motivation.* (pp. 237–288) Lincoln, NE: University of Nebraska Press.

Deci, E. L., Vallerand, R. J., Pelletier, L. G., & Ryan, R. M. (1991). Motivation and education: The self-determination perspective. *Educational Psychologist, 26*(3 & 4), 325–346.

DeSteno, D., & Salovey, P. (1997). Structural Dynamism in the Concept of self: A flexible model for a malleable concept. *Review of General Psychology, 1*(4), 389–409.

Dweck, C. S. (1986). Motivational processes affecting learning. *American Psychologist, 41,* 1040–1048.

Dweck, C. S. (1991). Self-theories and goals: Their role in motivation, personality and development. In R. Dienstbier (Ed.), *Nebraska symposium on motivation: Vol. 38. Perspectives on motivation.* Lincoln, NE: University of Nebraska Press.

Eccles, J. (1983). Expectancies, values, and academic behaviors. In J. T. Spence (Ed.), *Achievement and achievement motives: Psychological and sociological approaches* (pp. 75–146). San Francisco: W. H. Freeman.

Eccles, J. (1984). Self-perceptions, task perceptions, socializing influences, and the decision to enroll in mathematics. In M. W. Steinkamp & M. L. Maehr (Eds.), *Advances in motivation and achievement: Women in science* (Vol. 2, pp. 95–121). Greenwich, CT: JAI Press.

Eccles, J., Barber, B., Jozefowicz, D., Malenchuk, O., & Vida, M. (1999). Self-evaluations of competence, task values, and self-esteem. In N. G. Johnson & M. C. Roberts (Eds.), *Beyond appearance: A new look at adolescent girls* (pp. 53–83). Washington, DC: American Psychological Association.

Eccles, J. S., Early, D., Frasier, K., Belansky, E., & McCarthy, K. (1997). The relation of connection, regulation, and support for autonomy to adolescents' functioning. *Journal of Adolescent Research, 12*(2), 263–286.

Eccles, J. S., & Wigfield, A. (1995). In the mind of the actor: The structure of adolescents' achievement task values and expectancy-related beliefs. *Personality and Social Psychology Bulletin, 21*(3), 215–225.

Eccles, J. S., Wigfield, A., Midgley, C., Reuman, D., & Mac Iver, D. (1993). Negative effects of traditional middle schools on students' motivation. *Elementary School Journal, 93*(5), 553–574.

Epstein, J. A., Stokes, P. K., & Harackiewicz, J. M. (1987, August). *Affect and intrinsic interest: An arousal mediated model.* Paper presented at the annual meeting of the American Psychological Association, New York.

Figurski, T. J. (1987a). Self-awareness and other-awareness: The use of perspective in everyday life. In K. Yardley & T. Honess (Eds.), *Self and identity: Psychosocial perspectives.* New York: Wiley.

Figurski, T. J. (1987b, August). *The emotional contingencies of self-awareness in everyday life.* Paper presented at the annual meeting of the American Psychological Association, New York.

Fleming, J. S., & Courtney, B. E. (1984). The dimensionality of self-esteem: II. Hierarchical facet model for revised measurement scales. *Journal of Personality and Social Psychology, 46*(2), 404–421.

Ford, M. E. (1992). *Motivating humans: Goals, emotions, and personal agency beliefs.* Newbury Park, CA: Sage.

Frome, P. M., & Eccles, J. S. (1998). Parents' influence on children's achievement-related perceptions. *Journal of Personality and Social Psychology, 74*(2), 435–452.

Gardner, H. (1987, August). *Beyond modularity: Evidence from developmental psychology and neuropsychology.* Paper presented at the annual meeting of the American Psychological Association, New York.

Gardner, H. (1993). *Multiple intelligences: The theory in practice.* New York: Basic Books.

Gardner, H. (1995a). Reflections on multiple intelligences: Myths and messages. *Phi Delta Kappan, 77*(3), 200–209.

Gardner, H. (1995b). *Intelligence: Multiple perspectives.* Fort Worth, TX: Harcourt Brace College Publishers.

Giorgi, A. (Ed.) (1985). *Phenomenology and psychological research.* Pittsburgh, PA: Duquesne University Press.

Giorgi, A. (1990). *A phenomenological reinterpretation of the Jamesian schema for psychology.* Paper presented at the annual meeting of the American Psychological Association, Boston.

Green, D. P., & Salovey, P. (1999). In what sense are positive and negative affect independent? A reply to Tellegen, Watson, and Clark. *Psychological Science, 10*(4), 304–306.

Harre, R., & Secord, P. E. (1972). *The explanation of social behavior.* Oxford, England: Blackwell.

Harter, S. (1982). A developmental perspective on some parameters of self-regulation in children. In P. Karoly & F. H. Kanfer (Eds.), *Self-management and behavior change: From theory to practice* (pp. 165–204). New York: Pergamon Press.

Harter. S. (1985). Processes underlying self-concept formation in children. In J. Suls & A. Greenwald (Eds.), *Psychological perspectives on the self* (pp. 137–181). Hillsdale, NJ: Lawrence Erlbaum Associates.

Harter, S. (1987). The determinants and mediational role of global self-worth in children. In N. Eisenberg (Ed.), *Contemporary topics in developmental psychology.* New York: Wiley.

Harter, S. (1990, November). *Visions of self: Beyond the me in the mirror.* Presentation as University Lecturer of the Year, University of Denver.

Harter, S. (1992a). The relationship between perceived competence, affect, and motivation: Processes and patterns of change. In A. K. Boggiano & T. Pittman (Eds.), *Achievement and motivation: A social developmental perspective.* Cambridge: Cambridge University Press.

Harter, S. (1992b). Affective and motivational correlates of self-esteem. In R. Dienstbier (Ed.), *Nebraska symposium on motivation: Vol. 40. Developmental perspectives on motivation.* Lincoln, NE: University of Nebraska Press.

Harter, S. (1998). The development of self-representations. In W. Damon (Series Ed.) & N. Eisenberg (Vol. Ed.), *Handbook of child psychology: Vol. 3, Social, emotional, and personality development* (5th ed., pp. 553–617). New York: Wiley.

Harter, S. (1999). *The construction of the self: A developmental perspective.* New York: Guilford Press.

Harter, S., & Connell, J. P. (1984). A model of children's achievement and related self-perceptions of competence, control, and motivational orientation. *Advances in Motivation and Achievement, 3,* 219–250.

Harter, S., Whitesell, N. R., & Junkin, L. J. (1998). Similarities and differences in domain-specific and global self-evaluations of learning disabled, behaviorally disordered, and normally achieving adolescents. *American Educational Research Journal, 35*(4), 653–680.

Herzog, A. R., Franks, M. M., Markus, H. R., & Holmberg, D. (1998). Activities and well-being in older age: Effects of self-concept and educational attainment. *Psychology and Aging, 13*(2), 179–195.

Higgins, E. T. (1987). Self-discrepancy: A theory relating self and affect. *Psychological Review, 54,* 319–340.

Higgins, E. T. (1997). Beyond pleasure and pain. *American Psychologist, 52*(12), 1280–1300.

Howard, G. S. (1986). *Dare we develop a human science?* Notre Dame, IN: Academic Publications.

Inglehart, M. R., Markus, H., Brown, D. R., & Moore, W. (1987, May). *The impact of possible selves on academic achievement: A longitudinal analysis.* Paper presented at the Midwestern Psychological Association, Chicago.

Inglehart, M. R., Wurf, E., Brown, D. R., & Moore, W. (1987, August). *Possible selves and satisfaction with career choice—A longitudinal analysis.* Paper presented at the annual meeting of the American Psychological Association, New York.

Iran-Nejad, A. (1990). Active and dynamic self-regulation of learning processes. *Review of Educational Research, 60*(4), 573–602.

James, W. (1892), *Psychology: The briefer course.* NY: Henry Holt & Co.

Jennings, J. L. (1986). Husserl revisited: The forgotten distinction between psychology and phenomenology. *American Psychologist, 41,* 1231–1240.

Kanfer, R., Ackerman, P. L., & Heggestad, E. (1996). Motivational skills and self-regulation for learning: A trait perspective. *Learning and Individual Differences, 8,* 185–209.

Kanfer, R., & Heggestad, E. (1997). Motivational traits and skills: A person-centered approach to work motivation. In L. L. Cummings & B. M. Staw (Eds.), *Research in Organizational Behavior* (Vol. 9, pp. 1–57). Greenwich, CT: JAI Press.

Kanfer, R., & McCombs, B. L. (2000). Motivation: Applying current theory to critical issues in training. In S. Tobias & D. T. Fletcher (Eds.), *Handbook of Training* (pp. 85–108). New York: Macmillan.

Kohn, A. (1996). *Beyond discipline: From compliance to community.* Alexandria, VA: Association for Supervision and Curriculum Development.

Kuhl, J. (1985). Volitional mediators of cognition-behavior consistency: Self-regulatory processes and action vs. state orientation. In J. Kuhl & J. Beckmann (Eds.), *Action control: From cognition to behavior* (pp. 101–128). New York: Springer-Verlag.

Lambert, N., & McCombs, B. L. (1998). *How students learn: Reforming schools through learner-centered education.* Washington, DC: APA Books.

Levy, S. R., & Dweck, C. S. (1998). Trait-versus process-focused social judgment. *Social Cognition, 16*(1), 151–172.

Maden, S., Jussim, L., Keiper, S., & Eccles, J. (1998). The accuracy and power of sex, social class, and ethnic stereotypes: A naturalistic study in person perception. *Personality and Social Psychology Bulletin, 24*(12), 1304–1318.

Maehr, M. L. (1985). Meaning and motivation: Toward a theory of personal investment. In C. Ames & R. Ames (Eds.), *Research on motivation in education: The classroom milieu* (pp. 115–146). New York: Academic Press.

Manderlink, G., & Harackiewicz, J. M. (1984). Proximal versus distal goal setting and intrinsic motivation. *Journal of Personality and Social Psychology, 41*, 918–928.

Manicas, P. T., & Secord, P. F. (1983). Implications for psychology of the new philosophy of science. *American Psychologist, 38*, 399–413.

Markova, 1. (1987). Knowledge of the self through interaction. In K. Yardley & T. Honess (Eds.), *Self and identity: Psychosocial perspectives* (*pp.* 65–80). New York: Wiley.

Markus, H. R. (1998, August). *Our culture, our selves.* Invited address at the annual meeting of the American Psychological Association, San Francisco.

Markus, H. R., & Kitayama, S. (1991a). Culture and the self: Implications for cognition, emotion, and motivation. *Psychological Review, 98*(2), 224–253.

Markus, H. R., & Kitayama, S. (1991b). Cultural variation in the self-concept. In J. Strauss & G. R. Goethals (Eds.), *The self: Interdisciplinary approaches* (pp. 18–48). New York: Springer-Verlag.

Markus, H. R., & Kitayama, S. (1994). A collective fear of the collective: Implications for selves and theories of selves. *Personality and Social Psychology Bulletin, 20*(5), 568–579.

Markus, H. R., & Kitayama, S. (1998). The cultural psychology of personality. *Journal of Cross-Cultural Psychology, 29*(1), 63–87.

Markus, H., & Nurius, P. (1987). Possible selves: The interface between motivation and the self-concept. In K. Yardley & T. Honess (Eds.), *Self and identity: Psychosocial perspectives.* New York: Wiley.

Markus, H., & Ruvulo, A. (1990). Possible selves: Personalized representations of goals. In L. Pervin (Ed.), *Goal concepts in psychology* (pp. 211–241). Hillsdale, NJ: Lawrence Erlbaum Associates.

Markus, H., & Wurf, E. (1987). The dynamic self-concept: A social psychological perspective. *Annual Review of Psychology, 38*, 299–337.

Marsh, H. W. (1986). Self-serving effect (bias?) in academic attributions: Its relation to academic achievement and self-concept. *Journal of Educational Psychology, 78*(3), 190–200.

Marsh, H. W. (1990). *Self-Description Questionnaire (SDQ) II: A theoretical and empirical basis for the measurement of multiple dimensions of adolescent self-concept.* San Antonio, TX: Psychological Corp.

Marsh, H. W. (1993). Relations between global and specific domains of self: The importance of individual importance, certainty, and ideals. *Journal of Personality and Social Psychology, 65*, 975–992.

Marsh, H. W. (1994). Using the National Longitudinal Study of 1988 to evaluate theoretical models of self-concept: The Self-Description Questionnaire. *Journal of Educational Psychology, 86*, 439–456.

Marsh, H. W. (1995). A Jamesian model of self-investment and self-esteem: Comment on Pelham. *Journal of Personality and Social Psychology, 65*, 1151–1160.

Marsh, H. W., Byrne, B. M., & Shavelson, R. J. (1988). A multi-faceted academic self-concept: Its hierarchical structure and its relation to academic achievement. *Journal of Educational Psychology, 80*(3), 366–380.

Marsh, H, W., & Shavelson, R. (1985). Self-concept: Its multifaceted, hierarchical structure. *Educational Psychologist, 20*(3), 107–123.

Marsh, H. W., & Yeung, A. S. (1998). Longitudinal structural equation model of academic self-concept and achievement: Gender differences in the development of math and English constructs. *American Educational Research Journal, 35*(4), 705–738.

Martin, C. L., & Ruble, D. N. (1997). A developmental perspective on self-construals and sex differences: Comment on Cross and Madson. *Psychological Bulletin, 122*(1), 45–50.

Mayer, J. D., & Salovey, P. (1993). The intelligence of emotional intelligence. *Intelligence, 17*(4), 433–442.

Mays, W. (1985). Preface. In W.S. Hamrick (Ed.), *Phenomenology in practice and theory.* Dordrecht, The Netherlands: Martinus Nijhoff.

McCall, R. J. (1983). *Phenomenological psychology.* Madison: The University of Wisconsin Press.

McCombs, B. L. (1984). Processes and skills underlying continuing intrinsic motivation to learn: Toward a definition of motivational skills training interventions. *Educational Psychologist, 19*(4), 199–218.

McCombs, B. L. (1986). The role of the self-system in self-regulated learning. *Contemporary Educational Psychology, 11,* 314–332.

McCombs, B. L. (1991). The definition and measurement of primary motivational processes. In M. C. Wittrock & E. L. Baker (Eds.), *Testing and cognition* (pp. 62–81). Englewood Cliffs, NJ: Prentice Hall.

McCombs, B. L. (1994). Strategies for assessing and enhancing motivation: Keys to promoting self-regulated learning and performance. In H. F. O'Neil, Jr., & M. Drillings (Eds.), *Motivation: Research and theory.* Hillsdale, NJ: Lawrence Erlbaum Associates.

McCombs, B. L. (1995). Putting the learner and learning in learner-centered classrooms: The learner-centered model as a framework. *Michigan ASCD Focus, 17(1),* 7–12. *Special Issue, On the Learner, Learning and the Learner-Centered Classroom.*

McCombs, B. L. (1998). Integrating metacognition, affect, and motivation in improving teacher education. In B. L. McCombs & N. Lambert (Eds.), *Issues in school reform: Psychological perspectives on learner-centered schools* (pp. 379–408). Washington, DC: APA Books.

McCombs, B. L. (1999). What role does perceptual psychology play in educational reform today? In H. J. Freiberg (Ed.), *Perceiving, behaving, becoming: Lessons learned* (pp. 148–157). Alexandria, VA: Association for Supervision and Curriculum Development.

McCombs, B. L., & Lauer, P. A. (1997). Development and validation of the Learner-Centered Battery: Self-Assessment tools for teacher reflection and professional development. *The Professional Educator, 20*(1), 1–21.

McCombs, B. L., & Lauer, P. A. (1998, July). *The learner-centered model of seamless professional development: Implications for practice and policy changes in higher education.* Paper presented at the 23rd International Conference on Improving University Teaching, Dublin.

McCombs, B. L., & Marzano, R. J. (1990). Putting the self in self-regulated learning. *Educational Psychologist, 25*(1), 51–69.

McCombs, B. L., & Marzano, R. J. (in press). What is the role of the will component in strategic learning? In C. E. Weinstein & B. L. McCombs (Eds.), *Strategic learning: Skill, will, and self-regulation.* Hillsdale, NJ: Lawrence Erlbaum Associates.

McCombs, B. L., & Whisler, J. S. (1989). The role of affective variables in autonomous learning. *Educational Psychologist, 24*(3), 277–306.

McCombs, B. L., & Whisler, J. S. (1997). *The learner-centered classroom and school: Strategies for enhancing student motivation and achievement.* San Francisco: Jossey-Bass.

Menec, V. H., Hechter, F. J., & Perry, R. P. (1995, April). *Action control and self-efficacy: Their effects on self-regulatory strategies and achievement.* Paper presented at the annual conference of the American Educational Research Association, San Francisco.

Miller, R. B., & Brickman, S. (1997, March). *The role of future consequences in achievement motivation.* Paper presented at the annual meeting of the American Educational Research Association, Chicago.

Mills, R. C. (1991). A new understanding of self: The role of affect, state of mind, self-understanding, and intrinsic motivation. *Journal of Experimental Education, 60*(1), 67–81.

Mills, R. C. (1995). *Realizing mental health.* New York: Sulzburger & Graham.

Mills, R. C., Dunham, R. G., & Alpert, G. P. (1988). Working with high-risk youth in prevention and early intervention programs: Toward a comprehensive model. *Adolescence, 23,* 643–660.

Mischel, W. (1977). On the future of personality measurement. *American Psychologist, 32*(4), 246–254.

Mish, F. C. (Ed.) (1988). *Websters Ninth New Collegiate Dictionary.* Springfield, MA: Merriam-Webster.

Misiak, H., & Sexton, VS. (1973). *Phenomenological, existential, and humanistic psychology.* New York: Grune & Statton.

Moretti, M. M., & Higgins, E. T. (1999a). Internal representations of others in self- regulation: A new look at a classic issue. *Social Cognition, 17*(2), 186-208.

Moretti, M. M., & Higgins, E. T. (1999b). Own versus other standpoints in self-regulation: Developmental antecedents and functional consequences. *Review of General Psychology, 3*(3), 188–223.

Natsoulas, T. (1999). An ecological and phenomenological perspective on consciousness: Contact with the world at the very heart of the being of consciousness. *Review of General Psychology, 3*(3), 224–245.

Nicholls, J. G. (1983). Conceptions of ability and achievement motivation: A theory and its implications for education. In S. G. Paris, G. M. Olson, & H. W. Stevenson (Eds.), *Learning and motivation in the classroom.* Hillsdale, NJ: Lawrence Erlbaum Associates.

Nicholls, J. G. (1984). Achievement motivation: Conceptions of ability, subjective experience, task choice, and performance. *Psychological Review, 91,* 328–346.

Nicholls, J. G. (1987, August). *Motivation, values, and education.* Paper presented at the annual meeting of the American Psychological Association, New York.

Nyquist, L. V. (1986, August). *The dynamic self-concept: Cognitive and behavioral responses to challenge.* Paper presented at the annual meeting of the American Psychological Association, Washington, DC.

Paris, S. G., & Brynes, J. P. (1989). The constructivist approach to self-regulation and learning in the classroom. In B. J. Zimmerman & D. H. Schunk (Eds.), *Self-regulated learning and academic achievement: Theory, research, and practice* (pp. 169–209). New York: Springer-Verlag.

Paris, S. G., & Newman, R. S. (1990). Developmental aspects of self-regulated learning. *Educational Psychologist, 25*(1), 87–102.

Perry, N. E. (1998). Young children's self-regulated learning and contexts that support it. *Journal of Educational Psychology, 90*(4), 715–729.

Perry, K. E., Donohue, K. M., & Weinstein, R. S. (1999, March). *Young children's perceptions of learner-centered teaching practices: Meaningful predictors of early school success.* Paper presented at the annual meeting of the Society for Research in Child Development, New Orleans.

Perry, K. E., & Weinstein, R. S. (1998). The social context of early schooling and children's school adjustment. *Educational Psychologist, 33*(4), 177–194.

Pomerantz, E. M., & Ruble, D. N. (1997). Distinguishing multiple dimensions of conceptions of ability: Implications for self-evaluation. *Child Development, 68*(6), 1165–1180.

Pransky, G. S. (1998). *The renaissance of psychology.* New York: Sulzburger & Graham.

Purdie, N., & Hattie, J. (1996). Cultural differences in the use of strategies for self-regulated learning. *American Educational Research Journal, 33*(4), 845–871.

Reeder, G. D., McCormick, C. B., & Esselman, E. D. (1987). Self-referent processing and recall of prose. *Journal of Educational Psychology, 79*(3), 243–248.

Renkl, A. (1997, March). *Intrinsic motivation, self-explanations, and transfer.* Paper presented at the annual meeting of the American Educational Research Association, Chicago.

Rhodewalt, F. (1987, August). *Is self-handicapping an effective self-protective attributional strategy?* Paper presented at the annual meeting of the American Psychological Association, New York.

Richardson, J. T. E. (1999). The concepts and methods of phenomenographic research. *Review of Educational Research, 69*(1), 53–82.

Ridley, D. S. (1991). Reflective self-awareness: A basic motivational process. *Journal of Experimental Education, 60*(1), 31–48.

Robinson, D. N. (1987, August). *What moves us? A note on human motives.* Paper presented at the annual meeting of the American Psychological Association, New York.

Rosenberg, J. F. (1986). *The thinking self.* Philadelphia, PA: Temple University Press.

Ruble, D. N. (1987). The acquisition of self-knowledge: A self-socialization perspective. In N. Eisenberg (Ed.), *Contemporary topics in developmental psychology.* New York: Wiley.

Ruble, D. N., & Dweck, C. (1995). Self-conceptions, person conception, and their development. In N. Eisenberg (Ed.), *Social development* (pp. 109–139). Thousand Oaks, CA: Sage.

Ruvolo, A., & Markus, H. (1986, August). *Possible selves and motivation.* Paper presented at the meeting of the American Psychological Association, Washington, DC.

Ryan, R. M. (1991). The nature of the self in autonomy and relatedness. In J. Strauss & G. R. Goethals (Eds.), *The self: Interdisciplinary approaches* (pp. 208–238). New York: Springer-Verlag.

Ryan, R. M. (1992). A systemic view of the role of motivation in development. In R. Dienstbier (Ed.), *Nebraska symposium on motivation: Vol. 40. Developmental perspectives on motivation.* Lincoln, NE: University of Nebraska Press.

Ryan, R. M. (1995). Psychological needs and the facilitation of integrative processes. *Journal of Personality, 63*(3), 397–427.

Ryan, R. M., & Deci, E. L. (1996). When paradigms clash: Comments on Cameron and Pierce's claim that rewards do not undermine intrinsic motivation. *Review of Educational Research, 66*(1), 33–38.

Ryan, R. M., & Powelson, C. L. (1991). Autonomy and relatedness as fundamental to motivation and education. *Journal of Experimental Education, 60*(1), 49–66.

Salovey, P. (1987, August). *Mood, focus of attention, and self-relevant thought.* Paper presented at the annual meeting of the American Psychological Association, New York.

Salovey, P. (1992). Mood-induced self-focused attention. *Journal of Personality and Social Psychology, 62*(4), 699–707.

Sameroff, A. J. (1987). The social context of development. In N. Eisenberg (Ed.), *Contemporary topics in developmental psychology.* New York: Wiley.

Schunk, D. H. (1984, April). *Self efficacy and classroom learning.* Paper presented at the meeting of the American Educational Research Association, New Orleans.

Schunk, D. H. (1995). Inherent details of self-regulated learning include student perceptions. *Educational Psychologist, 30*(4), 213–216.

Schunk, D. H., & Zimmerman, B. J. (1998). *Self-regulated learning: From teaching to self-reflective practice.* New York: Guilford Press.

Shavelson, R. J., Hubner, J. J., & Stanton, G. C. (1976). Validation of construct interpretations. *Review of Educational Research, 46,* 407–441.

Showers, C., & Cantor, N. (1985). Social cognition: A look at motivated strategies. *Annual Review of Psychology, 36,* 275–305.

Spiegelberg, H. (1972). *Phenomenology in psychological psychiatry: A historical introduction.* Evanston, IL: Northwestern University Press.

Spielberger, C. D., Gorsuch, R. L., & Lushene, R. E. (1983). *Manual for the state-trait anxiety inventory.* Palo Alto, CA: Consulting Psychologists Press.

Srull, T. K., & Gaelick, L. (1983). General principles and individual differences in the self as a habitual reference point: An examination of self–other judgments of similarity. *Social Cognition, 2*(2), 108–121.

Stipek, D. (1998a). Differences between Americans and Chinese in the circumstances evoking pride, shame, and guilt. *Journal of Cross-Cultural Psychology, 29*(5), 616–629.

Stipek, D. (1998b). *Motivation to Learn. From theory to practice.* Boston, MA: Allyn and Bacon.

Tauer, J. W., & Harackiewicz, J. M. (1999). Winning isn't everything: Competition, achievement orientation, and intrinsic motivation. *Journal of Experimental Social Psychology. 35*(3), 209–238.

Turner, J., & Paris, S. G. (1995). How literacy tasks influence children's motivation for literacy. *Reading Teacher, 48*(8), 662–673.

Urdan, T. C., & Maehr, M. L. (1995). Beyond a two-goal theory of motivation and achievement: A case for social goals. *Review of Educational Research, 65*(3), 213–243.

Urdan, T., Pajares, F., & Lapin, A. Z. (1997, March). *Achievement goals, motivation, and performance: A closer look.* Paper presented at the annual meeting of the American Educational Research Association, Chicago.

Vispoel, W. P., & Boo, J. (1997, March). *Relations between domain specific and global aspects of self-concept in early adolescence: The moderating role of domain importance.* Paper presented at the annual meeting of the American Educational Research Association, Chicago.

Wang, M. C. (1983). Development and consequences of students' sense of personal control. In J. M. Levine & M. C. Wang (Eds.), *Teacher and student perceptions: Implications for learning* (*pp.* 213–247). Hillsdale, NJ: Lawrence Erlbaum Associates.

Wang, M. C. (1992). *Adaptive education strategies: Building on diversity.* Baltimore: Paul H. Brookes.

Werkmeister, W. H. (1940). *A philosophy of science.* Lincoln, NE: University of Nebraska Press.

Westphal, M. (Ed.) (1982). *Method and speculation in Hegel's phenomenology.* Atlantic Nishlords, NJ: New Jersey: Humanities Press.

Wheatley, M. J. (1994). *Leadership and the new science: Learning about organization from an orderly universe.* San Francisco, CA: Berrett-Koehler Publishers.

Wheatley, M. J. (1995, September). *Leadership and the new science.* Presentation transcribed as Professional Development Brief No. 3, California State Development Council.

Wheatley, M. J. (1999, July). *Reclaiming hope: The new story is ours to tell.* Summer Institute, Salt Lake City, UT: University of Utah.

Wheatley, M. J., & Kellner-Rogers, M. (1996). *A simpler way.* San Francisco: Berrett- Koehler Publishers.

Wheatley, M. J., & Kellner-Rogers, M. (1998). Bringing life to organizational change. *Journal of Strategic Performance Measurement,* April-May, 5–13.

Wigfield, A., Eccles, J. S., & Pintrich, P. R. (1996). Development between the ages of 11 and 25. In D. C. Berliner & R. C. Calfee (Eds.), *Handbook of educational psychology* (pp. 148–185). New York: Macmillan.

Williams, J. E. (1997, April). *Predicting students self-regulated learning: The roles of academic competence and self-determination.* Paper presented at the annual meeting of the American Educational Research Association, Chicago.

Wittrock, M. C. (1987, August). *The teaching of comprehension.* Paper presented at the annual meeting of the American Psychological Association, New York.

Wolters, C. A. (1998). Self-regulated learning and college students' regulation of motivation. *Journal of Educational Psychology, 90*(2), 224–235.

Zimmerman, B. J. (1985). The development of "intrinsic" motivation: A social learning analysis. *Annals of Child Development, 2,* 117–160.

Zimmerman, B. J. (1994). Dimensions of academic self-regulation: A conceptual framework for education. In D. H. Schunk & B. J. Zimmerman (Eds.), *Self-regulation of learning and performance: Issues and educational applications* (pp. 3–21). Hillsdale, NJ: Lawrence Erlbaum Associates.

Zimmerman, B. J. (1995). Self-regulation involves more than metacognition: A social cognitive perspective. *Educational Psychologist, 30*(4), 217–221.

Zimmerman, B. J., & Bandura, A. (1994). Impact of self-regulatory influences on writing course attainment. *American Educational Research Journal, 31,* 845–862.

Chapter 4

Social Cognitive Theory and Self-Regulated Learning

Dale H. Schunk
Purdue University

Current theoretical accounts of learning view students as active seekers and processors of information. Learners' cognitions can influence the instigation, direction, and persistence of achievement behaviors (Bandura, 1997; Schunk, 1995; Zimmerman, 1998).

This chapter discusses self-regulated learning from a social cognitive theoretical perspective. *Self-regulated learning* (SRL) refers to learning that results from students' self-generated thoughts and behaviors that are systematically oriented toward the attainment of their learning goals. SRL involves goal-directed activities that students instigate, modify, and sustain (Zimmerman, 1994, 1998); for example, attending to instruction, processing information, rehearsing and relating new learning to prior knowledge, believing that one is capable of learning, and establishing productive social relationships and work environments (Schunk, 1995). SRL fits well with the notion that rather than being passive recipients of information, students contribute actively to their learning goals and exercise control over goal attainment.

In the social cognitive theoretical framework, self-regulation is construed as situationally specific. This means that self-regulation is not a general trait or a particular level of development. Self-regulation is highly context dependent; people are not generally self-regulated or nonself-regulated. Learners are not expected to engage in self-regulation equally in all domains. Although some self-regulatory processes (e.g., goal setting) may generalize across settings, learners must understand how to adapt processes to specific domains and must feel efficacious about doing so.

This situational specificity is captured in Zimmerman's (1994, 1998) conceptual framework for studying self-regulation. In this view, there are six areas in which one can use self-regulatory processes: motives, methods, time, outcomes, physical environment, and social environment. Self-regulation is possible to the extent that learners have some choice in one or more of these areas. When all aspects of a task are predetermined, students may learn, but the source of control is external (i.e., teachers, parents, computers).

Initially I present a social cognitive theoretical overview of self-regulated learning. Key processes involved in SRL are discussed, along with supporting research. Implications of this view for how aspects of self-regulation are developed are discussed. The chapter concludes with a description of social cognitive principles being applied in a learning context to enhance students' achievement outcomes.

THEORETICAL OVERVIEW

Reciprocal Interactions

According to Bandura (1986), human functioning involves reciprocal interactions between behaviors, environmental variables, and cognitions and other personal factors (Fig. 4.1). This reciprocity is exemplified with an important construct in Bandura's theory: *perceived self-efficacy*, or beliefs about one's capabilities to learn or perform behaviors at designated levels. Research shows that students' self-efficacy beliefs influence such

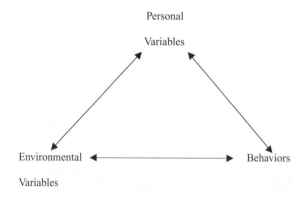

FIG. 4.1. Reciprocal Interactions in Human Functioning.

actions as choice of tasks, persistence, effort, and achievement (Schunk, 1995). In turn, students' behaviors modify their efficacy beliefs. For example, as students work on tasks, they note their progress toward their learning goals (e.g., completing sections of a term paper). Progress indicators convey to students that they are capable of performing well, which enhances self-efficacy for continued learning.

The interaction between self-efficacy and environmental factors was demonstrated in research on students with learning disabilities, many of whom hold low self-efficacy for performing well (Licht & Kistner, 1986). Individuals in students' social environments may react to them based on attributes typically associated with them rather than based on what students actually do. Teachers may judge such students as less capable than normally achieving students and hold lower academic expectations for them, even in content areas where students with learning disabilities are performing adequately (Bryan & Bryan, 1983). In turn, teacher feedback can affect self-efficacy. Persuasive statements (e.g., "I know that you can do this") can raise self-efficacy.

Students' behaviors and classroom environments influence one another. Consider a typical instructional sequence in which the teacher presents information and asks students to direct their attention to an overhead. Environmental influence on behavior occurs when students turn their heads without much conscious deliberation. Students' behaviors often alter the instructional environment. If the teacher asks questions and students give incorrect answers, the teacher may reteach some points rather than continue the lesson.

Enactive and Vicarious Learning

Learning is a change in behavior or behavioral potential brought about by intervening experiences. Enactive learning, or learning by doing, depends heavily on the consequences of one's actions. Actions that result in successes tend to be retained; those that lead to failures are discarded. Complex skills typically involve some enactive learning. Students may learn some components of a skill and not others. Guided practice of skills gives teachers the opportunity to provide corrective feedback and instruction.

What differentiates social cognitive theory from earlier reinforcement theories is not that people learn by doing but rather its explanation. Skinner (1953) postulated that skillful performances are gradually acquired through reinforcement of successive approximations to the target behavior, a process known as *shaping*. Cognitions may accompany behavioral change, but they do not influence it. Conversely, social cognitive theory contends that behavioral consequences serve as sources of information and motivation rather than as response strengtheners (Bandura, 1986). People selectively engage in cognitive activities that assist learning and are motivated to learn actions that they value and believe will lead to rewarding consequences.

Much human learning occurs in the absence of overt behavior, or vicariously by observing others, reading, watching TV and videos, surfing the web, and so forth. Vicarious learning accelerates learning and saves us from experiencing many negative consequences. We do not have to enter war zones to learn that they are dangerous; we observe their effects on the nightly news.

Cognitive skill learning often combines enactive and vicarious learning. In mathematics, students learn operations by observing teachers demonstrate their application. Students hone their skills through practice and feedback. Factors associated with the learning, such as the belief among observers that it is useful, can lead people to attend carefully to models and to cognitively and overtly rehearse their actions.

Learning and Performance

Social cognitive theory differentiates learning from performance of previously learned behaviors. By observing models, people can acquire knowledge that they may not demonstrate at the time of learning (Schunk, 1987). Some school activities (e.g., review sessions) involve performance of previously learned skills, but much time is spent on new learning. Students acquire *declarative knowledge* (facts, events of a story, organized passages), *procedural knowledge* (concepts, rules, algorithms), and *conditional knowledge* (when to employ declarative and procedural knowledge and why it is important to do so; Paris, Cross, & Lipson, 1984; Paris, Lipson, & Wixson, 1983). Each of these forms of knowledge can be acquired but not demonstrated when learning occurs. Thus, students may learn about the Apollo 11 flight to the moon in class and subsequently demonstrate their knowledge when they prepare a project for the science fair.

Modeling

Modeling refers to cognitive, affective, and behavioral changes that derive from observing models. *Models* are real or symbolic individuals or characters whose behaviors, verbalizations, and nonverbal expressions are attended to by observers and serve as cues for subsequent modeling (Schunk, 1987). According to Bandura (1986), modeling can serve different functions: acquisition of new behaviors (observational learning), strengthening or weakening of behavioral inhibitions (inhibition/disinhibition), and performance of previously learned behaviors due to prompting (response facilitation).

Response facilitation occurs when modeled actions serve as social prompts, as when one performs the actions of high-status models in the hope of obtaining approval. Inhibition/disinhibition involves strengthening or weakening of inhibitions for performing learned behaviors. Observing models perform threatening or prohibited activities without negative consequences can lead observers to perform the behaviors themselves; observing models punished for performing actions may inhibit observers' responding.

Observational learning occurs when observers display new behaviors that, prior to modeling, had no likelihood of occurring even with motivational inducements in effect. Observational learning through modeling is comprised of four processes: attention, retention, production, and motivation (Bandura, 1986). Observer *attention* to environmental events is necessary for them to be perceived. *Retention* includes coding and transforming modeled information for storage in memory, such as through rehearsal and linking new information to knowledge already in memory. There is debate whether knowledge ultimately is stored in memory exclusively in verbal form as propositions (units of information) or also in imaginal form; however, research shows that representing knowledge in imaginal form aids learning (Shepard, 1978). *Production* involves translating visual and symbolic conceptions of modeled events into behaviors. *Motivation* is necessary for observers to display actions learned observationally. Observers may be motivated because they see models rewarded, they believe that the learning is important, and so forth.

The functional value of behavior, or whether it results in success or failure or reward or punishment, affects observer modeling. Modeled actions are more likely to be performed if they previously led to rewarding outcomes than if they resulted in punishment, regardless of whether people experienced the consequences themselves or whether they observed modeled consequences. People also act in line with personal standards. They behave in ways they believe are acceptable and avoid what displeases them.

Modeling serves informational and motivational functions. Observing competent models perform actions that result in success conveys information to observers about the sequence of actions to use. Most social situations are structured so that the appropriateness of behaviors depends on such factors as age, gender, or status. By observing modeled behaviors and their consequences, people formulate outcome expectations, or beliefs about the likely outcomes of actions.

Perceived similarity between model and observer can inform people
of behavioral appropriateness and help them formulate outcome expectations (Schunk, 1987). Festinger (1954) hypothesized that when objective standards of behavior were unclear or unavailable, observers evaluated themselves through comparisons with others, and that the most
accurate self-evaluations derived from comparisons with those similar in
the ability or characteristic being evaluated. The more alike observers are
to models, the greater is the probability that similar actions by observers
are socially appropriate and will produce comparable results. Model attributes often predict the functional value of behaviors. Similarity should
be especially influential in situations where observers have little information about functional value. Modeled behaviors on tasks that observers
are unfamiliar with or those that are not immediately followed by consequences may be highly susceptible to influence by attribute similarity.

The motivational effects of vicarious consequences depend partly on
self-efficacy. Similarity to models constitutes a source of vicarious information for evaluating one's efficacy. Observing similar others succeed
can raise observers' self-efficacy and motivate them to try the task; they
are apt to believe that if others can do well, they can, too. Observing
similar others fail can lead people to believe they may lack the competence to succeed, which can dissuade them from attempting the task.
Model attributes often are predictive of capabilities. Similarity is most
influential when individuals are unfamiliar with the task or previously
experienced difficulties and hold low self-efficacy.

SUBPROCESSES OF SELF-REGULATED LEARNING

Self-regulation has been conceptualized as involving three key subprocesses: self-observation, self-judgment, self-reaction (Bandura, 1986;
Kanfer & Gaelick, 1986; Karoly, 1982). These subprocesses are not mutually exclusive but rather interact. While observing aspects of one's
behavior, one may judge them against standards and react positively or
negatively. One's evaluations and reactions set the stage for additional
observations of the same behavioral aspects or others. These subprocesses also do not operate independently of the learning environment;
environmental factors can assist the development of self-regulation.

Self-Observation

Behaviors can be assessed on such dimensions as quantity, quality, and
originality. Self-observation can inform and motivate. Information
gained is used to determine how well one is progressing toward one's

goals. Self-observation is most helpful when it addresses the specific conditions under which the behaviors occur. Such information is valuable in establishing a program of change. Students who notice that they accomplish less when they study with a friend than when they are alone may increasingly study by themselves.

Self-observation can motivate behavioral change. Keeping a record of what one does may prove illuminating. Many students with poor study habits are surprised to learn how much time they waste on nonacademic activities. Self-observation alone usually is insufficient; sustained motivation depends on outcome and efficacy expectations. For students to change their study habits, they need to believe that if they alter their habits they will accomplish more (outcome expectation) and that they can change those habits (self-efficacy).

Self-observation is aided with self-recording, where instances of the behavior are recorded along with such features as the time, place, and duration of occurrence (Karoly, 1982; Mace, Belfiore, & Shea, 1989). In the absence of recording, one's observations may not faithfully reflect one's behaviors due to selective memory.

Two important criteria for self-observation are regularity and proximity. Regularity means that behavior is observed on a continuous basis (i.e., hour by hour, day by day) rather than intermittently. Nonregular observation provides misleading results. Proximity means that behavior is observed close in time to its occurrence rather than long after it (e.g., recall at the end of the day what one did during the day). Proximal observations provide continuous information to use in gauging progress (Mace et al., 1989).

Self-Judgment

Self-judgment refers to comparing present performance with one's goal. Self-judgments can be affected by such factors as the type of standards employed, the properties of the goal, the importance of goal attainment, and the attributions made for outcomes.

Type of Standards.   Goals may involve absolute (fixed) or normative (relative to others) standards. Students whose goal is to complete six workbook pages in 30 minutes can gauge their progress against this absolute standard. Many grading systems are based on absolute standards (e.g., 90–100 = A). Normative standards often are acquired from observing models. Social comparisons with others allow people to determine the appropriateness of behaviors and evaluate their performances (Veroff, 1969). While working on an assignment, students might compare their progress with that of their peers to determine who will finish first.

Standards inform and motivate. Students who complete three pages in 10 minutes realize that they finished half of the work in less than half of the time. The belief that one is making goal progress enhances self-efficacy and sustains motivation. Students who find a task to be easy may think that they set their absolute goal too low and may set it higher the next time. Further, knowing that similar others performed a task can promote self-efficacy and motivation; students are apt to believe that if others can succeed, they can as well (Schunk, 1987).

Goal Properties. Goals exert their effects through their properties: specificity, proximity, difficulty level (Bandura, 1988; Locke & Latham, 1990). Goals that incorporate specific performance standards raise self-efficacy because progress toward an explicit goal is easy to gauge. General goals (e.g., "Do your best") do not enhance motivation. Proximal goals, which are close at hand, result in greater motivation than distant goals; it is easier to gauge progress toward the former. Students are not motivated by goals that they believe are too easy or overly difficult. Rather, a goal viewed as challenging but attainable can motivate and build a strong sense of efficacy.

Goal setting is especially influential with long-term tasks. For example, many students have self-doubts about completing a term paper. Teachers can assist by breaking the task into short-term attainable goals (e.g., select a topic, conduct research, write an outline). Students should feel efficacious about completing the subtasks, and attaining each subgoal helps develop their overall self-efficacy for completing the project.

Importance of Goal Attainment. Goal progress judgments are made for valued goals. People who care little about how they perform may not assess their performance (Bandura, 1997). Occasionally, goals that originally hold little value become more important when people receive feedback indicating that they are developing skill. Novice piano players initially may hold ill-defined goals (e.g., play better), but as piano skills develop, they will set specific goals (e.g., practice an hour a day, learn to play a particular piece) and regularly judge their goal progress.

Attributions. Attributions (perceived causes of outcomes) can affect expectations, behaviors, and affective reactions (Weiner, 1985). Achievement successes and difficulties often are attributed to such causes as ability, effort, and task difficulty. Children view effort as the prime cause of outcomes and ability as closely associated but with development, a distinct conception of ability emerges (Nicholls, 1978). With age, children's ability attributions increase in importance as an influence on expectancies, whereas children's effort attributions decline in importance (Harari & Covington, 1981). Success attributed to high effort should raise self-efficacy less than if minimal effort is required because the former implies that skills are not well developed (Bandura, 1986).

People take greater pride in their accomplishments when they attribute them to personal factors than when they attribute them to others. People also are more self-critical when they attribute failure to personal factors under their control (e.g., insufficient effort) than when they believe the factors were outside of their control (e.g., powerful others). Whether goal progress is judged as acceptable depends partly on its attribution. Students who attribute success to teacher help may feel inefficacious about performing well because they may think they cannot succeed on their own. Inadequate learning progress negatively affects motivation if learners believe they lack the ability to perform well.

Self-Reaction

Self-reactions to goal progress exert motivational effects (Bandura, 1986). Students who judge goal progress as acceptable and anticipate satisfaction from goal accomplishment feel efficacious about continuing to improve and motivated to complete the task. Negative evaluations will not necessarily decrease motivation if students believe they are capable of improving, such as by working harder. Motivation will not increase if students believe they lack the ability to succeed or to improve.

Instructions to people to respond evaluatively to their performances can affect motivation. People who believe they can perform better persist longer and work harder (Kanfer & Gaelick, 1986). Evaluations are not intimately tied to level of performance. Some students are content with a B in a course, whereas others want only an A. Assuming that people believe they are capable of improving, higher goals lead to greater effort and persistence than do lower goals (Locke & Latham, 1990).

In daily activities, people routinely make such consequences as work breaks, new clothes, and vacations contingent on task progress or goal attainment. Unlike reinforcement theories contending that consequences alter behavior, social cognitive theory postulates that the anticipation of consequences enhances motivation. Self- administered consequences motivate individuals even when external contingencies are in effect (Bandura, 1986). Grades are given at the end of a course, yet students set subgoals for accomplishing their coursework and reward and punish themselves accordingly.

Tangible consequences enhance self-efficacy when they are tied to students' actual accomplishments. Telling students they can earn rewards based on what they do can instill self-efficacy for learning. As they work at a task and note their progress, this sense of efficacy is validated. Receipt of the reward further validates efficacy because it symbolizes progress. When rewards are not tied to performance, they can convey negative efficacy information; students might infer that they are not expected to learn much because they do not have the necessary capability.

Cyclical Nature of Self-Regulation

The interaction of personal, behavioral, and environmental factors during self-regulation is a cyclical process because these factors typically change during learning and must be monitored (Bandura, 1986; 1997; Zimmerman, 1994). Such monitoring leads to changes in an individual's strategies, cognitions, affects, and behaviors.

This cyclical nature is captured in Zimmerman's (1998) three-phase self-regulation model. The forethought phase precedes actual performance and refers to processes that set the stage for action. The performance (volitional) control phase involves processes that occur during learning and affect attention and action. During the self-reflection phase, which occurs after performance, people respond to their efforts.

Various self-regulatory processes come into play during the different phases, as shown in Table 4.1 and summarized in the next section. Social cognitive theorists postulate that students enter learning situations with goals and varying degrees of self-efficacy for attaining them. During performance control, they implement learning strategies that affect motivation and learning. During periods of self-reflection, learners engage in the important process of self-evaluation, which is addressed later.

TABLE 4.1
Key Processes During Phases of Self-Regulation

Forethought	Performance Control	Self-Reflection
Goal setting	Social comparisons	Progress feedback & self-evaluation
Social modeling	Attributional feedback	Self-monitoring
	Strategy instruction & self-verbalization	Reward contingencies

LITERATURE REVIEW

This section presents a selective review of social cognitive research on self-regulation. A comprehensive review is beyond the scope of this chapter; readers should consult other sources (Bandura, 1986, 1997). Much social cognitive research applied self-regulatory principles to therapeutic contexts (e.g., weight loss, coping with fears). The research in this section focuses on self-regulation in educational learning settings. Although there is some overlap between areas, the review is organized according to Zimmerman's (1998) phases: forethought, performance control, self-reflection.

Forethought

Goal Setting. Goal setting is an integral aspect of the forethought phase of self-regulation. Allowing students to set learning goals can enhance their commitment to attaining them, which is necessary for goals to affect performance (Locke & Latham, 1990). Schunk (1985) found that self-set goals promoted self-efficacy. Children with learning disabilities in mathematics received subtraction instruction and practice over sessions. Some set performance goals each session; others had comparable goals assigned; those in a third condition did not set or receive goals. Self-set goals led to the highest self-efficacy and achievement. Children in the two goal conditions demonstrated greater motivation during self-regulated practice than did no-goal students. Self-set children judged themselves more confident of attaining their goals than did students in the assigned goals condition. Allowing students to choose their learning goals enhanced their self-efficacy for attaining them.

To test the idea that proximal goals enhance achievement outcomes better than distant goals, Bandura and Schunk (1981) provided children with subtraction instruction and self-regulated problem solving over sessions. Some pursued a proximal goal of completing one set of materials each session; a second group was given a distant goal of completing all sets of materials by the end of the last session; a third group was advised to work productively (general goal). Proximal goals led to the most productive self-regulated practice and to the highest subtraction self-efficacy and achievement; the distant goal resulted in no benefits compared with the general goal.

Schunk (1983c) tested the effects of goal difficulty. During a long division instructional program, children received either difficult but attainable or easier goals of completing a given number of problems each session. Within each goal condition, children either were given direct attainment information by an adult (i.e., "You can do this") or received social comparative information indicating that other similar children had been able to complete that many problems. Difficult goals enhanced motivation during self-regulated practice and achievement; direct goal attainment information promoted self-efficacy.

Social Modeling. Modeling studies provide evidence on how information conveyed socially can be internalized by students and used self-regulatively to produce greater learning. In addition to their benefits on learning, models convey that observers can succeed if they follow the same sequence. Students who believe they know how to perform a skill or strategy feel more efficacious and motivated to succeed (Schunk, 1987).

An important means of acquiring self-evaluative standards is through observation of models. Research shows that when children observe modeled standards, they are more likely to adopt them, and that model similarity can make adoption of standards more probable (Davidson & Smith, 1982).

In an early study, Zimmerman and Ringle (1981) showed that models can affect children's self-efficacy and achievement behaviors. Children observed adult models unsuccessfully try to solve a wire-puzzle problem for a long or short period; the models also verbalized statements of confidence or pessimism. Children who observed a pessimistic model persist for a long time lowered their self-efficacy judgments for performing successfully.

Schunk (1981) found benefits of modeling on children's mathematical skill learning. Children received either adult modeling or written instruction on long division, followed by guided and self-directed practice, over sessions. The adult model verbalized division solution steps while applying them to problems. Both treatments enhanced self-efficacy, persistence, and achievement, but modeling led to higher achievement and more accurate correspondence between self-efficacy and actual performance. Results of a path analysis showed that modeling enhanced self-efficacy and achievement, self-efficacy directly affected persistence and achievement, and persistence had a direct effect on achievement.

Schunk and his colleagues (Schunk & Hanson, 1985, 1989; Schunk, Hanson, & Cox, 1987) investigated the role of perceived similarity in competence by comparing mastery with coping models. Coping models initially demonstrate problems in learning but gradually improve and gain confidence. They illustrate how effort and positive thoughts can overcome difficulties. In addition to the modeled skills and strategies, observers learn and internalize these motivational beliefs and self-regulatory actions. Coping models contrast with mastery models, who demonstrate competent performance throughout the modeled sequence. In the early stages of learning, many students may perceive themselves more similar in competence to coping models.

Schunk and Hanson (1985) had children observe models solving subtraction problems. Peer mastery models solved subtraction problems correctly and verbalized statements reflecting high efficacy and ability, low task difficulty, and positive attitudes. Peer coping models initially made errors and verbalized negative statements, but then verbalized coping statements and eventually verbalized and performed as well as mastery models. After observing peer mastery, peer coping, adult mastery, or no model, children received instruction and self-regulated practice over sessions. Peer mastery and coping models increased self-efficacy and achievement better than adult or no models; adult-model children outperformed no-model students.

The lack of differences between the peer coping and mastery model conditions may have arisen because children previously had experienced success with subtraction. Any type of peer model might have raised efficacy, and children may not have internalized coping strategies and progress beliefs. Schunk, Hanson, and Cox (1987) further explored mastery–coping differences and found that observing peer coping models enhanced children's self-efficacy and achievement more than did observing peer mastery models. Unlike the Schunk and Hanson (1985) study, this project used fractions, a task at which children previously had not been successful. Coping models may be more effective when students have little task familiarity or have had previous learning difficulties. Schunk, Hanson, and Cox (1987) also found that multiple peer coping or mastery models promoted outcomes as well as did a single coping model and better than did a single mastery model. With multiple models, learners are apt to perceive themselves as similar to at least one model.

Schunk and Hanson (1989) investigated self-modeling, or cognitive and behavioral change brought about by observing one's own performances (Dowrick, 1983). Children were videotaped while solving mathematical word problems and then observed their tapes, after which they engaged in self-regulated practice. Subsequent self-modeling benefits were obtained as these children displayed higher self-efficacy, motivation, and self-regulated strategy use than did children who had been taped but did not observe their tapes and children who had not been taped.

Performance Control

Social Comparison. Social comparison conveys normative information that is used to assess one's capabilities. Schunk (1983b) compared the effects of social comparative information with those of goal setting during long-division instructional sessions. Half of the children were given performance goals each session; the other half were advised to work productively. Within each goal condition, half of the students were told the number of problems that other similar children had completed—which matched the session goal—to convey that the goals were attainable; the other half were not given comparative information. Goals enhanced self-efficacy; comparative information promoted self- regulated problem solving during the sessions. Students given goals and comparative information demonstrated the highest mathematical achievement. These results suggest that as students work on the task, they keep in mind the goal and comparative information. The perception of progress against these standards enhances motivation for self-directed learning and skill acquisition.

Attributional Feedback. Development of self-regulation is facilitated by providing learners with attributional feedback. Being told that one can achieve better through harder work can motivate one to do so and convey that one possesses the necessary capability (Dweck, 1975). Providing effort feedback for prior successes supports students' perceptions of their progress, sustains motivation, and increases self-efficacy for learning. Feedback linking early successes with ability (e.g., "That's correct. You're really good at this.") should enhance learning efficacy. Effort feedback for early successes may be more credible when students lack skills and must expend effort to succeed. As they develop skills, switching to ability feedback sustains self-efficacy and self-regulation.

Schunk (1982a) found that linking children's prior achievements with effort (e.g., "You've been working hard.") led to higher self-directed learning, self-efficacy, and achievement, compared with linking future achievement with effort (e.g., "You need to work hard."). Schunk (1983a) showed that ability feedback for prior successes (e.g., "You're good at this.") enhanced self-efficacy and achievement better than effort feedback or ability-plus-effort feedback. The latter children judged effort greater during self-directed learning than did ability-only students. Children in the combined condition may have discounted some ability information in favor of effort.

Schunk (1984b) periodically provided one group of children with ability feedback, a second group with effort feedback, and a third condition with ability feedback during the first half of the instructional program and effort feedback during the second half. The latter sequence was reversed for a fourth condition. Ability feedback for early successes led to higher ability attributions, self-efficacy and achievement, compared with effort feedback for early successes.

Schunk and Cox (1986) provided children with learning disabilities with subtraction instruction and self-directed practice. Students received effort feedback during the first or second half of the instructional program or no effort feedback. Each type of feedback promoted self-efficacy, achievement, and effort attributions better than no feedback. Students who received effort feedback during the first half of the program judged effort as a more important cause of success than did learners who received feedback during the second half. Given students' learning disabilities, effort feedback for early or later successes likely seemed credible because they realistically had to work hard to succeed. Over a longer period, effort feedback for successes on the same task could lead students to doubt their capabilities and wonder why they still have to work hard to succeed.

Collectively, the results of these studies suggest that the credibility of attributional feedback may be more important than the type of feedback. When feedback for success is credible, it is likely to enhance students' self-efficacy, motivation, and achievement. When it is not credible, students may doubt their learning capabilities, and motivation and achievement are apt to suffer.

Self-Verbalization of Strategies. Learners' self-verbalizations of self-regulatory strategies can guide their learning. Schunk (1982b) provided modeled instruction on long division and self-directed practice to children with low mathematical achievement. Adult models verbalized strategy descriptors (e.g., "multiple," "check") at appropriate places. During self-directed practice, some children overtly verbalized the descriptors, others constructed their own verbalizations (e.g., "How many times does 7 go into 22?"), those in a third group overtly verbalized strategies and self-constructions, and children in a fourth group did not verbalize.

Self-constructed verbalizations yielded the highest motivation during self-directed practice and mathematical achievement. Children who verbalized explicit strategies and self-constructions demonstrated the highest self-efficacy. Children's self-constructions typically included the strategies and were oriented toward successful problem solving.

Schunk and Cox (1986) examined the role of verbalization during learning of subtraction problem solution strategies among children with learning disabilities. While solving problems, continuous-verbalization students verbalized aloud their problem- solving operations, disconti-nued-verbalization children verbalized aloud during the first half of the instructional program but were asked to not verbalize aloud during the second half, and no-verbalization children did not verbalize aloud.

Continuous verbalization led to the highest self-efficacy and achievement. When instructed to discontinue verbalizing aloud, these students may have not continued to use the verbal mediators to regulate their academic performances. For verbal mediators to become internalized, students may need to be taught to fade overt verbalizations to a covert level. Such fading is an integral component of self-instructional training (Meichenbaum, 1977).

Self-Reflection

Self-Monitoring. The effects of self-monitoring have been studied extensively (Mace et al., 1989; Zimmerman, Bonner, & Kovach, 1996). In an early study (Sagotsky, Patterson, & Lepper, 1978), fifth- and sixth-grade students periodically monitored their work during mathematics sessions and recorded whether they were working on appropriate materials. Other students set daily performance goals, and students in a third condition received self-monitoring and goal setting. Self-monitoring significantly increased students' time on task and mathematical achievement; goal setting had minimal effects. Sagotsky, Patterson, and Lepper (1978) noted that for goal setting to affect performance, students initially need training on how to set challenging but attainable goals.

Schunk (1983d) provided subtraction instruction and self-directed practice over sessions to children who demonstrated low mathematical achievement. Self-monitoring students reviewed their work at the end of each session and recorded the number of pages they completed. External monitoring students had their work reviewed at the end of each session by an adult who recorded the number of pages completed. No monitoring students were not monitored and did not engage in self-monitoring. Self- and external monitoring enhanced self-efficacy and achievement better than did no monitoring; the former two conditions did not differ. The benefits of monitoring did not depend on instructional session performance because the three conditions did not differ in amount of work completed during self-directed practice. Monitoring of progress, rather than who performed it, enhanced children's perceptions of learning progress and self-efficacy for continued learning.

Reward Contingencies. Schunk (1983e) provided children with division instruction and self-directed practice opportunities over sessions. Performance-contingent reward children were told that they would earn points for each problem solved correctly and that they could exchange their points for prizes. Task-contingent reward students were told that they would receive prizes for participating. The effects of reward anticipation were disentangled from those of reward receipt by allowing students in the unexpected-reward group to choose prizes after completing the project. Performance- contingent rewards led to the greatest self-regulated problem solving and the highest division self-efficacy and achievement. Offering rewards for participation led to no benefits compared with merely providing instruction.

Schunk (1984a) compared the effects of performance-contingent rewards with those of proximal goals. Children received division instruction and self-directed practice over sessions. Some were offered performance-contingent rewards, others pursued proximal goals, and those in a third condition received rewards and goals. The three conditions enhanced motivation as evidenced by children's self-regulated problem solving during the sessions; combining rewards with goals resulted in the highest self-efficacy and achievement.

Progress Feedback and Self-Evaluation. As learners pursue goals, it is necessary that they believe they are making progress toward goal attainment. Learners can self- evaluate progress on tasks having clear criteria; however, on many tasks it is difficult to determine goal progress, especially when standards are not clear or progress is slow. Feedback indicating progress can substantiate self-efficacy and motivation. As learners become more skillful, they become better at self-evaluating progress.

Studies by Schunk and Swartz (1993a, 1993b; described in depth later) investigated how goals and self-evaluation affect achievement outcomes and self-regulation. Children received paragraph-writing instruction and self-directed practice over sessions. An adult modeled a writing strategy, after which children practiced applying it to compose paragraphs. Process-goal children were told to learn to use the strategy; product-goal children were advised to write paragraphs; general-goal students were told to do their best. Half of the process-goal students periodically received progress feedback that linked strategy use with improved performance (e.g., "You're doing well because you applied the steps in order").

The process goal plus feedback condition was the most effective, and some benefits were obtained from the process goal alone. Process goal plus feedback students outperformed product and general goal students on self-efficacy, writing achievement, self-evaluated learning progress, and self-regulated strategy use. Gains were maintained after 6 weeks; children applied self-regulated composing strategies to types of paragraphs on which they had received no instruction.

Schunk (1996) conducted two studies investigating how goals and self-evaluation affect SRL and achievement outcomes. In both studies, children received instruction and self-directed practice on fractions over sessions. Students worked under conditions involving either a goal of learning how to solve problems or a goal of merely solving them. In Study 1, half of the students in each goal condition evaluated their problem-solving capabilities after each session. The learning goal with or without self-evaluation and the performance goal with self-evaluation led to higher self-efficacy, skill, and motivation, than did the performance goal without self-evaluation. In Study 2, all students in each goal condition evaluated once their progress in skill acquisition. The learning goal led to higher motivation and achievement outcomes than did the performance goal.

These results show differential effects of self-evaluation as a function of its frequency. Frequent opportunities for self-evaluation of capabilities or progress raised achievement outcomes regardless of whether students received learning or performance goals. Conversely, infrequent opportunities for self-evaluation promoted self-regulated learning and self-efficacy only among students receiving learning goals. Under these conditions, self-evaluation may complement process goals better than product goals.

Schunk and Ertmer (1999) replicated these results with college students during instruction on computer skills. When opportunities for self-evaluation were minimal, the process goal led to higher self-efficacy, self-evaluated learning progress, and self-regulatory competence and strategy use; self-evaluation promoted self-efficacy. Conversely, frequent self-evaluation produced comparable outcomes when coupled with process or product goals.

IMPLICATIONS FOR DEVELOPMENT AND ACQUISITION

Self-regulation does not develop automatically with maturation nor is it acquired passively from the environment. The development and acquisition of self-regulatory skills are discussed in this section.

Phases of Self-Regulatory Development

Zimmerman and his colleagues formulated a social cognitive model of the development of self-regulatory competence (Schunk & Zimmerman, 1997; Zimmerman, 2000; Zimmerman & Bonner, in press). As shown in Table 4.2, the model predicts that academic competence develops initially from social sources and subsequently shifts to self-sources in a series of levels. Although there may be some overlap, the first two levels (observational and emulative) rely primarily on social factors, whereas by the second two levels (self-controlled, self-regulated), the source of influence has shifted to the learner.

Novice learners acquire skills and strategies well from social modeling, teaching, task structuring, and encouragement. At this observational level, students learn the major features of strategies but require practice with feedback to begin to develop the skills.

TABLE 4.2
Social Cognitive Model of the Development of Self-Regulatory
Competence

Level of Development	Social Influences	Self Influences
Observational	Models	
	Verbal Description	
Emulative	Social Guidance	
	Feedback	
Self-Controlled		Internal Standards
		Self-Reinforcement
Self-Regulated		Self-Regulatory Processes
		Self-Efficacy Beliefs

An emulative level is attained when the learner's performance approximates the general form of the model's. The learner is not copying the actions of the model, but rather emulates the model's general pattern or style. The major difference between the first two levels is that observational learning involves acquisition only at an observational level, whereas emulative learning also includes a performance capability.

These two sources of skill learning are primarily social because students require exposure to models for observational and emulative learning. Internalization of the skill or strategy being learned has begun, but this process increases with the shift to the third and fourth sources, which reside primarily within the learner.

The hallmark of the third, or self-controlled, level is the capability of learners to use the skill or strategy independently when performing related tasks. During this phase, the skill or strategy becomes internalized, although the learner's internal representation is patterned after the model's performance (i.e., covert images and verbal meanings). Learners have not developed an independent representation or begun to internally modify the performance based on what they believe will be most effective.

The final self-regulated level allows learners to adapt their skills and strategies systematically as personal and contextual conditions change. At this level, learners can initiate use of skills and strategies, incorporate adjustments based on features of the situation, and maintain their motivation through personal goals and a sense of self-efficacy for attaining them.

Triadic reciprocality is evident throughout the phases. Social factors in the environment influence behaviors and personal factors, which in turn affect the social environment. In the early stages of learning, teachers who observe problems in learners' performances of skills offer correction, learners who do not fully comprehend how to perform a skill or strategy at the emulative level may ask teachers for assistance, and learners' performances affect their self-efficacy. At more advanced levels, learners mentally and overtly practice skills and seek out teachers, coaches, and tutors to help them refine their skills.

Social influences do not disappear with advancing skill acquisition. Although self-controlled and self-regulated learners use social sources less frequently, they nonetheless continue to rely on them (Zimmerman, in press). In short, self-regulation does not mean social independence.

This is not a stage model, and learners may not necessarily progress in this fashion. Students without access to relevant models may nonetheless learn on their own. For example, one may learn to play a musical instrument "by ear" or develop a unique but successful method for solving mathematical word problems. Despite the frequent success of self-teaching, it fails to garner the potential benefits of the social environment on learning. Additionally, unless learners possess good self-regulatory skills, failing to use the social environment may severely limit their overall skill levels.

Developmental Considerations

Forethought Phase.   Children's capacity to learn from models depends on developmental factors (Bandura, 1986). Young children have difficulty attending to models for long periods and distinguishing relevant from irrelevant cues. The ability to process information also improves with development. Children develop a more extensive knowledge base to help them comprehend new information, and they become capable of using various memory strategies. Young children may encode modeled events in terms of physical properties, whereas older children represent information symbolically (e.g., language). Information acquired via observation cannot be performed if children lack the requisite physical capabilities. Production improves with development as children are better at translating into action information in memory, comparing performance with memorial representation, and correcting performance as necessary. Young children are motivated by immediate consequences; as they mature, they increasingly perform modeled actions that they find internally satisfying.

Young children have short time frames of reference and may not be fully capable of representing distant outcomes in thought. Proximal goals fit well with lesson planning in elementary classrooms; teachers plan activities around short blocks of time. Development improves the capabilities to represent longer term outcomes in thought and to mentally subdivide a distant goal into short-term goals.

Performance Control Phase.   The ability to use comparative information effectively depends on higher levels of cognitive development and experience in making comparative evaluations. Young children are egocentric in the Piagetian sense; the "self" dominates their cognitive focus and judgments (Higgins, 1981). Although children can evaluate themselves relative to others, they may not automatically do so. Children show increasing interest in social comparison with development and use such information to form self-evaluations of capabilities (Ruble, Boggiano, Feldman, & Loebl, 1980). By the fourth grade, children's performances on motor and academic tasks are influenced by peers' performances, whereas the behaviors of younger children are affected more by direct adult social evaluation (e.g., "You're good at this.").

The meaning and function of comparative information change with development and especially after entering school. Preschoolers actively compare at an overt physical level (e.g., amount of reward). Mosatche and Bragonier (1981) found that preschoolers' social comparisons primarily involved establishing how one was similar to and different from others, and competition that seemed to be based on a desire to be better than others, but that did not involve self-evaluation ("I'm the general; that's higher than the captain.").

The development of social comparison is a multistep process (Ruble, 1983). The earliest comparisons primarily involve similarities and differences but shift to a concern for how to perform tasks. Although first graders engage in peer comparison, it often is directed toward obtaining correct answers. Providing comparative information to young children may increase their motivation more for practical reasons than for acquiring information about personal capabilities. Telling young children who fail at a task that most other children also do poorly may not alleviate the negative impact of failure. After first grade, interest increases in determining how well peers are doing, and comparative information is used to evaluate one's capabilities (Ruble & Flett, 1988).

Young children view effort as the prime cause of outcomes; the concepts of effort and ability are intertwined (Nicholls, 1978). With development, a distinct conception of ability emerges. Ability attributions become increasingly important influences on self-efficacy, whereas effort as a causal factor declines in importance (Harari & Covington, 1981).

Self-Reflection Phase.   The process of comparing performances with goals in determining progress is affected by developmental factors. Children can easily over- or underestimate their capabilities. Progress misjudgments are likely when children learn some component subskills of a task but not others. In mathematics, students often employ "buggy algorithms," or erroneous strategies that produce solutions (Brown & Burton, 1978). Employing these can instate a false sense of competence. Other students may solve problems accurately but not feel efficacious because they are uncertain whether their answers are correct. Progress feedback is critical in these situations.

Children do not automatically keep goals in mind and self-evaluate progress. It helps to make goals explicit and to provide children with opportunities for self-evaluation of progress and capabilities. Children's self-efficacy is strengthened with tangible indicators of progress.

SELF-REGULATED STRATEGY USE IN THE CLASSROOM

This section exemplifies how social cognitive principles can be applied to foster self-regulatory skills in the classroom. The projects described in this section involved strategy instruction in paragraph writing with elementary school children (Schunk & Swartz, 1993a, 1993b). In particular, the interventions used goal setting, progress feedback, and self-evaluation of progress; the primary outcome variables were achievement, self-regulated strategy use, and self-efficacy.

Children received instruction and practice during twenty 45-minute sessions, over consecutive school days. The format for each session was identical. The first 10 minutes were devoted to modeled demonstration in which the teacher (a member of the research team) modeled the writing strategy by verbalizing the strategy's steps and applying them to sample topics and paragraphs. Students then received guided practice (15 minutes), during which time they applied the steps under the guidance of the teacher. The final 20 minutes of each session were for self-regulated practice; students worked alone while the teacher monitored their work.

The five-step writing strategy, which was displayed on a board in front of the room during the sessions, was as follows:

What do I have to do?

1. Choose a topic to write about.
2. Write down ideas about the topic.
3. Pick the main ideas.
4. Plan the paragraph.
5. Write down the main idea and the other sentences.

Four different types of paragraphs were covered during the instructional program; five sessions were devoted to each paragraph type. The four types of paragraphs were: descriptive, which discusses objects, events, persons, or places (e.g., describe a bird); informative, which conveys information effectively and correctly (e.g., write about something you like to do after school); narrative story, which contains events sequenced from beginning to end (e.g., tell a story about visiting a friend or relative); and narrative descriptive, which sequences steps in the correct order to perform a task (e.g., describe how to play your favorite game).

The daily content coverage was the same for each of the four types of paragraphs: session 1—strategy steps 1, 2, 3; session 2—strategy step 4; session 3—strategy step 5; session 4—review of entire strategy; session 5—review of entire strategy without the modeled demonstration. Children worked on two or three paragraph topics per session.

Children were assigned randomly to one of four experimental conditions: product goal, process goal, process goal plus progress feedback, or general goal (instructional control). Children assigned to the same condition met in small groups with a member of the research team.

Prior to the start of instruction, children were pretested on writing achievement and self-efficacy. At the start of the first instructional session for each of the four paragraph types, children received a self-efficacy for improvement test, which was identical to the self-efficacy pretest except children judged capabilities for improving their skills at the five tasks for the paragraph type to be covered during the next five sessions, rather than how well they already could perform the tasks. On completion of instruction, children received a posttest that was comparable to the pretest and also evaluated their progress in using the writing strategy compared with when the project began.

At the beginning of the first five sessions, the teacher said to children assigned to the process goal and to the process goal plus feedback conditions, "While you're working, it helps to keep in mind what you're trying to do. You'll be trying to learn how to use these steps to write a descriptive paragraph." These goal instructions were identical for the other sessions except the teacher substituted the name of the appropriate type of paragraph.

Children assigned to the product goal condition were told at the start of the first five sessions, "While you're working, it helps to keep in mind what you're trying to do. You'll be trying to write a descriptive paragraph." For the remaining sessions, the teacher substituted the name of the appropriate paragraph type. These instructions controlled for the effects of goal properties included in the process goal treatment.

The teacher said to general goal students at the start of every session, "While you're working, try to do your best." This condition controlled for the effects of receiving writing instruction, practice, and goal instructions, included in the other conditions.

Each child assigned to the process goal plus progress feedback condition received verbal feedback three or four times during each session. This feedback conveyed to children that they were making progress toward their goal of learning to use the strategy to write paragraphs. Teachers delivered feedback to each child privately during self-regulated practice with such statements as, "You're learning to use the steps," and, "You're doing well because you followed the steps in order." To ensure that feedback was credible, teachers provided feedback contingent on the child using the strategy properly. This goal- progress feedback is different from performance feedback, which all children received (e.g., "That's a good idea to include in your paragraph," "You need to write a sentence with this idea").

An important aim of these projects was to determine whether students would maintain their use of the strategy over time and apply it to types of paragraphs not covered during instruction. Maintenance and generalization were facilitated in several ways. The progress feedback was designed to convey to students that the strategy was useful for writing paragraphs and would help promote their writing achievement. By teaching the same strategy with four types of paragraphs, we showed how it was useful on different writing tasks. Finally, the periods of self-regulated practice provided independent practice using the strategy and built self-efficacy. Succeeding on one's own leads to attributions of successes to ability and effort and strengthens self-efficacy. Results from our projects showed that the process goal with progress feedback had the greatest impact on achievement and self-efficacy to include maintenance after 6 weeks and generalization to other types of paragraphs and that there were some benefits due to the process goal alone.

CONCLUSION

Social cognitive principles are useful for fostering self-regulatory skills in students. A solid theoretical foundation and a research base have been developed, and I anticipate that in the coming years we will add significantly to our knowledge about the operation of self-regulatory processes. I am confident that social cognitive researchers will play an active role in furthering our research knowledge and in developing new means for applying principles in learning settings to help students become better self-regulated learners.

REFERENCES

Bandura, A. (1986). *Social foundations of thought and action: A social cognitive theory.* Englewood Cliffs, NJ: Prentice Hall.

Bandura, A. (1988). Self-regulation of motivation and action through goal systems. In V. Hamilton, G. H. Bower, & N. H. Frijda (Eds.), *Cognitive perspectives on emotion and motivation* (pp. 37–61). Dordrecht, The Netherlands: Kluwer Academic.

Bandura, A. (1997). *Self-efficacy: The exercise of control.* New York: Freeman.

Bandura, A., & Schunk, D. H. (1981). Cultivating competence, self-efficacy, and intrinsic interest through proximal self-motivation. *Journal of Personality and Social Psychology, 41,* 586–598.

Brown, J. S., & Burton, R. R. (1978). Diagnostic models for procedural bugs in basic mathematical skills. *Cognitive Science, 2,* 155–192.

Bryan, J. H., & Bryan, T. H. (1983). The social life of the learning disabled youngster. In J. D. McKinney & L. Feagans (Eds.), *Current topics in learning disabilities* (Vol. 1, pp. 57–85). Norwood, NJ: Ablex.

Davidson, E. S., & Smith, W. P. (1982). Imitation, social comparison, and self-reward. *Child Development, 53,* 928–932.

Dowrick, P. W. (1983). Self-modelling. In P. W. Dowrick & S. J. Biggs (Eds.), *Using video: Psychological and social applications* (pp. 105–124). Chichester, England: Wiley.

Dweck, C. S. (1975). The role of expectations and attributions in the alleviation of learned helplessness. *Journal of Personality and Social Psychology, 31,* 674–685.

Festinger, L. (1954). A theory of social comparison processes. *Human Relations, 7,* 117–140.

Harari, O., & Covington, M. V. (1981). Reactions to achievement behavior from a teacher and student perspective: A developmental analysis. *American Educational Research Journal, 18,* 15–28.

Higgins, E. T. (1981). Role taking and social judgment: Alternative developmental perspectives and processes. In J. H. Flavell & L. Ross (Eds.), *Social cognitive development: Frontiers and possible futures* (pp. 119–153). Cambridge, England: Cambridge University Press.

Kanfer, F. H., & Gaelick, K. (1986). Self-management methods. In F. H. Kanfer & A. P. Goldstein (Eds.), *Helping people change: A textbook of methods* (3rd ed., pp. 283–345). New York: Pergamon.

Karoly, P. (1982). Perspectives on self-management and behavior change. In P. Karoly & F. H. Kanfer (Eds.), *Self-management and behavior change: From theory to practice* (pp. 3–31). New York: Pergamon.

Licht, B. G., & Kistner, J. A. (1986). Motivational problems of learning-disabled children: Individual differences and their implications for treatment. In J. K. Torgesen & B. W. L. Wong (Eds.), *Psychological and educational perspectives on learning disabilities* (pp. 225–255). Orlando: Academic Press.

Locke, E. A., & Latham, G. P. (1990) *A theory of goal setting and task performance.* Englewood Cliffs, NJ: Prentice Hall.

Mace, F. C., Belfiore, P. J., & Shea, M. C. (1989). Operant theory and research on self-regulation. In B. J. Zimmerman & D. H. Schunk (Eds.), *Self-regulated learning and academic achievement: Theory, research, and practice* (pp. 27–50). New York: Springer-Verlag.

Meichenbaum, D. (1977). *Cognitive behavior modification: An integrative approach.* New York: Plenum.

Mosatche, H. S., & Bragonier, P. (1981). An observational study of social comparison in preschoolers. *Child Development, 52,* 376–378.

Nicholls, J. G. (1978). The development of the concepts of effort and ability, perception of academic attainment, and the understanding that difficult tasks require more ability. *Child Development, 49,* 800–814.

Paris, S. G., Cross, D. R., & Lipson, M. Y. (1984). Informed strategies for learning: A program to improve children's reading awareness and comprehension. *Journal of Educational Psychology, 76,* 1239–1252.

Paris, S. G., Lipson, M. Y., & Wixson, K. K. (1983). Becoming a strategic reader. *Contemporary Educational Psychology, 8,* 293–316.

Ruble, D. N. (1983). The development of social-comparison processes and their role in achievement-related self-socialization. In E. T. Higgins, D. N. Ruble, & W. W. Hartup (Eds.), *Social cognition and social development* (pp. 134–157). New York: Cambridge University Press.

Ruble, D. N., Boggiano, A. K., Feldman, N. S., & Loebl, J. H. (1980). Developmental analysis of the role of social comparison in self-evaluation. *Developmental Psychology, 16,* 105–115.

Ruble, D. N., & Flett, G. L. (1988). Conflicting goals in self-evaluative information seeking: Developmental and ability level analysis. *Child Development, 59,* 97–106.

Sagotsky, G., Patterson, C. J., & Lepper, M. R. (1978). Training children's self-control: A field experiment in self-monitoring and goal-setting in the classroom. *Journal of Experimental Child Psychology, 25,* 242–253.

Schunk, D. H. (1981). Modeling and attributional effects on children's achievement: A self-efficacy analysis. *Journal of Educational Psychology, 73,* 93–105.

Schunk, D. H. (1982a). Effects of effort attributional feedback on children's perceived self-efficacy and achievement. *Journal of Educational Psychology, 74,* 548–556.

Schunk, D. H. (1982b). Verbal self-regulation as a facilitator of children's achievement and self-efficacy. *Human Learning, 1,* 265–277.

Schunk, D. H. (1983a). Ability versus effort attributional feedback: Differential effects on self-efficacy and achievement. *Journal of Educational Psychology, 75,* 848–856.

Schunk, D. H. (1983b). Developing children's self-efficacy and skills: The roles of social comparative information and goal setting. *Contemporary Educational Psychology, 8,* 76–86.

Schunk, D. H. (1983c). Goal difficulty and attainment information: Effects on children's achievement behaviors. *Human Learning, 2,* 107–117.

Schunk, D. H. (1983d). Progress self-monitoring: Effects on children's self-efficacy and achievement. *Journal of Experimental Education, 51,* 89–93.

Schunk, D. H. (1983e). Reward contingencies and the development of children's skills and self-efficacy. *Journal of Educational Psychology, 75,* 511–518.

Schunk, D. H. (1984a). Enhancing self-efficacy and achievement through rewards and goals: Motivational and informational effects. *Journal of Educational Research, 78,* 29–34.

Schunk, D. H. (1984b). Sequential attributional feedback and children's achievement behaviors. *Journal of Educational Psychology, 76,* 1159–1169.

Schunk, D. H. (1985). Participation in goal setting: Effects on self-efficacy and skills of learning disabled children. *Journal of Special Education, 19,* 307–317.

Schunk, D. H. (1987). Peer models and children's behavioral change. *Review of Educational Research, 57,* 149–174.

Schunk, D. H. (1995). Self-efficacy and education and instruction. In J. E. Maddux (Ed.), *Self-efficacy, adaptation, and adjustment: Theory, research, and application* (pp. 281–303). New York: Plenum.

Schunk, D. H. (1996). Goal and self-evaluative influences during children's cognitive skill learning. *American Educational Research Journal, 33,* 359–382.

Schunk, D. H., & Cox, P. D. (1986). Strategy training and attributional feedback with learning disabled students. *Journal of Educational Psychology, 78,* 201–209.

Schunk, D. H., & Ertmer, P. A. (1999). Self-regulatory processes during computer skill acquisition: Goal and self-evaluative influences. *Journal of Educational Psychology, 91,* 251–260.

Schunk, D. H., & Hanson, A. R. (1985). Peer models: Influence on children's self-efficacy and achievement. *Journal of Educational Psychology, 77,* 313–322.

Schunk, D. H., & Hanson, A. R. (1989). Self-modeling and children's cognitive skill learning. *Journal of Educational Psychology, 81*, 155–163.

Schunk, D. H., Hanson, A. R., & Cox, P. D. (1987). Peer-model attributes and children's achievement behaviors. *Journal of Educational Psychology, 79*, 54–61.

Schunk, D. H., & Swartz, C. W. (1993a). Goals and progress feedback: Effects on self-efficacy and writing instruction. *Contemporary Educational Psychology, 18*, 337–354.

Schunk, D. H., & Swartz, C. W. (1993b). Writing strategy instruction with gifted students: Effects of goals and feedback on self-efficacy and skills. *Roeper Review, 15*, 225–230.

Schunk, D. H., & Zimmerman, B. J. (1997). Social origins of self-regulatory competence. *Educational Psychologist, 32*, 195–208.

Shepard, R. (1978). The mental image. *American Psychologist, 33*, 125–137.

Skinner, B. F. (1953). *Science and human behavior.* New York: Macmillan.

Veroff, J. (1969). Social comparison and the development of achievement motivation. In C. P. Smith (Ed.), *Achievement-related motives in children* (pp. 46–101). New York: Russell Sage Foundation.

Weiner, B. (1985). An attributional theory of achievement motivation and emotion. *Psychological Review, 92*, 548–573.

Zimmerman, B. J. (1994). Dimensions of academic self-regulation: A conceptual framework for education. In D. H. Schunk & B. J. Zimmerman (Eds.), *Self-regulation of learning and performance: Issues and educational applications* (pp. 3–21). Hillsdale, NJ: Lawrence Erlbaum Associates.

Zimmerman, B. J. (1998). Developing self-fulfilling cycles of academic regulation: An analysis of exemplary instructional models. In D. H. Schunk & B. J. Zimmerman (Eds.), *Self-regulated learning: From teaching to self-reflective practice* (pp. 1–19). New York: Guilford Press.

Zimmerman, B. J. (2000). Attaining self-regulation: A social cognitive perspective. In M. Boekaerts, P. R. Pintrich, & M. Zeidner (Eds.), *Handbook of self-regulation* (pp. 13–39). San Diego, CA: Academic Press.

Zimmerman, B. J., & Bonner, S. (in press). A social cognitive view of strategic learning. In C. E. Weinstein & B. L. McCombs (Eds.), *Skill, will, and self-regulation.* Mahwah, NJ: Lawrence Erlbaum Associates.

Zimmerman, B. J., Bonner, S., & Kovach, R. (1996). *Developing self-regulated learners: Beyond achievement to self-efficacy.* Washington, DC: American Psychological Association.

Zimmerman, B. J., & Ringle, J. (1981). Effects of model persistence and statements of confidence on children's self-efficacy and problem solving. *Journal of Educational Psychology, 73*, 485–493.

Chapter 5

Self-Regulated Learning Viewed from Models of Information Processing

Philip H. Winne
Simon Fraser University
British Columbia

As the chapters in this book demonstrate, there are a variety of models to use in considering self-regulated learning (SRL). Each model offers an alternative perspective about SRL's parts, how self-regulation operates, what it accomplishes, and why it may succeed, falter, or fail. Variety does not lessen the utility or validity of any particular model. Rather, it stimulates comparison, reveals variance in qualities, and invites research that may unify or further differentiate features of SRL.

In this spirit, the lens I use to describe SRL in this chapter is information processing. Just as there are several models of SRL, there also is a family of models of information processing. Rather than delve into specifics that distinguish individual members in the family, I focus on the family as such so that issues of SRL can be placed in the foreground. First, I sketch essentials of theories about information processing. Then, I present a view of key features of self-regulated learning as information processing. This creates a platform for the third section where I examine research that investigates SRL viewed through the lens of information processing with a focus on current issues as well as targets for future research. I end with implications for instruction that flow from examining SRL through the lens of information processing.

THEORETICAL VIEWS OF INFORMATION PROCESSING

Educational psychology's model of information processing owes a great deal to mid-20th century work in the fields of computing and communications. In an influential book presenting a mathematical theory of information and communication, Weaver (Shannon & Weaver, 1949) offered a seminal definition of communication as "all of the procedures by which one mind may affect another" (p. 3). A communication event begins when a sender encodes information she or he knows into a message made up of symbols—dots and dashes of Morse code, articulated sounds (words) spoken in a lecture, characters printed in a book, underlines of hyperlinks on a web page, or organizations of lines in a diagram. The symbols are not the sender's information itself; rather, they re-present it. Weaver's theory included two critical ideas. First, there were degrees of information. Second, information *was* information only to the degree that the person receiving the sender's message perceived something *different* after decoding the symbols in the sender's message. This is what links Weaver's theory to education: every occasion for communicating information provides an opportunity for a receiver—a student, if you will—to learn. If the receiver does not learn something new, no information was communicated.

When a receiver notices a message, the symbols that represent the sender's information have to be interpreted or processed. Some messages involve minimal processing. An earsplitting clang communicates quite directly: "Jump!" In contrast, the graph of a quadratic inequality likely requires rather intense processing by most ninth-grade students but (we hope!) not very much by the algebra teacher.

Psychologists have devoted considerable energy to creating models of how information is processed to construct interpretations of symbols. All these models share three basic features. First, there are several virtual locations in the mind where processing is carried out. Each location is a kind of memory, and three are usually denoted: a sensory buffer, one for each of the human senses; working memory; and long-term memory. I describe these locations or types of memory as "virtual" because it's not clear yet whether there are specific physical places in the brain that correspond to each. The second basic feature of models of information processing is that there are several types of processes. One agreed-on example is the process of rehearsing. *Rehearsing* keeps information in a mental condition so you can reinspect it or deliberate about how to process it further. It is also one of the most reliable ways to store information for possible use later. The third basic feature of models of information processing is that there are different forms in which information is represented in memory. Some models suggest there may be as many representational forms as there are senses—kinesthetic, olfactory, visual, and so forth—plus one more: semantic. Semantic representational forms represent information that has meaning for us.

Memory and Information Processes

Locke (1690/1853) may have overstated the case when he described newborns as *tabula rasa*, or blank slates, but everyone agrees that, whatever their stock of initial knowledge, humans learn. Learning is a process or set of processes by which we acquire information. When we learn, information is encoded in a virtual location of memory called *long-term memory*. Information stored in long-term memory has the potential to be retrieved later. When it is retrieved or "brought to mind," that virtual location is called *working memory*, the spot where information becomes a topic of information processing.

People store a huge quantity of information in long-term memory. The topics of information are diverse, ranging from telephone numbers to political opinions to explanations for why a faucet drips to feelings about taking final examinations.

Models of information processing all share the assumption that all the information stored in long-term memory has a pattern. An image of that pattern is a *network*. Each knot in the network, called a *node of information*, is linked to one or several other nodes. Without those links, theoretically, there would be no way to retrieve information that had been stored in long-term memory.

Spreading activation (Anderson, 1991) is a model about how memory uses these links. Imagine working memory not as a location where information collects but, instead, as a metaphorical community of about a half-dozen simple robots that constantly commute from node to node in a network. Their paths from node to node are the links of long-term memory. Each robot receives input from just two sources: your continuously updated perceptions of your environment (sent to the robots from your sensory buffers), and the other robots wherever they are in the network of memory. When a robot receives a perception or "rides through" a node, it registers that information. Then, it uses what it registers to decide which of the available links to follow next. Almost instantaneously, the other robots also register that information and use it to determine which links they should ride next. At each instant, the collective "knowledge" shared among this community of robots is the information that is the content of working memory.

Spreading activation can be automatic so that some information comes to mind unbidden, "all-of-a-sudden." For example, as I walked past the library yesterday, I suddenly remembered a book I wanted to borrow. My perception that I was near the library had previously been linked to a proposition in my long-term memory about the book I needed. Without my "deliberation," one robot traveled the link from library to the book's title and—*voila!*—I remembered the book. McKoon and Ratcliff (1992) developed a model of automatic inferencing that explains this effect and extends it to tasks that have a direction or a goal, particularly reading. Such automatic inferencing, or nondeliberative spreading activation, is a defining feature of how we retrieve information from memory.

Nondeliberative retrieval is not always helpful. You might not want to recall your birth date when you intend to answer a teacher's question about phases in the water cycle. To account for how spreading activation retrieves particular information, another process is involved—monitoring.

Monitoring is a process that compares two chunks of information. It uses features that characterize one chunk of information as standards against which to compare the second chunk. In essence, monitoring reveals how well the target chunk measures up to the standard chunk's features in the same way that a student's project might be profiled relative to standards provided by a criterion-referenced scoring rubric. Monitoring creates new information: a list of the target chunk's features that do or do not match and, perhaps, the size or nature of discrepancies. This information becomes known to the robots out travelling the links of long-term memory. The links they travel next reflect what they "know" as a result of monitoring. In effect, they can search for a better match. According to this view, monitoring is a process that can lead to shifts in attention. Challenges in "paying attention" can arise when we monitor using inappropriate standards or when there are too many standards, as is explored later.

A synthesis of spreading activation and monitoring creates one of the most important information processes, searching or, as some theorists call it, retrieving. *Searching* accounts for how we retrieve particular information versus whatever information might be linked to a node. Sometimes, searching involves several cycles of retrieving, monitoring, and retrieving again.

To add a useful new chunk of information to long-term memory—to learn—new links have to be created in long-term memory. I label the process that manufactures links *assembling*. Other theorists (e.g., Anderson, 1991) use the term *encoding*. Blending the operation of assembling with rehearsing creates the process called *elaborative rehearsal* (Craik & Lockhart, 1972).

Some links are assembled automatically, without deliberation. The model of learning called classical or Pavlovian conditioning is an example. Loud clangs may be associated with just about any place or thing, and we subsequently can become a bit wary when we are in those places or near those things. This capability is probably the result of Darwinian selection whereby organisms, including human, with this ability to make links had better chances of survival. Other links, however, are created deliberately. An example is a first-letter acronym like ROY G BIV for colors of the visible spectrum. According to Anderson (1991), it is impossible to stop memory from assembling. It seems, then, that one key to effective learning is guiding learners, either instructionally or by means of their own self-regulation, toward assembling particular information using useful links.

A fifth basic process seems necessary on logical grounds, and there is solid empirical evidence for the inference that information in long-term memory can be represented in multiple formats. For instance, if you view a graph of a quadratic inequality, you might be able to represent the information in that image as an algebraic (symbolic) expression in your mind or using a few phrases of mathematical terminology. Some process—I call it *translating*—must account for our mental capability to use one representational format as a basis for creating another. One of these translations, from words to images and back again, forms an extensive literature (e.g., see Clark & Paivio, 1991). Hypothetically, translating may be a specialization of searching where the standards for monitoring information retrieved from long-term memory include criteria about alternative formats that represent that same information in another format or medium.

Altogether, then, I posit five fundamental types of information processes: Searching, Monitoring, Assembling, Rehearsing, and Translating (Winne, 1985). Using the first letter of each process's name, an acronym—SMART—can refer to the set. If you are storing SMART in your long-term memory, you are assembling links. You are also rehearsing the acronym SMART because I am repeating it here several times. As you encounter each occurrence, you might be monitoring how quickly you can recall each process that matches a letter in SMART. Forgotten what T links to? Perhaps you search for it. Because you are deliberately managing how you are changing long-term memory's network, you are self-regulating your learning.

Forms of Information

Information can be collected together and arranged to form complex patterns, sometimes called *chunks*. Examples are the steps involved in tying shoelaces or the web of events that historians chronicle as leading to the creation of the United Nations. When all the information that forms a chunk is cogently articulated and well learned, the whole set seems to be retrieved and used in other cognitive processing as a single unit. Notwithstanding this quality of chunks, even the simplest chunk of information can be analyzed into smaller parts or features by the links it has to other chunks. Whatever the "volume" of a particular chunk, links assemble it internally and articulate it to other chunks. In research that investigates SRL, three kinds of chunks are prominent: schemas, tactics, and strategies.

Schemas.   A great deal of the knowledge we have is about categories of things or events. Consider the category of introductory textbooks about educational psychology. Such textbooks have at least one and, often, several authors. They have a table of contents and usually two indexes, one by author of cited publications and one by topic. The book is divided into chapters, and chapters have parts. Typical parts are objectives, overview or introduction, the sections that make up the main body of the chapter, implications for classroom teaching, a summary, and practice test questions or suggested projects. There are almost always sidebars: charts, tables, diagrams, definitions of terms, and autobiographical sketches are common sidebars. Text cues are used throughout the book to signal special content: bold or colored words and phrases appear in paragraphs, headings divide sections, bulleted lists summarize critical elements, and numbered lists signal sequences.

A collection of features like this set that characterizes an educational psychology textbook is called a *schema*. Each feature in the schema—author, sections, sidebars, and so forth—is a *slot*. A slot is like an algebraic variable *x* for which a particular instance provides a value for the slot. The author slot might be equated to me. The slot for the author index might be nil if the book does not have that kind of index. When there is a most common or prototypical value for a slot, it is called a *default value*. The language of information processing says that, when a slot has a value, the slot has been instantiated—it now refers to a particular instance of all the values that slot might have. When all empty slots in schema are instantiated, it represents a complete, particular instance of all the possible instances the schema can catalog.

Schemas have three important properties. First, as chunks, memory's SMART processes "work" with or on whole schemas. Because a schema can be packed with a lot of information, a considerable amount of information is available for processing at any one time. This makes information processing efficient and we perceive it as easier. Second, schemas provide frameworks for recognizing new instances of information. I cannot read German, but I quite likely could recognize a German textbook about economics as a textbook because its superficial features can be nearly perfectly assembled into slots in my schema for an educational psychology textbook. Third, schemas are tools memory can use to make inferences. When explicit values are lacking for a slot, search can supply the prototypical value. When a sufficient number of slots or when an especially significant subset of a schema's slots have been instantiated, memory automatically fills in the remaining empty slots with default values. When you see a computer, you do not have to take it apart to infer that it has a computer chip in it.

Many schemas are formatted as a set of rules for carrying out tasks. For instance, chess experts have schemas that not only help them recognize strategic formations of chess pieces; their schemas also include sophisticated tactics for responding to those configurations. Baseball players have a schema that helps them recognize when a squeeze play is a possibility and what their role is in executing that play. Students have schemas for classroom lessons that describe how they are to participate (Winne & Marx, 1982).

Tactics.   A *tactic* is a particular form of schema that is represented as a rule in IF–THEN form, sometimes called a condition–action rule. IF a set of conditions is the case, THEN (and only then) is a particular action carried out. IF not, a learner's ongoing behavior or qualities of interacting with the task proceed unchanged. For instance, when I read a research article, IF I come upon the phrase, "In Figure 1...," I (a) stop reading the paragraph, (b) find the figure and (c) read its title, (d) examine the figure itself to understand what it is showing, (e) ask myself how what I have understood about the figure links to its title, and (f) try to assemble a link between what I understand about the figure and what I have read in the article so far. My tactic involves one simple condition but has multiple IFs. As my tactic also illustrates, a cognitive tactic can be a complex assembly that include multiple actions (THENs) in sequence.

I do not always understand what I am reading. When my comprehension falters, I follow a different tactic: IF I come upon the phrase, "In Figure 1..." and IF I'm not very sure I comprehend what I am reading at that point, I apply a different tactic. Instead of leaping to the figure, THEN I continue reading to the end of the paragraph and THEN I predict what the figure will show and, finally, THEN I enact the same tactic for "reading" the figure as when I understand what I'm reading. Linking this tactic to the one described in the preceding paragraph creates a system that produces a coordinated approach to reading. Straightforwardly, it's called a *production system* (Anderson, 1983).

Tactics can have multiple IFs that specialize or differentiate behavior. As tactics assemble more and diverse IFs, they become very sensitive to variations in the particular features that learners perceive about tasks. The name for a schema of IFs that affords this differential sensitivity is called *conditional knowledge.* Complex schemas of conditional knowledge allow tactics to be very discriminating about the context in which the actions assembled in them are enacted.

Contemporary theory suggests that conditional knowledge consists of two classes of information. "Cold" propositions describe what a task is about in a rational way. "Hot" propositions—efficacy expectations, outcome expectations, incentives associated with completing (or failing to complete) the task, and attributions—are motivational beliefs that give rise or link to affect (Pintrich, Marx, & Boyle, 1993; Winne, 1995, 1997; Winne & Marx, 1989). These hot propositions are discussed later in the section titled Representations of Information About SRL.

Strategies. Many SRL researchers do not distinguish between tactics and strategies. I do (Winne, 1995, 1996; see also Carver & Scheier, 1998; Schmeck, 1988). I characterize a *strategy* as a design or a plan for approaching a high-level goal, such as mastering a new software system or understanding the history of a political party. A strategy coordinates a set of tactics. Each tactic is a potential tool to use in carrying out a strategy, but not all tactics that make up the strategy are necessarily enacted. Carver and Sheier's (1998) model of self-regulation and its predecessor, Power's (1973) model, make a similar distinction between a principle, which is one's high-level goal, a program that provides a general course of action that relies on moment-to-moment decisions as the program is followed, and particular action sequences that make steps toward accomplishing the program. By distinguishing a strategy from a tactic, four critical qualities of strategies can be highlighted. Each quality has important implications for SRL that are discussed later.

First, strategizing precedes engagement. Strategic learners plan steps for a task before they act. Although tactics are plans, too, they are the simplest plans because they involve only one step, IF–THEN. (Remember that the conditional knowledge of IFs can be quite complex.) Tactics "pop up" when circumstances match conditions but, after a tactic has done its work, it's "done," too. Strategies have a broader influence. They characterize what might happen over a large portion of a task or over the course of a set of tasks.

Why is this plan-like quality of strategies important? Recall that information from long-term memory is brought to working memory by the automatic process of spreading activation and by searching. When a strategy—a schema of tactical options—is active in working memory, a learner is better prepared to explore what this task may be like and how it might be better addressed before starting to work on it per se. The strategy as plan provides standards for monitoring thought experiments, better preparing the learner for self-regulation when work actually begins.

Like the author who develops an outline and refines it before drafting a complex essay about sex education, strategies serve as guides for multipart projects that span periods of time beyond the immediate present.

Because strategies are made up of alternative tactics for engaging with a task, putting a strategy to work calls for making decisions about which tactic to use next as work unfolds on a task. Strategies elaborate the go–no go decision encapsulated in an IF–THEN tactical unit to accommodate that decision making. To do this, tactical units within a strategy elaborate the IF–THEN tactic to a more complex form: IF–THEN–ELSE. IF conditions are met, THEN enact a particular tactic; ELSE use a different tactic.

A second quality of strategies follows from their being built from IF–THEN–ELSE representations. Having an alternative ELSE to use knits together a pattern for working through a task that explicitly involves monitoring key junctures in the task. In other words, strategies also increase attention. As long as the total volume of information in working memory does not become too great, chances of success increase with attention to a task.

A third quality of a strategy also is the result of its IF–THEN–ELSE units. Work on a task that is more than one step "deep" will generate information—feedback—as each step is completed (Butler & Winne, 1995; Carver & Scheier, 1998). Such feedback may originate with the student at midpoints in navigating a task when, for example, monitoring creates profiles that compare attributes of the present state of work relative to the attributes of a goal. Somewhere in the middle of researching environmental issues, for instance, a student may monitor the large number of issues that are being identified and their present lack of articulation. Such attributes do not fit well with the goal of producing a one-page synopsis for tomorrow's earth science seminar. Or, feedback may be provided by the environment, as when a computer program does not run or a peer makes a suggestion about a project. Whatever its source, feedback updates the task's conditions at each step of engagement. Because an IF–THEN–ELSE unit of a strategy includes an alternative action—the ELSE—it is more flexible than a tactic. A strategy provides means for adapting work on a task based on feedback that becomes available. This feature complements the notion of a strategy as a design. Better designs are flexible, and strategies are flexible because of the ELSE in their IF–THEN–ELSE structure. Thus, strategies are a hallmark of sophisticated SRL.

The fourth distinctive quality of a strategy also follows from its IF–THEN–ELSE structure. If applying different tactics changes conditions of the task in different ways—that is, if different tactics lead to different feedback—a strategy has potential to provide richer (i.e., more) information to a learner than a tactic can provide. If an IF–THEN tactic works, it works. If it fails, it fails, but the learner has little additional information to use choosing another tactic that might be effective—there is no ELSE. In contrast, if a strategy's THEN succeeds, the learner has a potential to know that the action linked to the ELSE wasn't needed. The conditions of the strategy can be updated to reflect whatever specifics differentiate this present situation from a more general one where either the THENs or the ELSEs might have been appropriate. In this case, beyond merely knowing that the tactic linked to THEN worked, feedback indicates that the tactic linked to ELSE was not necessary. In this way, a strategy's structure inherently provides for enhancing conditional knowledge about the tactics embedded in the strategy. The more discriminating one's conditional knowledge, the greater the capacity to regulate one's approaches to learning.

Control Models of Information Processing and the Drive to Learn

A prominent family of information processing models assigns a key role to the concept of control. Control in the sense these models intend is not about holding dominion over something else or having authority. Rather, it is about giving direction to behavior (Miller, Galanter, & Pribram, 1960; Carver & Scheier, 1998), that is, guiding information processing toward a goal held in the mind of a purposeful student.

The IF–THEN–ELSE structure of strategies sets the stage for exercising control. After we have classified a task or a midpoint in a big job based on current information (its conditions), memory may offer us a choice: follow the activities described in the THEN of the strategy or actions associated with the ELSE. Which provides the better path toward achieving our goal? Monitoring the profile of attributes that describes the goal relative to our forecast about progress by following THEN versus ELSE leads us to that choice. When we choose, we have exercised control: the next thing we do, be it THEN or ELSE, is guided by the result of our monitoring.

As often as not, the information created by monitoring is probably not so precise and unambiguous that the choice of whether to follow what is available as THEN or ELSE is unequivocally one or the other. Even if we wanted our cognitive life to be so precise, it probably is not (Butler & Winne, 1995; Winne & Perry, 1999). For reasons of pure self-interest, it behooves us to figure out how to boost the precision of comparisons that monitoring generates between products, actual or predicted, and standards. We often do that by adding further conditions, more IFs, to increase our powers to discriminate. The more detailed our rules for classifying conditions, the more precisely we can match the best action to the variety of tasks we face. When we succeed, we learn how to reach goals more effectively (Winne, 1995). Control theories of information processing thus lead to a provocative inference about motivation: We should be concerned not so much about how to begin learning something as how to steer toward learning information that is useful and valued. In this sense, theories of information processing that highlight issues of cognitive control are fundamentally theories about agency.

KEY INFORMATION PROCESSES IN SELF-REGULATED LEARNING

Models of SRL are variations on a theme. To organize my analysis of SRL viewed from a perspective of information processing, I introduce a model Hadwin and I codeveloped (Winne & Hadwin, 1998a; see Fig. 5.1). Our model characterizes SRL as an event that spans three necessary phases and sometimes includes a fourth phase. Within each phase, information processes construct information products. Those products have one of four possible topics:

- Conditions. These describe resources available for work on a task and constraints that may affect information processing. Among the most significant of resources is prior knowledge—information that is already stored in long-term memory.
- Products. A product is new information created when information processes—searching, monitoring, assembling, rehearsing, and translating (SMARTs)—manipulate existing information. Successive products build toward the goal that completes a task. Products may reside and remain entirely in memory, as when we run a "thought experiment," or products may take shape in the environment, such as the first paragraph of an assigned essay or the results of a statistical analysis from a computer.
- Standards. These are qualities that products are supposed to have. A schema made up of standards is a goal.
- Evaluations. Evaluations are products created by monitoring. They characterize the fit between standards and products. As already noted, evaluations can be created by the learner or they can be provided from the environment.

By collecting the set of SMART information processes into a one-word category called *operations*, an entire task can be summarized by the first-letter acronym COPES—Conditions, Operations, Products, Evaluations, and Standards are the elements a student COPES with to learn. COPES represents five slots in a particular kind of schema, a *script*, for working on a task.

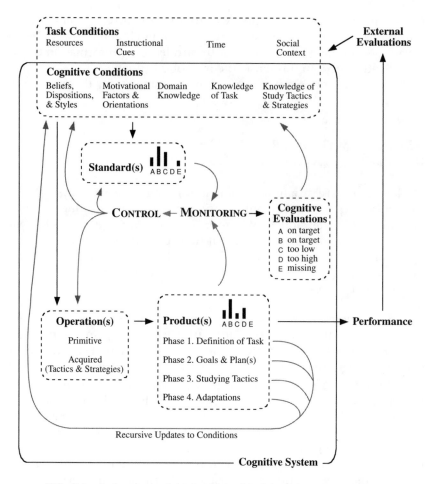

FIG. 5.1. A 4-stage model of self-regulated learning. From Winne, P. H., & Hadwin, A. F. (1998) "Studying as Self-Regulated Learning." In D. J. Hacker, J. Dunlosky, & A. C. Graesser (Eds.), *Metacognition in educational theory and practice.* Hillsdale, NJ: Lawrence Erlbaum Associates. Reprinted with permission.

Also shown in Fig. 5.1 are two events that form the hub of SRL, metacognitive monitoring and metacognitive control. Metacognitive monitoring is the pivot on which SRL turns because it creates opportunities to change tactics, to control how a task might be better dealt with than at the moment. Carver and Scheier (1998) used the term *comparator* to emphasize that monitoring compares current conditions to standards, setting the stage for metacognitive control to exercise agency by changing the tactics or even the strategy for working on at task. In Carver and Scheier's model, agency is realized in an output function that puts a change into effect. Arrows in Fig. 5.1 depict paths along which information travels to create updates as phases change over time as a student engages with a task.

Phase 1: Defining the Task

In Phase 1, the learner processes information about the conditions that characterize an assigned task or a self-posed task. This information processing constructs a perception that defines what the task is (Butler & Winne, 1995; Winne, 1997; Winne & Marx, 1977). Two main sources of information contribute to definitions of a task. *Task conditions* refer to information about the task that the learner interprets based on the outside environment. Examples are a teacher's directions for a homework assignment, a peer's quizzical look when the teacher goes over those directions, or the presence of worked out examples in the book chapter. *Cognitive conditions* refer to information the learner retrieves from long-term memory. Such information might include a student's estimate of prior knowledge in this task's domain, an attribution that describes ability (as opposed to, say, effort or luck) that accounts for success at tasks typical of this domain, or a memory of feeling anxious about tasks like this. Once information about task conditions and cognitive conditions is active in working memory, the student amalgamates it to construct an idiosyncratic definition of the task at hand. This product of Phase 1 is listed in the Products box of Fig. 5.1.

Students probably generate at least two definitions of any task. One is a "default" or prototypic definition. It characterizes what the task is like under usual circumstances, and it most likely includes a routine tactic or strategy for addressing the task (see the next section about Phase 2). Students probably have a prototypical understanding of homework assigned in, say, math—how difficult problems are, whether the book's worked-out examples can always be matched to the types of problems in the homework set, and so forth.

The second definition is what the task is when atypical conditions are perceived to apply. For example, suppose that, instead of setting problems to be solved, the math homework calls for students to create problems so that just one particular method is required to solve each problem. Perhaps the student has little experience with this kind of task. It is likely to be perceived as more difficult.

The reason I hypothesize the existence of two definitions of a task is to acknowledge that students are agents. It is necessary on logical grounds that agents have choices, so there must be a choice. A student facing math homework that requires creating method-specific problems might follow the directions as given by the teacher. However, there is always another option—dismissing the task (see Winne, 1997). Choosing to skip a task can also express SRL, though not in a form intended by teachers.

The Role of Monitoring.   The definition of a task that a student generates can be metacognitively monitored relative to standards. To illustrate this, Fig. 5.1 shows five abstract standards labeled A, B, C, D, and E in the box labeled Standards. Suppose the student is reviewing during a homework session on trigonometric identities. The first sentence of the textbook chapter asks, "Can you recall the definition of the cosine of an angle?" The student searches long-term memory for that definition but cannot retrieve it. Under these conditions, the student might conclude that this task is going to be quite difficult because it depends on having already mastered a lot of domain knowledge about trigonometry. The tall bar for B in the Product(s) box of Fig. 5.1 represents this high level of knowledge called for according to the student's interpretation. In everyday language, the student believes that learning in this domain depends a lot on how much you already know.

Most tasks probably have multiple standards in the student's definition of a COPES script that describes the task. Typical examples might be the precision necessary in answers, thoroughness of process, belief that ability in this subject area is incremental (achievable with effort) versus static, and emphasis on speed of execution. These standards might be represented in Fig. 5.1 as facets A, C, D, and E that, along with B, the necessary prior knowledge, constitute the student's full definition of this task's standards. Monitoring the fit of each condition of this task against each of these standards may lead to metacognitive control that recycles through Phase 1 to redefine the task. For example, suppose standard D refers to an epistemological belief about the worth of spending effort to review class notes before tackling the assigned problems at the end of a textbook chapter. The student's initial standard for this was zero—just dive into the homework. However, because the student failed to retrieve the definition of cosine, the task might now be viewed as a bit harder, one where there may be a correlation between effort and success. The student may exercise metacognitive control, choosing to reevaluate the task's conditions in terms of how much effort is required. This develops a new definition of the task. Metacognitive monitoring and control in other phases of Winne and Hadwin's (1998) model would follow a similar structure.

Phase 2: Setting Goals and Planning How to Reach Them

In Phase 2, the learner frames a goal and assembles a plan to approach it. We view goals as multifaceted or multivariate profiles of standards (Butler & Winne, 1995; Winne & Hadwin, 1998a). The profile can be pictured as the shape of a line created by connecting the top of each bar labeled A, B, C, D, and E in the Standards box of Fig. 5.1. Each standard in a goal's profile is a value against which products can be monitored throughout the task. By cycling through Phase 2 again, goals can be updated as work on the task itself proceeds in Phase 3. Once goals are active, completing an instantiation of the COPES script for this task, memory may automatically retrieve tactics or strategies coupled to them (McKoon & Ratcliff, 1992). Plans constituted this way are a common sign of expertise.

For example, suppose the student's trigonometry homework is unusual. Instead of being assigned problems to solve, the student's assignment is to invent one problem to illustrate each of several unique methods for solving a family of problem types. One plan for this atypical assignment might be to make a list of each unique method, examine each method on the list to infer unique qualities a problem should have if it can be solved only by that method, then create a problem that requires qualities particular to that method. Call this the deductive plan.

Another approach might be quite different: Make up any problem, solve it, then identify the method used. If the method differs from any methods used to solve any problems previously made up, add this problem to the "done" pile, then randomly make up another problem, and so on. This can be called the inductive plan.

If the student's goal includes a facet that specifies how long searches of memory should take before trying a different approach (or dismissing the task entirely as "too hard"), a student who begins with the deductive plan might reevaluate its utility if it fails to create enough problems soon enough. This shows how monitoring in the next phase of the model, enacting tactics, can cycle back to Phase 2 in a self-regulated way.

Phase 3: Enacting Tactics

When the student begins to apply tactics and strategies that were identified in Phase 2, this marks the transition into Phase 3. In Phase 3, work on the task itself is done. Search tactics copy information into working memory from long-term memory that relates to the student's definition of task. Other tactics, previously built up by coupling SMART operations and knowledge of the subject area, construct information to make progress on the task. The deductive plan our student enacts is a good illustration.

Each product created by carrying out a tactic or a strategy has facets that, like goals, can be modeled in the shape of a profile. In Fig. 5.1, the shape of the profile in the Products box is a bit different from the shape of the goal profile in the Standards box. Monitoring compares the shapes of these profiles or the relative heights of specific bars representing particular facets, and this generates internal feedback. Our student working on making up trigonometry problems that illustrate specific methods for solving these types of problems used the results of this comparison to shift from the deductive plan to another, the inductive plan. Metacognitive monitoring of progress resulted in applying metacognitive control.

Phase 4: Adapting Metacognition

Phase 4 is optional. Here, the student makes major adaptations to schemas that structure how self-regulating is carried out. This is accomplished in three ways: (a) by *accreting* (or deleting) conditions under which operations are carried out or by adding or replacing operations themselves; (b) by *tuning* conditions that articulate tactics in strategies; or, (c) by significantly *restructuring* cognitive conditions, tactics, and strategies to create quite different approaches to addressing tasks (after Rumelhart & Norman, 1978; see Winne, 1997).

In the example of the student and the trigonometry problems, it seems plausible that two important changes to overall SRL might evolve. First, in characterizing the conditions of new problem-solving tasks, the student might not be more inclined to consider two types of plans, deductive as well as inductive. Second, having experienced success with switching from an initial plan to an alternative, the facet in the goal that relates to "how much effort to apply before switching plans" might change to a lower threshold—switch sooner.

Although Fig. 5.1 and my presentation so far might imply that SRL unfolds linearly, in a standard sequence that marches through the phases in numeric order, this is likely not the case. SRL is recursive. Recursive means that products created by information processing can become inputs to subsequent information processing. SRL is recursive in two ways. First, information produced in a phase may be monitored and the results fed back into that same phase, creating a second cycle of the same phase. Second, the information product created by monitoring in a given phase may feed back into a prior phase, as when a judgment about how well a tried and true plan worked in Phase 3 invites the student to recalibrate initial perceptions about the task's difficulty or complexity that was constructed in Phase 1. In this sense, SRL is weakly sequenced. Once an initial perception of a task is generated in Phase 1, information generated subsequently in any subsequent phase may jump phases, forward or backward, or recurse to create another cycle of information processing in the same phase.

The Centrality of Monitoring and Feedback in SRL

Metacognitive monitoring is the key to self-regulating one's learning (Butler & Winne, 1995; Winne, 1996, 1997) because without the cognitive evaluations it creates about differences between a current profile of work on a task and goals that specify standards for a satisfactory product, there is no guidance about how to regulate learning. Like other information processing operations, monitoring produces information. Its form is a list of matches and mismatches between (a) the standards for a task and (b) a representation in working memory of the product(s) of (a phase of) a task. As illustrated earlier, when a student develops a definition of a task in Phase 1, that perception may be monitored relative to memories about similar prior tasks. In Phase 3, monitoring operations contrast the products that have been created so far in the task against standards (goals) framed in Phase 2. The products of monitoring (labeled Cognitive Evaluations in Fig. 5.1) can update any or all of: (a) task conditions, for example, if the student is prompted to ask a question of the teacher that leads to a change in resources provided for the task; (b) cognitive conditions, for instance, when a student revises motivational elements that bear on the task; (c) standards (goals) the student assigns to the task, and (d) products generated in a first cycle of cognition or on the basis of recursive cognition, for instance, changing the tactics selected for approaching the goal. Within limits of cognitive resources—the student's knowledge and working memory capacity—and given particular external task conditions—resources, instructional cues, time, and social factors—these updates afford potential for the student to exercise metacognitive control that adapts engagement in midtask.

RESEARCH ON INFORMATION PROCESSING IN SELF-REGULATED LEARNING

Although there has been much research on SRL and its relationship(s) to achievement, there has not been much research investigating properties of SRL as information processing per se. In this section, several topics of research are reviewed to shed light on this topic and raise important areas for new research. Those topics are: working memory capacity, representations of information involved in SRL, and judgment or decision making that frames subsequent engagement with a task.

Memory Capacity and SRL

There is a ubiquitous constraint on information processing that arises because working memory can simultaneously process only a limited number of chunks of information. Working memory's capacity or span is typically estimated at between four and seven chunks, but the actual number depends on individual differences such as the student's age, qualities of the chunks themselves, and the complexity of SMART information processing that works on the chunks in working memory. When processing is more than just rehearsing, Sweller, van Merrienboer, and Pass (1998) suggested the information capacity of working memory reduces to approximately three chunks. This limited capacity of working memory to process information can be accommodated three ways: reducing demands of the task, schematizing and automating information, and off-loading information from memory to the environment. Each has implications for SRL.

Effects of Task Demand.   When tasks are complicated, they absorb the capacity of working memory, leaving little and sometimes insufficient capacity to apply to self-regulating. A study reported by Biemiller, Shany, Inglis, and Meichenbaum (1998) illustrated how individual differences in knowledge of a domain typically correlate inversely with the demands a task makes on learners. It also shows how task demands can vary across different settings.

Biemiller and his colleagues observed children during independent mathematics activities in second-grade, third-grade, and fourth-grade classrooms. The researchers first asked the children to nominate peers with whom they wanted to work on math, peers who would be a good source of help in math, who in the class best understands what to do in math, and peers who had lots of good ideas for things to do in math activities. Based on these peer nominations, the researchers created low, middle, and high groups that subsequently were shown to differ, as expected, in both achievement and IQ.

Biemiller et al. then recorded instances of self-regulatory speech, talk that reflects both a child's willingness (motivation) and capability to monitor progress on a task and regulate work on it to reach goals. For instance, self-directed questions about math ("Did I forget to check any of these?") and about monitoring progress ("Now, that part's done.") were deemed to reflect self-regulation. Although some of these utterances may be indicative of private thoughts, it is also probable many were meant to inform and solicit help from a partner or comment on a partner's work. These kinds of talk were distinguished from social talk not related to the speaker's current task, remarks that reiterated the answer to a task, or negotiations with the teacher or a partner about how the difficulty of a task might be lowered (e.g., "Can I do just this one?").

There were two contexts for these observations. In the first, students worked alone at their seats in a regular classroom on a common set of problems. Because the problems varied in difficulty and because students also varied in their level of competence, higher ability students had an easier set of problems overall, whereas lower ability students worked mostly on problems that were quite difficult for them. The second setting was a laboratory context where students worked in pairs. A significant difference in the lab setting was that each pair of students worked on a set of 10 word problems that were matched to the pair's level of ability.

The study revealed clear differences. Working solo in the classroom, the high achievement/ability group averaged 57 self-regulatory sentences per hour, statistically different from 8 self-regulatory sentences for the middle group and 16 for the low group. In the lab context, where children worked in pairs on problems matched to their ability, differences between the groups disappeared. More significantly, the rate of self-regulatory sentences increased enormously to 177 for the low group, 199 for the middle group, and 222 for the high group.

This study suggests an interesting interaction. During independent seatwork in a whole class setting, self-regulation overall was low for middle and low ability students compared to students with higher ability. Theoretically, middle and low ability students' working memory was "overloaded" due to the difficulty of problems and distractions in the room, so they had little resource to devote to self-regulation. Students with a better grasp of the subject matter, in contrast, could use that knowledge to relieve some of the load on working memory, thereby freeing resources to apply to self-regulation. However, in the lab setting where problems were differentially assigned to match each student's grasp—that is, the problems were within each student's zone of proximal development—two effects were observed. First, the frequency of self-regulation substantially increased. Second, ability level did not moderate the tendency to engage in self-regulation as in the classroom setting. The first effect shows that self-regulation is not rare or necessarily special (Winne, 1995). The second effect indicates that, when working memory is not overloaded but is appropriately challenged by work on a task, self-regulation intensifies.

In general, tasks where a learner's competence is appropriately challenged provide inherently greater affordance for SRL. When the rudiments of expertise are lacking, however, tasks become unduly difficult for two reasons. First, the learner cannot retrieve knowledge that completes the task directly; and, second, generating a solution is overly challenging because the expert's schemas that could do that are not readily available. Thus, when expertise is not adequately developed, learners who try to self-regulate during challenging tasks need to allocate working memory to self-regulating, leaving too little available to work on the task per se.

A study by Kanfer and Ackerman (1989, Experiment 1) illustrated this situation. They examined how Air Force personnel juggled cognitive resources as they learned a fast-paced, complex skill in a computer simulation—pretending to be an air traffic controller whose job was to land airplanes. A general finding of their research was that, until sufficient domain knowledge and skill was available, the more participants monitored in the service of self-regulating learning, the worse their safety record in landing planes. A similar finding emerged from research by Cooper and Sweller (1987; see also Sweller et al., 1998) in which eighth- and twelfth-grade students learned to solve algebra problems.

These several studies provide grounds for inferring a basic principle: When promoting SRL is an objective, instruction should not make multiple demands on working memory's limited capacity. Specifically, avoid requiring learners to search too deeply for knowledge or schemas to do work on tasks.

Research on goal-free problem solving (see Sweller et al., 1998) suggests a plan about how to do this. The basic idea is to present students with problems to solve that have two attributes. First, if they engage in SMART thinking using their prior knowledge, the problems should be solvable. Second, problems should be designed so that there are several variables (or solutions) that could be solved for, rather than just one. For example, instead of setting a problem like, "Find angle G given information about these two congruent triangles," set the problem like this: "There are several unknowns in this figure. Solve for anything you can." This way, students can increase information about the overall problem as they add solutions to it. In general, the more information in the conditions of COPES (provided it is relevant), the better. Under these conditions, students can explore schemas in a manner where they can avoid overloading memory. A further benefit of goal-free problem solving is that students also can schematize information and automate tactics as they build up understanding about the relations among elements of a type of problem. This issue is next.

Schematizing and Automating.   As noted earlier, another way the limits of working memory capacity can be stretched is when chunks of information represent a large volume of information in a unitized form. Such chunks contain a rich bundle of conditional knowledge plus automated tactics or strategies for processing information. Sweller et al. (1998) considered schemas with these qualities to be "prime goals of instruction" (p. 258).

Although such a chunk may be complex, if it is well learned and well articulated with other chunks, it can still be processed as a single chunk. An example suggested in this chapter is SMART, an acronym for five cognitive processes and the descriptions of each. You probably have not yet learned this chunk to the degree necessary for it to make minimal demand on working memory, but other mnemonics you may know probably have that quality, such as ROY G BIV (the colors of the visible spectrum in order of decreasing wavelength) or Chief SOH CAH TOA (that provides a common structure of the trigonometric relations in the form of sine = opposite ÷ hypotenuse, and so on).

A chunk made up of simple descriptions, like SMART, could be augmented with tactics to become a tool for SRL. For instance, if monitoring reveals a lack of comprehension as you read the next paragraph, you might search for information related to the topic being presented, monitor for text cues, assemble the main idea of that paragraph with this one, and so on. Suppose SMART became a checklist for reviewing information students had previously studied—for example, "Have I assembled basic lists into more useful organizational forms like concept maps?" and "Did I test my searches for key concepts?" Such a schema might be further assembled with other study tactics to regulate entire study sessions.

Schematizing and practicing in this way to automate a network of conditional knowledge plus tactics poses a considerable task. The result of such schematizing and automating is expertise. For tasks like playing the violin, winning chess matches, and playing tennis, it is achieved only after approximately 10,000 hours or 250 40-hour work weeks (Ericsson, Krampe, & Tesch-Römer, 1993).

There is not yet much research that reveals the nature of conditional knowledge students use in SRL. In an early study, Marx and I (Winne & Marx, 1982) observed lessons in fourth-, fifth-, and seventh-grade classrooms, then interviewed students about their participation. The students described complex arrangements of conditional knowledge they understood about how their teachers led lessons and tactics they adopted for learning in relation to their teacher's instructional cues. Students discriminated a variety of cues used in regulating their engagement. However, they also reported that the complexity of material and its pace of presentation could interfere with their attempts to regulate engagement. This is indirect evidence of less-than-complete schematization for the structures of lessons. As well, Marx and I observed significant individual differences among students in the content, reliability, and usage patterns of these students' schemas, further evidence that schematization varied among students.

Pressley and his colleagues (see Pressley, Van Etten, Yokoi, Freebern, & Van Meter, 1998) reported that conditional knowledge for SRL is rich among college students. Students differentiate conditions for taking particular types of notes in lectures, recording different types of material based on expectations for tests, studying for tests, and managing time and motivation. However, the degree to which these schemas are unitized, which determines their draw on the limited resources of working memory during SRL, is unknown.

We can borrow from research on learning to solve problems in areas like physics and trigonometry to develop a sharper picture of how SRL can be facilitated. Solving problems is enhanced when problem solvers can bring schematized and automated routines to bear. When unitized and automated schemas are lacking, problem solvers often adopt a means–ends approach (Sweller et al., 1998). In this approach, operations are performed to reduce differences between the current state of problem solving and the goal (solution). The nature of the remaining differences is monitored, and another operation is applied to further reduce the difference between the current state of problem solving and the goal (solution). This process of applying means to successively approximate the end (goal) parallels the four phases of SRL described in the 4-phase model Hadwin and I proposed (Winne & Hadwin, 1998a).

Means–ends analysis takes a heavy toll on working memory's resources. First, it requires that successive operations in an overall attack on a problem be carried out step-by-step. Second, it requires maintaining in working memory (rehearsing) a list of features that describe each successive approximation to the solution. Without that information, the problem solver has inadequate bases for searching for the next operation to apply in trying to make progress toward solving the problem. Having to rehearse items on this list to keep them active is direct evidence that the learner lacks a schema for solving the problem. Were that schema unitized and available, the separate items on that list could be represented in a single unit, the schema. Facing all this work, despite its challenges, may be a good thing because it gives the learner incentive to simplify it, that is, to unitize the schema (Anderson, 1991). However, it does make for arduous learning.

When learners have to use problem-solving methods such as means–ends analysis to self-regulate, they may over-challenge the capacity of working memory. In theory, this is especially the case in phase 4 of the 4-phase model where adaptations to self-regulation are the focus (Winne, 1997). However, there are several ways to deal with this (see Sweller et al., 1998) and, perhaps, facilitate SRL as well (Winne, 1995, 1997).

When the subject is not too challenging, learners can profit by having clear standards against which to monitor their grasp of the subject and their methods of learning. A good example is provided in a study by Morgan (1985). In a year-long educational psychology course, four groups participated in his experiment. In addition to a control group, who participated in the course without any intervention, three other groups were trained to set goals. Once each week, one group set daily goals for how long to study and then, each day they studied, they recorded whether they met that goal. A second group set an overall goal, such as "Learn the material," for each session they studied and then recorded whether they met it. The last group created specific behavioral objectives for each study session by specifying conditions, products, and standards (from the COPES script) and logged whether they met those objectives at the end of each study session. At the end of the whole course, the last group of students, who set specific goals, learned more than any of the other groups. Students who set goals about how long to study did study longer, but learned no more than a control group who "just studied." Why? Goals framed in terms of time do not provide subject-matter relevant standards for monitoring. What about the group who set general goals? They, too, had inadequate standards for monitoring the quality of learning. Thus, having the right kind of goals can facilitate self-regulation that underlies achievement.

What about when the material is complicated and challenging? Here, having goals can be detrimental to SRL. There are at least three elements to this story. First, I previously introduced Sweller et al.'s (1998) findings about the goal-free effect where students are provided no particular goals about what to solve for in physics or algebra problems. This boosts opportunity to schematize information for solving similar types of problems because students can use whatever elements of the schemata they have. That makes more efficient use of working memory's limited resources, reserving some for enhancing the schemata.

Kanfer and Ackerman's (1989, Experiment 2) study of Air Force personnel using a computer simulation to learn the complicated and time-pressured skill of landing airplanes adds to Sweller et al.'s (1998) principle about goal-free problems. Based on a prior experiment, Kanfer and Ackerman already knew that rule-based skill in landing planes generally began to be unitized after a particular number of experiences. So, for the first few trials in Experiment 2, they simply suggested that their participants try to do their best. Then, at the point where participants were predicted to be making the transition from using rules in a memory-consuming, step-by-step way to using unitized rules, the researchers changed goals from "do your best" to specific challenging ones. This switch resulted in better performance compared to participants who began working at the start under the draw of specific challenging goals.

Finally, studies by Zimmerman and Kitsantas (1997, 1999) showed how to complete the process of unitizing and automating schemas. In their studies of a motor skill (dart throwing) and an academic skill (combining sentences in preparation for writing compositions), they examined the effects of shifting goals from those that describe the product within the COPES script for a task (e.g., use the minimum number of words possible in combining sentences) to goals that describe a standards for operations (or processes, as they call them; e.g., practice the key steps in the method for combining sentences) within the COPES script. In their study, Zimmerman and Kitsantas (1999) compared four groups of learners. One group was not given any explicit goals. A second group was provided a product goal and the third group was given an operations goal. The fourth group was first given a product goal that was switched to an operations goal once students had unitized the schema. Students who were assigned shifting goals did better than those assigned operations goals, and both outperformed students with product goals.

In summary, schematizing then automating schemas with embedded tactics is a key to providing students with sufficient cognitive resources to engage in productive SRL. The small set of studies presented here conforms with theoretical predictions made (Butler & Winne, 1995) about self-generated feedback being a pivot for SRL. Understandings about how to preserve memory's limited resources are an important step forward in understanding how SRL works and how its development can be fostered (see also Winne, 1997).

Off-loading. The third way that the capacity of working memory can be extended is by storing information outside the mind where it can be referenced if needed but not clutter working memory if it is not. Examples are notes that students take to record information in a lecture, a calculator that "knows" the square root algorithm, and even the proverbial string around the finger. Planned off-loading is an excellent example of self-regulation.

Several studies of learning to use tactics and employing them selectively examined or directly manipulated off-loading information involved in SRL. The study by Morgan (1985), previously described, provided some indirect evidence. His experiment involved four groups of undergraduates enrolled in a year-long course in educational psychology: a control group, a group that set specific objectives, a group that set general goals, and a group that set goals for how long they would study. The latter three groups wrote out their goals and recorded whether they met them.

Goals are standards against which studying can be monitored, and writing them into a notebook is equivalent to off-loading those standards to an external record. Morgan's findings showed that the group who set goals for how long they should study did study approximately 30 minutes more than the other groups, all of which studied about the same. This is evidence of self-regulating effort. On the final examination in the course, students who daily set and monitored specific behavioral objectives for the conditions, products, and standards of COPES scripts for studying outscored the other groups. If SRL is a benefit to learning, this is indirect evidence that off-loading standards used in monitoring helped free resources in memory that students could apply to learning per se, rather than constantly maintaining standards used in monitoring studying.

A study by De La Paz, Swanson, and Graham (1998) showed a direct effect of off-loading information involved in SRL. They investigated processes used by a dozen eighth-grade students with learning difficulties as they made revisions to compositions. In this study, information about tactics for SRL was off-loaded by providing students with cards that provided external representations of tactics for: (a) comparing drafts against standards, (b) diagnosing weaknesses at both local and global levels of their compositions, and (c) selecting tactics to repair shortcomings. To search for (diagnose) shortcomings, students also could select from among any of several cards describing standards and, once instances in their essay were identified as falling short of a particular standard, any of several other cards describing tactics for operating on the composition to improve it. This instructional design not only off-loads information but also incorporates a partially goal-free approach to SRL as students had several options for tactics, presented by the cards, rather than just one to use. Both features reduce demands on the limited resources of working memory. The joint effects of off-loading values for slots in COPES scripts and reducing cognitive load by allowing work to proceed relatively goal free enhanced students' use of appropriate tactics for revising their work.

Representations of Information About SRL

Under the lens of information processing, schemas involved in SRL have a standard format: IF–THEN–ELSE. All schemas classify an experience as a particular something based on bits of information that discriminate one experience from another. When the experience is a task to be carried out, a schema's IFs can refer to either or both of the task's conditions and its standards, C and S elements of a full COPES script for the task.

Standards typically describe the product created by working on the task. They can also refer to qualities of information processes, such as the time a SMART operation should require to "run" or the number of cycles an operation should run. The contents of slots for THENs and ELSEs are actions. These animate the schema, equipping it with the power to act. Acts may remain totally cognitive, ranging from discrete SMARTs to complex cognitive strategies. Alternatively, THENs and ELSEs may manifest as a physical behavior, such as clicking a selected (monitored) hyperlink on a page in the World Wide Web.

A challenge to the family of information processing models has been to incorporate motivation. Commonly, motivation refers to any or all of: internal conditions or mental constructs that influence which tasks students choose to pursue or reject; temperamental qualities of engaging in a task, such as intensity, carefulness, and the like; and one's persistence at a task. All three kinds of information discriminate tasks—for example, tasks that really cannot be passed over, that merit our devoted attention, or that will entail many trials and adjustments based on feedback about errors.

Some IFs in schemas for SRL refer to information of just these sorts, information that concerns what motivation is (Winne & Marx, 1989). Alongside "cold" cognitive conditions, such as whether a new software word processor has an easy-to-use help feature, schemas for SRL include "hot" motivational conditions, such as whether one is intrinsically interested in learning all the subtle tricks of using new software (Pintrich, Marx, & Boyle, 1993). Because the synthesis of hot plus cold IFs is the trigger for THENs or shunting to ELSEs in schemas for SRL, information processing about tasks is intrinsically "motivational processing," too (Winne & Marx, 1989; see also Borkowski & Burke, 1996).

A simple but possibly profound deduction follows by viewing schemas for SRL as a fusion of information–motivational processing. Except for "primitive" emotional content, such as fundamental preferences (see Zajonc, 1980) or arousal associated with a startle response, this view of schemas that regulate learning invites viewing issues of motivation just like issues of information processing about a topic like history (Winne & Marx, 1989). If that is the case, motivational features of SRL could be investigated and explained using widely researched models of information processing that address facets of cognitive life such as limited capacity working memory, expertise, and metacognition.

Motivation in Schemas. On completing phases 1 and 2 of the 4-phase model depicted in Fig. 5.1—generating a perception of a task, and developing plans for reaching goals—a student will have constructed a personalized COPES script for addressing the task at hand (Winne & Marx, 1977). Theoretically, four main categories of motivationally related information for SRL (Winne, 1997) are included in this script: outcome expectations, judgments about efficacy, attributions, and incentives. Together, these form a basis for generating a fifth description of the task, its utility. Utility is a summary position about the overall usefulness of this task versus alternatives.

SRL means adapting to circumstances that unfold when products do not meet standards. More sophisticated forms of SRL investigate more than one option for operations. This requires predicting the likelihood that alternative tactics and strategies can create products that do meet standards. Once a forecast has been made about the degree to which each potential product (or performance; see Bandura, 1997) matches standards, it is then possible to search memory—to predict—the various outcomes to one's self that are associated with each product. This prediction is an *outcome expectation*. Like any other "kind" of information, an outcome expectation can play the role of an IF that triggers a search of memory for what THEN will be the case. According to contemporary theories of motivation, information returned to working memory by a search like this concerns three main topics.

Each outcome has some kind of or degree of value to the learner. Because the product has not yet been created, that value is not yet realized. It's an *incentive* the learner anticipates.

An *efficacy expectation* is an estimate of the probability that a learner is able to carry out operations specified in a COPES script to create the product called for by the task's standards. Efficacy expectations can be directly recalled in phase 1 of the 4-phase model if the learner is very familiar with the task. In this case, the learner is expert in this task and a COPES script appropriate to it is automatically forthcoming from long-term memory. Otherwise, when tasks are novel, efficacy expectations are generated in phase 2 when a plan is assembled about operations for dealing with the task.

The topic of *attributions* is a third kind of information about a task. Its topic is the reason or the cause for one's success (or failure) at the task. Typical attributions are to ability, effort, luck, and difficulty of the task (see Pintrich & Schunk, 1996).

When memory automatically fills in values of slots in a COPES script for a task (Winne, 1997; see also McKoon & Ratcliff, 1992), outcome expectations, incentives, efficacy expectations, and attributions add motivationally "hot" information to what might otherwise be a "cold" cognitive structure (Pintrich, Marx, & Boyle, 1993). In just the same way that SRL might use "cold" facts or interpretations in a COPES script as grounds for metacognitive monitoring or the target of metacognitive control, it also can use and adapt motivational elements that concern the tasks learners select, their temperament, and their persistence (Garcia & Pintrich, 1994). Thus, the information processing view of SRL can stretch to give an account of the volitional features of task engagement, that is, how learners develop and apply control over their motivation and emotion in tasks.

Options Afford Decisions.   How does a learner decide which script to follow? To make such decisions—that is, to self regulate—it is logically necessary that alternative scripts be represented in a way that allows them to be compared (Winne, 1997; see also Byrnes, 1998). The four motivationally related IFs—outcome expectations, incentives, efficacy expectations, and attributions—might provide just the right kind of rulers for measuring one script against another.

There is overwhelming evidence that each of these kinds of information is individually significant in motivated behavior and in SRL (Bandura, 1997; Winne, 1997). Although we do not have a good model for how learners amalgamate these four facets to reach a judgment favoring one COPES script over another, I suggest labeling that amalgam the *utility* of the script. In other words, utility is the degree to which a script is believed to achieve all goals the learner holds in phase 2 of the 4-phase model of SRL. Choosing one script for engaging with a task—self-regulating one's engagement—means choosing the script that promises the greatest utility (Winne, 1997; see also Baron, 1994; Byrnes, 1998). I suggest another first-letter acronym, AEIOU, to represent jointly all four motivationally related slots in a COPES script—Attributions, Efficacy judgments, Incentives, Outcome expectations—plus the Utility a script has (Winne, 1997; Winne & Marx, 1989).

An important finding about utility was reported in several lines of research: learners self-regulate their choices for scripts according to their idiosyncratic views of utility rather than ours. A compelling example is students who adopt self-handicapping approaches to academic work such as procrastinating, purposefully avoiding tasks, or setting unachievable goals (see Covington, 1992). For example, a study by Wood, Motz, and Willoughby (1998) reported that students deliberately selected scripts that they realized were less effective or appropriate for tasks they undertook. Also, Garner (1990) posited that students purposefully select scripts that are less complex, a stance that I believe reflects a general disposition to balance effort against incentives (Winne, 1997), that is, to satisfice (Simon, 1953).

Decision Making as the Basis of Metacognitive Control

Previously, I described metacognitive monitoring as the key to SRL. It creates a profile of evaluations that characterizes the utility of the COPES script the learner is following at present. Having created this evaluation, the learner is poised to self-regulate, to persist with the current script because its utility is sufficient or to search for and select a new script to try because its utility is deemed better than the current script's. Making a selection between these alternatives sets metacognitive control in motion and amounts to making a decision, "... the essence of intelligent, purposeful behavior" (Slovic, 1990, p. 89) such as SRL.

We infer that students do make decisions like this, and various studies (e.g., Wood et al., 1998; see also Zimmerman & Martinez-Pons, 1988) demonstrate it. However, there is almost no research on decision making in the context of SRL in academic tasks. Related research I have reviewed (Winne, 1997, 1999) can be summarized briefly in terms of three broad issues. First, in choosing among tactics or strategies to use in tasks, young children (Klayman, 1985) and college students (Wood et al., 1998) appear to seek a satisficing balance between powerful or accurate approaches on one hand, and controlling the effort involved in enacting those approaches on the other hand. Second, accompanying this disposition among some students may be a belief that effort probably is not necessary for some tasks (Schommer, 1994). Finally, younger and older students alike may be somewhat to moderately unreliable in estimating the utility of alternative approaches to tasks (Byrnes, 1998). If these findings generalize validly to students' SRL, the upshot is that decision making about matters attending SRL will be just as fraught with hazards as decision making in other areas (see Baron, 1994; Stanovich, 1999; Winne, 1997).

CoNoteS2: A Design for Supporting SRL Based on Information Processing Theory

Hadwin and I (Winne & Hadwin, 1998b) used a general programming system dubbed *STUDY* (Winne & Field, 2000) to prototype CoNoteS2, a software system designed to support students' SRL and simultaneously serve as a laboratory for researching SRL. Figures 5.2, 5.3, and 5.4 show representative tools CoNoteS2 provides students for studying textbook chapters.

On the right side of Fig. 5.2, CoNoteS2 displays a section of the chapter students are studying; hence, we refer to this kind of window as a *section*

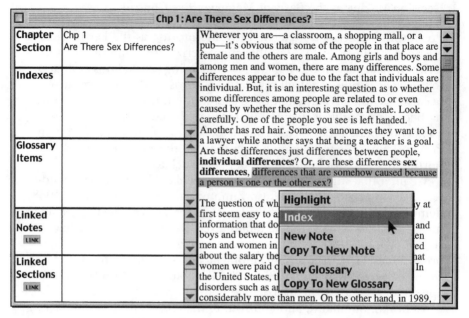

FIG. 5.2.   The section window in CoNoteS2.

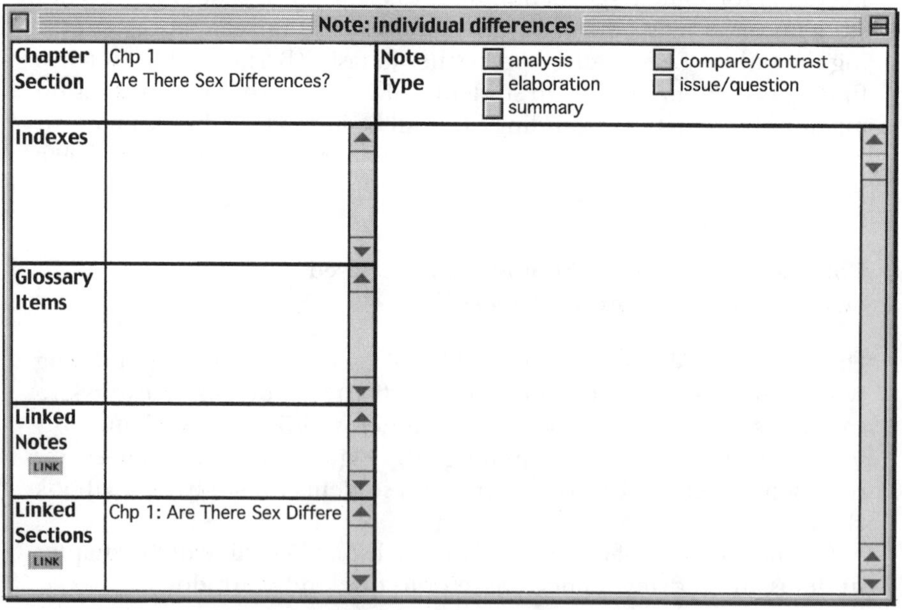

FIG. 5.3.   The notes window in CoNoteS2.

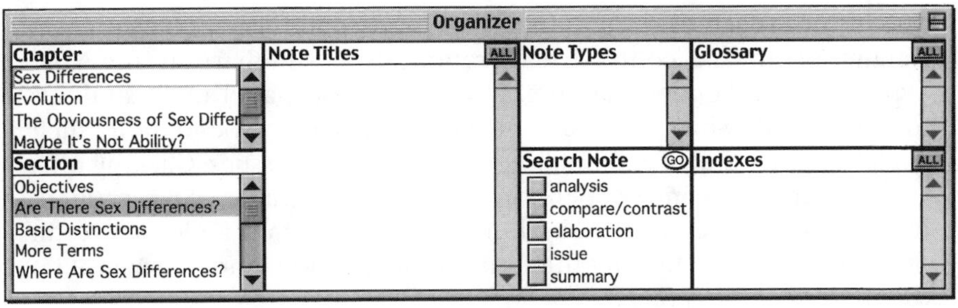

Organizer			
Chapter	**Note Titles**	**ALL** **Note Types**	**Glossary** **ALL**
Sex Differences ▲		▲	▲
Evolution			
The Obviousness of Sex Differ			
Maybe It's Not Ability? ▼		▼	▼
Section		**Search Note** GO	**Indexes** **ALL**
Objectives ▲		☐ analysis	▲
Are There Sex Differences?		☐ compare/contrast	
Basic Distinctions		☐ elaboration	
More Terms		☐ issue	
Where Are Sex Differences? ▼		▼ ☐ summary	▼

FIG. 5.4.   The organizer window in CoNoteS2.

window. The left half of every chapter's section windows is divided into five vertically stacked panels. Except for the top panel, where CoNoteS2 shows the titles of the present chapter and chapter section, these panels display information the student constructs using tools CoNoteS2 provides. For example, Fig. 5.2 shows the student beginning to create an index term for text highlighted in the section. That index term will appear in the Indexes panel. If the student clicks that term, CoNoteS2 will scroll to and highlight the text the student indexed. The Glossary Items panel works similarly for terms the student adds to a glossary. In the window (not shown) where students enter the glossary term and create its definition, they are explicitly cued to elaborate that information by creating an example.

Using the pop-up menu for text selected in a chapter section, students can create notes using a note window shown in Fig. 5.3. On the way to a note window, CoNoteS2 requires students to create a title for each note and posts it to the Linked Notes panel in the section window. This title is a hyperlink to the note. Clicking it tells CoNoteS2 to scroll to the text in the chapter's section that the note is about, highlight it, and simultaneously open the note the student made.

The note window in Fig. 5.3 shows the title of the note ("individual differences") in its top bar, and the chapter and section where it was created in the top left panel. In the large blank area at the right, students enter a note. In a note, they can create indexes and glossary items, link this note to other notes, and link a note from one chapter section to other sections. Above the notetaking area is a panel with checkboxes where students classify each note according to the type of information it contains. CoNoteS2 forces students to choose at least one note type before allowing students to continue studying.

The student keeps track of all this work in a continually visible Organizer window shown in Fig. 5.4. By clicking on a chapter and then a chapter's section, the student tells CoNoteS2 to display for that section all notes' titles, glossary terms, and indexes in that section. Clicking on the title of a specific note identifies the type(s) of information it contains (analysis, compare/contrast, elaboration, issue, summary) in the Note Types panel and opens that note. The Search Note panel allows students to view all note windows for one or several particular types of note, such as all the notes that are summaries or that deal with issues. Clicking on a glossary term or an index opens the window where that item was created, highlights the relevant text, and, if the clicked item is a glossary term, opens the window showing the term, its description, and an example if the student created one.

Support for SRL

CoNoteS2 has an number of scaffolds or ways to support students in self-regulating learning. Here, I illustrate some that are already implemented in the software and forecast others on our drawing board.

Phases 1 and 2: Defining the Task, and Setting Goals and Planning. A studying session with CoNoteS2 begins in the Organizer window where the student selects a chapter and then a section. Any note titles, glossary entries, and indexes created in a preceding study session for that section are posted in their respective panels.

The Organizer window was designed to support students in some elements of phases 1 and 2 of our 4-phase model of SRL: defining the task, and generating goals and plans. It also provides a method for reducing demands on working memory's limited capacity later in studying, during phase 3.

Types of information that notes might contain, listed in the Search Note panel, are products created when students apply particular study tactics (operations) to engage in a task of analyzing information or creating a summary. Reminding students of these common studying tasks invites searching long-term memory for schemas that contain conditions for metacognitively monitoring information in the chapter relative to whether it should be analyzed or summarized. Those conditions are IFs that differentially trigger tactics for creating, say, an analysis versus a summary. Rehearsing already available schemas is a simple form of planning. If the chapter's author provides objectives for studying, shown in the Section panel of Fig. 5.4, the student can develop plans that are more sensitive (discriminating) about particular tactics' applicability to studying *this* chapter. If the student has not yet automated these studying schemas, this information can be off-loaded into a note. In creating that note, the student is rehearsing the schema, adding to expertise at studying, as well as assembling the objectives with schemas for common studying tasks like analyzing, comparing/contrasting, and so forth. By indexing these planning notes, the student can assemble a single chunk with a coherent, chapter-sensitive trigger for metacognitively monitoring while studying the chapter's sections.

Phase 4: Adapting Metacognition.   Research (Rabinowitz, Freeman, & Cohen, 1993; see also Winne, 1995) suggests that students may not put effective tactics to use if the effort to use those tactics seems too much. By avoiding such tactics, however, students ironically preclude the very practice that leads to automaticity and expertise with them. We are presently designing additions to CoNoteS2 that theoretically should help students avoid this self-handicapping approach to studying.

In an experiment where undergraduates used CoNoteS2, we predicted that the study tactic of indexing information would be perceived as having high utility and, therefore, it would be used often. We were wrong—students very rarely created indexes (Winne, Hadwin, McNamara, & Chu, 1998). On reflection, two features of the task of creating an index might explain our finding. First, students likely have almost no experience indexing materials, particularly as a method for studying. Inviting them to self-regulate use of this novel tactic while studying complex material probably parallels the situation in Kanfer and Ackerman's (1989) study where self-regulating faltered while learners were challenged to develop skills in air traffic control. Second, unlike Kanfer and Ackerman's study, where the motivational descriptions of air traffic control might be relatively clearer, students might have a rather empty AEIOU schema about indexing as a tactic for studying.

Using features that STUDY provides, CoNoteS2 might be modified to count notes as a student makes them and to observe for each note whether the student indexes information in it. When the count of notes exceeds some value, say 10, and the count in indexes in notes remains below a threshold, say 2, CoNoteS2 might interrupt studying the chapter with a brief tutorial about indexing. First, the benefits—outcomes and potential incentives—of making indexes would be described. Next, referring to the 10 notes created so far, CoNoteS2 might guide the student to recognize that considerable effort has already been applied but that this new tactic, indexing, could make that effort even more productive. That is, the attribution in this instance is that effort, in the form of making indexes, contributes to success. Mixed into this presentation are examples of indexing that rehearse conditions for indexing usefully as well as how to make an index. CoNoteS2 concludes the tutorial with a summary about the tactic of indexing. This summary is added to the students' notes and indexed as "indexing."

Thereafter, when the student starts to make a note, CoNoteS2 automatically pops up a reminder about indexing—the aforementioned note—and, when the student is done with that new note, it asks the student to rate the current level of skill in indexing. This is a subtle way to involve the student in generating an efficacy expectation for future notes and reexamining or rehearsing the conditions that apply to making a useful index, two essentials in adapting self-regulation about study tactics. If the tutorial was effective, and as the student gains skill in indexing, the tactic's automaticity should develop along with increasing judgments about its utility. In this process, CoNoteS2 has guided the student to adapt schemas, beginning with a fusion of skills with motivational elements, for self-regulating studying.

CONCLUSIONS

An information processing view of SRL is based on two fundamental qualities of how learners think. First, memory has limited resources to devote to tasks. The chunk is the unit used to measure that capacity regardless of how much information a chunk contains. Memory's limitations can be virtually extended by packing lots of information into the chunks it handles. Second, schemas that include tactics and strategies provide a very resourceful way to represent information about self-regulating one's engagement in tasks. In particular, schemas provide a meeting ground where cold cognition and hot motivation can integrate to provide personal guidance for how to self-regulate learning. Using these pervasive features found in the information processing view of SRL, we can understand better how SRL is challenging and how instruction can be designed to provide opportunity for students to practice more effective forms of SRL. Work on software systems such as CoNoteS2 provides a laboratory for strengthening the span between information processing-based theory about SRL and practice, as well as stimulating further refinements in both.

ACKNOWLEDGMENT

Work on this chapter was supported by a grant from the Social Sciences and Humanities Research Council of Canada, #410-98-0705.

REFERENCES

Anderson, J. R. (1983. *The architecture of cognition.* Cambridge, MA: Harvard University Press.
Anderson, J. R. (1991). The adaptive nature of human categorization. *Psychological Review, 98,* 409–429.

Bandura, A. (1997). *Self-efficacy: The exercise of control.* New York: W. H. Freeman.

Baron, J. (1994). *Thinking and deciding.* Cambridge, UK: Cambridge University Press.

Biemiller, A., Shany, M., Inglis, A., & Meichenbaum, D. (1998). Factors influencing children's acquisition and demonstration of self-regulation on academic tasks. In D. H. Schunk & B. J. Zimmerman (Eds.), *Self-regulated learning: From teaching to self-reflective practice* (pp. 203–224). New York: Guilford.

Borkowski, J. G., & Burke, J. E. (1996). Theories, models, and measurements of executive functioning. In G. R. Lyon & N. A Krasnegor (Eds.), *Attention, memory, and executive function* (pp. 235–261). Baltimore: Paul H. Brookes.

Butler, D. L., & Winne, P. H. (1995). Feedback and self-regulated learning: A theoretical synthesis. *Review of Educational Research, 65,* 245–281.

Byrnes, J. P. (1998). *The nature and development of decision making: A self-regulation model.* Mahwah, NJ: Lawrence Erlbaum Associates.

Carver, C. S., & Scheier, M. F. (1998). *On the self-regulation of behavior.* New York: Cambridge University Press.

Clark, J. M., & Paivio, A. (1991). Dual coding theory and education. *Educational Psychology Review, 3,* 149–210.

Cooper, G., & Sweller, J. (1987). Effects of schema acquisition and rule automation on mathematical problem-solving transfer. *Journal of Educational Psychology, 79,* 347–362.

Covington, M. V. (1992). *Making the grade: A self-worth perspective on motivation and school reform.* Cambridge, UK: Cambridge University Press.

Craik, F. I. M., & Lockhart, R. S. (1972). Levels of processing: A framework for memory research. *Journal of Verbal Learning and Verbal Behavior, 11,* 671–684.

De La Paz, S., Swanson, P. N., & Graham, S. (1998). The contribution of executive control to the revising by students with writing and learning difficulties. *Journal of Educational Psychology, 90,* 448–460.

Ericsson, K. A., Krampe, R. Th., & Tesch-Römer, C. (1993). The role of deliberate practice in the acquisition of expert performance. *Psychological Review, 100,* 363–406.

Garcia, T., & Pintrich, P. R. (1994). Regulating motivation and cognition in the classroom: The role of self-schemas and self-regulatory strategies. In D. H. Schunk & B. J. Zimmerman (Eds.), *Self-regulation of learning and performance: Issues and educational applications* (pp. 127–153). Hillsdale, NJ: Lawrence Erlbaum Associates.

Garner, R. (1990). When children and adults do not use learning strategies: Toward a theory of settings. *Review of Educational Research, 60,* 517–529.

Kanfer, R., & Ackerman, P. L. (1989). Motivation and cognitive abilities: An integrative/aptitude-treatment approach to skill acquisition [Monograph]. *Journal of Applied Psychology, 74,* 657–690.

Klayman, J. (1985). Children's decision strategies and their adaptation to task characteristics. *Organizational Behavior and Human Decision Processes, 35,* 179–201.

Locke, J. (1690/1853). *An essay concerning human understanding.* London: W. Tegg.

McKoon, G., & Ratcliff, R. (1992). Inference during reading. *Psychological Review, 99,* 440–466.

Miller, G. A., Galanter, E., & Pribram, K. H. (1960). *Plans and the structure of behavior.* New York: Holt, Rinehart & Winston.

Morgan, M. (1985). Self-monitoring of attained subgoals in private study. *Journal of Educational Psychology, 77,* 623–630.

Pintrich, P. R., Marx, R. W., & Boyle, R. A. (1993). Beyond cold conceptual change: The role of motivational beliefs and classroom contextual factors in the process of conceptual change. *Review of Educational Research, 63,* 167–199.

Pintrich, P. R., & Schunk, D. H. (1996). *Motivation in education: Theory, research, and applications.* Englewood Cliffs, NJ: Prentice-Hall.

Powers, W. T. (1973). *Behavior: The control of perception.* Chicago: Aldine.

Pressley, M., Van Etten, S., Yokoi, L., Freebern, G., & Van Meter, P. (1998). The metacognition of college studentship: A grounded theory approach. In D. J. Hacker, J. Dunlosky, & A. C. Graesser (Eds.). *Metacognition in educational theory and practice* (pp. 347–366). Hillsdale, NJ: Lawrence Erlbaum Associates.

Rabinowitz, M., Freeman, K., & Cohen, S. (1993). Use and maintenance of strategies: The influence of accessibility to knowledge. *Journal of Educational Psychology, 84,* 211–218.

Rumelhart, D. E., & Norman, D. A. (1978). Accretion, tuning, and restructuring: Three modes of learning. In J. W. Cotton & R. Klatzky (Eds.), *Semantic factors in cognition* (pp. 37–53). Hillsdale, NJ: Lawrence Erlbaum Associates.

Schmeck, R. R. (1988). Individual differences and learning strategies. In C. E. Weinstein, E. T. Goetz, & P. A. Alexander (Eds.), *Learning and study strategies. Issues in assessment, instruction, and evaluation* (pp. 171–191). San Diego, CA: Academic Press.

Schommer, M. (1994). Synthesizing epistemological belief research: Tentative understandings and provocative conclusions. *Educational Psychology Review, 6,* 293–319.

Shannon, C. E., & Weaver, W. (1949). *The mathematical theory of communication.* Urbana, IL: University of Illinois Press.

Simon, H. A. (1953). *Models of man.* New York: Wiley.

Slovic, P. (1990). Choice. In D. N. Osherson & E. E. Smith (Eds.), *An invitation to cognitive science: Vol. 3. Thinking.* (pp. 89–116). Cambridge, MA: MIT Press.

Stanovich, K. E. (1999). *Who is rational? Studies of individual differences in reasoning.* Mahwah, NJ: Lawrence Erlbaum Associates.

Sweller, J., van Merrienboer, J. J. G., & Paas, F. G. W. C. (1998). Cognitive architecture and instructional design. *Educational Psychology Review, 10,* 251–296.

Winne, P. H. (1985). Steps toward promoting cognitive achievements. *Elementary School Journal, 85,* 673–693.

Winne, P. H. (1995). Inherent details in self-regulated learning. *Educational Psychologist, 30,* 173–187.

Winne, P. H. (1996). A metacognitive view of individual differences in self-regulated learning. *Learning and Individual Differences, 8,* 327–353.

Winne, P. H. (1997). Experimenting to bootstrap self-regulated learning. *Journal of Educational Psychology, 89,* 397–410.

Winne, P. H. (1999, June). *Children's decision making skills and the development of self-regulated learning.* Paper presented at the meeting of the Canadian Association for Educational Psychology, Sherbrooke, Québec.

Winne, P. H., & Field, D. (2000). *STUDY: An environment for authoring and presenting adaptive learning tutorials* (version 3.5) [computer program]. Simon Fraser University, Burnaby, BC.

Winne, P. H., & Hadwin, A. F. (1998a). Studying as self-regulated learning. In D. J. Hacker, J. Dunlosky, & A. C. Graesser (Eds.). *Metacognition in educational theory and practice* (pp. 277–304). Hillsdale, NJ: Lawrence Erlbaum Associates.

Winne, P. H., & Hadwin, A. F. (1998b, August). *Using CoNoteS2 to study and support self-regulated learning.* San Francisco, CA: International Association of Applied Psychology.

Winne, P. H., Hadwin, A. F., McNamara, J. K., & Chu, S. T. L. (1998, April). An exploratory study of self-regulating learning when students study using CoNoteS2. In S. Tobias (Chair), *Metacognition: Assessment and training.* San Diego, CA: American Educational Research Association.

Winne, P. H., & Marx, R. W. (1977). Reconceptualizing research on teaching. *Journal of Educational Psychology, 69,* 668–678.

Winne, P. H., & Marx, R. W. (1982). Students' and teachers' views of thinking processes for classroom learning. *Elementary School Journal, 82,* 493–518.

Winne, P. H., & Marx, R. W. (1989). A cognitive processing analysis of motivation within classroom tasks. In C. Ames & R. Ames (Eds.), *Research on motivation in education* (Vol. 3, pp. 223–257). Orlando, FL: Academic Press.

Winne, P. H., & Perry, N. E. (1999). Measuring self-regulated learning. In M. Boekaerts, P. Pintrich, & M. Zeidner (Eds.), *Handbook of self-regulation* (pp. 531–566). Orlando, FL: Academic Press.

Wood, E., Motz, M., & Willoughby, T. (1998). Examining students' retrospective memories of strategy development. *Journal of Educational Psychology, 90*, 698–704.

Zajonc, R. B. (1980). Feeling and thinking: Preferences need no inferences. *American Psychologist, 35*, 151–175.

Zimmerman, B. J., & Kitsantas, A. (1997). Developmental phases in self-regulation: Shifting from process to outcome goals. *Journal of Educational Psychology, 89*, 29–36.

Zimmerman, B. J., & Kitsantas, A. (1999). Acquiring writing revision skill: shifting from process to outcome self-regulatory goals. *Journal of Educational Psychology, 91*, 241–250.

Zimmerman, B. J., & Martinez-Pons, M. (1988). Construct validation of a strategy model of student self-regulated learning. *Journal of Educational Psychology, 80*, 284–290.

Chapter 6

Volitional Aspects of Self-Regulated Learning

Lyn Corno
Teachers College, Columbia University

Conceptions of self-regulation during learning emphasize the actions a person takes to carry out intentions. The underlying psychological processes that guide these actions are volitional. However, the volitional aspects of self-regulated learning (SRL) remain ill-understood and implicit in many operationalizations. A look forward to the next generation of research suggests the benefits of a better understanding of modern theories of volition.

In an early article Mandinach and I (Corno & Mandinach, 1983) described the role of SRL in acquiring knowledge of school subjects. We adopted concepts from information-processing theory, and argued that self-regulation in school learning reflects students' use of higher level processes to orchestrate and control their concentration, motivation, and affect. We defined SRL as "an effort put forth by students to deepen and manipulate the associative network in content areas, and to monitor and improve that deepening process" (p. 95).

This initial definition made some assumptions. For one thing, it assumed that students seek to understand subject matter content rather than simply committing it to memory. In giving meaning to a subject and monitoring their understanding, students engage important volitional functions. Self-monitoring protects concentration and motivation when intrusions arise in the outer (task) environment, or internally (e.g., as when interest or mood shifts).

Efforts to learn the content material, in part, involve surveying and sampling from available resources. However, resourcefulness here implies more than task-management; it includes self-management, or efficiently handling personal resources as well. This, too, is an aspect of volitional functioning.

Another assumption of our early definition was that students differ in propensities for self-regulated learning—that is, in their knowledge of and tendencies to use SRL in school learning. Such propensities confer advantages, particularly when a learning situation suggests the need for extra effort or support. Even students with above-average cognitive ability need to bring self-regulation to bear on many school tasks. Thus, SRL is not to be equated with cognitive–intellectual ability. Neither does SRL follow predictably from expectation or hope for success. Often, a person calls up personal resources when hope stands on shaky ground (Corno, 1994). SRL cannot then be exclusively cognitive or motivational; it has volitional aspects that weigh in as well.

With the internalization of learning strategies, and self- and task-management, a person comes to use SRL according to situational demand (Corno, 1986). SRL is thus part skill (overlearning provides benefits), and part workstyle (not every student brings SRL propensities to tasks). These refinements in our early definition retain its ties to volition, while also distinguishing SRL from manifestations of personality or temperament over which people have little control (e.g., reflectivity).

Volition has special relevance in education. Many school and classroom learning situations invite or demand volitional control while constraining other behavior. Paying attention, listening, and answering questions are expected in classrooms, yet, when peers work collaboratively, observe models, or change learning stations, potential diversions abound. Observations of classrooms confirm that students confront a range of distractions, even during relatively controlled, teacher-led instruction (Doyle, 1983). Studies of problem solving, when students work individually, reflect similar attentional demands and likewise emphasize the need for coping. A given task, viewed by some students as difficult, may be equally hard to tackle for a student who perceives it as busy work (Stanford Aptitude Seminar, in press).

Beyond situational demands and constraints, students have diverse capabilities, motives, and goals; their levels of commitment vary for goals that teachers establish. As interests and values wax and wane, students' initial intentions and efforts may either escalate or degrade. Some classroom settings and actions by teachers undermine students' best intentions to learn, such as when students feel they have been treated unfairly (McCaslin & Good, 1996). The ability to maintain concentration in the face of obstacles is a fundamentally volitional aptitude for many tasks of schooling. In our framework, volition is a necessary but insufficient condition for SRL and is given special status as the key to follow-through.

This chapter first presents some general theory on volition, establishing its importance for ongoing research on self-regulation in school learning. Next examples of volitional subprocesses and strategies in academic learning are discussed. Several lines of investigation in educational psychology connect to these volitional aspects of SRL. Finally, I describe some research directed at a better understanding of volition in academic settings and how education might promote it.

MODERN THEORY OF VOLITION

Brief History

The construct of volition fared poorly throughout the history of psychology. Early 20th-century debates among German psychologists questioned its theoretical value. Some theorists equated volition with motivation, or saw the latter as more inclusive. Others found volition either derivative of basic processes, such as emotions or simple cognitions, or merely the manifestation of instrumental conditioning.

In part these problems were tied to ambiguities in colloquial conceptions of volition as willpower or strength of will. Modern volition theory disentangles volitional processes from the vague notion of willfully resisting temptation. Effective use of volitional processes confers advantages. For example, selectively strengthening intentions protects them from interference, thus serving a practical purpose. Similarly, taking immediate action toward goals helps a person avoid the traps of procrastinating. Understanding the processes that underlie action control begins to set volition apart from motivation.

Until the 1980s, the term *volition* appeared rarely in psychological research and related writings on education (Snow, 1986). The current revival is due in large part to efforts by German psychologist Julius Kuhl.[1]

---

[1]It is fitting that Germany again offers us the construct of volition when her debates did away with it in the first place. Lest we think for a moment, however, that issues of will are somehow linked to German culture, I hasten to point out that early essays on the Puritan ethic spoke of willpower as "proof" of divine worth. Cotton Mather said we should "Prove virtue by denying pleasure." A "no pain, no gain" view of volition is not what modern volitional theory posits, however, as we shall see. In addition, our all-American favorite, John Dewey, wrote an essay on interest and volition that denigrates the "willpower" sense of the term (see Dewey, 1974).

Kuhl made a convincing case for resurrecting an early, unconventional theory developed by Ach (1910). Ach handled the definitional difficulties of volition by distinguishing it clearly from motivation: *Motivation* generates the impulse or intention to act; *volition* controls intentions and impulses so that action occurs. Motivational and volitional processes are therefore related but conceptually distinct and imply different points of intervention. Kuhl (1985) added the idea of reconceptualizing volition within a general information-processing theory, and operationalized the construct as *learned volitional strategies* or *action control.*

Kuhl's Theory and Its Application in Education

Kuhl and Beckmann (1985) collected data on volitional processes in many domains of everyday life from overeating to coping with tragedy, including academic learning. Most of the Kuhl–Beckmann volume reported short-term experiments with adult participants who performed tasks that appear artificial compared to most school tasks, homework assignments, or jobs in work settings (Corno & Kanfer, 1993).

Elsewhere (Corno, 1986; Corno & Randi, 1999) Kuhl's theory was applied to the particular case of academic self-regulation. Some of that writing bears repeating here. The ideas are complex and evolving, and researchers are reluctant to return to discarded theoretical constructs if there is a simpler convincing viewpoint. Kuhl demonstrated that there is both theoretical and functional utility to remaking the construct of volition, particularly in the case of academic learning.

Kuhl (1985) conceptualized volition after Ach (1910) as consisting of "postdecisional, self-regulatory processes that energize the maintenance and enactment of intended actions" (p. 90). Postdecisional, volitional, and action control processes were interchangeable for Kuhl, who considered self-regulatory processes as a broader category. Self-regulatory processes that are motivational precede or impact decisions about to be formed—including, for example, expected consequences, or judgments about the value of a course of action. Volitional processes come into play *after* a decision is made to learn or complete an academic task.

In education, motivational processes *promote* an intention to learn or to carry out a task, mediating the formation of decisions about work. Volitional processes *protect* the intention to learn from competing action tendencies and other potential distractions, mediating the enactment of decisions about work. Although volitional processes are central to self-regulation, other processes, such as task appraisals made in relation to performance, contribute to self-regulation in learning (see Zimmerman, chapter 1, this volume; Stanford Aptitude Seminar, in press).

According to Beckmann and Kuhl (1984):

> Kuhl... postulated that the presence of sufficient motivation and sufficient ability alone are not enough for the actual performance of an intended action unless the action consists of mere routine behavior or is controlled by external forces. When a person intends to perform a certain action, he or she is often subject to various external and/or internal forces which arouse alternative action tendencies. To ensure that the intended action rather than one of the competing action tendencies will be executed, the former has to be selectively strengthened and protected against interference until it is performed. In his theory of action control, Kuhl (1984) presumes that the efficiency of the process of action control is affected by two different states of the organism, i.e., action vs. state orientation (p. 226).

Action- versus state-orientation is defined as a relatively stable disposition that persons manifest in situations that require coping. For example, Kuhl (1981) demonstrated that extended exposure to uncontrollable aversive events, coupled with a tendency to focus on these events rather than on an appropriate plan of action, results in an inability to act. He called this inhibition a *state* orientation. In contrast, when adult subjects are asked to think aloud while solving problems, or to plan a given course of action, they often can be oriented to take immediate *action*.

Dispositional action-orientation tendencies in adults can be measured by questionnaire. The Action-Control Scale (ACS) includes three 20-item subscales for performance, failure, and decision-making situations. One item from the ACS *performance* subscale is, "When I've finished an excellent piece of work," (either) "I like to do something else for a while," or "It makes me want to do some more in the same area." One item from *the failure* scale is, "When my work is labeled 'unsatisfactory,'" (either) "Then I really dig in" or "At first I am stunned." An item from the *decision* scale is, "If I had work at home" (either) "I would often have problems getting started" or "I would usually start immediately." Each subscale asks respondents to provide information about work, leisure, and social activities.

Although Kuhl's theory explained the general case, and much of his early research related action orientation tendencies to behavior, his recent work turned to process explanations in the person–situation interface. Using personality-systems interaction (PSI) theory, Kuhl (1996, 2000) conceptualized different modes of volitional control, allowed for the operation of volition below the level of consciousness, and undertook studies of the conditions under which the different modes operate.

For example, Kuhl made no assumption that all classroom tasks demand deliberate volitional control; features of tasks can supplant the need for a student to protect learning goals. Motivational enhancements such as fantasy elements or games function to make learning goals so appealing that a student can concentrate on other aspects of self-regulation (Lepper & Malone, 1987). In another sense, a task can seem to "complete itself" when there is sufficient challenge and interest-appeal (Csikszentmihalyi, 1975). Conscious mechanisms for self-control—what Kuhl (2000) called the "inner dictatorship" (p. 115)—then yield to an openness to self-related thoughts and emotions—the "inner democracy" (p. 115). In this case, the volitional program runs as if on autopilot.

Hypothetical situations in which some form of volition is likely to be in demand include the following:

- Students are required to complete assigned tasks and are not free to choose other actions at that time.
- There is sufficient "noise" in the classroom/task environment to distract students from task-related goals that they have elected to undertake.
- Other interests and subjective goals compete with the intent to work or learn, thereby dividing student attention.
- Students develop performance anxiety that obstructs or interferes with the wish to take action. Students then may be "held up" by a rising sense of self-consciousness that suggests the need for volitional control.
- When students believe they possess the skills to perform a task, yet sense the need for deliberate effort to achieve success, then protective moves again are likely to be made. (Bandura, 1986; see Schunk, chapter 4, this volume).

The first two situations emphasize features of external, task environments. The remaining situations describe unions of persons and situations. For example, self-consciousness would be hypothesized to occur when a student perceives a task as difficult and public performance is a requirement. Conditions like these characterize many academic learning and study situations, thereby inviting a mantle of volitional control.

The distinction between motivation and volition should now be clear: Motivational aspects of learning and performance, such as interests and goals, shape intentions and establish commitments. Motivationally relevant cognitions, such as perceptions of efficacy and attributions for past performance, can either fuel task involvement or bring it to a halt. Volition becomes important partly *because* intentions are fragile and people often waver on commitments. The volitional aspects of SRL help a person give priority to commitments, and function to steer involvement along.

Practical Utility

Why volition is useful in education should be evident if one considers for a moment what life in classrooms would be like without student volition. That is why kindergarten teachers, primed to confront pandemonium, work out classroom reward systems for adherence to rules of conduct and strive to develop their students' self-control. As youngsters move along in years, becoming increasingly able to manage schoolwork, their performance continues to benefit from refinements in volitional control. By internalizing school rules and eventually assuming personal responsibility, a student learns to handle the growing complexities of academic study and achievement (Winne, 1995). Again, Kuhl (2000) would say that the form of volition develops from that of inner dictator to more of an inner democracy.

Teachers speak of specific cases, but volitional control issues sometimes dominate entire classrooms, or spill over to the larger school community. The so-called "motivational" problems in America's urban schools are well documented and growing (Brophy, 1998). However, the tendency for teachers and scholars to classify volitional issues together with motivational problems is mainly out of convention and does little to help in dealing with either. Factors that influence students' intentions to learn and concentrate may be less amenable to educational intervention than postdecisional, volitional factors.

Utility for Theory and Research

Why volition is useful from the standpoint of scientific psychology is perhaps less obvious but no less important. As Snow (1986) argued, reintroducing the volitional construct deepens psychological theory, permitting a better understanding of how cognition, affection, and conation work together (Hilgard, 1980; see also Snow & Farr, 1987, p. 33).

Another ancient construct only recently brought back into modern theory, conation is defined as the state of unrest that characterizes both motivation and volitional functions. It thus integrates components of motivation and volition, forcing study of their interaction. Like volition, conation has yet to be embraced by some researchers; however, there is no denying the theoretical symmetry and parsimony of three basic psychological functions. What is more, when the full range of conative processes is studied in conjunction with cognition, and when affect is seen as central and not peripheral to performance, human behavior and performance can be better explained (Corno, in press; Snow, Corno, & Jackson, 1996). For example, striving toward clearly established goals may result in success even when cognitive processing and affective engagement are inadequate. However, many goals will not be reached without striving, and striving is meaningless without goals.

Theory in specialty areas such as social psychology is also evolving. The best example may be Bandura's theory of social learning and behavior change, now complicated and enriched by a focus on social–cognitive processes (Bandura, 1993; Zimmerman, chapter 1, this volume). The evolution of a process-theoretic viewpoint in social psychology permits a healthy alignment with developmentalists who have long held that the internalization of behavior and thinking modeled by others (i.e., social construction) is a keystone in cognitive–social development (McCaslin and Hickey, chapter 7, this volume; Vygotsky, 1962; Wertsch, 1979). When one believes, with Bandura (1974), that humans are "partial architects of their own destinies" (p. 867), then there is no need to side philosophically with determinism or free will. Instrumental contingencies become internalized over the course of development to regulate action; but humans also apply appropriate instrumentalities purposefully as situations demand. Having volition can then be seen as the tendency to mobilize and maintain self-regulation in given situations, not simply as the manifestation of learned contingencies.

The reintroduction of volition to theory and research in educational psychology is also important given the rising stature of motivation as a recent interest of educational researchers (compare Ames & Ames, 1984 with Pintrich & Schunk, 1996). Theoretical contributions from American psychologists, including Weiner, Bandura, and Deci, have fueled solid lines of continuing research on attributions, self-efficacy, and the educational environments that affect self-regulation directly. Just as Kuhl (1985) reconceptualized Ach's theory of volition in information processing terms, so these psychologists reach down to the processes involved in traditional motivation theories. Performance attributions, expectations, self-observations, and self-evaluations are no longer defined as cognitions with motivational overtones, but actually recognized as processes combining both functions. Because none of these cognitive–motivation theories *focuses on* postdecisional processes that protect intentions to learn, however, the particular problem of volition goes unaddressed.

One reason to rectify this situation is the potential for teaching children rudiments of volitional control, when it seems impossible to change their prior reinforcement histories with school. Prior performances in a variety of more or less academic situations shape both attributions and beliefs about efficacy for school-related work; better volitional control mediates these relations. Equally difficult to accomplish, some feel, are the changes to instruction and organization of educational settings recommended by Deci and Ryan (1985), changes that allow students and

TABLE 6.1
Categories of Volitional Control and Specific
Volitional Control Strategies

I. Covert processes of self-control

A. Control of cognition
  1. Attention control*
  2. Encoding control*
  3. Information-processing control*
B. Emotion control*
C. Motivation control
  1. Incentive escalation*
  2. Attribution
  3. Instruction

II. Overt processes of self-control: Environmental control

A. Control of the task situation
  1. Task control
  2. Setting control
B. Control of others in the task setting
  1. Peer control
  2. Teacher control

Note. *Volitional controls identified by Kuhl
(1985); in this article Kuhl equated motivation control with incentive escalation, and did not distinguish the subprocesses of environmental control.

teachers more equivalent control. This, of course, is an empirical matter,
which is the final reason to revive volition in educational research—to
spawn studies that might resolve this and other issues.

Volitional Subprocesses of SRL

Elsewhere (Corno, 1986; Corno & Randi, 1999) examples were given
of six ways students can use volitional control strategically. Table 6.1
presents an expanded list of Kuhl's six volitional strategies, organized by
categories of volitional subprocesses.

Asterisks mark Kuhl's (1985) six strategies in the table. Several of these
involve efforts to control covert, internal processes. Controlling attention to information and encoding, for example, is a form of metacognition. Likewise, by consciously controlling emotion and thinking ahead
to positive or negative outcomes, an individual can manage the affective
and motivational aspects of learning and performance. How to engage in
successful self-control has been a focus of cognitive–behavioral interventions in the field of clinical psychology for some time (see Meichenbaum,

1977). Another way of viewing volitional controls, then, is at a meta-level; they are aspects of *self- and task-management* that facilitate learning indirectly (see Dansereau, 1985; Thomas, Strage, & Curley, 1988).

Volitional strategies are trainable. Kuhl's research (see Kuhl, in press) even manipulates strategy use experimentally and assesses the conditions under which volition will be called into play. An important issue with respect to training volitional strategies is that these are subtle aspects of mental functioning that vary across learners and may be disrupted (at least temporarily) during early learning. Intervention with young learners is therefore promising. Although there is a certain parallel in cognitive strategy instruction (Pressley et al., 1995; Weinstein & Mayer, 1986), strategic volition may be less amenable than most cognitive strategies to short-term training.

Volition continues to develop through adolescence based on a growing awareness of one's own functioning, including cognition, motivation, and affection. This developmental process is heavily influenced by socialization practices in the home and elsewhere (Kuhl & Kraska, 1989; Kuhn & Ho, 1980). It therefore seems likely that successful volitional strategy training will involve the kind of naturalistic guidance, or participant modeling instruction, that has come to characterize more effective forms of cognitive and metacognitive strategy training (Collins, Brown, & Newman, 1989; Corno & Randi, 1999; McKeachie, Pintrich, & Lin, 1985; Paris, Byrnes, & Paris, chapter 8, this volume; Pressley et al., 1995).

The second major category shown in Table 6.1 reflects efforts to control the self by controlling one's environment. Human factors research emphasizes the value of modifying or adapting the person–task interface for more effective or efficient performance. Some people instinctively modify poorly designed tasks, by streamlining steps, for example, or reorganizing priorities. Others cleverly manipulate other people in the task situation to help them get work done. Combining these strategies is one way to reduce excessive task demands — streamline the task, but also seek assistance, and find a way to hush-up distracting peers. The general category of environmental control includes all of these things.

Each of the entries in Table 6.1 can be illustrated further as they might be observed in classroom tasks. To take first the area of covert self-control, such actions as diverting one's eyes from the class clown or tuning out excess noise would be examples of *attention control*. *Encoding control* involves selectively thinking about those aspects of a task that facilitate completion. Thus students can opt to rehearse only the material on which they will be tested, or plan out steps for completing a task mentally. *Information-processing control* is, in Kuhl's (1985) terms, the "definition of stop rules for information processing" (p. 106). A student who processes information efficiently (or makes decisions efficiently) quickly assesses steps needed to perform a task and then gets down to business, thus "optimizing the motivational power of the intent" to learn (p. 106).

One may also, as Waters and Andreassen (1983) suggested, avoid adopting a style that overtaxes the processing system, or elect a brief timeout from a tedious task as a way of regrouping and refreshment. This example suggests a different way of looking at some students' so-called "off-task" behavior. Mobilizing volitional processes when situations demand maximizes the efficiency of information processing, supports the intention to learn, and increases the liklihood of follow-through on tasks. One could think of strategic volition as a way to insure the smooth running of an easily crashed central processor.

To control negative affect during learning, students may inhibit or alter detrimental emotional states such as worry. *Emotion control* may involve using positive inner speech to help maintain task engagement: "I can't worry about this; I can't get irrational." It might also include admonishments that produce sufficient guilt to carry a person through, or converting an unpleasant emotion to one that is more agreeable. A student could cope with the anxiety associated with waiting for test results by thinking of interesting and relaxing things, for example.

For Kuhl, *motivation control* reflects prioritization of intentions; in school, learning intentions, for example, must be given priority over other, competing intentions. It may be preferable to socialize with friends, but doing homework has to come first after school. Sensing a lapse of motivation for completing a given task, a student can think ahead to the consequences of failing and the pleasure that will come instead with success. In some publications, Kuhl called such thinking *incentive escalation* (see Kuhl, 1984). Zimmerman and Pons (1986) used the similar idea of *self-consequences* to represent both imagined and actually arranged outcomes. Both of these terms are more descriptive than the term *motivation control*, which is a more general category that subsumes several other subprocesses (just as we saw with control of cognition).

Research has identified some of these motivation-control subprocesses. In addition to incentive escalation (or control of expected outcomes and values), a student can control motivation with an accurate analysis of causality ("I know this material, and how to approach it;" or, "I failed, but I can succeed next time if I study better"). Self-instructing also works wonders: "I missed most of these; reread closely and take notes." Later on I shall discuss variations on each of these subprocesses.

The overt processes of self-control reflect strategic control of the environment. These are more easily assessed than the covert strategies, and probably develop naturally in students' home and school environments. For example, doing homework provides an opportunity for many children to learn to manage time and create a proper workspace (Xu & Corno, 1998). In Kuhl's taxonomy of volitional controls, environmental control is the most amenable to direct intervention (Kuhl, 1984). Again, environmental control includes both changes to be made in task situations (i.e., changing the task itself or the task setting, such as where and when a task is completed), and changes in the behavior of other people who support the task (i.e., typically, teachers and peers).

Individuals can also arrange environmental contingencies to help themselves complete difficult tasks. For example, a student can set proximal subgoals for a task, rather than more distal commitments that would be harder to carry out. Similarly, there is value to self-rewards for hard work and imposed penance for dawdling. These changes help students gain control of the *task outcome*. *Controls in the task setting* are different and involve, for example, asking permission to move away from noisy peers, or using a calculator, word processor, or other equipment in the interest of efficiency. Students may also manipulate their own intentions in more subtle ways, for example, by surrounding themselves with hard-working peers, or asking a good friend to provide social support and avoid references to past failures. Such controls complement direct efforts to obtain extra assistance or favors from teachers, and fall into the subclass *control of others in the task setting*. They enhance concentration and affect as well as control behavior.

VOLITION-RELATED RESEARCH ON SRL

Three types of studies reflect the range of research being conducted to capture SRL in academic settings. Various *descriptive* studies identify and document self-regulation moves by students during regular academic tasks. Some of these show evidence of strategic volition. Second, *correlational* research relates self-regulation (and volitional controls) to student aptitude profiles, task factors, and performance outcomes such as academic achievement. The correlational studies distinguish SRL from general cognitive ability and document its independent contributions to school performance outcomes for different types of tasks. Third, there is a growing body of *experimental* research on tasks designed to elicit or teach students various aspects of self-regulation; here, researchers compare the performance of experimental groups to that of controls who receive different tasks. Classroom experiments vary task and instructional conditions to promote self-regulation directly and assess resultant academic performance.

Some Leads from Descriptive Studies

In many descriptive studies of learning and performance, evidence of volition is implicit; detective work is needed to find it. For example, Dyson (1987) conducted an in-depth analysis of the "spontaneous talk" of eight elementary students during language arts periods taught by the same teacher. As the children interacted with their peers to complete writing assignments, they were audiotaped. Dyson then combined these protocol data with participant observation records to conceptualize student collaborative effort. Her data show students spontaneously using volitional control to complete school tasks effectively.

In language arts, there was evidence that students (a) asserted themselves to manage peers ("I was sitting here"), (b) were self-congratulatory ("I knew that"), and (c) anticipated audience reactions to their own written work. Noting that something might be "hard" for readers to understand was a student move Dyson interpreted as an incentive to rewrite. The study documents the importance of active mental and environment control to effective written work. And yet, volition was not implicated per se.

In a different vein, a descriptive study by Johnston (1985) documented the *lack* of effective self-regulation in the academic efforts of reading-disabled adults. Johnston used a case analysis method, and held interactive assessment sessions with three males in which he elicited think-aloud reports and oral reading performance. The think-aloud protocols included spontaneous introspections and retrospections. In addition to the conceptual problems his respondents displayed, Johnston noted extensive use of dysfunctional styles of coping. These included, for example, bluffing, avoiding the teacher, and listening for oral instructions.

Such moves allowed participants to function in society even though they were largely illiterate. The coping style also effectively prevented efforts these men may have made to overcome their illiteracy, and so proved self-handicapping in the long run. Johnston also noted the frequency with which such coping was accompanied by negative affective responses (debilitating anxiety and stress).

One implication is that overcoming the problem of adult reading difficulty may require self-management interventions in addition to improvements in reading skills. For example, students can learn how to cope with failure effectively, through balanced performance attributions that suggest a second try. Persistence is more likely when past failures can be attributed, for example, to multiple causes, only some of which can be personally controlled (e.g., "Perhaps I didn't try hard enough, but I was also given poor instruction.)" In recent investigations of the workstyles of learning disabled students, Butler (1996) specifically targeted volitional deficiencies as potentially critical areas for intervention.

Rohrkemper (1986) conducted still another type of descriptive study. She interviewed urban elementary school students with different levels of academic ability as they completed math problems of varying difficulty. Her interest was in examining "inner speech" accompanying problem solving, under easy and more difficult conditions. Eighty-four students, balanced by mathematics ability and gender, participated. A structured questionnaire/interview asked students to identify things they might "say to themselves" while solving particular mathematics problems. Categories of statements included motivational remarks as well as self-instruction (e.g., "I take my time and try to figure the problem out;" I make a plan.)" The strategic self-instruction reflected some of the aspects of motivation control previously defined.

These students used inner speech to regulate task performance irrespective of individual differences in ability and gender. There were differences in the amount and type of inner speech, depending on task difficulty: Less inner speech occurred on difficult tasks, and more self-related (as opposed to task-related) speech occurred during easy tasks. Again, the study shows that self-regulatory statements specifically referring to volitional controls occur spontaneously among students at this age level, even among those with different ability profiles. McCaslin and Hickey, (chapter 7, this volume) now refer to volitional controls in their continuing work on inner speech in self-regulated learning.

A final descriptive account derives from data by Leinhardt and Putnam (1987), who produced videotapes of fifth-grade students as they learned about astronomy under different instructional treatments. The videotape data again show spontaneous use of self-regulation and a clear instance of encoding control: One student said, in an interview during which he viewed a videotape of his class lesson in mathematics, "Well, I was thinking about... what she was saying because it was something new so I had to keep my eyes on it 'cause this is on our MAP test... it's kind of important" (p. 575). Again, however, the term *volition* was not in the language these researchers used to interpret data.

The Bulk of the Work: Correlational Studies

Correlational work dominates SRL research, as evidenced from national studies (see Jan Simons & Beukhof, 1987) to international handbooks (Boekaerts, Pintrich, & Zeidner, 2000). However, some research takes up questions of volition directly. For example, DeWitte and Lens (in press) investigated academic procrastination in college students using self-reports. They also measured study intentions, time spent studying, student's perspectives on studying, and optimism as a personality trait. Correlational analyses showed that optimistic procrastinators postpone their intentions to study with little guilt whereas pessimistic procrastinators feel badly. An additional finding was that persistence of procrastinators and their performance on an open-ended response question benefitted from a focus on details of the task, rather than a broad perspective on studying. In this research, both personality and workstyle mediated performance.

Such direct investigation of volitional questions contrasts with the frequently-cited correlational research of Zimmerman and his colleagues who used a structured interview procedure to measure SRL. Zimmerman and Pons (1986) asked eighty students from higher and lower tracks of a suburban high school to "indicate the methods they used to participate in class, to study, and to complete their assignment" (p. 617). The interview included specific examples from classroom learning, homework, and studying for tests. Student responses were coded into various categories of self-regulated and nonself-regulated learning. At least 5 of the 14 categories of SRL identified reflected processes of volitional control, although the authors did not use this term in their description. There were, for example, instances of students rearranging the task environment to make learning easier, seeking information and social assistance, selecting out more from less important material to study, and imagining or actually arranging positive and negative outcomes for working.

Results showed that frequency of SRL strategy use significantly distinguished higher from lower achievers. Overall, regression analyses showed self-reported use of SRL to account for 36% to 41% of the variance in both verbal and quantitative standardized test scores; this was over and above percentages accounted for by parent level of education and gender. Zimmerman and Pons produced a more refined measure of SRL, as well as good evidence (despite their lack of reference) for the practical and theoretical value of SRL's volitional aspects (see Zimmerman, chapter 1, this volume for an update).

Another type of correlational study is illustrated by Blumenfeld and Meece (1988), who categorized middle-school science lessons by difficulty level, type of social organization, and procedural complexity using field observations. These different lesson types were then distinguished by the extent to which they produced or lessened involvement and cognitive engagement, as reported by 191 students in questionnaires and interviews. The student self-report data again included questions about SRL strategy use during the lessons observed. Only one of these questions, regarding help seeking, was volitional.

Although reported strategy use in this study related significantly to students' perceptions of lesson involvement, strategy use was unrelated to performance outcomes such as test scores and grades. Among several possible explanations the authors provided for these results were a lack of correspondence between what is demanded in lessons and what is tested, and a lack of student ability to *employ* strategies on tests. This latter hypothesis raises the possibility that volitional strategies are most predictive of performance outcomes, and yet again these were underrepresented on the researchers' strategy questionnaire.

Measures that tap volitional components directly need to be placed in a correlational network with other indicators of SRL strategy use. Bembenutty and Karabenick (1998) obtained self-reports of SRL from college students and related these to measures of "academic delay of gratification." They conceived academic delay as a likely outcome of successful SRL strategy use. Their delay scale asked students to report on met deadlines, library use, peer interactions, and studying, for example. Students with higher delay scores showed more constructive motivation and better strategy use, but the strongest correlations appeared between delay scores and students' reports of how they used their time and studied. Again there is the suggestion that elements of volition play an important role in academic work.

Perhaps the most direct measure of volition related to schooling is McCann's (1999) Academic Volitional Strategies Inventory. Included are questions beginning with the stems "I tell myself..." and "I think about..." and ending with "you can do it!" or "get to it and concentrate..." Each item reflects strategies represented in Table 1. McCann's dissertation, using the Inventory with a sample of 246 college students and a causal correlational analysis, found course grades to be enhanced through cognitive engagement, which in turn was supported by volitional control.

The Rare Experiments

Three experimental studies illustrate what is possible with experimental research in education, although well-designed experiments remain rare.

Shapiro (1988) conducted a semester-long dissertation study with a sample of 156 remedial mathematics students in a large urban college. The treatment was a specially designed textbook providing worked examples of algebra problems these students encountered in their remedial coursework. In early lessons of the text, problems were accompanied by strategic problem-solving statements, as well as various volitional prompts.

For example, a problem included suggestion of an efficient problem-solving algorithm as well as the idea that students should pay careful attention to the information given. Some problems also suggested ways to handle frustration and points at which the student might want to try another solution. Such prompts were "faded" in later lessons, but the text left space for students to record their own efforts and tactics. Homework assignments on parts of the text, criterion-referenced, and standardized posttests served as dependent measures.

The textbook was randomly assigned to classes in an experimental group; a traditional text, covering identical content, was used by classes in a comparable control group taught by the same instructor. Nested ANOVAs controlling for teacher differences showed results favoring the treated group to be statistically significant for all measures (effect sizes averaged .40). This study showed that students can be taught by text to use the cognitive and volitional strategies that mark SRL in basic algebra, and that strategy use results in higher achievement.

Shapiro dealt with all the obstacles confronting experimental field research and still produced supportive results; moreover, her little-known study demonstrated that strategy use can be learned through *textbook* instruction alone and does not necessarily require teacher intervention.

Another type of experiment, which should be seen more frequently, examined aptitude-instructional treatment interactions in the acquisition of strategic planning knowledge and self-regulatory skills in an intellectual computer game. Mandinach (1987) gave 48 urban junior high school students after-class instruction in a "hunt-the-monster" computer problem-solving game. Students either (a) explored the game's parameters with minimal intervention by the instructor (they used a "discovery learning" approach); or (b) they received modeling in optimal moves along with instructor-guided practice and gradually faded prompts.

Students representing different levels of cognitive–intellectual ability were assigned randomly to treatments and attended several individual sessions with the experimenter. A variety of process and outcome measures reflecting strategic planning and follow-through ranged from "hard data" such as computer-generated response latencies, error patterns, and game scores, to transfer tasks and qualitative field notes, student drawings, and spontaneous verbalizations. A combination of latency data and student self-statements served as indicators of self-regulation and its volitional aspects.

Results showed that higher ability students significantly outperformed lower ability students on gaming measures and transfer tasks. Higher ability students also gave more evidence of self-regulation, on average, than lows. All students, regardless of ability, performed best in the participant-modeling treatment; however, this main effect was not statistically significant. An interaction effect showed that lower ability students, in particular, benefitted from modeling; their performance was markedly lower in discovery learning.

Mandinach concluded from these data that ability differences influenced profitability from the game-playing instruction. Although able players demonstrated more evidence of self-regulation on average, some higher ability players never displayed evidence of self-regulated learning. Mandinach did not compare frequencies of volitional strategies with those of other SRL strategies, however.

In a follow-up to this experiment, Mandinach (Mandinach & Linn, 1986; 1987) conducted qualitative case studies of the higher ability students she considered "superstars" by virtue of their performance on this task. She found that extensive use of self-regulation and strategic planning knowledge defined the work efforts of these individuals. Thus, it again appears that strategic self-regulation can be learned by a particular form of instruction targeting specific academic tasks.

This study adds the caveat that *able students* will use SRL strategies readily. Because a "read only" version of instruction was not provided, we have no way of knowing whether a guided-modeling computer text akin to Shapiro's math textbook would produce results similar to Mandinach's experimenter-directed instruction.

A final type of experimentation is illustrated by a line of recognized research by Scardamalia and Bereiter on the teaching of elementary writing and composition (Scardamalia & Bereiter, 1983; 1985; 1993). This work, like Shapiro's and Mandinach's, exemplifies the current style of experimentation in education, where instructional treatments are based on analyses of the underlying cognitive and self-regulatory skills necessary to perform a particular task as reflected in protocols of "experts" at work. Also like Shapiro and Mandinach, Scardamalia and Bereiter provided instruction that modeled expert self-regulation during writing, and guided performance, with gradually reduced support.

These authors focused on instruction in the planning, writing, and revising phases of written composition. Teachers addressed each phase separately, initially with teacher–learner interaction, and later requested that students "fly solo." Students received examples of statements they could say to themselves to aid with idea generation and improved writing techniques; many of these statements were self-regulatory or volitional in nature (Scardamalia & Bereiter, 1985). Think-aloud protocols, obtained following instruction while students produced written work, gave evidence of strategy use. The quality of written products for students working under experimental and comparable control conditions was then compared.

Several related experiments are reported in the examples just cited, all of which demonstrate significant effects favoring elementary students instructed in the manner described. Positive effects appear on the quality of strategies reflected in protocols, on time spent in planning, and on the quality of text produced.

There is a notable method of successful instruction common to all the experiments described, suggesting the conditions under which self-regulatory skills can be learned. Collins, Brown, and Newman (1989) singled out work by Palinscar and Brown and Scardamalia and Bereiter (along with Schoenfeld, 1985) as examples of this form of instruction. Elsewhere, I (Corno, 1987) listed some of the different names for this type of instruction, including "participant modeling" (after Bandura, 1977), and "cognitive apprenticeship" (Collins, Brown, & Newman, 1989):

> There are two key reasons for [Scardamalia & Bereiter's] success. First... their methods help students build a new conception of the writing process. Students initially consider writing to be a linear process of knowledge telling. By explicitly modeling and scaffolding expert processes, they are providing students with a new model of writing that involves planning and revising. Most children found this view of writing entirely new.... Moreover, because students rarely if ever see writers at work, they tend to hold naive beliefs about the nature of expert writing... Live modeling helps convey... struggles, false starts, discouragement, and the like. Modeling also demonstrates for students that in evolving and decomposing a complex set of goals for their writing, expert writers often treat their own thoughts as objects of reflection and inquiry... (p. 13)

The result is budding self-regulation. It remains to be shown whether or not volitional and other aspects of SRL can be learned in the absence of modeling, and the extent to which live models are necessary with younger students.

I have illustrated the range and types of research that contribute to a better understanding of SRL and how it intersects with volitional control. A key question for this early generation of SRL research was, "What aspects of self-regulation are most relevant for academic work, and how can these best be taught to students for whom they might be of benefit?" Descriptive research on processes used by more effective learners to complete academic tasks helped to answer the first part of this question. The second part is addressed by exploring the ways students use and acquire self-regulatory propensities naturally, through socialization and modeling. Later studies that inculcate strategies by training or naturalistic instruction will develop attunements for self-regulated learning.

EXAMINING OTHER EVIDENCE OF VOLITION
IN CLASSROOMS

The previous section described work that touches on volitional aspects of self-regulation more or less indirectly. Our research at Teachers College during the past decade centered squarely on volitional strategies in classroom tasks. We began with a microanalysis of descriptive data in a few small sample studies and moved to experimental designs. Our method in the descriptive studies was to control enough task variables so volition would likely be important to success, and to search for varied evidence of volitional strategy use by students as they complete tasks. We assumed, following Kuhl (in press), that different task conditions (i.e., products, operations, and resources; see Doyle, 1983) will influence student use of volition.

One dissertation study 6 weeks long involved an analysis of peer distractions as students worked cooperatively in small groups. Panagiotopolous (1986) observed 21 fifth graders in a self-contained public school classroom in the Bronx. Students were ethnically mixed and performing slightly above average on standardized achievement tests.

Several of Kuhl's situations that induce volition were designed into the tasks for this study: The tasks were required by the teacher, who expected completion during the time allotted with all of the potential distractions that collaborative work provides. In addition, the work was familiar to students, and pitched at a moderately low difficulty level (tasks involved alphabetization, dictionary use, arithmetic, etc.). The cooperative task used Slavin's (1983) Student Teams-Achievement Divisions, in which teams cooperate in the completion of predesigned, objectives-based materials. As recommended by Slavin, teams were balanced on indicators of academic performance, gender, and ethnicity. Teams completed the same materials in 30-minute sessions that were audiotaped and later transcribed. The verbal protocol data reflect task-management as well as task-completion processes.

Our interest was in the extent to which students enlisted volitional control to complete assigned tasks as a group, under otherwise regular classroom conditions. The intent was to see which, if any, of the strategies these fifth graders had internalized through their own experiences, that is, which would appear without prompting. We hoped then to use that information as scaffolds for teaching other strategies that might require direct development or training.

A test battery, administered prior to the study, served as a classification device. We measured two aspects of students' general intellectual ability using a test of analytical reasoning (Raven, 1958), and the verbal and mathematics subscales of the California Achievement Test

(CTB/McGraw-Hill, 1977). In addition, to obtain an index of motivation, we measured perceived competence using Harter's (1979) *Perceived Competence Scale for Children,* cognitive and general-competence subscales.

Two major aspects of these data are of interest. Some of the data are described in detail to illustrate another form of evidence for volition that can be obtained from classroom research.

First, coded transcripts from all six cooperative sessions were used to classify data into categories reflecting the ways that students worked in groups. Independent coders reached 100% agreement when classifying each segment of the transcript as "main task" and "alternative task." Agreement reached 92% in classifying "main task" remarks as either task-"management" or "completion"' activities. *Task-management* activities involved volitional controls such as tracking and gathering information for completing the task, moving oneself and other students along in their respective roles, checking progress, handling distractions, motivating oneself and others, and the like. *Task-completion* activities involved moves to actually *do* the task, such as subtracting or adding out loud during math tasks and repeating the alphabet aloud during alphabetization. A third main task category was defined as *instruction* to show the amount of times that one student instructed another, which, incidentally, also served volitional functions.

We computed mean percentages of verbal activity for all cooperative sessions in language and math. Students were involved in alternative tasks 20% to 25% of the time, and instructing one another less than 5% of the time. By far the bulk of their main task work in both subject areas was management activity. Students spent two thirds of their total time, on average, managing the task at hand. Moves to complete the task that were verbalized (students were specifically asked to say their answers out loud) amounted to 5% to 9% of time spent, with the larger percentage being in math.

A second aspect of the data of interest are segments of verbal protocols that reflect volitional control. We culled the protocols to locate segments illustrating the use of volitional strategies identified by Kuhl (1985) and listed in Table 6.1. We cross-coded the transcripts until we reached agreement on categorizations. The intent was to show students using volitional control in a group setting to move assigned tasks along.

I begin with an illustration of the types of evidence we identified, and then discuss some of the important roles students assume when working cooperatively. Our data provide a different way of viewing the roles of *task master* and *instructor* in cooperative-learning activities. Because we have data on each student's cognitive ability and perceived competence, we may also see which types of students were more inclined to use volitional control in this setting. This may result in hypotheses for future, more comprehensive examinations of individual differences in volitional control.

Types of Evidence

Sections from a representative transcript in mathematics show how students used several volitional tactics to move the task along. The groups were given answer sheets for the task, and told to check and help one another. The question, then, is what procedures for task management could be observed apart from checking and merely helping?

Anne:	Come on, let's work. You work.
Paul:	Okay. Eight times five is...
Honey:	Five times eight...
Paul:	Is forty.
Anne:	Don't tell him! He has to work it himself.
Honey:	Okay.
Anne:	Five times eight is...
Paul:	...is forty.
Paul:	It's forty! It's right. It's right!
Anne:	Oh, yeah!
Paul:	Five times one is five plus four is nine.
Sal:	Gotta round it to the nearest ten.
Paul:	That too.
Sal:	Zero times five. What's zero times five?
Anne:	How did you get nine hundred for that?
Sal:	Ten. Zero.
Paul:	Why'd you ask me if you knew? You don't know how to do nine hundred?
Anne:	I don't understand. Wait a minute. Ms. Panagiotopoulos! I can't understand this. I did all of this.
Sal:	Where's Honey? Honey, you got the answers? Let me see...
Ms.P:	Who's got the answers in your group?
Sal:	Her.
Anne:	Me.
Honey:	Me.
Anne:	You want to sit next to me?
Paul:	Naw, you give me your paper.

Sal: Paul, you know that. You know it, Paul.

Paul: I know it, but. . . I forgot we add the two.

Sal: My God, you're on number five. Well, I'm only on
          number six.

Honey: You better stop, Sal.

Anne: Eight times six? Oh yeah. Forty-eight. Why are you
          asking me? Why don't you ask yourself? Count on
          your fingers. Oh, I hate this so much.

Paul: I love it so much. Oh, this is very nice.

Anne: I like it and I hate it.

This passage shows a prevalence of environmental control. Peer control is used here by Paul, Sal, and Anne to keep themselves on task. These students successfully protect their own time by warding others off ("Why'd you ask me. . .?"). Getting hold of the answer sheet is one way to check one's own work. Paul uses knowledge of successful results to self-motivate ("It's right!"). Anne also uses information-processing control when she urges everyone (herself included) to work. Anne's comments reflect self-attributions, attempted teacher control, and emotion control.

When students work together in groups, they use a number of different techniques to keep one another going. Some of these techniques provide more encouragement than others. The use of informed feedback, self-attribution, and specific suggestions for how to attack the task are all constructive ways of motivating oneself and others (Brophy, 1998). Some students used these techniques spontaneously in their groups.

Anne, who used self-attribution, emotion control, and instruction as motivational tools, displayed average ability and high perceived competence on the pretest. Paul scored highly on the ability measures, but low in perceived competence. Paul's behavior pattern was to self-motivate, bring emotion to the task, and try to control his peers. Sal, who evidenced peer-control as well, scored average on ability and low on perceived competence.

Little can be made of these data on individual differences except to look across other segments of the transcript for similar patterns and other sensible relationships. Discernable patterns might be used to form hypotheses for future investigations. A more immediate implication is that strategies used by a few students in group work are simultaneously observed by the others, creating the possibility for vicarious learning through observation of a model (Bandura, 1986). One could also envision a computer programmed to help students make different types of motivational statements to themselves when they falter, hesitate, or express negative emotions.

Two Leadership Roles in Cooperative Learning: Active Steps to Insure One's Own Learning

A second excerpt from a mathematics transcript paints a different picture. In this session, Honey assumes a leadership role we referred to as "task master:" She tries hard to move the group along:

Honey:	(To the group) He does all of it. Do all of it. Do the first, no, do the first row and then you check it. Do the next row and then you check it. No, don't do that. Do the first row, okay?
Michelle:	Right?
Honey:	Five is four: two, five; three, one. Right. Now do that. I said do the whole row. You checked it?
Phillip:	Yeah.
Honey:	You sure? Everything's right?
Phillip:	Every single thing.
Honey:	Check it. 'Kay? This is wrong.
Phillip:	Yeah, that's wrong.
Michelle:	Wait a minute. Let me just do the last one.
Honey:	Hurry, hurry, hurry, hurry.
Phillip:	Right? You check it? No, you didn't check it.
Honey:	Now, say the numbers. Start from the beginning. Say the numbers and he'll see if it's right or wrong. 'Kay? No, no, no, no! Like this, watch. 'Kay? Number four, two, three, one. Right. Let's don't say nothing cause we might get in trouble with this. (*Honey just had Michelle answer two questions for her.*)

One interpretation of Honey's behavior is that it mimics the way a person in authority behaves. Persons in authority cajole, badger, direct, entrap ("You sure? Everything's right?"), and model ("Like this, watch.") to get something done. Parents, teachers, and employers act this way often, and Honey has learned to do it well. She recapitulates it for us when placed in an authoritative role. Honey scored high in ability and average in perceived competence.

Children internalize the motivation controls displayed by parents and other authority figures and call them up themselves when managing their own tasks (Xu & Corno, 1998). Indeed, some researchers see social interactions as the developmental experiences necessary for the flowering of volitional control (Wentzel, 1991). Most important here, however, is the fact that *by managing others, Honey also manages herself.* Her active efforts at task management protect her own intention to concentrate; it is hard to get distracted when you are the task master.

Two interesting questions for future research are, then: How do students learn or develop volition from early social interactions with authority figures and older siblings; and How might parents and teachers emphasize the more positive, caring forms of motivation control with children (i.e., incentive escalation, attribution, instruction), rather than cajoling and badgering? Noddings (1984) argued that teachers can model the caring aspects of motivation at the same time that they teach subject matter. This suggestion deserves systematic investigation.

Transcripts from our study also present examples of students we identified as exceptional "teachers." Because it is part of the ethic of cooperative learning to help others, some students naturally assume a teaching role (Webb, 1983, 1992). As with the role of task master, assuming a teaching role during cooperative learning is another active way for a student to protect concentration. Insuring that everyone understands the task and carries out actions to complete it also insures one's own understanding and contribution. A close examination of the remarks made by one of these identifiably "good teachers" provides a second example of how taking an active role during cooperative learning also insures one's own learning.

Shpresa, a girl of average ability and average perceived competence, was told by others that she was a good teacher. The following are examples of Shpresa's teaching in math and language:

Shpresa:	Wait, wait, you did it wrong.
Henry:	Who me?
Shpresa:	The directions say you must, you must write your estimate and multiply, then you must write the answer.
Henry:	I got it right. No doubt about it.
Jackie:	So, shut up.
Shpresa:	No, you round, you round to the nearest hundred.
Henry:	You check.
Michelle:	Eight times five?
Shpresa:	You're supposed to know that, Michelle. The fives are the easiest. It's forty, right? You have to write the zero first right over here. Okay, now. One times five.

Michelle:	One times five.
Henry:	Shpresa, let me have the answer sheet. The teacher made a mistake.
Shpresa:	I know she made a mistake on, uh, four.
Shpresa:	You see? Would you be quiet? I wrote it easier for her. Eight times three so I wrote three eights. Eight plus eight is sixteen...
Ms. P:	Maybe she can't see your handwriting because you're sitting on that side.
Michelle:	Eight and seven you can't do. Okay.
Shpresa:	How'd you get that? How'd you, how'd you get twenty-five?
Ms. P:	Good teacher! Wow!
Salvatore:	Four. Six. Shpresa's a good teacher. Did you hear that?
Shpresa:	Okay, Michelle. Okay, listen. You have to all, all's you have to do is add. You estimate to the nearest ten thousand. If it says, listen um, if it says, if it says like six thousand by itself, then you can't estimate to the nearest ten, you just have to leave six thousand.

And in language arts:

Shpresa:	Come here. I'll, I'll help, do you understand?
Dina:	No.
Shpresa:	Okay, come here. Come sit here.
Shpresa:	Come here. See? You know, the *shwa* sound.
Salvatore:	(*Gasps*) You got the answer sheet?
Dina:	Shpresa, is this *nit* or *night?*
Shpresa:	I can't tell you.
Salvatore:	*Night.* She don't know her long I's and everything. She don't...
Shpresa:	You have to look over here. You have to look and you'll see, you'll see the things that uh, uh. Okay.
Salvatore:	I'm doing that.
Shpresa:	It says over, you could see it over here, the *shwa* sound. The *shwa*'s like this way. Where's the *shwa?* Where is it?

Salvatore:	You're a good teacher. (Shpresa laughs.)
Shpresa:	Okay. Joseph, you did pretty good on it. Do you know what to do, Adriano?
Adriano:	Huh?
Shpresa:	You almost finished?
Adriano:	No.
Shpresa:	You don't have to rush, you can take your time.

At the beginning of the math passage, Shpresa uses knowledge of results and direct instruction to control Henry's actions ("Wait, you did it wrong. The directions say..."). In so doing, she repeats the task's directions to herself. Later, in response to Michelle's question, Shpresa is at first admonishing with her attributions ("You're supposed to know that..."), but quickly offers some concrete suggestions that simplify the task (task control) and encourage Michelle to go on to the next item. When Henry asks for the answer sheet because he suspects a teacher error, Shpresa shows him that she has *already* identified the error herself.

This move sets Shpresa up as an authority over and above the instructional role she adopts. Taking control by simplifying the task for another student is again evident: Shpresa says, "I wrote it easier for her," and describes why this is so. This models the strategy of simplifying the task, thus providing other students with an example of one means to gain control. The teacher also suggests the idea of changing the setting (which again gains control) when she encourages Shpresa to move closer to the student she is helping. The excerpt from language sessions shows Shpresa modeling, self-checking, simplifying the task, using incentives ("Come here, I'll help..."), repeating directions, and offering positive reinforcement.

Again, these important instructional actions provide models that other students can use, and insure Shpresa's own involvement at the same time. If more students could learn to become "task masters" and "teachers" in cooperative learning, there might be fewer lapses in task-oriented behavior. This is not to suggest that every student must be a leader, but rather that there is room for more than one leader, and that the leadership roles in cooperative learning serve the volitional functions of protecting one's own task-related behavior as well as that of others.

Individual Differences in Volition

We can only speculate about individual differences based on data from this study. In examining the students who assumed leadership roles during cooperative learning, a pattern emerged. Six of the 21 students in the sample tended to assume either the task master or instructor role consistently. Honey and Anne, for example, were task masters in all sessions observed; Shpresa and Louis were always instructing. The tendency to assume these roles did not appear to be related to ability measures in our data—among the six students, all ability levels were observed. However, little can be made of this finding because previous research on cooperative learning *has* found higher ability students to display more helping behavior and instruction than lower ability students (Webb, 1992).

Perceived self-competence was high, on average, among the six students observed in our study. Assuming task-master or instructor roles in cooperative learning may thus relate to perceived ability to perform in school. This is an hypothesis derived directly from Kuhl's (2000) theory, which posits perceived ability as one condition for volitional control. The precise nature of this relationship sorely needs delineation. The relationship between efficacy and volitional control may be curvilinear, for example, and this makes theoretical sense (Stanford Aptitude Seminar, in press). There is likely to be an optimal amount of efficacy or personal confidence for given tasks or situations, with either an excess or a deficiency being potentially detrimental. We do not see indications here that "task-master" profiles differed from those of "instructors" in our data, although that, too, would be an interesting question for future research.

Our individual difference data are typical of those obtained in classroom research studies, namely, standardized measures of cognitive ability and self-concept. It would be interesting to add a version of Kuhl's action-orientation scale to this database. Kuhl (1982) found positive correlations between his dispositional measure and measures of test anxiety and achievement motivation on the order of .20. Because the action-orientation scale is specifically designed to tap into a personality factor related to behavioral indicators of volition, its validity could exceed that of other measures in predicting volitional strategy use in classroom tasks. A revised action-orientation scale that includes only items pertaining to classroom or academic tasks, and is valid and reliable for use by a younger population, would make a contribution. Based on knowledge of the students in our small sample who assumed leadership roles, we expect that action orientation would predict these tendencies more than the kinds of individual difference measures we obtained.

For example, classroom experiments could investigate relationships between student ACS scores and their performance under different academic tasks at different grade levels. Tasks could be designed or selected to create decision conflicts, as some experiments have done. Students of different orientation levels could be asked to think aloud, following

Kuhl (1981), while researchers observe their relative use of volitional controls under different conditions (e.g., when tasks vary in difficulty, interest, or support). A valid action-control scale would also be a useful way to augment standardized tests with noncognitive data.

Data from this study provide one lens on volition. Individual volition may be less important in completing cooperative tasks than when students work alone; cooperation allows students to protect each other's efforts, as just described. It is tempting to assume that the need for volition arises most when there is no one available but oneself to get a job done (when the task is not controlled by external forces). Nonetheless, we saw the kinds of distractions that peer work provides; students in this study were not equally oriented toward completing the assigned task in cooperative groups. There was a good deal of bantering coded as "alternative-task" behavior that would have been coded as "off task" in research focused on other processes.

A major limitation of verbal-protocol data is that the most expressive students are the ones displaying strategy use. Zimmerman and Pons (1986) handled this problem by attaching a 4-point scale to their interview protocol that asked each student to rate *frequency* of strategy use. This measure was a better predictor of student performance than counts of strategies mentioned in the interview. A computer could also elicit a similar rating.

To overcome verbal bias in cooperative audio transcripts, stimulated recall interviews might be used. For example, the audiotape could be played back to students who vary in verbal fluency. The interview would ask for their thoughts during the session. This method of data collection is labor-intensive. However, another dissertation by Xu (1994; see Xu & Corno, 1998) made profitable use of stimulated recall interviews following videotapes of third graders doing homework with their parents. Parents and children had different interpretations of the stresses and strains produced by homework, and the videotapes provided good opportunities for parents to explain the ways they tried to help. In some cases, there was clear evidence that children began to internalize parental modeling of volitional controls.

Further study is needed of how volitional control develops naturally in real-world instructional environments and imposed situations such as doing homework (Corno, 1994; Turner et al., 1998). For example, Bullock & Lutkenhaus (1988) examined volitional development in toddlers at play and work in the laboratory. Results showed predictable shifts in volition-related behavior, even during play, as children approached 3 years of age. The children's growth in volitional control related positively to measures of self-involvement, general self-regulation, and cognitive change.

THE ONGOING RESEARCH AGENDA

There are several agenda items for the next generation of research on volition in academic learning. A mapping is needed of the range of classroom tasks and situations that afford opportunities for volitional control by students (Mischel & Shoda, 1998). Students may or may not use volitional processes when working individually, in the absence of joint control. Some features of tasks will demand volition more than others; for example, tasks that hold little intrinsic interest for students would be difficult to complete. Boredom may operate, or not completing them may be reinforcing somehow (Wolters, 1998). Research needs to demonstrate the utility of volitional control in different classroom tasks.

There is also a need to follow studies like Zimmerman and Pons (1986) to learn how best to measure classroom strategy use, including performance-based indicators that are nonverbal (see Pressley et al., 1995). Studies like Mandinach's provide some nice leads; Mandinach required students to teach back what they had learned about the computer game (in this case, to a researcher). All students thus displayed performance evidence, not just those inclined to be verbal.

A recurrent topic has been the important educational outcomes that can be predicted reliably by use of volitional strategies. Task engagement and timely completion of tasks are important consequences of volitional management described in many other chapters in this volume. More than 20 years ago, classroom research substantiated the powerful link between student engagement and academic achievement (Berliner, 1979). What other affective and cognitive payoffs might there be to having volitional control in classrooms (Rohrkemper & Corno, 1988; Stanford Aptitude Seminar, in press)? What may be the downside risks (McCaslin & Good, 1996)?

Sorely needed are more and better experimental manipulations of volition in the educational arena. Can we induce action orientation easily, as Kuhl (1981) did with adults, in school children? Will asking them to think aloud while solving programs in a natural classroom setting be effective? What of the suggestion that computers could be programmed to remind users to self-reward, or press on to the next item when too much time has elapsed; or to rehearse, self-check, and the like (Scardamalia & Bereiter, 1993)? What effects might exposure to such a virtual parent have on student learning? Will this kind of volitional modeling be internalized for later use? Can students who lack volition learn it under these conditions? Or is social interaction with a human model who demonstrates volitional strategy use under difficult conditions important for some learners?

An another dissertation from our project by Trawick (1990) involved underprepared college students in a remedial counseling program at a local community college. She instructed students in positive self-speech and environmental controls that aid in managing academic work. She role-played things to do when facing a final exam, when choosing between a dinner date and homework, when concentration buckles during class, etc.. These role-play scenes were vehicles for delivering instruction in volitional strategy use, as well as measurement procedures for assessing learned strategies. However, not all of her students benefitted equally.

In further work, Randi and I (Corno & Randi, 1999; Randi & Corno, 1999) designed classroom tasks for elementary and secondary students that demand volition. Our "curriculum-embedded approach" to teaching SRL centers on the close match between the inherent messages of the quest genre, or literary "journey tale," and modern conceptions of volition. In future studies, teachers will attempt to develop an intellectual understanding of academic volition in their students, and the research design will vary high- and low-demand tasks systematically.

CONCLUSION

This chapter characterized the role of volition in conceptions of SRL. Volition is a propensity on which people differ. Many school situations demand volition, and volitional control is an important product of education (Corno, in press; Stanford Aptitude Seminar, in press). Volitional aspects are implicit in most assessments and existing studies of SRL, but evidence of volition is sufficiently important, both in theory and empirically, to be given more explicit attention than it has in years past.

We enrich scientific theory with clear concepts and integration. The promise of different and better assessment procedures and more interpretable relationships among interacting constructs likewise embellishes research. Ultimately, it may be possible to account for and redress some important issues in educational performance by understanding the common underpinnings of effective interventions such as cognitive-behavioral therapies and cognitive-emotional strategy training in schools. It will be similarly important to achieve a better integration of social-cognitive theories of motivation and theories of volition in SRL.

In the area of volitional control, practical implications abound. Conscious use of volitional strategies can assist individuals to protect their best-laid plans—whether the plan is for a researcher to produce written work while teaching graduate courses and raising children, for a student to follow a teacher's agenda when other interests loom large, or for a teacher to modify distracting mannerisms. When I talk to an audience about theory and research on volition, I find that people want to improve their own volitional capabilities; they are eager to refine volitional skills and become more resourceful. We look forward to future research that shows them how.

REFERENCES

Ach, N. (1910). *Uber den willensakt und das temperament.* [On the will and temperament]. Leipzig, Germany: Quelle & Meyer.

Ames, C., & Ames, R. (Eds.) (1984). *Student motivation.* New York: Academic Press.

Bandura, A. (1974). Behavior theory and the models of man. *American Psychologist, 29(12),* 859–869.

Bandura, A. (1977). Self-efficacy: Toward a unifying theory of behavioral change. *Psychological Review, 84,* 191–215.

Bandura, A. (1986). *Social foundations of thought and action: A social cognitive theory.* Englewood Cliffs, NJ: Prentice-Hall.

Bandura, A. (1993). Perceived self-efficacy in cognitive development and functioning. *Educational Psychologist, 28,* 117–148.

Beckmann, J., & Kuhl, J. (1984). Altering information to gain action control: Functional aspects of human information-processing in decision-making. *Journal of Research in Personality, 18,* 224–237.

Bembenutty, H., & Karabenick, S. A. (1998). Academic delay of gratification. *Learning and Individual Differences, 10,* 329–346.

Berliner, D. C. (1979). Tempus educare. In P. L. Peterson & H. J. Walberg (Eds.), *Research on teaching* (pp. 120–135). Berkeley, CA: McCutcheon.

Blumenfeld, P. C., & Meece, J. L. (1988). Task factors, teacher behavior, and student involvement and use of learning strategies in science. *The Elementary School Journal, 88,* 235–250.

Boekaerts, M., Pintrich, P., & Zeidner, M. (Eds.). (2000). *Handbook of self-regulation.* San Diego: Academic Press.

Brophy, J. (1998). *Motivating students to learn.* Boston: McGraw-Hill.

Bullock, M., & Lutkenhaus, P. (1988). The development of volitional behavior in the toddler years. *Child Development, 59,* 664–674.

Butler, D. L. (1996). Promoting strategic content learning by adolescents with learning disabilities. *Exceptionality Education Canada, 6,* 131–157.

Collins, A., Brown, J. S., & Newman, S. E. (1989). Cognitive apprenticeship: Teaching the crafts of reading, writing, and mathematics. In L. B. Resnick (Ed.), *Knowing, learning, and instruction: Essays in honor of Robert Glaser* (pp. 453–494). Hillsdale, NJ: Lawrence Erlbaum Associates.

Corno, L. (Ed). (in press). Conceptions of volition: Theoretical investigations and studies of practice [Special double issue]. *International Journal of Educational Research, 33* (7, 8).

Corno, L. (1986). The metacognitive control components of self-regulated learning. *Contemporary Educational Psychology, 11,* 333–346.

Corno, L. (1987). Teaching and self-regulated learning. In D. C. Berliner & B. V. Rosenshine (Eds.), *Talks to teacher* (pp. 249–266). New York: Random House.

Corno, L. (1994). Student volition and education: Outcomes, influences, and practices. In D. H. Schunk & B. J. Zimmerman (Eds.), *Self-regulation of learning and Performance: Issues and educational applications* (pp. 229–251). Hillsdale, NJ: Lawrence Erlbaum Associates.

Corno, L., & Kanfer, R. (1993). The role of volition in learning and performance. In L. Darling-Hammond (Ed.), *Review of research in education* (pp. 301–341). Washington, DC: American Educational Research Association.

Corno, L., & Mandinach, E. B. (1983). The role of cognitive engagement in classroom learning and motivation. *Educational Psychologist, 18*, 88–108.

Corno, L., & Randi, J. (1999). A design theory for classroom instruction in self-regulated learning? In C. M. Reigeluth (Ed.), *Instructional-design theory and models: A new paradigm of instructional theory, Vol. II* (pp. 293–317). Mahwah, NJ: Lawrence Erlbaum Associates.

Csikszentmihalyi, M. (1975). *Beyond boredom and anxiety.* San Francisco: Jossey-Bass.

CTB/McGraw-Hill. (1977). *The California Achievement Test.* New York: Author.

Dansereau, D. F. (1985). Learning strategy research. In J. W. Segal, S. F. Chipman, & R. Glaser (Eds.), *Thinking and learning skills (Vol.* 1, pp. 209–240). Hillsdale, NJ: Lawrence Erlbaum Associates.

Deci, E. L., & Ryan, R. M. (1985). *Intrinsic motivation and self-determination in human behavior.* NY: Plenum.

Dewey, J. (1974). *On education: Selected writing.* Chicago: University of Chicago Press.

DeWitte, S. & Lens, W. (in press). Optimistic and pessimistic academic procrastination as a function of a student's action identification level. *International Journal of Educational Research, 33*(8).

Doyle, W. (1983). Academic work. *Review of Educational Research, 53*, 159–199.

Dyson, A. H. (1987). The value of "time off task": Young children's spontaneous talk and deliberate text. *Harvard Educational Review, 57*, 396–421.

Harter, S. (1979). *Perceived competence scale for children. Denver*, CO: University of Denver Seminary.

Hilgard, E. R. (1980). The trilogy of mind: Cognition, affection and conation. *Journal of the History of the Behavioral Sciences, 16*, 106–117.

Jan Simons, P. R., & Beukhof, G. (Eds.). (1987). *Regulation of learning.* Den Haag, The Netherlands: Instituut voor Onderzoek van het Onderwijs.

Johnston, P. H. (1985). Understanding reading disability. *Harvard Educational Review, 55*, 153–177.

Kuhl, J. (1981). Motivational and functional helplessness: The moderating effect of state versus action orientation. *Journal of Personality and Social Psychology, 40(l)*, 155–170.

Kuhl, J. (1984). Volitional aspects of achievement motivation and learned helplessness: Toward a comprehensive theory of action-control. In B. A. Maher (Ed.), *Progress in experimental personality research* (Vol. 13, pp. 99–171). New York: Academic Press.

Kuhl, J. (1985). Volitional mediators of cognition-behavior consistency: Self-regulatory processes and action versus state orientation. In J. Kuhl & J. Beckmann (Eds.), *Action control: From cognition to behavior* (pp. 101–128). West Berlin: Springer-Verlag.

Kuhl, J. (1996). Who controls whom when "I control myself"? *Psychological Inquiry, 7*, 61–68.

Kuhl, J. (2000). A functional-design approach to motivation and self-regulation: The dynamics of personality systems interactions. In M. Boekaerts, P. R. Pintrich, & M. Zeidner (Eds.), *Handbook of Self-regulation* (pp. 111–169) San Diego: Academic Press.

Kuhl, J. (in press). The volitional basis of personality systems interaction theory: Applications in learning and treatment contexts. *International Journal of Educational Research, 33*(7).

Kuhl, J., & Beckmann, J. (Eds.). (1985). *Action control: From cognition to behavior.* West Berlin: Springer-Verlag.

Kuhl, J., & Kraska, K. (1989). Self-regulation and metamotivation: Computational mechanisms, development, and assessment. In R. Kanfer, P. L. Ackerman, & R. Cudeck (Eds.), *Abilities, motivation, and methodology: The Minnesota Symposium on individual differences* (pp. 343–368). Hillsdale, NJ: Lawrence Erlbaum Associates.

Kuhn, D., & Ho, V. (1980). Self-directed activity and cognitive development. *Journal of Applied Developmental Psychology, 1*, 119–133.

Leinhardt, G., & Putnam, R. T. (1987). The skill of learning from classroom lessons. *American Educational Research Journal, 24,* 557–588.

Lepper, M. R., & Malone, T. W. (1987). Intrinsic motivation and instructional effectiveness in computer-based education. In R. E. Snow & M. J. Farr (Eds.), *Aptitude, learning, and instruction* (Vol. 3, pp. 223–254). Hillsdale, NJ: Lawrence Erlbaum Associates.

McCaslin, M. M., & Good, T. (1996). The informal curriculum. In D. Berliner & R. C. Calfee (Eds.), *Handbook of educational psychology* (pp. 622–670). New York: Macmillan.

McCann, Erin J. (1999). *The assessment and importance of volitional control in academic performance.* Unpublished doctoral dissertation, University of Texas at Austin.

Mandinach, E. B. (1987). Clarifying the "A" in CAI for learners of different abilities. *Journal of Educational Computing Research, 3,* 113–128.

Mandinach, E. B., & Linn, M. C. (1986). The cognitive effects of computer learning environments. *Journal of Educational Computing Research, 2,* 411–427.

Mandinach, E. B., & Linn, M. C. (1987). Cognitive consequences of programming: Achievements of experienced and talented programmers. *Journal of Educational Computing Research, 3,* 53–72.

McKeachie, W. J., Pintrich, P. R., & Lin, Y. (1985). Teaching learning strategies. *Educational Psychologist, 20,* 153–161.

Meichenbaum, D. (1977). *Cognitive behavior modification.* New York: Plenum.

Mischel, W., & Shoda, Y. (1998). Reconciling processing dynamics and personality dispositions. *Annual Review of Psychology, 49,* 229–258.

Noddings, N. (1984). Caring: *A feminine approach to ethics and moral education. Berkeley:* University of California Press.

Panagiotopolous, J. (1986). *Cognitive engagement variations among students and classroom tasks.* Unpublished doctoral dissertation, Teachers College, Columbia University, New York.

Pintrich, P. R., & Schunk, D. H. (1996). *Motivation in education: Theory, research, and applications.* Englewood Cliffs, NJ: Prentice-Hall.

Pressley, M., Woloshyn, V., Burkell, J., Cariglia-Bull, T., Lysynchuk, L., McGoldrick, J. A., Schneider, B., Snyder, B. L., & Symons, S. (1995). *Cognitive strategy: Instruction that really improves children's academic performance* (2nd ed.). Cambridge, MA: Brookline Books.

Randi, J., & Corno, L. (1999). Teacher innovations in self-regulated learning. In M. Boekaerts, P. Pintrich, & M. Zeidner (Eds.), *Handbook of self-regulation* (pp. 651–685). New York: Academic Press.

Raven, J. C. (1958). *Standard progressive matrices.* New York: Psychological Corporation.

Rohrkemper, M. M. (1986). The functions of inner speech in elementary school students' problem-solving behavior. *American Educational Research Journal, 23,* 303–315.

Rohrkemper, M., & Corno, L. (1988). Success and failure on classroom tasks: Adaptive learning and classroom teaching. *The Elementary School Journal, 88,* 297–313.

Scardamalia, M., & Bereiter, C. (1983). The development of evaluative, diagnostic, and remedial capabilities in children's composing. In M. Martten (Ed.), *The psychology of written language: A developmental approach* (pp. 67–95). London: John Wiley.

Scardamalia, M., & Bereiter, C. (1985). Fostering the development of self-regulation in children's knowledge processing. In S. F. Chipman, J. W. Segal, & R. Glaser (Eds.), *Thinking and learning skills: Current research and open questions* (Vol. 2, pp. 563–577). Hillsdale, NJ: Lawrence Erlbaum Associates.

Scardamalia, M., & Bereiter, C. (1993). Technologies for knowledge-building discourse. *Communications of the ACM, 36*(5), 37–41.

Schoenfeld, A. H. (1985). *Mathematical problem solving.* New York: Academic Press.

Shapiro, L. J. (1988). *Effects of written metacognitive and cognitive strategy instruction on the elementary algebra achievement of college students in a remedial mathematics course.* Unpublished doctoral dissertation, Teachers College, Columbia University, New York.

Slavin, R. (1983). *Cooperative learning.* New York: Longman.

Snow, R. E. (1986, April). *Cognitive-instructional-differential psychology in Western Europe.* Invited address to the Annual Meeting of the American Educational Research Association, New Orleans, LA.

Snow, R. E., Corno, L., & Jackson, D. N. III (1996). Individual differences in affective and conative functions. In D. C. Berliner & R. C. Calfee (Eds.). *Handbook of educational psychology* (pp. 243–310). New York: Macmillan.

Snow, R. E., & Farr, M. J. (Eds.). (1987). *Aptitude, learning, and instruction* (Vol. 3). Hillsdale, NJ: Lawrence Erlbaum Associates.

Stanford Aptitude Seminar (in press). *Remaking the concept of aptitude: Extending the legacy of Richard E. Snow.* Mahwah, NJ: Lawrence Erlbaum Associates.

Thomas, J. W., Strage, A., & Curley, R. (1988). Improving students' self-directed learning: Issues and guidelines. *The Elementary School Journal, 88,* 313–327.

Trawick, L. (1990). *Effects of a cognitive-behavioral intervention on the motivation, volition, and achievement of academically underprepared college students.* Unpublished doctoral dissertation. Teachers College, Columbia University, New York.

Turner, J. C., Cox, K. E., DiCintio, M., Meyer, D. K., Logan, C., & Thomas, C. T. (1998). Creating contexts for involvement in mathematics. *Journal of Educational Psychology, 90,* 730–745.

Vygotsky, L. S. (1962). *Thought and language.* Cambridge, MA: MIT Press.

Waters, H. S., & Andreassen, C. (1983). Children's use of memory strategies under instruction. In M. Pressley & J. R. Levin (Eds.), *Cognitive strategy instruction: Psychological foundations* (pp. 3–24). New York: Springer-Verlag.

Webb, N. M. (1983). Predicting learning from student interaction: Defining the interacting variables. *Educational Psychologist, 18,* 33–42.

Webb, N. M. (1992). Testing a theoretical model of student interaction and learning in small groups. In R. Hertz-Lazarowitz & N. Miller (Eds.), *Interaction in cooperative groups* (pp. 102–119). Cambridge, England: Cambridge University Press.

Weinstein, C. F., & Mayer, R. F. (1986). The teaching of learning strategies. In M. C. Wittrock (*Ed.*), *Handbook of research on teaching* (3rd ed., pp. 315–327). New York: Macmillan.

Wentzel, K. R. (1991). Relations between social competence and academic achievement in early adolescence. *Child Development, 62,* 1066–1078.

Wertsch, J. (1979). From social interaction to higher psychological processes: A classification and application of Vygotsky's theory. *Human Development, 22,* 1–22.

Winne, P. H. (1995). Inherent details in self-regulated learning. *Educational Psychologist, 30,* 173–187.

Wolters, C. A. (1998). Self-regulated learning and college students' regulation of motivation. *Journal of Educational Psychology, 90,* 224–235.

Xu, J. (1994). *Doing homework: A study of possibilities.* Unpublished doctoral dissertation. Teachers College, Columbia University, New York.

Xu, J., & Corno, L. (1998). Case studies of families doing third grade homework. *Teachers College Record, 100,* 402–436.

Zimmerman, B. J., & Pons, M. M. (1986). Development of a structured interview for assessing student use of self-regulated learning strategies. *American Educational Research Journal, 23,* 614–629.

Self-Regulated Learning and Academic Achievement: A Vygotskian View

Mary McCaslin
University of Arizona

Daniel T. Hickey
The University of Georgia

In this chapter, we first outline the context of emergent Vygotskian theory in the Soviet Union of the 1920s, because a theory about social mediation and the historical nature of consciousness demands a historical perspective. Second, we focus on three interdependent concerns within a Vygotskian perspective: multiple functions of language, internalization processes and the nature of change, and methodology and unit of analysis. Within each concern, we briefly address related constructs in theory and practice. Third, we present a model of co-regulated learning as one way to organize modern classroom research and illustrate the kinds of questions and methods that can emerge within a socioconstructivist framework in classroom research.

HISTORICAL CONTEXT OF VYGOTSKIAN THEORY

Vygotsky's ideas were the product of the unique circumstances that existed in post-revolutionary Russia, making him "one of the figures in intellectual history who might have never been" (Werstch, 1985, p. 1). The ready embrace of Vygotskian practices by Western educators shows that his notions are easily grasped and generally compatible with contemporary educational goals. However, as Davydov and Raddizikovski (1985) pointed out, "Beneath the external simplicity of Vygotsky's formulation is hidden a subtext with profound implications. In order to analyze the specifics of Vygotsky's ideas, one must follow an indirect path, beginning with a general context of Soviet Psychology at the time" (p. 35).

A discussion of Vygotsky necessarily involves a discussion of Marx because Vygotsky was an avowed Marxist and his theory was a noteworthy attempt to operationalize the Marxist analysis of social change. Indeed, Vygotsky was a pioneer of Marxist psychology. Thus, one reason Vygotsky's notions have high "face-validity" in contemporary contexts is because they have been, in a sense, "sanitized" by multiple iterations in Western practice (Bruner, 1984).

Three tenets of Marxism concerning language, consciousness, and the process of change are discussed briefly to suggest their central role in Vygotsky's thinking (Vygotsky, 1962; 1978). First is Vygotsky's elaboration on Engels' conception of human labor and tool use as the means by which man changes nature, and in doing so, changes himself. Engels' (1890) theory of human evolution proposed that language developed as a result of human activity and the need for cooperative labor. Vygotsky extended this conception to include the use of signs more broadly, including writing and numbers. The use of signs changes human kind in the same fashion as the use of the tools of labor changed humankind in the manner typically associated with Engels. In short, the use of signs is what distinguishes humans from animals (for extended discussion, see Slobin, 1966).

Second, Marx defined consciousness as a property of the human brain that was the result of a gradual accumulation of small quantitative changes, which account for a qualitative change (see also Gray, 1966). Furthermore, consciousness is an active constructor of experience and organizes and controls behavior. It is the ability to control one's behavior that frees the individual from specific situations. Self-control enables socially meaningful activity. One is able to anticipate, plan, and direct one's actions toward nonimmediate goals. For Marx, this ability to plan, to imagine, and to formulate a course of action *before* implementation was peculiar to humans (see Marx, 1867).

The third basic Marxist tenet that influenced Vygotsky's perspective is the dialectic process, as advanced initially by Hegel (1949). The dialectical method involves the notion that movement (or progress) is the result of the conflict of opposites. Thus, the dialectic is that process by which contradictions are seen to merge and transcend into a higher truth. The dialectic implies growth; there is a hierarchical ordering in thesis, antithesis, and synthesis. Though Hegel himself avoided these terms, they are helpful in understanding his concept. The *thesis* is some idea or historical movement. This idea has within itself incompleteness that gives rise to opposition, or an *antithesis*, a conflicting idea or movement. As a result of the conflict, a third point of view arises, a *synthesis*, that overcomes the conflict by reconciling this at a higher level of truth, the thesis contained in both the thesis and antithesis. As extended by Marx and Engels, it informs how to change the world, not merely interpret it (Marx, 1844; Marx & Engels, 1888).

In the aftermath of the October 1917 revolution, the new Soviet government faced the task of extensive reorganization, and most intellectual and scientific energy was devoted to furthering Socialist ideals. In revolutionary times, total rejection of the status quo *is* status quo. In the Soviet Union, however, the situation was more complex because of the embodiment of the Marxist doctrine sketched here. The doctrine has obvious appeal to a new government faced with the task of reeducating a huge peasant class in order to shape it into *vosepatanii novova Sovetskovo cheloveka*, the character of the new Soviet man. Such a person would need to cope with rapid change while simultaneously instigating that change.

We return to Vygotsky, who arrived on the scene in 1924 at the Second Psychoneurological Congress in Leningrad. The prevailing psychological view at that time did not attend to subjective experience. Vygotsky nonetheless challenged the dominant view by speaking of the relation between conditioned reflexes and conscious human behavior. Arguing that a "scientific" psychology could not ignore the "fact" of consciousness (Wertsch, 1985), Vygotsky argued strenuously for a "nonreflexilogical scientific psychology" that would be "developmental, address the relationship between higher and lower mental functions, and take 'socially meaningful activity' as an explanatory principle" (Kozulin, 1986, p. xvii).

On the strength of his 1924 remarks, Vygotsky was invited to join the Institute of Psychology in Moscow. His partnership there, with Luria and Leontiev, which Luria referred to as the *troika*, continued until Vygotsky's death a decade later. It is during this time that Vygotsky formulated his ideas on the social mediation of learning and the role of consciousness, within a decidedly Marxist perspective. Luria (1979) recalled:

> ... in Vygotsky's hands, Marx's methods of analysis did serve a vital role in shaping our course. Influenced by Marx, Vygotsky concluded that the origins of higher forms of conscious behavior were to be found in the individual's social relations with the external world. But man is not only a product of his environment, he is also an active agent in creating that environment. ... We needed, as it were, to step outside the organism to discover the sources of specifically human forms of psychological activity (p. 43).

Hence, by going "outside the organism," Vygotsky went beyond the biological processes that he believed to dominate only at birth and examined the individual's mediation of experience, an experience that is at once cultural, in that it represents socially structured tasks and tools, and historical, in that it reflects the "storehouse" of what we today call *semantic knowledge* (language-based information), *learning to learn* strategies and procedures (e.g., rehearsal, elaboration), and *metacognitive awareness* (conscious monitoring of one's cognitive strategies). Luria (1979) discussed this storehouse as having ". . . enormously expanded man's powers, making the wisdom of the past analyzable in the present and perfectible in the future" (p. 44). The contrast between Luria's image of the realm of psychology and information-processing theorists' dispassionate and bounded discussion of the function of metacognition that has dominated educational psychology since the 1980s may provide the reader with some feeling for the social–political context of Soviet psychology.

VYGOTSKY'S THEORY OF LANGUAGE

Engels' theory of the evolution of language posited that communicative, social language evolved from and with human labor and was peculiarly human—it is what distinguishes human from animal. Similarly, Pavlov (1927) made the critical distinction between what he termed the *first* (perceptual) and *second* (linguistic) *signal systems*. Pavlov observed the abrupt nature of human conditioning and the nongeneralizability of animal classical conditioning data to humans. He hypothesized that the second signal system was the cause of differences between human and animal learning and that, whereas in one sense speech has removed man from reality, in another, ". . . it is precisely speech which has made us human" (as quoted in Slobin, 1966, p. 112).

Thus, for Pavlov, as for Engels, speech was peculiar to humans. In interaction with the first signal system (perception), speech allowed *mastery of* the environment as opposed to *control by* its stimulus properties. Language, then, is responsible for the human ability to direct and mediate behavior. The mediational and self-directive role of the second signal system became the cornerstone of Vygotsky's research and theorizing.

Multiple Functions

Vygotsky was concerned with the multiple functions of semantic, meaningful language—what Pavlov termed the second signal system—and how this occurs naturally and acquires two distinct functions: communication with others and self-direction (see also Zivin, 1979). At birth the human infant is controlled by biology and the first signal system, the physical properties of the environment. Initially, the child reacts to words not by their meanings, but by their sounds, that is, by their physical stimulus properties. James Joyce, also writing in the early 1900s, vividly conveyed the stimulus properties of language development in the life of Stephan Dedalus. The novel begins with infant Stephan's story: "Once upon a time and a very good time it was there was a moocow coming down along the road..." (1976, p. 1). Throughout childhood, young Stephan works to make meaning of adults and events in his life. He tells of Aunt Dante: "And when Dante made that noise after dinner and then put her hand to her mouth: that was heartburn" (p. 11).

As the child's language develops, words gradually acquire meaning independent of their stimulus properties. Stephan the young schoolboy reflects on calling a fellow student a suck. "Suck was a queer word. The fellow called Simon Moonan that name because Simon Moonan used to tie the prefect's false sleeves behind his back and the prefect used to let on to be angry. But the sound was ugly. Once he had washed his hands in the lavatory of the Wicklow Hotel and his father pulled the stopper up by the chain after and the dirty water went down through the hole in the basin. And when it had all gone down slowly the hole in the basin had made a sound like that: suck. Only louder" (p. 11).

After repeated exposure to word meanings by *other persons* in their social–instructional environments, children subsequently become able to expose *themselves* to word meanings and thereby direct their own behavior. Stephan is late for lights out. "His fingers trembled as he undressed himself in the dormitory. He told his fingers to hurry up" (p. 18). But children bring their everyday understandings to the acculturation process; they do not simply imitate or replicate others. Joyce continued; "He had to undress and then kneel and say his own prayers and be in bed before the gas was lowered so that he might not go to hell when he died" (p. 18). Thus, the child acquires the facility to direct and control his own behavior as well as communicate with others through language. Through collaboration with others, the child integrates his everyday concepts and understandings with the scientific concepts of his culture—to the enrichment of the culture (see also Yowell & Smylie, 1999).

The developmental sequence of the two functions of language, communication with others and self-direction, is from social or interpersonal to self-directive or intrapersonal. The implications of this progression are critical. Language acquires two distinct functions, but the social environment is the source of both external communication and internal self-direction. The second signal system, which makes us uniquely human, is embedded in the cultural, historical, and social language environment.

The structure and function of social communication and internal self-direction differ, however. Inner speech, in contrast to the grammatically correct communicative speech, is more economical. As it branches off communicative (external) speech, ultimately the "speech structures mastered by the child become the basic structures to his thinking" (Vygotsky, 1962, p. 51). Inner speech, then, is the opposite of external speech. External speech involves turning thought into words, whereas inner speech involves turning words into thought (Vygotsky, 1962, p. 131). Inner speech is thinking in pure meanings; it is the link between the second signal system of the social world and the thought of the individual. Because of the evolution of language, from first to second signal system, Vygotsky could claim (as quoted by Leontiev & Luria, 1968, p. 342) that by mastering nature (through the second signal system) we also master ourselves.

Contrasting Historical Positions

Vygotsky's theoretical interests in language development are frequently confused with the interests of two colleagues, Luria and Piaget, who were also working on language development in the 1920s and 1930s. Vygotsky differed from Luria in the area of focus and methodology and from Piaget in theory development and data interpretation.

A. R. Luria. In contrast to Vygotsky, who focused on the semantic and self-directive capacity of the second signal system, Luria focused on the child's *transition from* the first to the second signal system. Thus, Luria examined the stimulus properties of language, those impulse qualities that also can regulate behavior through sound and conditioning, and designed conditions that would elicit a transition from one signal system to the other. His research methods involved a degree of intrusiveness and direct experimental manipulation. In contrast, Vygotsky's studies were confined to observations of what he considered naturally occurring self-directive speech, what Piaget called *egocentric speech,* which consists of words spoken aloud in the presence of others. It resembles social or communicative speech, but does not require a response or even the attention of a listener.

Jean Piaget. It is probably fair to say that Vygotsky's theorizing about the emergent dual function of language owed much to his disagreement with Piaget (1983) on the source and function of egocentric speech. Although Vygotsky felt Piaget had revolutionized child study, he disagreed with Piaget's basic premise: that the earliest forms of thought are autistic, with logic occurring sometime later, and egocentric speech the connective link. Vygotsky's disagreement fueled a line of research that replicated Piaget's clinical method and setting, but added difficult elements that would frustrate the child so that "by obstructing his free activity we made him face his problems" (Vygotsky, 1962, p. 16). Results indicated that children's egocentric speech increased when faced with difficulties.

Vygotsky, like Piaget, interpreted this as support for the premise that speech is an expression of the process of becoming aware. Vygotsky also maintained, however, that egocentric speech becomes an instrument in the seeking and planning of a solution to a problem. It is self-directive. In contrast to Piaget, Vygotsky did not consider egocentric speech ultimately to be "corrected" and, thus, to disappear, but rather to be the transition between external and inner speech. It already serves the function of inner speech, but remains similar to social speech in its structure. As inner speech develops, egocentric expression decreases because "behind the symptoms of dissolution lies a progressive development, the birth of a new speech form," that is, inner speech (Vygotsky, 1962, p. 135). Thus, the progression of multiple functions of language is from social to egocentric to inner speech.

Modern Considerations for Practice

Confusions about historical theorists are evident in modern educational practice. Vygotsky, Piaget, and Dewey are the developmental triumvirate for educators. This is especially evident in movements like Whole Language in reading and recommended practice by the National Council of Teachers of Mathematics (1990). Each theorist is valued because of his interactive, dialectical approach to development, position on activity as a basic unit of meaning, and is a child advocate concerned with educational opportunities that afford the development of mental structures. Vygotsky went so far as to claim that "passivity of the student is the greatest sin from a scientific point of view, since it relies on the false principle that the teacher is everything and the pupil is nothing" (as quoted in Bozhovich & Slavina, 1968, p. 165).

Readiness. The enactment of each theorist differs in important ways, however, especially when comparing a Vygotskian classroom with a Piagetian one (see McCaslin, 1989 for extended discussion). Differences in practice related to interpretation of egocentric speech are relatively straightforward, but consider the notion of readiness. Vygotsky was involved in curriculum; Piaget was not. Thus, curricular enactments of Piaget have been formulated by others. Piaget's theory of stage development and processes of adaptation have been interpreted to mean that teachers meet the child at his or her developmental level and provide a stimulus that initiates an optimum amount of disequilibrium. The goal is to engage the learner in activity that is more supportive of accommodation (modification of existing cognitive structures) than of assimilation (incorporation of new concepts into existing structures) processes. The locus of concern is inside the learner's head; the process of concern is learner adaptation. Piaget's learner engages a private inner struggle to achieve equilibrium between his current schemata and schemes (roughly, knowledge structures and procedures) and the challenges perceived in the task.

In contrast, Vygotsky did not adhere to the development-precedes/allows-learning progression of Piaget. Nor did he believe it was possible to directly influence or affect another. For Vygotsky, authentic educational activities were those opportunities in which a learner was engaged with a task beyond his or her immediate capability (the "zone of proximal development") with a facilitator (a more capable peer or adult), constructs to which we return. The locus of concern is social, the "socially situated" learning; the process of concern is "emergent interaction" (Wertsch & Stone, 1985). Vygotsky's learner engages a perceived task that also is mediated socially. His learner is guided and supported by and participates in a social–instructional environment that seeks to develop mental structures via personal relationships embedded in a shared activity—that seeks to acculturate as well as stimulate mental structures.

Social Learning. The unique capacities of human language (e.g., Bruner, 1965, 1972) would become central to U.S. psychology in the 1960s and 1970s and severely diminish the relevance of animal research in understanding human experience and learning. American psychologists of the time also introduced new models of causation. Interactionism (Mischel, 1977) and reciprocal determinism (Bandura, 1978), for example, seriously diluted the power of the environment to affect humans. Translations of Vygotskian theory (Vygotsky, 1962) and Soviet uses of group learning, social modeling, and character education (Bronfenbrenner, 1962) were readily available in the academy in the 1960s (MIT Press and American Psychologist, respectively). Knowledge of Soviet developmental theory and educational practice and changing and challenging conceptions of humans and their relation to their world occurred at a time in U.S. history of rapid social change and high expectations for social engineering. There might not have been a revolution, but it was going to be a Great Society.

The emergent synthesis of these forces included a focus on the nature of social relationships in human experience (McCaslin & DiMarino-Linnen, 2000). Thus, there is considerable common ground between the inherently social nature of learning in a Vygotskian perspective and the social modeling features of social learning theory (e.g., Palincsar & Brown, 1984). Both theories attend in some manner to interpersonal dynamics, guided demonstration, and scaffolding "in-the-moment," for example.

One should not overlook an essential difference, however. Vygotsky's socially mediated learning was essential to the *collectivism* that was to be at the core of Soviet socialism: "the ZPD [Zone of Proximal Development] is a direct expression of the way in which the division of labor should work in a collective society" (Bruner, 1984, p. 95). In contrast, in modern social learning theory, socially mediated learning is essential to self-reliance and self-interest that are the core of American *individualism*. Self-control is Vygotsky's path to socially meaningful activity; in contrast, socially meaningful activity is social learning theory's path to self control—and personal freedom (Bandura, 1997). It is quite a different trajectory from the sociocultural model and the division of labor in society.

DYNAMICS OF CHANGE: PROCESSES OF INTERNALIZATION

The sequence of language development, from interpersonal and communicative with others to intrapersonal and self-directive, squarely locates the emergent capacity for "self-regulation" in the interpersonal realm. Vygotskian theory adheres to cultural–historical evolution and the development of consciousness; thus the role of the social environment is preeminent. Vygotskian theory (Luria, 1969) ". . . conceives of mind as the product of social life and treats it as a form of activity which was earlier shared by two people (originated in communication), and which only later, as a result of mental development, became a form of behavior within one person" (p. 143). The psychology of the individual is a multiplicative product of his social encounters. Hence, higher psychological processes begin in the social world.

Emergent Interaction

Emergent interaction was coined by Wertsch and Stone (1985) to capture the dynamics of internalization of the interpersonal realm in the Vygotskian perspective. An understanding of the emergence of self-directive inner speech requires an appreciation of emergent interaction, the process of internalization that integrates the multiple social–instructional environments in the child's experience—the interpsychological, cultural world—with the child's natural developmental processes and understandings. Internalization, then, is not replication, extension, or mere "introjection" of the external. Rather, it is inherently social and interactional, and at its core is the mastery of signals—language.

This conception of internalization embeds the individual within his or her culture; it blurs the distinction between self and other that is more readily accepted in mainstream American psychology. Within a

Vygotskian framework, the interplay of the social–historical and the natural in the formation of consciousness informs questions about the relationship between social cognition and intrapersonal awareness and understanding. The individual is intricately a part of the perceived social world; thus self-knowledge is not independent of knowledge of others. One could argue then, and we do, that reports about self are not interpretable without a context of "perception of others" within which to analyze them; nor is a student's specific intrapersonal approach and response apparent in a learning situation without understanding the interpersonal influences of home and school. Later we illustrate these assertions and suggest a model of "co-regulation" wherein teachers (as well as parents) might better structure relationships and opportunities in classrooms to facilitate student internalization of social supports and promote what we call *adaptive learning* (McCaslin & Good, 1996b). Adaptive learning involves the internalization of goals, the motivation to commit, challenge, or reform them, and the competence to enact and evaluate those commitments (McCaslin & Murdock, 1991).

Modern Considerations for Practice

The stress on social and emergent interaction is obviously compatible with the social and political goals of the Soviet Union of the early 20th century. It is compatible with contemporary Western educational goals as well. When Bronfenbrenner (1962) introduced American psychologists to the Soviet notion of group competition to motivate individuals, there was considerable post-Sputnik interest in Soviet psychology and education. These strategies have transferred quite readily to the American classroom, although labels have not. Procedures termed *group competition* in the Soviet Union are termed *cooperative learning* in the United States.

Zone of Proximal Development (ZPD). Vygotsky's constructs were gladly received in the educational community, most notably his notions of peer facilitation and the Zone of Proximal Development, as previously mentioned. Vygotsky identified this zone as a sort of gap or the difference between what a learner cannot do alone yet can do with help from a teacher or more capable peer. The basic tenet of this construct is that tasks that learners can initially do only with assistance, they come to do independently as they incorporate the structure or the scaffolding of the assistance. Scaffolding suggests moveable and malleable supports that are faded when superfluous. American psychologists and subsequently educators have stressed peer facilitation as well, most notably in the enthusiasm for small-group learning of the past two decades.

Essential to a Vygotskian perspective, however, is the relationship between the coparticipants. As Yowell and Smylie (1999) noted, "It is within close personal relationships marked by support of student autonomy, intersubjectivity, and intelligent sympathy that effectively scaffolded interactions between teachers and students can occur" (p. 475). Students and teachers *mutually regulate* the ZPD; ZPD is not a top-down notion of change. The goal of scaffolding in the ZPD is to foster meaningful connections between the teacher's cultural knowledge and the everyday understandings and experiences of students. The goal of structural support in the ZPD is not simply student adoption of adult or cultural knowledge. As Yowell and Smylie continued, student movement in the ZPD "represents an emergent and imaginative understanding of concepts learned in collaboration with the adult (p. 478)." The ZPD is about the enrichment of the culture as well as empowerment of the individual. The individual does not submit to the cultural authority, but renders culture yet more meaningful.

Politics and School Reform.   Vygotskian theory is a theory about fundamental change through the internalization of the social–instructional environment (SIE). It at once empowers the SIE and the individual, a provocative formula for education. A Vygotskian perspective is inherently political. This is not unique to Vygotsky—all psychological theories are inherently political. Perhaps the construct of self-regulation simply magnifies the broader issue. For example, one goal of SRL research may be to enhance the development of self-regulated learning for the purpose of individual empowerment, to free the individual from the immediate environment by promoting self-direction and planfulness. Another may be to free the SIE from responsibility for the individual: SRL suggests that learners can teach themselves. Yowell and Smylie (1999) suggested a third potential goal of SRL: character education and the promotion of student self-control and "conformity through repeated messages" (p. 481). For some character educators, SRL is all about obedience. As Kilpatrick claimed, "Sometimes compulsion is what is needed to get a habit started" (1992 in Yowell and Smylie, 1999, p. 481).

Modern school reform is all about holding students accountable for their lack of cross-national competitiveness. Hard work, high expectations, and higher standards are the panacea. Students who are unable to profit from instruction, or who are unable to compensate for inadequate instruction—who cannot teach themselves—are to be retained if unable to perform on mandated tests even so. It may be easier and less expensive in the short term to expect students to compensate for inadequate instruction, expose them to sheer repetition until they do, or remove them from the educational setting altogether (Bryk, 1999) than to fund instructional improvement.

In short, it seems especially problematic that educators remain unaware of educational and political dynamics in their work, because a bits-and-pieces approach in the classroom in the belief that one is politically neutral often results in applications that are anything but neutral. The cooperative group of homogeneous high-ability learners is an obvious example. One *can* simply implement tools like the Zone of Proximal Development or "peer facilitation" without an understanding of the emergent interpsychological developmental premise that underlies them; however, theoretical justification *cannot* be claimed. Educators' decontextualization of theoretical concepts does not promote an informed understanding of motivated classroom learning. Neither does a diffusion of teacher responsibility in the name of constructivist theory. Too many teachers (and teacher educators) capitulate to the "idiosyncratic constructions of intrinsically motivated" students for whose learning they therefore cannot be held accountable. A political naivete that surrenders the work of the public school to others—some of whom may be more interested in school failure or self-promotion (e.g., Berliner & Biddle, 1995; Good & Braden, 2000 respectively) than in motivated classroom learning—is dangerous. Educators are essential participants in the education of youth; they must rise to and accept the informed responsibility of that occasion.

METHODOLOGICAL ISSUES AND THE UNIT OF ANALYSIS

The study of naturally occurring self-directive inner speech that originates in the interpersonal realm within a theoretical framework of "emergent interactionism" places considerable demands on the researcher to design informative methodology. It is seldom achieved now, with all the technical advances in tools and accrued wisdom of the past 80 years. It was not readily obtained by Vygotsky, either. A recurring argument among Vygotskian scholars concerns inconsistencies in Vygotsky's research in meeting the demands of his theory. Davydov and Radzikhovski (1985), among others, have distinguished "between Vygotsky the methodologist and Vygotsky the psychologist."

Informative Data

Vygotsky the methodologist did not readily accept elicited behavior as indicative of behavior that occurs naturally. He opposed subjective and introspective reports and would not directly ask a subject to report his or her thoughts. He did manipulate task structures, however, and would change a task to increase its frustrating potential, thus requiring self-directive speech. Vygotsky's rejection of direct-questioning techniques meant that he confined his research on self-directive inner speech to observations of egocentric speech in difficult, novel, or frustrating task conditions. Because he considered egocentric speech to be self-directive speech on its way inward, he had to *infer* the dynamics of inner speech from these observations.

Vygotsky the psychologist voiced concern about the false dichotomy of affect *or* intellect that characterized much of psychology at the turn of the century and that continues today:

> We have in mind the relation between intellect and affect. Their separation as subjects of study is a major weakness of traditional psychology since it makes the thought process appear as an autonomous flow of "thoughts thinking themselves," segregated from the fullness of life, from the personal needs and interests, the inclinations and impulses, of the thinker.... [The present approach] demonstrates the existence of a dynamic system of meaning in which the affective and the intellectual unite.... It permits us to trace the path from a person's needs and impulses to the specific direction taken by his thoughts, and the reverse path from his thoughts to his behavior and activity (Vygotsky, 1962, p. 8).

Thus, although Vygotsky's own research did not address the interplay of the affective with the intellectual, he recognized the need to examine their organization—that is, their dialectical integration—and the futility of examining either facet in isolation from the other and from their emergent interactional origins with the SIE.

Unit of Analysis

Vygotsky's concern with the integration of the affective and intellectual did not lead him to a concern with the structure and nature of tasks that would afford that integration. What is now seen as a major shortcoming in Vygotsky's theorizing likely stems from his shortcomings as a methodologist. Although Vygotsky used difficult tasks to stimulate egocentric speech, he did not appreciate their theoretical implication, and instead viewed them as a discrete tool.

Vygotsky (1962) had set out to establish a unit of psychological analysis that differed from the elemental approach that "analyzes complex psychological wholes into elements" (p. 3). He posited instead the notion of unit, "... a product of analysis, which, unlike elements, retains all the properties of the whole and which cannot be further divided without losing them" (p. 4). Vygotsky believed that the basic unit of verbal thought that met these requirements was word meaning.

Tool-mediated, goal-directed action as the basic unit of analysis is consistent with Vygotsky's discussion of the study of internal processes. His concern with the limits of introspection and subjective report led him to consider ways to externalize internal processes, "connecting it with some outer activity," because only then would objective functional analysis be possible (Vygotsky, 1962, p. 132). It is perhaps useful to once again consider the distinction between Vygotsky the methodologist and Vygotsky the theoretician. Here we see that his research methods embodied the notion of task to allow examination of self-directive speech rising to the occasion of tool mediation. In this instance, however, Vygotsky the theorist failed to rise to the occasion of his methodology.

Modern Considerations for Practice

Researchers continue the struggle to understand basic relations among affective and intellectual processes within the dynamics of emergent interaction. Recognition of the fullness of Vygotsky's theory has diminished the utility of mainstream psychology research tools such as group comparison and one-shot sampling designs. For some modern theorists, constructs like "individual difference" and "independence" are as troubling as introspective reports were to Vygotsky.

Construct Relationships. Integrating affect and intellect in the pursuit of human activity is not an easy task, and the researcher's conception of causality within the integration is essential. For example, Strong (1958) attempted to integrate "will with skill" with adults in the workplace. His model envisioned skill as the fuel for motivation In contrast, in the 1980s, attempts to integrate classroom will and skill essentially viewed motivation as the commitment or self-control that afforded the cognition (see Corno & Mandinach, 1983; Corno & Rohrkemper, 1985; Paris, 1988; Rohrkemper & Bershon, 1984; Rohrkemper & Corno, 1988). These do not seem to be minor differences of emphasis. Teach Strong's worker and motivation will follow; motivate modern students and they will learn. Diagnosis of failure is less benign: Strong's worker needs more help; modern students lack commitment and self-control.

Yowell and Smylie (1999) used a Vygotskian perspective to consider self-regulation as it is developed and enacted at multiple levels, intrapsychological and interpersonal interactions of activity. This includes the internalization that occurs within close, personal relations, the empowerment afforded by contingent social environments, and the future orientation that resides within the broader contexts of social capital. They outlined indicators that identify critical relations at each level, and used this model to consider various school-based interventions and educational practices. Yowell and Smylie (1999) suggested that successful scaffolding within adult–child interaction may actually involve two experts and two novices. Whereas children are likely to be experts in their social environment and the various contingencies placed on their behavior, adults likely are novices regarding the contingencies in the child's social environments. Conversely, adults are experts in the long-term consequences of actions and strategies that promote positive outcomes; children likely are novices in these domains. Their analysis demonstrated that such a characterization of self-regulation drives a richer and potentially more useful conceptualization of self-regulation and related constructs such as autonomy and intersubjectivity.

Activity Theory.   Wertsch (1985), like Zinchenko (1985), claimed that developments within semiotics have challenged the position of word meaning as the basic unit of analysis in psychology, and offered instead the construct of "activity" that embodies tool mediated, goal-directed action. This notion was developed extensively by one of Vygotsky's students, Leontiev, within *activity theory* (e.g., 1974–1975; 1978; also Kozulin, 1986). In this theory, human activity provides the link between the individual and society. According to Leontiev (1974–1975), *activity* is defined by its real or material *object,* its "real motive . . . a need or desire to which it always answers" (p. 22). Activity is composed of goal-directed processes known as *actions,* "a process that is structured by a mental representation of the result to be achieved, i.e., a process structured by a conscious *goal*" (p. 22). Activity theory presumes that motives and goals emerge and exist within the sociocultural realm, rather than as a property of the individual, and that activity, actions, and operations are interdependent and cannot be analyzed in isolation; "Objects themselves can become energizers, goals, and tools only within a system of human activity. Out of the context of this system they lose their being as energizers, as goals, or as tools" (Leontiev, 1974–1975, p. 28–29).

Wertsch (1985) maintained that the construct of activity applies "to the interpsychological as well as the intrapsychological plane, and it provides an appropriate framework for mediation" (p. 208). Like Vygotsky and Leontiev, many contemporary theorists (e.g., Lave, 1988; Rogoff, 1990) presume that cognitive activity is so context bound that one can never distinguish between the individual's cognitive ability, the individual's affective state, the context in which activity takes place, and the activity itself. Rogoff (1990) argued that while "events and activities are organized according to goals . . . . mental processes cannot be dissected apart from the goals to be accomplished and the practical and interpersonal actions used" and that "meaning and purpose are central to the definition of all aspects of events or activities and cannot be separated by summing the features of the individual and the features of the context" (p. 29). From this perspective, constructs such as motivation cannot be distinguished from the larger realm of activity, and the individual's activity cannot be distinguished from the larger sociocultural context. One can only study the larger sphere of human activity—in Leontiev's words, "laying bare [activity's] inner relations" (p. 28). Easier said than done.

Research within a Vygotskian tradition may well involve multiple methods, emergent constructs, and evolving questions. Work related to self-regulated learning, for example, includes group and task comparisons and case study designs. Conceptions of self-directive behavior have emerged as identity activity, and questions of how to predict SRL have evolved into questions of how to promote it through authentic relationships with students that are characterized by challenging support and contingent feedback. The ultimate goal of research in this tradition remains constant, however. SRL is instrumental to socially meaningful activity; SRL not only empowers the individual, it enriches the culture. Even so, there is much to learn from the wealth of SRL research in other traditions and constructs in related areas of study (e.g., attribution theory, parenting styles). The model of co-regulated learning presented next is one attempt to illustrate this utility.

CO-REGULATED LEARNING

Co-regulation is based on three fundamental concepts that we define within the context of classrooms (see McCaslin, 1996; McCaslin & Good, 1996a; 1996b for extended discussion). First, the basic unit of analysis is the relationship with and among individuals, objects, and settings. Relationship replaces conceptions of individuals or tasks as the basic unit of classrooms, achievement or work as their basic goal, and settings as simply places where it all happens. Second, students' basic task is coordination of multiple social worlds, expectations, and goals. Achievement is only one aspect of being a student; being a student is only one aspect of being a child. Students live in multiple social worlds (e.g., home, neighborhood, school) that do not always provide support and safety. Students are members of multiple groups that may well hold noncompatible, unattainable, or unpalatable expectations. Students negotiate more than school demands and even within school, expectations may differ (e.g., Brantlinger, 1993). Students seek multiple goals and negotiate assigned tasks and expectations for multiple reasons with varying commitment. They need to learn "goal coordination" to identify and evaluate the array of goals and tasks they engage, their interrelationships, and strategies to prioritize and optimize among them (see also Dodge, Asher, & Parkhurst, 1989).

Third, goal coordination is learned. It is difficult. It is easier to get off track than to get back on (Corno, 1993). Teachers' basic task is to provide supportive scaffolding and affording opportunities to promote student mediation processes of motivation, enactment, and self-evaluation. Co-regulation among teachers, students, and opportunities is the link to eventual student "self"-regulation, within a particular context. McCaslin and Good (1996b) noted:

> Thus, co-regulated learning replaces an exclusive focus on students who are more or less willing (in protest or in self-protection) and able (because of degree of prior knowledge or cognitive or metacognitive strategies) to learn.... It also replaces an exclusive focus on societal expectations and prejudicial opportunities that promote a conception of student as beneficiary or victim that distract those who would seek change from the emergent interaction of student characteristics with the educational context (p. 660).

In co-regulation, the "ultimate goal of the educational system" is not "to shift to the individual the burden of pursuing his own education" as claimed by John W. Gardner, former Secretary of Health, Education, and Welfare (in Zimmerman & Schunk, 1989, dedication page). Co-regulation connotes shared responsibility; the goal is self-regulation that is instrumental to socially meaningful activity that ultimately enriches the culture.

Table 7.1 (McCaslin & Good, 1996b) delineates students' intrapersonal or "self"-regulatory processes that co-regulation is meant to promote. We use it to organize our presentation of research examples within a sociocultural perspective and illustrate the contributions of research in other traditions. Within each arena, constructs are organized to suggest dynamic tensions between intrapersonal and interpersonal interactions.

Motivation

Two powerful theories dominate motivational research in classrooms. First, attribution theory (Weiner, 1986), focuses on the "look back" to understand why an event has occurred. Much classroom research has profited from this framework, both in achievement (e.g., Ames, 1992) and affiliation (e.g., Goodenow & Grady, 1992; Rohrkemper, 1984, 1985) domains. Understanding how individuals "look back" renders their

TABLE 7.1
Co-regulated Learning: A Heuristic Model of Intrapersonal Processes Afforded by the Social/Instructional Environment (SIE) of Classrooms

| MOTIVATION | | ENACTMENT | | EVALUATION | |
| | | Overt and Covert Strategies | | Self-Evaluation Of Progress | Teacher Evaluation Of Student Progress |
Motive	Goal Setting	SIE-Directed	Intrapersonally Directed	Assessment TOTE—Interim, Final	Assessment of Progress, Product
Needs/wishes/desires Interests	Individual goal(s): difficulty level of attainment, specificity, timing, etc.	Other-involved (e.g., assistance, assertion, equity)	Self-involved (e.g., affect, volition, goal, motive reconsideration)	Affect Attributions	Affect Attributions
Knowledge about/relations among self, task, situation	Goal relationships (e.g., instrumentality of proximal/distal goals) Goal coordination strategies (e.g., integration, modification) Periodic goal review (e.g., recommitment, reformulation, rejection)	Setting-involved (e.g., transform objects, control setting features)	Task-involved (e.g., cognitive, metacognitive strategies, goal refinement)	Decision re persistence: (e.g., continue, modify, or cease)	Decision re instruction: (e.g., continue, modify, or cease)
Attributions					
Efficacy Expectations				Attributional interpretation, immediate and delayed (for future related: goals, tasks, Self)	Attributinal consequences, immediate and delayed (e.g., opportunities, tasks, assessment, accountability)

→Artifacts

assessment ↔ congruence

Note.   Source: McCaslin, M., & Good, T. (1996). The informal curriculum. In D. Berliner & R. Calfee (Eds.), *The Handbook of Educational Psychology* (1st ed., pp. 622–670). New York: American Psychological Association/Macmillan.

emotion and behavior predictable. Attribution theory typically has little interest in individual differences; situations rule the attributional process (Graham & Weiner, 1996). The second, efficacy theory (Bandura, 1997), is more focused on the "look forward," setting goals, maintaining focus, and evaluating progress. Much classroom research has examined linkages among goals, perceived progress, and self-efficacy (e.g., Schunk, 1981). At the core of the goal-setting and goal-seeking individual is personal agency. Efficacy theory is all about individual differences.

In a sociocultural analysis, attribution and efficacy theories both inform the emergent interaction of motivational dynamics, which are the stuff of identity. Attribution theory is one vehicle for understanding motivation as the internalization of sociocultural norms (we suggest this is one reason the "situation rules") and personal agency is one way to organize reciprocal selectivity in seeking, setting, or settling for available opportunities (the reciprocity of "individual differences"). Consideration of their merger brings the reader closer to the construct of emergent interaction in the formation of identity within a sociocultural approach. Another step includes consideration of multi-layered context.

Penuel and Wertsch (1995) illustrated identity formation in a Vygotskian framework that also is informed by Erikson's (1968) notions of identity. Like Vygotsky, Erikson embedded sociocultural, historical and psychological contexts. Vygotsky, however, did not specifically study identity formation. Penuel and Wertsch (1995) argued that human action is the starting point and examined identity formation, that is, developing commitments, in Erikson's basic domains of fidelity, values, ideology, and work. They stated:

> It is for this reason we suggest that identity be conceived as a form of action that is first and foremost rhetorical, concerned with persuading others (and oneself) about who one is and what one values to meet different purposes: express or create solidarity, opposition, difference, similarity, love, friendship, and so on. It is always addressed to someone, who is situated culturally and historically and who has a particular meaning for individuals. The most basic point about identity we could make from this approach is, as Erikson might put it, both simple and difficult to achieve: Identity is about realizing and transforming one's purposes, using signs to accomplish meaningful action (p. 91).

McCaslin and Murdock (1991) studied identity formation in the context of two sixth-grade students, one boy and one girl of similar achievement, members of the same (small city) class (see McCaslin & Murdock [1991] for full selection criteria). Both students are members of working-class families; they live in the same neighborhood. Their parents' managerial styles differ, however. Nora's parents are what Baumrind (1987) described as traditional, Julio's parents are authoritarian–restrictive. Case studies of each were constructed from parent, teacher, and student (multiple) interviews, classroom journals, and process-tracing protocols of problem-solving tasks of varying difficulty. Here we emphasize the power of the emergent interaction construct in understanding SRL and identity development.

The cases illustrate how students come to terms with conflicting allegiances, limited time, and bounded energy. They also illustrate the evolving (in)congruence between home and school expectations. Julio believes that learning takes time and work and help. He has internalized his home learning that stresses obedience and reliance on others rather than one's self—strategies with increasingly diminishing returns as he moves through the grades. Nora has internalized her home learning that stresses self-reliance, "seeing through and following through" for self and others: commitment, responsibility and priority. She discounts her ability and inflates her self-reliance. In contrast to Julio, Nora's home learning serves her better in the later grades than in the earlier, where Julio's help-seeking was valued more than Nora's private puzzling-out. For Julio, it is the reverse. Julio's help-seeking is no longer valued in Grade 6. His help-seeking behavior now signals immaturity or inattention to his teachers and classmates, rather than motivation to learn—SIE messages that confuse, sadden, and anger him.

McCaslin & Murdock (1991) selected these two cases from a larger study including parent beliefs about learning, motivation, their child, and the school. McCaslin and Infanti reviewed the entire group of parent interviews (N = 45) and were struck by the extent to which parents, in general, surrendered authority to their child's school and appeared to accept a role of "outsider" in their child's educational experience. The result was a study of parent identity as a societal construction that is influenced by formal educational policy documents, popular women's magazines, academic research, and educational practice (McCaslin & Infanti, 1998). In the main, modern U.S. culture apparently believes and communicates that too many parents are either incompetent or unwilling to support the work of the schools. The parents of Julio and Nora and the parents of their children's classmates give authority to the school; they do not give up on schooling. Even so, perceived parent neglect of their children's education is part of the sociohistorical context of today's students.

In brief, within a sociocultural perspective, SRL is inherently affective and motivational. Motivation is all about identity, identity is all about personal activity that emerges within a historical cultural context, and a historical cultural context also immerses the significant others in our lives who challenge or validate our emergent identity. A sociocultural model of motivation looks beyond the individual to "know" her beliefs about herself and her experience, her goals, and how she might prioritize and coordinate among them. Identity also informs enactment strategies (that are more and less efficacious) and self-evaluation (that is more and less realistic).

Enactment

We conceptualize *enactment* as those overt and covert strategies directed at self or other control. We include fellow participants and objects (e.g., task and setting features) in the "other" of the social–instructional environment. Thus, we include in enactment those constructs that are often studied independently. We include, for example, self-control strategies like cognitive strategies, metacognitive strategies, volitional control strategies, inner speech, and taking control of emotion when frustrated or beset by tedium. We also include other-control strategies geared to persons, settings, and tasks, such as seeking help when confused, changing small groups when distracted, and starting the problem from the end rather than the beginning when in a rut. Integration of multiple overt and covert constructs allows realization of the wealth of extant research that may well lead to more integrative conceptions of enactment in future study (see Nuthall, 1997, for an extensive review and integration of these literatures). Our organization also underscores the dialectic tensions between intrapersonal and interpersonal interactions.

As we discussed, within a Vygotskian tradition, enactment strategies integrate the affective with the intellectual and are understood within the construct of activity, as "tool-mediated, goal-directed action" (Wertsch, 1985; Zinchenko, 1985). Thus, opportunity is an inherent feature of enactment. The integration of intrapersonal affective and intellectual processes with opportunities was one focus of a program of research within a Vygotskian perspective with elementary school children (Bershon, 1987; Fields, 1990; McCaslin & Murdock, 1991; McCaslin Rohrkemper, 1989; Rohrkemper, 1986; Rohrkemper & Bershon, 1984; Rohrkemper, Slavin, & McCauley, 1983; Segal-Andrews, 1991, 1994). Briefly, tasks that appear to promote—require and challenge—the most efficacious integration of affective and intellectual processes and strategies are those that are subjectively of moderate difficulty. Subjectively perceived moderate-difficulty tasks appear to have the aura of "should" about them; they are similar to something done before yet solution is not certain. They are the "tip of my tongue" of problem solving. It is their very familiarity that increases arousal—and attempted strategies.

In contrast, tasks that are subjectively too easy do not require effortful cognition and importantly, do not promote refinement of strategies or emotion. Those perceived as too difficult are similarly limiting. Too-difficult tasks are beyond learner expectation and accessibility; thus, they do not promote strategic refinement. Rather, they may well afford learner adaptive fantasy and creativity or maladaptive behavior (e.g., resignation or withdrawal without substitution; resentment-fueled alienation). One implication of this research is the design of classroom tasks, opportunities, and assessment procedures that promote and support the adaptive integration of the affective *with* the intellectual.

Evaluation

The third arena of student intrapersonal processes that teachers co-regulate involves the opportunity for and instruction in self-evaluation. Self-evaluation of personal progress is a central feature of social learning theory. In a Vygotskian tradition, self-evaluation is as much about personal meanings and affect as it is about progress toward standards, especially those set by others (i.e., tasks vs. goals). Thus the TOTE (test-operate-test-exit) unit (Miller, Galanter, & Pribram, 1960) to represent this process in Table 7.1 is less than ideal for representing self-evaluation by students who feel as well as think about how they are doing and why they are doing it. Opportunity is central to a Vygotskian perspective. We briefly note three types of opportunities from which knowledge of self might emerge: task design, instructional pacing, and assessment procedures. Task features differ in the extent to which they afford student self-evaluation. For example, tasks designed with subgoals or steps allow interim progress checks. Settings differ in evaluation affordance. Quickly paced classrooms, for example, do not allow time for self-reflection. Some students may profit from "time off self," whereas others may find that speed accelerates their anxiety. Finally, assessment procedures differ in what is learned about performance. Individually referenced assessment enhances self-evaluation more than socially comparative assessment, which can be especially detrimental to less able learners while simultaneously exacerbating the elitism often associated with ability in classrooms (Krampen, 1987).

In addition to the intended and unintended messages embedded in evaluation opportunities in classrooms, co-regulation of student self-evaluation considers as well deliberate instruction in self-evaluation. For example, Russian educators (Zuckerman, 1994) teach self-evaluation as early as first grade to promote students' active participation in their own learning. "Introduction to school life" attempts first to change students' private intrapersonal perceptions of deficiency into active interpersonal opportunities; to change "I can't do this" into "What help do I need." Second, it teaches realistic self-evaluation in situations that involve an objective criterion (vs. opinions). Zuckerman (1994) emphasized the match between students' self-evaluation and teacher evaluation, independent of level of attainment. If teacher and student evaluation coincide, the child is praised for realistic self-evaluation—even if both agree this is a C. The goal is realism. Students' over- and underevaluations are confronted.

"Introduction to school life" seems a provocative co-regulation strategy to support the internalization of standards of excellence while socially situating learning and assessment. Importantly, student self-evaluations need to be realistic if they are to serve mental health and learning. In a model of co-regulation, realistic self-evaluations also are key to adaptive learning. Realistic self-evaluation serves realistic goal setting and thus the very opportunities that challenge and refine enactment strategies that merge the affective with the intellectual.

CLOSING COMMENTS

In this chapter we attempted to make a Vygotskian or sociocultural approach to SRL accessible to the Western reader. At the same time that we highlighted how this approach differs from more typical self-regulation understandings, we also attempted to link Vygotskian or sociocultural constructs with others in the self-regulation literature. We hope that one result is stimulation of research ideas, methods, and constructs. We believe that research in this tradition will promote and challenge meaningful educational opportunities and supportive co-regulating classroom relationships. Our goal is to empower students and to enrich the culture. Our students deserve nothing less. Our culture should settle for nothing less.

REFERENCES

Ames, C. (1992). Classrooms: Goals, structures, and student motivation. *Journal of Educational Psychology, 84*, 261–271.

Bandura, A. (1978). The self system in reciprocal determinism. *American Psychologist, 33*, 344–358.

Bandura, A. (1997). *Self-efficacy: The exercise of control.* New York: W. H. Freeman & Co.

Baumrind, D. (1987). A developmental perspective on adolescent risk taking in contemporary America. In C. Irwin Jr., (Ed.), *Adolescent social behavior and health,* (pp. 93–126). San Francisco: Jossey-Bass.

Berliner, D., & Biddle, B. (1995). *The manufactured crisis: Myths, fraud, and the attack on America's public schools.* New York: Addison-Wesley.

Bershon, B. L. (1987). *Elementary school students' reported inner speech during a cooperative problem-solving task.* Unpublished doctoral dissertation, University of Maryland-College Park.

Bozhovich, L. I., & Slavina, L. S. (1968). Fifty years of Soviet psychology of childrearing. *Soviet Psychology, 7*(1), 3–22.

Brantlinger, E. A. (1993). *The politics of social class in secondary school: Views of affluent and impoverished youth.* Teachers College Press: NY.

Bronfenbrenner, U. (1962). Soviet methods of character education: Some implications for research. *American Psychologist, 17*, 550–564.

Bruner, J. S. (1965). The growth of the mind. *American Psychologist, 20*, 1007–1017.

Bruner, J. S. (1972). Nature and uses of immaturity. *American Psychologist, 27*, 687–708.

Bruner, J. S. (1984). Vygotsky's zone of proximal development: The hidden agenda. *New Directions for Child Development, 23*, 93–97.

Bryk, A. (1999, October). *Issues in school reform.* Pittsburgh, PA: National Academy of Education Annual Meeting.

Corno, L. (1993). The best-laid plans: Modern conceptions of volition and educational research. *Educational Researcher, 22*, 14–22.

Corno, L., & Mandinach, E. (1983). Student interpretive processes in classroom motivation. *Educational Psychologist, 18*, 88–108.

Corno, L., & Rohrkemper, M. (1985). The intrinsic motivation to learn in classrooms. In C. Ames & R. Ames (Eds.), *Research on motivation in education: The classroom milieu* (pp. 53–90). Orlando, FL: Academic Press.

Davydov, V. V. & Raddzikhovski, L. A. (1985). Vygotsky's theory and the activity-oriented approach in psychology. In J. Wertsch (Ed.), *Culture, communication, and cognition: Vygotskian perspectives* (pp. 66–93). New York: Cambridge University Press.

Dodge, K. A., Asher, F. R., & Parkhurst, J. T. (1989). Social life as a goal-coordination task. In C. Ames & R. Ames (Eds.), *Research on motivation in education: Vol. 3. Goals and cognition* (pp. 107–135). New York: Academic Press.

Engels, F. (1890). Socialism: Utopian and scientific. Reprinted from the authorized English edition of 1892, in R. C. Tucker (Ed.), (1972). *The Marx-Engels reader* (pp. 605–639). New York: Norton.

Erikson, E. (1968). *Identity: Youth and crisis.* New York: Norton.

Fields, R. D. (1990). *Classroom tasks, children's control perceptions, and their relation to inner speech.* Unpublished doctoral dissertation, Bryn Mawr College, Bryn Mawr, PA.

Good, T., & Braden, J. (2000). *The great school debate: choice, vouchers, and charters.* Mahwah, NJ: Lawrence Erlbaum Associates.

Goodenow, C., & Grady, K. (1992). The relationship of school belonging and friends' values to academic motivation among urban adolescents. *Journal of Experimental Education, 62*, 60–71.

Graham S., & Weiner, B. (1996). Theories and principles of motivation. In D. Berliner & R. Calfee (Eds)., *Handbook of Educational Psychology* (pp. 63–84). New York: Macmillan.

Gray, J. (1966). Attention, consciousness, and voluntary control of behavior in Soviet psychology. In N. O'Connor (Ed.), *Present-day Russian psychology* (pp. 1–38). London: Pergamon.

Hegel, G. W. F. (1949). *The phenomenology of the mind.* London: G. Allen & Unwin. (Original work published 1807).

Joyce, J. (1976). *James Joyce: A portrait of the artist as a young man.* New York: Penguin. (Original work published 1916).

Kozulin, A. (1986). The concept of activity in Soviet psychology: Vygotsky, his disciples, and critics. *American Psychologist, 41*, 264–274.

Krampen, G. (1987). Differential effects of teacher comments. *Journal of Educational Psychology, 79*, 137–146.

Lave, J. (1988). *Cognition in practice.* Cambridge: Cambridge University Press.

Leontiev, A. N. (1974–1975, Winter). The problem of activity in Soviet psychology. *Soviet Psychology*, 4–33.

Leontiev, A. N. (1978). *Activity, consciousness, and personality.* Englewood Cliffs, NJ: Prentice Hall.

Leontiev, A. N., & Luria, A. R. (1968). The psychological ideas of L. S. Vygotsky. In B. B. Wolman (Ed.), *Historical roots of contemporary psychology* (pp. 338–367). New York: Harper & Row.

Luria, A. R. (1969). Speech development and the formation of mental processes. In M. Cole & L. Maltzman (Eds.), *A handbook of contemporary Soviet psychology* (pp. 121–162). New York: Basic Books.

Luria, A. R. (1979). *The making of mind: A personal account of Soviet psychology* (M. Cole & S. Cole, Eds.). Cambridge, MA: Harvard University Press.

Marx, K. (1844). Critique of the Hegelian dialectic and philosophy as a whole. In R. C. Tucker (Ed.), (1972) *The Marx-Engels reader* (pp. 7–10). New York: Norton.

Marx, K. (1867). *Capital.* Selections from Volume I from the English text of 1887 as edited by Engels, in R. C. Tucker (Ed.) (1972). *The Marx-Engels reader* (pp. 191–327). New York: Norton.

Marx, K., & Engels, F. (1888). Theses on Feuerbach. Reprinted from the version edited by Engels and included with F. Engels & L. Feuerbach, in R. C. Tucker (Ed.) (1972). *The Marx-Engels reader* (pp. 107–109). New York: Norton.

McCaslin, M. (1989). Whole language: Theory, instruction, and future implementation. *Elementary School Journal, 90*(2), 223–230.

McCaslin, M. (1996). The problem of problem representation: The summit's conception of student. *Educational Researcher, 25,* 13–15.

McCaslin Rohrkemper, M. (1989). Self-regulated learning and academic achievement: A Vygotskian view. In B. Zimmerman & D. Schunk (Eds.), *Self-regulated learning and academic achievement: Theory, research, and practice* (pp. 143–168). New York: Springer.

McCaslin, M., & DiMarino-Linnen, E. (2000). Motivation and learning in school: Societal contexts, psychological constructs, and educational practices. In T. Good (Ed.), *Schooling in America: Yesterday, today, and tomorrow, 100th Yearbook of the National Society for the Study of Education* (pp. 84–151). Chicago: University of Chicago Press.

McCaslin, M., & Good, T. (1996a). *Listening in classrooms.* New York: HarperCollins.

McCaslin, M., & Good, T. (1996b). The informal curriculum. In D. Berliner & R. Calfee (Eds.), *Handbook of Educational Psychology* (pp. 622–673). New York: Macmillan.

McCaslin, M., & Infanti, H. (1998). The generativity crisis and the "scold war": What about those parents? *Teachers College Record, 100,* 275–296.

McCaslin, M., & Murdock, T. B. (1991). The emergent interaction of home and school in the development of students' adaptive learning. In M. L. Maehr & P. R. Pintrich (Eds.), *Advances in motivation and achievement* (pp. 213–259). Greenwich, CT: JAI Press.

Miller, G. A., Galanter, E., & Pribram, K. H. (1960). *Plans and the structure of behavior.* New York: Holt.

Mischel, W. (1977). On the future of personality measurement. *American Psychologist, 32,* 246–254.

National Council of Teachers of Mathematics. (1991). *Professional standards for teaching mathematics.* Reston, VA: Author.

Nuthall, G. (1997). Understanding student thinking and learning in the classroom. In B. Biddle, T. Good, & I. Goodson (Eds.), *International handbook of teachers and teaching* (Vol. I, pp. 681–768). Dordrecht, the Netherlands: Kluwer.

Palincsar, A., & Brown, A. (1984). Reciprocal teaching of comprehension fostering and monitoring activities. *Cognition and Instruction, 1,* 117–175.

Paris, S. (1988, April). *Fusing skill with will: The integration of cognitive and motivational psychology.* Address presented at the annual meeting of the American Educational Research Association, New Orleans.

Pavlov, I. (1927). *Conditional reflexes.* London: Oxford University Press.

Penuel, W., & Wertsch, J. (1995). Vygotsky and identity formation: A sociocultural approach. *Educational Psychologist, 30,* 83–92.

Piaget, J. (1983). Piaget's theory. In P. Mussen (Ed.), *Handbook of child psychology* (4th ed., Vol. 1). New York: Wiley.

Rogoff, B. (1990). *Apprenticeship in thinking. Cognitive development in social context.* New York: Oxford University Press.

Rohrkemper, M. (1984). The influence of teacher socialization style on students' social cognition and reported interpersonal classroom behavior. *Elementary School Journal, 85,* 245–275.

Rohrkemper, M. (1985). Individual differences in students' perceptions of routine classroom events. *Journal of Educational Psychology, 77,* 29–44.

Rohrkemper, M. (1986). The functions of inner speech in elementary students' problem solving behavior. *American Educational Research Journal, 23,* 303–313.

Rohrkemper, M., & Bershon, B. (1984). The quality of student task engagement: Elementary school students' reports of the causes and effects of problem difficulty. *Elementary School Journal, 85,* 127–147.

Rohrkemper, M., & Corno, L. (1988). Success and failure on classroom tasks: Adaptive learning and classroom teaching. *Elementary School Journal, 88,* 299–312.

Rohrkemper, M., Slavin, R., & McCauley, K. (1983, April). *Investigating students' perceptions of cognitive strategies as learning tools.* Paper presented at the annual meeting of the American Educational Research Association, Montreal.

Schunk, D. (1981). Modeling and attributional effects on children's achievement: A self-efficacy analysis. *Journal of Educational Psychology, 73,* 93–105.

Segal-Andrews, A. M. (1991). *Intrapersonal functioning and interpersonal context: A proposed model of interaction from a Vygotskian perspective.* Unpublished doctoral dissertation, Bryn Mawr College, Bryn Mawr, PA.

Segal-Andrews, A. M. (1994). Understanding student behavior in one fifth-grade classroom as contextually defined. *Elementary School Journal, 95,* 183–197.

Slobin, D. (1966). Soviet psycholinguistics. In N. O'Connor (Ed.), *Present-day Russian psychology* (pp. 109–151). London: Pergamon.

Stevenson, H. (1970). Learning in children. In P. Mussen (Ed.), *Carmichael's manual of child psychology* (3rd ed., Vol. 1, pp. 849–938). New York: Wiley.

Strong, E. K. (1958). Satisfactions and interests. *American Psychologist, 13,* 449–456.

Vygotsky, L. S. (1962). *Thought and language.* Cambridge, MA: MIT Press.

Vygotsky, L. S. (1978). *Mind in society: The development of higher psychological processes.* Cambridge, MA: Harvard University Press.

Weiner, B. (1986). *An attributional theory of motivation and emotion.* New York: Springer-Verlag.

Wertsch, J. (Ed.). (1985). *Culture, communication, and cognition: Vygotskian perspectives.* New York: Cambridge University Press.

Wertsch, J., & Stone, C. (1985). The concept of internalization in Vygotsky's account of the genesis of higher mental functions. In J. Wertsch (Ed.), *Culture, communication, and cognition: Vygotskian perspectives.* New York: Cambridge University Press.

Yowell, C. & Smylie, M. (1999). Self-regulation in democratic communities. *The Elementary School Journal, 99,* 469–490.

Zimmerman, B. J., & Schunk, D. H. (Eds.) (1989). *Self-regulated learning and academic achievement: Theory, research and practice, Progress in cognitive development research.* New York: Springer-Verlag.

Zinchenko, V. P. (1985). Vygotsky's ideas about units for the analysis of mind. In J. Wertsch (Ed.), *Culture, communication, and cognition: Vygotskian perspectives.* New York: Cambridge University Press.

Zivin, G. (Ed.). (1979). *The development of self-regulation through private speech.* New York: Wiley.

Zuckerman, G. (1994). A pilot study of a 10-day course in cooperative learning for beginning Russian first graders. *Elementary School Journal, 94,* 405–420.

Chapter 8

Constructing Theories, Identities, and Actions of Self-Regulated Learners

Scott G. Paris
University of Michigan

James P. Byrnes
University of Maryland

Alison H. Paris
University of Michigan

Self-regulated learning (SRL) has been a popular topic within educational psychology during the past 20 years, partly because a fundamental goal of education is to promote students who use learning strategies effectively, appropriately, and independently. Much of the enthusiasm for SRL in the 1980s was focused on the acquisition and use of strategies for learning and studying. Some studies were developmental analyses of the strategies that students use. In general, SRL was more evident among adolescents than children and more likely to be used effectively by higher achieving than lower achieving students (Zimmerman, 1989). Other studies included interventions designed to promote SRL. For example, instructional research showed that students could be taught to use effective strategies for reading, writing, and mathematics when provided with metacognitive insights and social supports (Graham & Harris, 1994; Palincsar & Brown, 1984; Paris, Cross, & Lipson, 1984; Pressley, Woloshyn, & Associates, 1995). Thus, becoming a strategic and independent learner was fostered by scaffolded support, discussions about strategies and how to use them, and making visible the tactics of effective problem solving.

Paris and Byrnes (1989) painted these accomplishments in a constructivist frame that emphasized how children acquired and applied cognitive strategies and how SRL was embedded in children's emerging theories of themselves, learning, and the tasks of schooling. Ten years later, there is abundant research on the development of children's theories, strategies, and motivation that underlie SRL, but the interpretive framework of constructivism has changed considerably. We begin this chapter by locating the new tenets of constructivism and the interpretive framework that we apply to SRL. Then we examine the kinds of theories that children construct about themselves and academic learning. In the final section, we consider the dynamics of SRL, specifically, how beliefs and desires can turn theories into actions, and how actions can promote desired identities.

THE NEW CONSTRUCTIVISM

Dividing recent research into the new and the old versions of constructivism is not just an arbitrary historical categorization. The brand of constructivism popular in the United States from the 1960s through the 1980s was the culmination of the cognitive revolution in psychology. It was individualistic in both interpretation and method. The "new" constructivism of the 1990s embedded thinking and learning in social situations and practices so that both interpretation and method are necessarily contextualized (Lave, 1993). DeCorte, Greer, and Verschaffel (1996) described these conceptual differences as the first and second waves of the cognitive revolution. The second wave of constructivism was a reaction against "solo cognition" (cf. Rogoff, 1990) and included expanded emphases on the importance of features of cultures and contexts that had been noted by Bronfenbrenner, Cole, Vygotsky, Dewey, Bartlett, and others.

Our original chapter (Paris & Byrnes, 1989) was a product of the first wave of constructivism and decidedly solitary, partly because that was our charge in that volume. We summarized some of the key principles of "solo" constructive thinking in the following statements:

- There is an intrinsic motivation to seek information.
- Understanding goes beyond the information given.
- Mental representations change with development.
- There are progressive refinements in levels of understanding.
- There are developmental constraints on learning.
- Reflection and reconstruction stimulate learning.

These principles, derived from work by Bruner, Piaget, and others, remain viable for constructivist approaches to learning and development, but the second wave has added additional interpretive principles. We note five of them briefly in the following points because they enlarge the interpretive framework for constructivist views of SRL.

- Learning is situated in social and historical contexts that shape the content and processes of thinking. This claim is the basic criticism of solo cognition and argues for the contextualized interpretations of all learning. These contexts are not just definitions of problem spaces for task analyses, rather they are socially constructed positions, both physical and psychological, that constrain, afford, and support particular actions over others. Cobb and Bowers (1999) pointed out that this difference in the root meaning of context underlies some of the conflicting claims between classical positions of solo (e.g., Anderson, Reder, & Simon, 1996) versus situated (e.g., Greeno, 1997) views of learning.

In our analysis of SRL, it is important to acknowledge that the kinds of strategies, behaviors, and affect that are desirable (in the eyes of students or teachers) are the "things" to be regulated and are specified by significant others such as parents, peers, and classroom teachers. The new constructivism highlights the relativism of any list of SRL behaviors because the actions to be regulated and the goals to be pursued are specified by particular social roles and situations. For example, being obedient and deferent might be desirable among Japanese students whereas being assertive and inquisitive might be desirable for students in other countries. We contend that the what, how, why, and when questions surrounding SRL must be constructed by individuals in their unique situations and any interpretation of how they serve self or regulating functions must attend to the environmental circumstances and individual histories of the students.

- Practical activities in local communities impart procedures, tools, values, and customs to newcomers who strive to become members of the communities. Research by Rogoff (1990) and Lave (1993) revealed the importance of practices for enculturating individuals into communities. Just as children learn to sew, bake tortillas, or take care of pets as part of routine practices at home, students learn to behave and conform to the practices at school. A theory of practice is thus an ecological or phenomenological accompaniment to a theory of learning because children's SRL is an adaptive response to their environmental demands. The sociocognitive view of constructivism maintains that these practices change with history, culture, and participants—again emphasizing the relativism of SRL. For example, students can create different ideas about their own ability depending on the school practices for academic assessment and evaluation. Private, noncompetitive, self-referenced assessment promotes students' ideas about the importance of personal growth and mastery whereas norm-referenced, comparative, and public evaluations of abilities promotes students' ideas about winning classroom competitions and enhancing relative status among peers.

Participation is a key process in the enculturation into membership. One of the fundamental differences between successful and unsuccessful students is their access to effective learning practices because unequal access leads to different patterns of appropriation and use. Preschoolers who do not practice school-like routines of joint reading, asking and answering questions, being obedient and compliant, and sharing appropriately with others are not prepared for the demands of school and cannot participate in sustained learning–teaching episodes. They are also likely to elicit disapproval from peers and teachers in schools and endure more daily social sanctions rather than cognitive lessons. Whether the barriers to learning in school are erected by cultural experiences, SES, unavailable parents, or language differences, the lack of participation in academic practices interferes with achievement in school. Lave and Wenger (1991) described the process of moving from the periphery to the center of social practices based on legitimate peripheral participation (LPP). We contend that some students remain on the periphery of academic circles and do not participate in practices that give rise to effective learning strategies. Thus, they cannot construct the same identities, values, and expectations for SRL actions nor enact them as well as students who are supported for these practices.

• Self is constructed by the individual and by the surrounding social groups. Practices and tools used within communities or schools impact what is available and valuable for students to appropriate. Students acquire the cultural capital of their local groups, which may entail the values and identities associated with sports, music, academic achievement, membership in cliques or gangs, and so on. Each group proscribes specific practices and values that become the behaviors to be appropriated, that is, imitated, monitored, and regulated in order to have the visible appearance of group membership. In this way, group membership has direct consequences on a student's sense of competence and personal identity as well as on the behaviors that ought to be regulated. We emphasize the act of becoming a self-regulated person as part of the development of the individual in a group. The student is object as well as subject, shaped by others as well as an agent of self-regulation. Becoming a student is thus one aspect of identity development during middle childhood and adolescence that is grounded in social situations (Erikson, 1968; Paris & Cunningham, 1996). As we illustrate later, whether students are regulated toward behaviors condoned by teachers or not is a matter of the identities that students are trying to assume and the practices that exemplify those aspired identities.

Because schooling coincides with rapid developmental changes during childhood, children's educational experiences have profound impacts on their many senses of self. The most marked outcome is a sense of one's own ability or self-competence, but there are related self-referenced processes such as self-efficacy and self-control. These properties of the active agent can yield more general outcomes such as feelings of self-esteem and self-worth. Harter (1999) distinguished two meanings of self according to a distinction made originally by James (1890). The self as subject, the I-self, is an active knower with:

"(1) self-*awareness*, an appreciation of one's internal states, needs, thoughts, and emotions; (2) self-*agency*, the sense of the authorship over one's own thoughts and actions; (3) self-*continuity*, the sense that one remains the same person over time; and (4) self-*coherence*, a stable sense of the self as a single, coherent, bounded entity" (Harter, 1999, p. 6).

In contrast, Harter described the "self as object" as the Me-self, with components that include the "material me," the "social me," and the "spiritual me." The Me-self is the result of observation and analysis, the object of thought, whereas the I-self is the analyzer and agent of thought. Current views of constructivism conflate the two aspects of self. In fact, the classic view of solo cognition described by Anderson, Reder, and Simon (1996) focuses on the Me-self and the cognitive features and outcomes of cognition as they impact the individual whereas the situated view of learning locates learning in activities where the I-self is the agent of reasoning. This source of difference in meanings between the two positions was noted by Cobb and Bowers (1999) according to a difference in actors' or observers' perspectives, perhaps another way of denoting subjective versus objective views of self in learning research. For our purposes, it is essential to examine both meanings of self in SRL because students increasingly reflect on their cognitive selves as both objects and agents in their educational endeavors.

• People construct personalized interpretations of their own lives and actions that reflect coherence and optimism. We believe that students understand themselves partly in relation to their own histories and anticipated futures. Looking forward and backward in one's own life shapes the actions that we characterize as SRL because students are regulated toward specific practices, identities, and goals. Autobiographical interpretation can be both a personal psychological process of constructing meaning from experiences and an external analytical tool for understanding SRL. If notions of self are constructed by individuals in social situations and communities, then self-analyses are personalized and idiographic to some extent (Ferrari & Mahalingham, 1997). Markus and Nurius (1986) suggested that people envision multiple selves that are possible: "Self-schemas are constructed creatively and selectively from an individual's past experiences in a particular domain. They reflect personal concerns of enduring salience and investment, and they have been shown to have a systematic and pervasive influence on how information about the self is processed" (p. 955). Students amalgamate available data about their abilities as they draw evidence from teachers, peers, and self-interpretations of their own behavior. They organize this information into coherent representations of who they are and who they want to become.

•   Thinking and learning usually are adaptive and beneficial, but they can lead to maladaptive thoughts and actions, too. Two core premises of classical constructivism are that (a) children represent their experiences in the form of interconnected knowledge structures and belief systems and (b) adaptation changes knowledge and beliefs, usually to be more coherent, more in accord with reality, and more beneficial for the functioning of the person. Whereas the first premise is an enduring part of constructivism, the second has been modified to reflect self-serving conceptions of mental representations. Adaptation involves dynamic processes of changing representations so that environmental success becomes more likely (Anderson, 1990; Byrnes, Miller, & Reynolds, 1999; Halford, 1999). This view leads one to expect the following sorts of outcomes. First, children's knowledge and beliefs become more finely attuned to the "reality" of situations such as academic environments, but as those environments change, so do children's knowledge and beliefs. There is progressive and adaptive fit with environmental demands. Second, the occurrence of an experience matters less than the person's interpretation of that event because the subjective experience is represented cognitively and emotionally. Third, individual differences in interpretations of events can lead to maladaptive tendencies, especially when the short-term benefits or fit of misconceptions lead to long-term liabilities such as avoidance of challenges and deep understanding.

GOALS AND FUNCTIONS OF SELF-REGULATED LEARNING

In the context of SRL, the actions that become regulated promote the person's status, success, or well-being. Consider three questions about the functional coherence of SRL. First, why regulate ones' actions? There can be many reasons to direct learning to specific ends. We emphasize that the motives for regulating one's actions are based on desires for recognition and self-enhancement through positive self-presentation. In other words, children learn to act deliberately in ways that are admired by others, for example, as the "smart student." This can lead to positive evaluations by self and others. However, what actions are chosen to enact what kinds of identities to which social group are highly personal. For example, when a teacher asks a question to the class, one student may raise a hand with the correct answer, another student may mutter an expletive, and another student may shout out a derisive comment. Each action might be regulated by the individual to impress a particular audience and enhance that person's reputation as smart, tough, or funny. Only situated and autobiographical analyses can reveal the motives for the different actions.

Second, how do students acquire regulative strategies? Students learn particular strategies for SRL through both invention and instruction. Sometimes they are told how to solve problems, read text, and write reports with formulaic tactics; sometimes they adapt heuristic routines for their own styles; and sometimes they invent and apply idiosyncratic approaches. Regardless of origin, these practices become part of students' epistemological beliefs about learning that can become deeply ingrained. These practices may be unique and ineffective but steadfastly used. Common examples among adolescents include studying in crowded, noisy places or reading with loud music playing in the background or cramming at the last minute. The strategies may be resistant to instruction if they have been effective periodically in the past. In a parallel manner, children may learn social roles by either instruction or invention. Subsequent reinforcement of those roles will lead to more enduring practices that sustain those identities.

Third, what are the consequences of being a self-regulated learner? The consequences of SRL are usually considered to be better learning and higher achievement, but nonacademic orientations must be noted as well. Students who strive to act in specific ways for particular outcomes and audiences gain recognition from self and others for specific identities. We should not overlook the motivation for students to be self-regulated as highly personalized desires to be regarded by peers as a particular type of person. Too often, traditional accounts of SRL have assumed that students want to use effective strategies and want to be high achievers and they only lack knowledge about how to do so. Our account is decidedly different. We emphasize that students are regulated in their actions in order to enhance their social presentations to others so that they act like X in order to be recognized as a good X. If acting like X leads to positive acceptance, it is likely that students will direct their behavior and learning to become a better X. If the consequences of SRL are not positive, then students are likely to choose a different identity rather than become unregulated. Whether the aspired X is an identity valued by peers, parents, teachers, or self depends on many factors. Children and adolescents may pursue multiple identities, perhaps simultaneously, so their behaviors are regulated by their emerging knowledge about social identities and their growing abilities to convey those impressions.

Higgins (1991) described a stage model of how children construct ideal self-representations and how they pursue them. During early childhood, there is increased sensitivity to the goals and standards held by others and children are motivated to meet these standards and display their competence. In middle childhood, there is a shift from external expectations to "self-guides" and children pursue their idealized selves. However, they become vulnerable to noticing discrepancies between ideal and actual views of self and the results can lead to depression or loss of self-worth. Higgins (1991) said that if children feel that they cannot be the person they *want* to be, sadness and dejection ensue. If they feel they cannot be the person they *ought* to become, however, then they feel anxious and threatened. Such negative reactions can lead to self-regulative actions such as lowered expectations, social avoidance, or helplessness instead of the positive aspirations that children enact when they feel successful in achieving their desired or obliged senses of self. It is the goals of "want" and "ought" that establish the paths for the content and processes of self-regulation.

SRL entails enactment of behaviors that allow the student to be recognized as a distinct individual, perhaps the prankster, the good student, the slacker, or the jock. Indeed, regulation is a consequence, not necessarily the cause, of trying to act according to the roles and rules of a desired identity, one of the possible selves that students try on and try out, in specific situations. Students may experiment with multiple possible identities to gauge reactions from valued others and judge the consequences of various self-presentations. Coherence and regulation of behavior is a consequence of trying to convey a specific identity to others. The distinction is subtle but important. We believe that people do not try to act in a self-regulated manner because regulation is good as an end in itself but rather, they try to act in the manner of a desired identity that results in coherent and regulated actions. Put another way, it is the striving to become a person with specific abilities and identities that organizes a person's knowledge, beliefs, and actions. Regulation is derived from and consequential to identity strivings. Thus, new interpretive frameworks that are grounded in autobiographical interpretation are needed such as life course theory (Elder, 1998) and narrative analyses (Bruner, 1986). Harter (1999) showed the value of such analyses in the following quote:

> In developing a self-narrative, the individual creates a sense of continuity over time as well as coherent connections among self-relevant life events. In constructing such a life story, the I-self is assigned an important agentic

role as author, temporally sequencing the Me-selves into a coherent self-narrative that provides meaning and a sense of future direction" (p. 334).

EMERGING THEORIES OF SELF, REGULATION, AND LEARNING

Harter (1999) claimed that from a cognitive-developmental perspective, the construction of self-representations is inevitable. She said, "... our species has been designed to actively create *theories* about the world, to make *meaning* of one's experiences, including the construction of a theory of self" (p. 8). We agree that children try to make sense of themselves and their worlds, and the ways that they organize the evidence is abstracted into different theories with age and experience. This position has been called *theory theory* because it posits that children's knowledge organization can be studied in ways analogous to the ways that scientists accumulate data, organize abstractions, and create and test theories. Gopnik and Wellman (1994) identified explicitly the features of children's theories that make their knowledge more than loose generalizations or scripts:

> ...children's theories should involve appeal to abstract unobservable entities, with coherent relations among them. Theories should invoke characteristic explanations phrased in terms of these abstract entities and laws. They should also lead to characteristic patterns of predictions, including predictions about new types of evidence and false predictions. Finally, theories should lead to distinctive interpretations of evidence; a child with one theory should interpret even fundamental facts and experiences differently than a child with a different theory. This distinctive pattern of explanation, prediction, and interpretation is among the best indicators of a theoretical structure, and it provides a way of distinguishing the theory theory from its competitors" (p. 262).

In this section, we gather evidence that suggests that children construct theories about learning and education, particularly self-referenced theories about SRL. The theories are aspects of the Me-self, but the processes of creating and testing the theories are functions of the I-self. Both are developing concurrently throughout K–12 education so that new I-self abilities to reflect, analyze, and control thinking will be reflected in changing Me-self theories about competence, efficacy, and identity. The emerging theories of self are intertwined with developing theories about the environment and others (i.e., social cognition) so that children's theories about SRL become more conditional, contextual, and relativistic. We believe that children create theories for foundational domains (Wellman & Gelman, 1992) and that theories about learning are part of children's psychological theories.

Most attention in cognitive development research has been paid to children's emerging theories of mind from 2 to 5 years of age. The focus of much research has been on children's discrimination of the mental from the physical world and differentiation of one's own mind from others' minds. We think similar processes of discrimination and differentiation operate in older children's construction of theories about learning and specifically about academic learning in school. The following section captures the main abstractions and developmental changes in children's theories that are relevant to SRL: self-competence, self-control, academic tasks, and instrumental learning strategies.

THEORIES OF SELF-COMPETENCE

Although there are many developing theories about the self that are relevant to children's SRL, children's beliefs about ability and effort are predominant influences on children's perceptions of their own competence. Years of workbooks, social comparisons, and external evaluations provide continuous data for children to ascertain their relative strengths and weaknesses in the classroom. During elementary school, children learn how to accumulate and interpret this evidence, which results in a progressive fitting and refitting between these external markers of competence and children's constructions of their Me-selves (Paris & Cunningham, 1996). Competence perceptions have strong influences on children's motivation and regulation of actions in the classroom. Children who perceive themselves as competent are more likely to persist when they confront difficulties and to use the abilities and strategies that they possess (Harter, 1990; Pintrich & Schrauben, 1992). Conversely, perceptions of incompetence undermine motivation to tackle new tasks and erode efforts to complete ongoing tasks, even if one's underlying ability is high (Pressley & McCormick, 1995).

Research has shown that children's perceptions of their academic abilities decline precipitously during school (Eccles & Roeser, 1999; Nicholls, 1984). Children enter school with highly positive views of their own competence, often in excess of their objective skills (Pressley & Ghatala, 1989). As early as third grade, however, such optimistic beliefs begin to wane, and many students significantly underestimate their abilities relative to their teachers' more objective estimates (Eccles, Wigfield, Harold, & Blumenfeld, 1993; Juvonen, 1988; Stipek & McIver, 1989). By ages 11 or 12, self-perceptions of competence decrease further (Wigfield et al., 1996). The junior high school transition apparently brings a dramatic decline in ratings of self-perceived ability, perhaps because of changes in schools and classes with new peers that increase social comparisons (Eccles, Midgley et al., 1993). In addition, these declines are often more evident for girls than for boys (Cole, Martin, Peeke, Serocynski, & Fier, 1999; Phillips & Zimmerman, 1990). Thus, children's academic paths and eventual career options can be shaped by the theories that they construct about their own abilities.

Factors That Underlie Changes in Competence Perceptions

What accounts for these substantial changes in self-perceptions of academic ability? Three developmental factors are critical: conceptual changes in children's understanding of ability and effort; changing educational practices and cues for assessing competence; and increasing opportunities to form distorted, often deleterious, theories of ability and effort.

Changing Theories. First, there is a developmental change in the way that children conceptualize academic abilities and effort (Covington, 1987). A child's theory of ability provides answers to the question "How good am I?" and a child's theory of effort answers questions such as "How hard should I try?" The answers to these questions yield a network of constructed beliefs and attitudes about ability and effort. Young children's theories of academic ability are tied to their theories about effort. In the early elementary school grades, many children equate effort or outcome with ability, and they believe that trying hard leads to improvements in ability (Nicholls, 1990). In their original formulation, Dweck and Elliott (1983) characterized young children as "incremental theorists" because these children believe that intelligence is a direct consequence of effort. It was argued that, by 10 to 12 years of age, many students become "entity theorists" who believe that some students have more intelligence than others and that effort cannot overcome these differences. Students who hold entity theories, and also believe that they do not have much intelligence themselves, may exhibit lower effort and declining self-efficacy in school. A recent study, however, found that most students tend to hold a mixture of entity and incremental beliefs (Cain & Dweck, 1995).

In addition to undifferentiated concepts of ability and effort, young children confuse several other concepts with ability. For example, it was found that most young children do not differentiate academic and social competence (Stipek & Tannatt, 1984), many first graders claim that sharing is a quality that distinguishes between average and smart people (Yussen & Kane, 1985), and preschoolers often equate difficulty with ability (Nicholls, 1990). As children get older, they gain an increasing understanding of the differences between these concepts. By 12 years of age, children clearly distinguish skill and luck outcomes, believing that effort only affects outcomes on skill tasks. They also gradually acquire an objective and then a normative concept of difficulty that is separate from ability (Nicholls, 1990). By 10 to 11 years of age, children begin to differentiate the concepts of effort and ability, often regarding them as independent, and by early adolescence, ability is regarded as a capacity that varies among people, the entity theory of ability (Licht, 1992; Nicholls, 1990; Nicholls & Miller, 1984).

A negative consequence of this conceptual advance, however, is heightened sensitivity to one's relative standing among peers and to social comparisons (Nicholls, 1990), resulting in the belief that effort signals low ability. Trying hard begins to take on a negative connotation as young adolescents begin to realize that success with greater effort indicates lower ability. Chapman and Skinner (1989) found that age-related changes in youngsters' preference to be diligent versus not display hard work were associated with their developing understanding of the perceived trade-off between effort and ability. In a similar vein, it was found that fourth- and sixth-grade students desired to portray themselves as effortful to peers, whereas eighth graders were more reluctant to convey to their popular peers that they study hard (Juvonen & Murdock, 1995). According to Ames (1992) and Maehr and Midgley (1991), peer norms are cultivated that promote beliefs that one should not try hard, and many choose not to show that they work hard because of fear of peer rejection (Brown, 1993). Besides, high achievement without perceived effort is regarded as a sign of high ability rather than luck, whereas failure without effort is regarded as a sign of laziness or low task value rather than low ability.

Along with the negative connotation that effort begins to have by fourth or fifth grade, children's theories of ability become differentiated by domain. For example, ability-related academic self-perceptions are differentiated into at least two domains, math and verbal, as well as a general school self-concept (Marsh, 1990; Marsh, Byrne, & Shavelson, 1988). It was also evident that fifth graders differentiated four self-perceptions within academic domains: perceived ability, expectancies for the near future, expectancies for the distant future and causal attributions to ability (Simpson, Licht, Wagner, & Stader, 1996). Wigfield et al. (1996) examined a number of domains (math, reading, music, sports, and general ability) and found that children's responses became more finely tuned and more correlated with external estimates of competencies with increasing age. This domain specificity indicates that students distinguish their competence in different tasks, which helps students to maintain differentiated self-concepts as opposed to generalized high or low feelings of adequacy. Differentiated perceptions of ability also allow the regulation of different effort expenditures across domains so that SRL may be expected to vary by domain as children become older and more experienced.

Changing Environments.   Classroom practices also change as students get older. One result is new and public criteria for self-evaluation that often lead to declines in competence perceptions. Young children believe that completing tasks indicates mastery and mastery is good evidence of competence. Young children are also influenced greatly by social praise and believe they are competent if they receive positive evaluations and praise from other people. The tasks and evaluation practices of the early grades facilitate this optimistic approach that effort and social competence can compensate for ability. Conversely, grades, tokens, and rewards given in the classroom provide distinctive information about performance. For example, Stipek and Daniels (1988) found that children in highly academic kindergartens, where evaluative feedback was very salient, had lower self-perceptions of competence than children in regular kindergartens. In general, however, self-ratings of competence are not related to grade until third or fourth grade (Nicholls, 1978) and are not highly correlated with teacher ratings until the fifth grade (Harter, 1982). As children progress through school, they are exposed to distinct performance evaluations as well as an increase in practices such as ability grouping. Normative and public evaluations increase the opportunities for social comparisons and gradually replace effort as the basis for self-perceived competence. These practices also contribute to the gradual differentiation of self-concept by academic domain because students receive different patterns of evaluation by subject area. Although younger children may have exerted equal effort across domains and considered their abilities equal, as they get older, they may notice that different evaluations given similar efforts indicates lower ability in some subjects.

Distorted Theories.   As classroom practices change and children construct theories of effort that are distinct from their theories of ability, they encounter increasing opportunities to form erroneous concepts and distorted theories. We cite five well-known examples in the literature. First, Marsh (1990) showed that students develop a tendency to accept responsibility for their successes while blaming failures on other people or external circumstances. He labeled this phenomena the Self-Serving Effect or SSE. A second way that children protect their self-perceptions is through disengagement. Certain students, known as *self-worth protective students*, will voluntarily withdraw effort in achievement situations in which poor performance is likely to be attributed to low ability (Thompson, Davidson, & Barber, 1995). A third distortion in children's theories of effort concerns the well-known phenomena of learned helplessness (Abramson, Seligman, & Teasdale, 1978). Students give up trying to control their outcomes when they mistakenly believe that further effort is futile.

A fourth factor that influences children's theories of effort and ability involves the classroom climate and instructional dynamics. For example, teachers' praise has a strong influence on children's theories of effort and ability. If teachers praise randomly selected students for their high ability, other students lower perceptions of their own abilities. Pintrich and Blumenfeld (1985) found that teachers' praise was highly correlated with students' self-perceptions of ability but not effort at second and sixth grade. Work criticism was highly correlated with their effort. Thus, teachers' praise leads to students' hypotheses of who is smart, but teachers' criticism leads to hypotheses about who is lazy. The fifth factor concerns the provision of assistance. Although teacher assistance is often provided to weaker students, it need not be treated as a sign of student weakness. One of the characteristic signs of a competent decision maker is knowing when to seek help and from whom (Byrnes,1998; Newman, 1998). Too often, students avoid asking for help because they are afraid they will be judged to be incompetent by their peers.

Children's theories of ability and effort reflect constructive principles outlined at the beginning of the chapter. Their theories occur early in their school experiences, are modified in response to changing I-self abilities as well as changes in their school environments, may be adaptive or maladaptive, and have direct impact on how they act in school. The clearest indicator may be the effort they expend to succeed, but their theories also are evident in the values they attach to school subjects and their feelings of self-worth. Harter (1999) said that self-processes serve organizing, motivating, and self-protective functions and these self-processes are consistent with the emerging theories that children entertain about self and school. Young children are protected from defensive motivational patterns that undermine SRL by their tendency to hold an undifferentiated concept of effort and ability, rate their ability highly, and expect to succeed as long as they exert the effort (Cain & Dweck, 1995; Paris & Newman, 1990). However, as children's theories become more differentiated and lead to distinctive views of their competence by domain, children form notions of their possible selves that channel their efforts into particular tasks where they expect to succeed and to derive satisfaction. SRL becomes increasingly more situated, personal, and dependent on how ability and effort are differentiated.

THEORIES OF AGENCY AND CONTROL

In addition to theories of ability and effort, children develop theories about their agency and control as they accumulate evidence about the success of their attempts to control academic situations. The notion of personal agency was articulated in detail by Bandura (1997). In attempting to bridge the gulf between cognitive and action theories, Bandura (1986) stated candidly, "Thought affects action through the exercise of personal agency. People use the instrument of thought to comprehend the environment, to alter their motivation, and to structure and regulate their actions" (p. 1). Personal agency means that people take responsibility for their actions and ascribe success and failure to the goals they choose, the resources they mobilize, and the effort they expend. Perceived self-efficacy is a critical component of personal agency because perceptions of one's ability to behave in a particular way establishes one's expectations and motivation. Children who judge themselves to have high self-efficacy participate in academic tasks more readily, choose challenging tasks, work harder, persist in the face of failure, and achieve at a higher level (Pintrich & Schunk, 1996; Schunk & Zimmerman, 1997). Bandura (1997) cited a variety of evidence to show that perceptions of self-efficacy can influence cognitive development and functioning. The basic axiom of agency is that a strong belief in one's ability to use specific actions effectively enhances successful performance. High self-efficacy also brings pride, satisfaction, and positive affect.

What kinds of factors promote positive beliefs in personal agency? One factor is success. Practice at a task with continued success brings feelings of mastery and satisfaction and the belief that similar tasks can be mastered easily in the future (Stipek & Hoffman, 1980). Consistent with the trend toward increased social comparison, students may raise their efficacy by comparing their performances with those of others (Schunk, 1987). A second factor is feedback. Positive feedback reinforces self-efficacy and helps students set goals that are challenging yet attainable (Zimmerman & Kitsantas, 1997). A third factor is observational learning. Observers may raise their self-efficacy by witnessing similar peers succeed at a task, although the effects of such changes in self-efficacy may be negated after observers fail to perform the task as successfully as the models whom they viewed (Schunk & Zimmerman, 1997). A fourth factor that often contributes to positive self-efficacy perceptions is social persuasion. Students often receive persuasive information from teachers, parents, and peers that they are capable of performing a task (Schunk & Zimmerman, 1997). For example, a teacher might encourage a child by saying, "You can figure this word out if you just think about what the rest of the sentence means." The construction of a belief in personal agency depends on the interpretation of success. But task performance and mastery, observation, and persuasion by others that students have the capability, and that success is due to their intelligence and hard work, are the foundations of agency beliefs that contribute to self-competence.

Some researchers consider perceptions of efficacy or agency to be generalized perceptions of ability, perhaps synonymous with domain-specific self-concepts. But others, such as Skinner (1996), consider *agency beliefs* as the specific expectations that people hold about the extent to which a potential means is available to a particular agent. Thus, agency beliefs reflect the link between self and means (*agent–means* beliefs) whereas *control beliefs* refer to the extent to which people believe they can successfully produce desired outcomes and avoid undesired ones. These refer to the link between self and goal, labeled *agent–ends beliefs* by Skinner. *Means–ends beliefs* reflect the instrumental connection in this triadic framework. In a study using factor analyses of interviews with children, Skinner, Chapman, and Baltes (1988) found that these three sets of beliefs are independent contributors to children's self-regulated learning.

We believe that children do construct beliefs about the control they can exercise in their environments. Certain outcomes become desirable or unattainable based on their beliefs, which contribute directly to their theories of ability and effort. Independent goal selection and motivation to pursue goals is unlikely unless students have strong beliefs that they can control their actions to obtain those goals (Johnston & Winograd, 1985). As we see later, maladaptive learning often results from erroneous beliefs that students cannot control their access to legitimate goals of education. Children's beliefs about their agency and control are a major part of their emerging theories about learning. Their perceived self-efficacy to create change, as well as their beliefs about the control they exert over desired outcomes, are both necessary for the enactment of self-regulated behavior. Even if children aspire toward valued educational identities, they will not attempt to fulfill them unless they believe they have the control and the agency to be successful (Cullen, 1985).

THEORIES ABOUT SCHOOLING AND ACADEMIC TASKS

Children begin school with a naïve view of what they will learn and how long it will take. As they encounter changing academic tasks and methods of evaluation, they form more definitive concepts about the nature of schooling and the tasks they confront. Theories of schooling are critical because they interact with theories of self-competence and control. In this section, we consider two aspects of students' theories of schooling: the goals they choose and the structure of tasks.

Students' Goal Orientations

Self-regulated learning requires that students choose appropriate goals as the objects of their effort. Unfortunately, young children begin school with little notion of discrete task goals. For example, many 5-year-olds do not know that reading involves decoding print rather than viewing pictures to tell a story. Bondy (1990) reported that many first graders believe that reading is merely saying the words on the page. Beginning and poor readers often focus on word calling, decoding, and literal interpretation of text rather than understanding that the primary goal of reading is the construction of meaning. Goals of correct pronunciation require different strategies than goals for elaborating and integrating ideas in text (Paris, Wasik, & Turner, 1991).

In a similar vein, young children do not understand the goals of writing as learning the rules of composition for self-expression (Scardamalia & Bereiter, 1986). Nor do most elementary-school children understand that the goal of mathematics is to understand relationships among numbers (Resnick, 1987). Instead, they focus attention on the activities that define the domain such as worksheets and drill exercises. Thus, in some classrooms, mathematics often becomes a dreary set of procedures to be followed in a mindless fashion rather than a set of principles to be understood. In reading, writing, and mathematics, children's theories of academic tasks as skill-based, ritualized procedures interferes with a conceptual understanding of the task and the goals of learning (e.g., Turner, 1995).

Within the classroom setting, the goals that students adopt are often described as "mastery" or "performance" goals (Ames, 1992). Students adopting a mastery goal orientation focus on developing new abilities, enhancing self-competence, mastering challenging tasks, and trying to gain understanding (Dweck & Leggett, 1988, Maehr & Midgley, 1991). In contrast, performance goals emphasize improving status, trying to better normative performance standards, and enhancing one's status by comparison to others' performance. Other theorists have used different names to label similar constructs, such as "learning" and "performance" goals (Dweck & Leggett, 1988; Elliott & Dweck, 1988), "ego-involved" and "task-involved" goals (Nicholls, 1983), or "task-focused" and "ability-focused" goals (Maehr & Midgley, 1991). More recently, mastery and performance goals have been further differentiated into approach and avoidance dimensions. Elliot and Church (1997) stated that "Mastery and performance approach goals are characterized as self-regulation according to potential positive outcomes (task mastery and normative competence, respectively)"; whereas "performance avoidance goals are characterized as self-regulation according to potential negative outcomes" (p. 218). Most current conceptualizations of motivational goals also incorporate mastery avoidance goals, which entail a focus on avoiding misunderstanding, not learning, or not mastering the task (Pintrich, 2000). Performance avoidance is like "fear of failure" and mastery avoidance is like "fear of success." Both kinds of beliefs derive from personal theories of self-competence and the anticipated attributions for success and failure. Both can lead to self-inhibition to protect self-worth.

Much research has been conducted comparing the differential effects of mastery versus performance goals on self-competence, motivation, and achievement behaviors. Research shows that mastery goals are linked to positive, adaptive patterns of attributions (Ames, 1992; Dweck & Leggett, 1988) where students are more likely to make effort attributions for both success and failure (Pintrich & Schunk, 1996). Conversely, students with performance goals tend to make ability attributions for success and failure and see effort and ability as inversely related. Students with mastery goals spend more time on tasks, exhibit more persistence (Ames, 1992; Elliott & Dweck, 1988), and have higher levels of cognitive engagement, especially the use of deeper processing strategies and self-regulated learning strategies (Pintrich & De Groot, 1990). In addition to attributional patterns and motivational behaviors, mastery and performance goals have been associated with different affective outcomes. Mastery goals lead to more pride, satisfaction, intrinsic interest, and positive attitudes about learning tasks (Ames, 1992; Pintrich, 2000).

Although traditional theories of achievement motivation distinguish mastery and performance goals, and place greater value on mastery, the possibility of a benefit of multiple goal adoption was recently acknowledged. Harackiewics and Baron (1998) found that mastery and performance goals had independent, positive effects on interest and performance, respectively, and they contended that both goals can enhance intrinsic motivation if they facilitate task completion and promote a sense of competence. How multiple goal adoptions operate and interact with SRL at different stages of learning and skill development is an interesting question open for investigation. We believe that students pursue different, and perhaps multiple, goals according to situational features of the activity as well as according to their own dispositions and personalities (Wentzel, 1996). For example, as a student named John works on a mathematics assignment, he may observe other students complete the assignment quickly. If John is struggling with the assignment, he may make an attribution about his own ability, decide to avoid trying to complete the task successfully, and instead, cheat or fake the answers so he can turn in the assignment quickly with the appearance of having the ability to complete the task with ease. In this hypothetical case, John shifted from goals based on mastery approach to mastery avoidance to performance approach coupled with social enhancement. Our point is that goals emerge as students engage in tasks, and the conditions surrounding the task may influence their emerging theories of the task and their competence and be reflected in their evolving goal orientations.

Motivation is Rooted in Academic Tasks

Where do these different goal orientations come from? Many researchers suggest that goals arise from the structure of classroom experiences. For example, variety, diversity, challenge, control, and meaningfulness are task dimensions that have been shown to influence the adoption of mastery goals (Blumenfeld, 1992; Meece, 1991). Conversely, when teachers structure classroom tasks that emphasize competition, rote procedures, and management, students are likely to perceive tasks as busy work, to focus on task completion, and to engage in superficial manners (Blumenfeld, Hamilton, Bossert, Wessels, & Meece, 1983; Doyle, 1983). Such activities encourage students to construct theories of academic tasks that lead to minimal and hasty engagement in learning. Superficial approaches to classroom tasks are fostered by teachers who give many similar tasks to students to complete, especially tasks that are "closed" instead of "open-ended" (Turner, 1995). Closed tasks include worksheets, rote recall, and little creativity. In contrast, open-ended tasks include projects, research, and interpretation.

Paris and Turner (1994) summarized the central features of open-ended tasks that promote intrinsic motivation according to easily remembered constructs involving the letter "C": *constructing* personal meaning, *choosing* how to approach and solve a task, seeking *challenging* tasks, *controlling* strategies for success, *collaborating* with others, and deriving *consequences* from performance that enhance self-efficacy. Turner, Meyer, Cox, Logan, DiCintio, and Thomas (1998) analyzed the conditions leading to high involvement of fifth and sixth graders in mathematics and found that high involvement and positive affect were most evident in classrooms where teachers negotiated understanding, transferred responsibility to students, and fostered intrinsic motivation. Involvement was much lower in classrooms where teachers used Initiation–Response–Evaluation sequences, focused on extrinsic motivation, and had few challenging tasks.

We want to call attention to two critical characteristics of children's theories about tasks in school. First, they search for problem isomorphs to minimize effort. As students become familiar with academic problems, they recognize similarities in the demands of worksheets, basal reading lessons, social studies passages, story problems, and other traditional academic tasks. Recognition of the similarities in structure and required responses to tasks elicits particular strategies and goals. The second characteristic is the construction of algorithms and habits to complete tasks quickly. Most academic tasks elicit a high degree of proceduralization from students. As they encounter similar tasks, they transfer habitual procedures, partly because of economy of effort and partly because of cognitive accuracy. Many students develop effective problem-solving strategies for completing workbook assignments, oral reading, story problems, and other tasks. However, others develop maladaptive strategies to minimize task involvement. For example, by fourth or fifth grade, most students learn that many questions on reading tests can be answered without reading the passage and that it saves time to try to answer the questions *before* reading the passage. Teachers promote the use of mindless procedures through their emphasis on compartmentalized tasks and subjects in school. Thus, both good and bad intentions motivate children to search for algorithms and procedures to accomplish tasks quickly, but only some conditions promote involvement and mastery orientations.

Clearly, children's theories of academic tasks depend on years of experience. As they become more familiar with repeated activities, they can recognize similarities among problems, thus eliciting appropriate problem-solving strategies. By 12 to 13 years of age, children recognize the structure of various texts and apply relevant strategies to them. However, in reading, mathematics, and other subject areas, children often devise "buggy algorithms" or idiosyncratic procedures applied erroneously to difficult problems (Resnick, 1987; VanLehn, 1990). The motivation for inventing these faulty procedures is partly a best-guess procedure of applying well-practiced procedures to new situations. Although the misapplied procedures are sometimes humorous, they can lead to enduring maladaptive patterns of learning and motivation.

THEORIES OF STRATEGIES

Self-regulated learning is intentional and resourceful; students must learn to use a wide variety of strategies independently in the classroom. Some strategies organize information processing whereas other strategies help to manage time, motivation, and emotions (Weinstein & Mayer,

1986). Some strategies are performed mentally and some are external strategies such as note taking. Some strategies are specific to situations and tasks whereas others can be general heuristics. Despite the variety of learning strategies, certain characteristics are shared among them (see Paris & Lindauer, 1982). First, strategies are deliberate actions performed to attain particular goals. Second, they are invented or generated by the person and involve both agency and control rather than compliance or mindless rule following. Third, strategies are selectively and flexibly applied; they involve both cognitive skill and motivational will. Fourth, strategies are often socially assisted tactics for problem solving that become independent, especially when related to academic learning tasks. Fifth, although strategies are important trouble-shooting tactics and are often consciously applied or shared, the preferred developmental fate of strategies involves both automatization and transfer to a variety of tasks (Paris & Winograd, 1990).

Some strategies develop early and the rudiments of strategic behavior are evident long before children begin school. Wellman (1988) argued that 2- to 5-year-old children develop a rich variety of strategies that are frequently used for remembering objects and events. From daily tasks, like searching for toys and remembering to brush one's teeth, emerge fundamental concepts of strategies that include an understanding that strategies are goal-directed, instrumental, and depend on personal effort or agency (Paris, Newman, & Jacobs, 1985). During school years, children's strategies reflect advances in cognitive development. For example, elaborate techniques for remembering, communicating, and attending develop between 5 and 12 years of age (Schneider & Bjorklund, 1997; Brown, Bransford, Ferrara, & Campione, 1983; Paris & Lindauer, 1982). School experiences also cultivate specific strategies for reading, writing, computing, studying, and taking tests (Pressley & Levin, 1987; Weinstein & Mayer, 1986). Thus, cognitive development, practice with academic tasks, and specific instruction all facilitate the development of cognitive strategies for academic learning.

What kinds of information do children include in their theories about strategies? First, children develop an awareness of what strategies are (declarative knowledge). There is a conceptual understanding of the functions and purposes of a repertoire of strategies. Students who are taught process-writing approaches understand that planning and revising are critical strategies for composing (Scardamalia & Bereiter, 1986). Second, students understand how to use strategies (procedural knowledge). They develop procedural knowledge about the requisite actions. Repeated practice with procedures for solving tasks in school may give rise to explicit procedural knowledge as well as a conceptual understanding of strategies. Third, children begin to understand when and why strategies are effective (conditional knowledge). This aspect of strategy understanding may be fundamental for children's spontaneous transfer of appropriate strategies. For example, Paris, Newman, and McVey (1982) found that children who received explanations about the importance and utility of memory strategies continued to use them without instructions, whereas other children reverted to their previous nonstrategic behavior and lower levels of recall. O'Sullivan and Pressley (1984) also found that children who received explanations regarding when and why to apply effective strategies for a paired-associate task performed significantly better than children who were simply taught to use the method. Pressley, Ross, Levin, and Ghatala (1984) found that conditional knowledge helped children choose between more and less efficient strategies. Fabricius and Hagen (1984) observed that children who attributed successful recall to their card-sorting strategies continued to use the strategies in subsequent tasks to facilitate memory.

Most research on cognitive strategies during the 1970s and 1980s emphasized the importance of children's understanding declarative, procedural, and conditional knowledge for effective maintenance and generalization of the tactics. The development of strategic reading appears to depend on students' progressive understanding of the nature and usefulness of strategies that aid comprehension (Paris, Lipson, & Wixson, 1983). However, strategic behavior involves more than simply knowledge or metacognition about strategies. Children's theories of strategies must be joined with their theories of self-competence, effort, and academic tasks in order to be manifested in self-regulated learning. Knowledge needs to be translated into action with appropriate intentions and volitional control (Corno, 1989).

Our review showed that children acquire a great deal of information about their own abilities, the nature of tasks they confront in classrooms, and how they manage their effort and strategies to accomplish particular goals. These theories are often analyzed separately by researchers, and they may be discrete initially for young children. A central task of development is to integrate the information about the various components that influence SRL. Cognitive constraints on language and information processing may affect the development of children's theories of cognitive processes. Children's theory building is also constrained by task specificity. Children's early experiences with reading, writing, and arithmetic that require intentional learning and self-regulated behavior may be limited to a few formal tasks, settings, and people. Thus, the data available for theory building may not be representative and may take on distorted significance.

FROM THEORIES TO ACTIONS

Knowing is not sufficient grounds for acting. This problem persists for many accounts of SRL and might apply to "theory theory" positions also, so it is worth comment. We think that many accounts of SRL involve definition and description of various processes of self-management with less attention given to dynamic processes of regulation. For example, many accounts of SRL, especially those from an information processing perspective, identify important components such as attributions, self-observations, goals, and strategies and show how each can influence the effectiveness of students' learning. However, the components are analytical devices for description, and they do not show how these components are related in the mind of the learner. Models depicting boxes connected by arrows are mechanical and do not show the interactions among variables. Models with boxes within boxes or boxes connected by two-headed arrows simply assert complex interactions. Such models create a large list of possible components and possible relations in SRL that are not comparable or testable across models.

Furthermore, many accounts ignore the self in SRL (cf. McCombs & Marzano, 1990) when the components are all descriptions of prerequisite knowledge without an agent. As Vygotsky pointed out, such models lack purpose and human interactions. Regarding the separation of intellect and affect, Vygotsky (1986) said, "Their separation as subjects of study is a major weakness of traditional psychology, since it makes the thought process appear as an autonomous flow of thoughts thinking themselves, segregated from the fullness of life, from the personal needs and interests, the inclinations and impulses, of the thinker" (p. 10). This criticism is a variation on the familiar criticisms of cognitive models such as homunculi guiding thinking or regressive causality of one type of thinking causing another that causes another. It is a problem for SRL theories because without an agent with will and emotion, the models are cold and static (Paris, 1988). Knowledge may be a prerequisite for action, but knowing does not impel action by itself. There is no causal mechanism within a knowledge-bound theory.

These problems of knowledge-driven systems could threaten theory theory positions also unless there are additional explanatory frameworks introduced. Wellman (1988) proposes a causal connection from thought to action based on the child's belief–desire–action. Believing in X motivates the pursuit of Y, which leads to action Z. It is the "knowledge turned desire" construct that attaches motivation to the theory. We advocate a similar causal framework for understanding SRL in order to solve the problem of why people act in particular ways that are self-regulated. Our proposal, however, is not restricted to acting in prosocial ways to apply "good" strategies for academic learning alone. Instead, we propose a general view of why people act in coherent and consistent ways and suggest that the label of SRL that is used to describe their actions is not the motive for action but a description of the resulting behaviors. People do not strive to be regulated nor does knowledge about SRL alone motivate people to enact their knowledge. Motivation for SRL cannot be reduced to direction, instruction, or support from others, either, because then it would not be *self*-regulated. So, we are left with the task of identifying the motivation for SRL that is internal, self-determined, constructed, and causal. We propose identity confirmation as an underlying motive.

Seeking and Confirming Senses of Self

SRL is adaptive because it is the person's responses to changing environmental demands and opportunities according to the individual's abilities and theories. The regulated aspects of children's behavior in schools, we contend, is partly due to their strivings to be regarded or represented in certain ways, certain possible selves and aspired identities. This may be an implicit aspect of young children's behavior in school, but it becomes more deliberate and organized with increasing age as children's theories become more differentiated and their notions of Me-selves become more conscious. By middle school and high school, most adolescents are highly regulated toward patterns of behavior that increase their own self-worth in their communities of valued others. For many, the academic orientation of SRL is consistent with models of achievement-oriented students. Rohrkemper and Corno (1988) described such students as those who, "... strive, seek goals that involve mental risks, and can learn from their mistakes—students who have the capacity to *respond* flexibly and proactively to stressful situations and also to *initiate* tasks that challenge their own abilities—these are students who assume control of their own learning" (p. 299).

Strivings, whether for academic success or other purposes, include the motivating conditions of want and desire fueled by feelings of efficacy and ought (Bandura, 1997; Higgins, 1991). We speculate that students exhibit regulated actions as they try out various personas and the roles associated with them. The desire that motivates action is the effort to be like a desired or aspired "self" such as the smart student, the fast work-finisher, or the quiet-serious intellectual. These possible selves all lead to self-regulated actions typically associated with good strategy users, good students, and the laundry list of good SRL. Yet, the aspired self could also include identities rejected by teachers but supported by some peers, such as the practical joker, the bully, the liar, or the cheat. Regardless of the particular identity that the person is trying to enact, the actions are intended to confirm this specific Me-self for the audience of others as well as for the individual. Seeking to try out and confirm a social role is the desire–action link. Striving to make the ideal self the ought self turns belief into pursued actions (Higgins, 1991). In any case of trying to confirm a notion of Me, the critical dynamic motive that relates desire to action is self-regulated. The process of self-regulation thus must be separated from the values of the actions or the social acceptability of the aspired identity.

The result of regulated actions must be evaluated partly by the reactions of others and partly by self-evaluations. If a student tries to act in a way that shows disrespect for authority and personal bravado, such as refusing to follow a teacher's demand, the student might be held in high or low regard by various peers. The hypothetical student must judge the reactions of valued and nonvalued peers, as well as teachers and parents, to determine whether this particular act and its associated identity leads to increased or decreased social esteem. Those acts that confirm an identity and are also rewarded by others are likely to be repeated and internalized. Thus, the strength of the link between desired identity-regulated actions is influenced by the consequences of personal and social evaluations. When disapproval, sanctions, or neglect follow an attempt to "be like X," then a new identity might be tried out. This is the link between beliefs and desires. As students hypothesize and fantasize about who they are, who they might become, and who others might admire, they try out various identities, roles, and behaviors. These are the "pretensions" described by James (1890), the "possible selves" described by Markus and Nurius (1986), and the self-construals noted by Boekaerts (1998). Students have constellations of emerging beliefs about these personas. The belief that a specific identity might be perceived positively by others leads to the desire to try that identity on, which in turn leads to regulated actions. Confirmation or disconfirmation of the aspired Me stimulates the ensuing regulated actions according to the same dynamic relations. The result is a series of experiments with different identities in different social situations with different audiences. Those experiments that lead to success, in terms of positive affect, are likely to be sustained, but the processes of self-evaluation, interpretation of feedback, confirmation of aspired identities, and perseverance of regulated actions are complex.

Examples of Identity Strivings

Our ideas about SRL being derived from personal attempts to try out and confirm possible social identities is grounded in a constructivist framework of personal knowledge, but we want to add the sociocultural axioms noted earlier as part of the second wave of constructivism. We provide three examples of variations in SRL that emanate from distinctive views of the Me-self. Consider first the identity of academic nonachievers, low achievers, or anti-achievers. Regardless of the labels we attach to students who resist socially sanctioned roles and behaviors in school, the dynamics of their identities may be similar and equally self-regulated. For example, students who are not successful in school may disdain identities linked with grades, achievement, and adult approval or expectations for future schooling because they all evoke anxiety about possible failure. These threats to self-esteem can be avoided with adoption of identities that eschew achievement and efforts to be good students and thus they choose alternative identities based on resistance to achievement. Their behaviors may exhibit defiance to authority in school, denial of academic goals, refusal to use strategies for learning and studying, and avoidance of mastery goals. They all preclude effort that might lead to failure and redirect efforts to enhancing identities based on nonachievement in school. When the efforts are redirected to socially sanctioned values such as athletics or music, adult and peer approval may follow, but when efforts are redirected to antisocial behaviors such as delinquency or drug use, then peer group approval may become the sustaining influence. The end result is highly regulated individuals who act in ways that undermine effort and success in school as a defensive maneuver to enhance alternative identities.

A second example of the dynamics of identity confirmation for SRL is evident in group stereotyping. Consider gender differences in mathematics achievement. This well documented effect has been interpreted as arising from parental and teacher beliefs that are transmitted to students (Eccles & Roesser, 1999). For example, if girls are thought to have more difficulty with math, then they may attribute success to transitory effort and failure to enduring low ability, whereas boys make the opposite attributions, namely, success is due to high math ability and failure is due to a temporary lack of effort. Such attributional patterns can nurture distinct beliefs about competence and thus lead to different investments or effort, different evaluations of the subject matter, and different expectations for success (Eccles & Roeser, 1999). School may foster confirmation of boys' identities as math able and girls' identities as math handicapped, a stereotype that is inaccurate but threatening. Spencer, Steele, and Quinn (1999) showed that inferior performance of women on difficult math problems could be exaggerated if the stereotypical gender differences were emphasized or eliminated if the expected gender differences were dispelled.

The same dynamic may operate for stereotypes based on race. The well known "stereotype threat" effect demonstrates that individuals perform worse when they believe that their identity is negatively stereotyped in a domain and that task failure will confirm that stereotype (Steele, 1997). This effect has been shown to lower the standardized test scores of African-Americans dramatically. It is clear that achievement strivings in school, the backbone of SRL, can be impaired when students feel that their performance will confirm a negative stereotype. Individuals caught in stereotyped threat predicaments may find it more adaptive in the short term to avoid achievement strivings, which is perhaps why women have often avoided math courses and minorities devalued academic success. Thus, the desire–action link is volitional and regulated, but it may reveal adaptive patterns influenced by links between beliefs and actions such as expectancies and stereotyped threats.

The third example reflects the influence of social, cultural, and historical forces on identity confirmation. We believe that there is not a list of effective SRL actions that all students follow because there are different goals for students based on different notions of identity. The clearest examples of these differences are in cultural comparisons. American students are enculturated into academic environments where individual achievement is prized. Most accounts of SRL are based on this American view of achievement so they value cognitive strategies, social comparison, and competition that enhance individual success. However, non-Western views of education and human development do not value individualism to the same extent. Asian and Polynesian cultures, for example, place higher values on collaboration, teamwork, family, and cooperation. In school contexts, students are supported for social identities based on these values rather than the individual success of American students. Therefore, the regulated actions associated with different aspired identities are different among students in Asia and the United States. Boekaerts (1998) argued that these cultural differences in self-construals lead to "personal stakes" and self-actualizing goals among Western students and to "collective interest" and self-harmonizing goals among Asian students.

Implications of Identity Construction and Confirmation for SRL

How is this proposal different from other explanations of SRL? First, and most importantly, we believe that the actions of SRL are derived from developing theories about the self. The Me-self is a developmental construction that begins in infancy and continues throughout the life-span. Theories about academic competence, tasks, goals, strategies, standards, agents, and so forth are rooted in larger psychological theories about self and learning. Thus, emerging theories about SRL are part of the theory theory in cognitive development. Second, the emerging theories are constructed from internal and external sources of information. Internal notions about possible selves interact with external feedback from others about personal talents so that the range of hypothesized and aspired identities is shaped by age and social environments. Third, the dynamics of SRL are enacted through belief–desire–action sequences in which students experiment with various identities and their roles. Confirmation and approbation for some roles over others leads to winnowing and perseverance of supported identities. Thus, SRL is not about acquiring strategies for learning as much as it is about becoming a specific kind of person who uses particular behaviors in a regulated way.

Fourth, the dynamics of acting according to aspired identities is the root motive for SRL. Actions in pursuit of or derived from different identities will vary tremendously and, thus, so will demonstrations of SRL. Part of the variability is due to age and emerging sophistication of academic theories. Part of the variability is due to situations because some environments elicit, support, and privilege some identities over others. These could include peer, familial, and cultural environments that provide social guides for the development of self-guides in identity development. Part of the variability may be by domains because students recognize where their efforts pay off and where they do not, so they invest selectively by academic domains and personal talents. Finally, part of the variability in observed SRL is due to personal strivings to adopt multiple identities. As students experiment with alternative roles, they may discover the need to act differently to satisfy distinct identities according to achievement, race, gender, athletics, and so on. They learn to monitor and regulate their behaviors according to the immediate situation and audience and may switch among different sets of behaviors for the different roles. This is highly self-regulated, but the behaviors and identities that are being controlled are variable.

Fifth, the processes of self-regulation may be normative according to developmental constraints on theorizing about self and according to constraints on self-referenced processes of evaluation and regulation, but the consequences of the constructed self may be idiosyncratic (Harter, 1990). Individual differences emerge in SRL because students are trying to assert their unique Me-selves for their own confirmation and for the approval from others. They may construct their identities as students according to beliefs transmitted by parents, teachers, and peers, and they may create stereotypical senses of Me that include race, gender, and culture as much as academic achievement. This makes the separation of identity development and SRL impossible because the behaviors pursued in school are manifestations of whom students are trying to become. It also makes clear that SRL cannot be taught as a curriculum of "good strategies" removed from the goals, roles, and identities of students. How and why students exercise self-control of their academic behavior must be explained with reference to personal development. Thus, SRL is autobiographical in the ongoing construction of self and any attempts to understand or manipulate how students regulate their behavior in schools requires analyses, as well as interventions, that are attuned to the personal, historical, and developmental features of the individual.

CONCLUSIONS

Earlier in this chapter, we noted that a fundamental goal of education is to promote students who use learning strategies effectively, appropriately, and independently. We showed how constructivist approaches to SRL can be useful for understanding individual and developmental differences in the attainment of this goal. We suggested that children are naturally inclined to construct explanatory frameworks and to make sense of their educational experiences. When things go right (i.e., they are given multiple opportunities to succeed, scaffolded interpretations of their performance, culturally meaningful and challenging tasks, and encouragement to pursue positive possible selves), children construct theories of competence, tasks, and selves that foster the acquisition and use of adaptive learning strategies. When things go wrong, however, we showed that children construct theories that foster the acquisition and use of maladaptive learning strategies and inappropriate goals. In essence, theories are the conceptual and conditional knowledge that are the bases for procedural knowledge. The strategic and regulated features of what children do, especially in school, is largely a function of what they understand about themselves and school-related tasks.

We also suggested that the motives for enacting conceptual knowledge are rooted in children's beliefs and desires. Specifically, children believe that some actions are warranted in situations, and the actions are typical of people with particular identities. They desire to try out those identities or to be perceived as a person with those actions and thus they are motivated to engage or sustain specific behaviors. The beliefs about what should be done in academic situations and what kind of person is signaled by those actions are not always accurate or clear to children so even when they try to enact their beliefs, they may behave inappropriately by some standards. However, it is important to note that the I-self regulates the behaviors to exhibit the desired or aspired Me-self. The chain of events in the beliefs–desires–actions sequence provides the conceptual knowledge (i.e., children's emerging theories), the overt behaviors (i.e., strategies and actions), and the connecting motives (i.e., desires and aspirations) of SRL. In closing, it is important to note that the constructivist perspective on SRL provides a powerful lens to study the confluence of multiple aspects of children's motivation and learning in specific environments.

REFERENCES

Abramsom, L. V., Seligman, M. P., & Teasdale, J. D. (1978). Learned helplessness in humans: Critique and reformulation. *Journal of Abnormal Psychology, 87*, 49–74.

Ames, C. (1992). Classroom: Goals, structures, and student motivation. *Journal of Educational Psychology, 84*, 261–271.

Anderson, J. R. (1990). *The adaptive character of thought.* Hillsdale, NJ: Lawrence Erlbaum Associates.

Anderson, J. R., Reder, L. M., & Simon, H. A. (1996). Situated learning and education. *Educational Researcher, 25*(4), 5–11.

Bandura, A. (1997). *Self-efficacy: The exercise of control.* New York: W.H. Freeman.

Blumenfeld, P. C. (1992). Classroom learning and motivation: Clarifying and expanding goal theory. *Journal of Educational Psychology, 84*(3), 272–281.

Blumenfeld, P. C., Hamilton, V. L., Bossert, S. T., Wessels, K., & Meece, J. (1983). Teacher talk and student thought: Socialization into the student role. In J. M. Levine & M. C. Wang (Eds.), *Teacher and student perceptions: Implications for learning* (pp. 143–192). Hillsdale, NJ: Lawrence Erlbaum Associates.

Boekaerts, M. (1998). Do culturally-rooted self-construals affect students' conceptualizations of control over learning? *Educational Psychologist, 33*(2/3), 87–108.

Bondy, E. (1990). Seeing it their way: What children's definitions of reading tell us about improving teacher education. *Journal of Teacher Education, 41*, 33–45.

Brown, A. L., Bransford, J. D., Ferrara, R. A., & Campione, J. C. (1983). Learning, remembering, and understanding. In J. H. Flavell & E. M. Markman (Eds.), *Carmichael's manual of child psychology* (Vol. 1, pp. 77–166). New York: Wiley.

Brown, B. B. (1993). School culture, social policies, and the academic motivation of U.S. students. In T. M. Tomlinson (Ed.), *Motivating students to learn: Overcoming barriers to high achievement* (pp. 63–98). Berkeley: McCutchan.

Bruner, J. S. (1986). *Actual minds, possible worlds.* Cambridge, MA: Harvard University Press.

Byrnes, J. P. (1998). *The nature and development of decision-making: A self-regulation perspective.* Mahwah, NJ: Lawrence Erlbaum Associates.

Byrnes, J. P., Miller, D. C., & Reynolds, M. (1999). Learning to make good decisions: A self-regulation perspective. *Child Development, 70*, 1121–1140.

Cain, K. M., & Dweck, C. S. (1995). The relation between motivational patterns and achievement cognitions through the elementary school years. *Merrill-Palmer Quarterly, 41*, 25–42.

Chapman, M., & Skinner, E. A. (1989). Children's agency beliefs, cognitive performance, and conception of effort and ability: Individual and developmental differences. *Child Development, 60*, 1229–1238.

Cobb, P., & Bowers, J. (1999). Cognitive and situated learning perspectives in theory and practice. *Educational Researcher, 28*(2), 4–15.

Cole, D. A., Martin, J. M., Peeke, L. A., Serocynski, A. D., & Fier, J. (1999). Children's over- and underestimation of academic competence: A longitudinal study of gender differences. *Child Development, 70*(2), 459–473.

Corno, L. (1989). Self-regulated learning: A volitional analysis. In B. J. Zimmerman & D. H. Schunk (Eds), *Self-regulated learning and academic achievement: Theory, research, and practice* (pp. 111–141). New York: Springer-Verlag.

Covington, M. V. (1987). Achievement motivation, self-attributions and exceptionality. In J. D. Day & J. G. Borkowski (Eds.), *Intelligence and exceptionality: New directions for theory, assessment and instructional practices* (pp. 173–213). Norwood, NJ: Ablex.

Cullen, J. L. (1985). Children's ability to cope with failure: Implications of a metacognitive approach for the classroom. In D. L. Forrest-Pressley, G. E. MacKinnon, & T. G. Waller (Eds.), *Metacognition, cognition, and human performance* (Vol. 2, pp. 267–300). Orlando, FL: Academic Press.

DeCorte, E., Greer, B., & Verschaffel, L. (1996). Mathematics learning and teaching. In D. Berliner & R. Calfee (Eds.), *Handbook of Educational Psychology* (pp. 491–549). New York: Macmillan.

Doyle, W. (1983). Academic work. *Review of Educational Research, 53,* 159–200.

Dweck, C. S., & Elliott, E. S. (1983). Achievement motivation. In P. Mussen (Ed.), *Carmichael's manual of child psychology* (Vol. 4, pp. 643–691). New York: Wiley.

Dweck, C., & Leggett, E. L. (1988). A social cognitive approach to motivation and personality. *Psychological Review, 95,* 256–273.

Eccles, J., Midgley, C., Wigfield, A., Buchanan, C., Reuman, D., Flanagan, C., & MacIver, D. (1993). Development during adolescence: The impact of stage-environment fit on young adolescents' experiences in schools and families. *American Psychologist, 48,* 90–101.

Eccles, J. S., & Roeser, R. W. (1999). School and community influences on human development. In M. H. Bornstein & M. E. Lamb (Eds.), *Developmental Psychology: An advanced textbook* (pp. 503–555). Mahwah, NJ: Lawrence Erlbaum Associates.

Eccles, J., Wigfield, A., Harold, R. D., & Blumenfeld, P. (1993). Age and gender differences in children's self and task perceptions during elementary school. *Child Development, 64*(3), 830–847.

Elder, G. H. (1998). The life course as developmental theory. *Child Development, 69*(1), 1–12.

Elliot, A. J., & Church, M. A. (1997). A hierarchical model of approach and avoidance achievement motivation. *Journal of Personality and Social Psychology, 72*(1), 218–232.

Elliott, E. S., & Dweck, C. S. (1988). Goals: An approach to motivation and achievement. *Journal of Personality and Social Psychology, 54,* 5–12.

Erikson, E. H. (1968). *Identity: Youth and crisis.* New York: W.W. Norton.

Fabricius, W. V., & Hagen, J. W. (1984). Use of causal attributions about recall performance to assess metamemory and predict strategic memory behavior in young children. *Developmental Psychology, 20,* 975–987.

Ferrari, M. & Mahalingham, R., (1997). Personal cognitive development and its implications for teaching and learning. *Educational Psychologist, 33*(1), 35–44.

Gopnik, A., & Wellman, H. M. (1994). The theory theory. In L. A Hirschfeld & S. A. Gelman (Eds.), *Domain specificity in cognition and culture* (pp. 257–293). New York: Cambridge University Press.

Graham, S., & Harris, K. R. (1994). The role and development of self-regulation in the writing process. In D. H. Schunk & B. J. Zimmerman (Eds.), *Self-regulation of learning and performance: Issues and educational applications* (pp. 203–228). Hillsdale, NJ: Lawrence Erlbaum Associates.

Greeno, J. G. (1997). On claims that answer the wrong question. *Educational Researcher, 26*(1), 5–17.

Halford, G. S. (1999). The properties of representations used in higher cognitive processes: Developmental implications. In I. E. Sigel (Ed.), *Development of mental representation* (pp. 147–168). Mahwah, NJ: Lawrence Erlbaum Associates.

Harachiewicz, J. M., & Baron, K. E. (1998). Rethinking achievement goals: When are they adaptive for college students and why? *Educational Psychologist, 33*(1), 1–21.

Harter, S. (1982). The perceived competence scale for children. *Child Development, 53,* 87–97.

Harter, S. (1990). Causes, correlates and the functional role of global self-worth: A life-span perspective. In R. Sternberg & J. Kolligian, Jr., (Eds.), *Competence considered* (pp. 67–98). New Haven, CT: Yale University Press.

Harter, S. (1999). *The construction of self.* New York: Guilford Press.

Higgins, E. T. (1991). Development of self-regulatory and self-evaluative processes: Costs, benefits, and tradeoffs. In M. R. Gunnar & L. A. Sroufe (Eds.), *Self processes and development: The Minnesota Symposia on Child Development* (Vol. 23, pp. 125–166). Hillsdale, NJ: Lawrence Erlbaum Associates.

James, W. (1890). *Principles of psychology.* Chicago: Encyclopedia Britannica.

Johnston, P., & Winograd, P. (1985). Passive failure in reading. *Journal of Reading Behavior, 17,* 279–301.

Juvonen, J. (1988). Outcome and attributional disagreements between students and their teachers. *Journal of Educational Psychology, 80*(3), 330–336.

Juvonen, J., & Murdock, T. (1995). Grade-level differences in the social value of effort: Implications for self-presentation tactics of early adolescents. *Child Development, 66,* 1694–1705.

Lave, J. (1993). The practice of learning. In S. Chaiklin & J. Lave (Eds.), *Understanding practice: Perspectives on activity and context* (pp. 3–32). New York: Cambridge University Press.

Lave, J., & Wenger, E. (1991). *Situated learning: Legitimate peripheral participation.* New York: Cambridge University Press.

Licht, B. G. (1992). The achievement-related perceptions of children with learning problems: A developmental analysis. In D. H. Schunk & J. L. Meece (Eds.), *Student perceptions in the classroom* (pp. 247–266). Hillsdale, NJ: Lawrence Erlbaum Associates.

Maehr, M. L., & Midgley, C. (1991). Enhancing student motivation: A school-wide approach. *Educational Psychologist, 26,* 399–426.

Markus, H., & Nurius, P. (1986). Possible selves. *American Psychologist, 41,* 954–969.

Marsh, H. W. (1990). The structure of academic self-concept: The Marsh/Shavelson model. *Journal of Educational Psychology, 82,* 623–636.

Marsh, H. W., Byrne, B. M., & Shavelson, R. J. (1988). A multi-faceted academic self-concept. Its hierarchical structure and its relation to academic achievement. *Journal of Educational Psychology, 80,* 366–380.

McCombs, B. L., & Marzano, R. J. (1990). Putting the self in self-regulated learning: The self as agent in integrating will and skill. *Educational Psychologist, 25*(1), 51–69.

Meece, J. (1991). The classroom context and children's motivation goals. In M. Maehr & P. Pintrich (Eds.), *Advances in achievement motivation research* (Vol. 7, pp. 261–286). Greenwich, CT: JAI Press.

Newman, R. S. (1998). Students' help-seeking during problem solving: Influences of personal and contextual goals. *Journal of Educational Psychology, 90,* 644–658.

Nicholls, J. G. (1978). The development of the concepts of effort and ability, perceptions of own attainment, and the understanding that difficult tasks require more ability. *Child Development, 49,* 800–814.

Nicholls, J. G. (1983). Conceptions of ability and achievement motivation: A theory and its implications for education. In S. Paris, G. Olson, & H. Stevenson (Eds.), *Learning and motivation in the classroom* (pp. 211–237). Hillsdale, NJ: Lawrence Erlbaum Associates.

Nicholls, J. G. (1984). Achievement motivation: Conceptions of ability, subjective experience, task choice, and performance. *Psychological Review, 19,* 308–346.

Nicholls, J. G. (1990). What is ability and why are we so mindful of it? A developmental perspective. In R. J. Sternberg & J. Kolligan (Eds.), *Competence considered* (pp. 11–40). New Haven, CT: Yale University Press.

Nicholls, J. G., & Miller, A. T. (1984). Development and its discontents: The differentiation of the concept of ability. In J. G. Nichols (Ed.), *Advances in motivation and achievement* (Vol. 3, pp. 185–218). Greenwich, CT: JAI Press.

O'Sullivan, J. T., & Pressley, M. (1984). Completeness of instruction and strategy transfer. *Journal of Experimental Child Psychology, 38,* 275–288.

Palincsar, A. S., & Brown, A. (1984). Reciprocal teaching of comprehension-fostering and comprehension-monitoring activities. *Cognition and Instruction, 1,* 117–175.

Paris, S. G. (1988). Fusing skill and will in children's learning and schooling. Paper presented at the American Educational Research Association, New Orleans.

Paris, S. G., & Byrnes, J. P. (1989). The constructivist approach to self-regulation and learning in the classroom. In B. Zimmerman & D. Schunk (Eds.), *Self-regulated learning and academic achievement: Theory, research, and practice* (pp. 169–200). New York: Springer-Verlag.

Paris, S. G., Cross, D. R., & Lipson, M. Y. (1984). Informed strategies for learning: A program to improve children's reading awareness and comprehension. *Journal of Educational Psychology, 76,* 1239–1252.

Paris, S. G., & Cunningham, A. E. (1996). Children becoming students. In D. Berliner & R. Calfee (Eds.), *Handbook of Educational Psychology* (pp. 117–147). New York: Macmillan.

Paris, S. G., & Lindauer, B. K. (1982). The development of cognitive skills during childhood. In B. Wolman (Ed.), *Handbook of developmental psychology* (pp. 333–349). Englewood Cliffs, NJ: Prentice-Hall.

Paris, S. G., Lipson, M. Y., & Wixson, K. K. (1983). Becoming a strategic reader. *Contemporary Educational Psychology, 8,* 293–316.

Paris, S. G., & Newmann, R. S. (1990). Developmental aspects of self-regulated learning. *Educational Psychologist, 25,* 87–102.

Paris, S. G., Newman, R. S., & Jacobs, J. E. (1985). Social contexts and functions of children's remembering. In C. J. Brainerd & G. M. Pressley (Eds.), *The cognitive side of memory development* (pp. 81–115). New York: Springer-Verlag.

Paris, S. G., Newman, R. S., & McVey, K. A. (1982). Learning the functional significance of mnemonic actions: A microgenetic study of strategy acquisition. *Journal of Experimental Child Psychology, 34,* 490–509.

Paris, S. G., & Winograd, P. W. (1990). How metacognition can promote academic learning and instruction. In B. J. Jones & L. Idol (Eds.), *Dimensions of thinking and cognitive instruction* (pp. 15–51). Hillsdale, NJ: Lawrence Erlbaum Associates.

Paris, S. G., Wasik, B. A., & Turner, J. C. (1991). The development of strategic readers. In R. Barr, M. Kamil, P. Mosenthal, & P. D. Pearson (Eds.), *Handbook of reading research,* (2nd ed., pp. 609–640). New York: Longman.

Paris, S. G., & Turner, J. C. (1994). Situated motivation. In P. Pintrich, D. Brown, & C. Weinstein (Eds.), *Student motivation, cognition, and learning: Essays in honor of Wilbert J. McKeachie* (pp. 213–237). Hillsdale, NJ: Lawrence Erlbaum Associates.

Phillips, D. A., & Zimmerman, M. (1990). The developmental course of perceived competence and incompetence among competent children. In R. J. Sternberg & J. Kollogian (Eds.), *Competence considered* (pp. 41–66). New Haven, CT: Yale University Press.

Pintrich, P. R. (2000). The role of goal orientation in self-regulated learning. In M. Boekaerts, P. Pintrich, & M. Zeidner (Eds.), *Handbook of self-regulation* (pp. 452–502). NY: Academic Press.

Pintrich, P., & Blumenfeld, P. (1985). Classroom experience and children's self-perceptions of ability, effort, and conduct. *Journal of Educational Psychology, 77,* 646–657.

Pintrich, P. R., & De Groot, E. V. (1990). Motivational and self-regulated learning components of classroom academic performance. *Journal of Educational Psychology, 82*(1), 33–40.

Pintrich, P. R., & Schrauben, B. (1992). Students' motivational beliefs and their cognitive engagement in classroom academic tasks. In D. H. Schunk & J. L. Meece (Eds.), *Student perception in the classroom* (pp. 247–266). Hillsdale, NJ: Lawrence Erlbaum Associates.

Pintrich, P. R., & Schunk, D. H. (1996). *Motivation in education.* Englewood Cliffs, NJ: Prentice Hall.

Pressley, M., & Ghatala, E. S. (1989). Metacognitive benefits of taking a test for children and young adolescents. *Journal of Experimental Child Psychology, 47*(3), 430–450.

Pressley, G. M., & Levin, J. R. (1987). Elaborative learning strategies for the inefficient learner. In S. J. Ceci (Ed.), *Handbook of cognitive, social, and neuropsychological aspects of learning disabilities* (pp. 175–212). Hillsdale, NJ: Lawrence Erlbaum Associates.

Pressley, M., & McCormick, C. B. (1995). *Advanced educational psychology for educators, researchers, and policy-makers.* New York: Harper Collins.

Pressley, G. M., Ross, K. A., Levin, J. R., & Ghatala, E. S. (1984). The role of strategy utility knowledge in children's decision making. *Journal of Experimental Child Psychology, 38,* 491–504.

Pressley, M., Woloshyn, V., & Associates. (1995). *Cognitive strategy instruction that really improves children's academic performance* (2nd ed.). Cambridge, MA: Brookline.

Resnick, L. B. (1987). *Education and learning to think.* Washington, DC: National Academy Press.

Rogoff, B. (1990). *Apprenticeship in thinking: Cognitive development in social context.* New York: Oxford University Press.

Rohrkemper, M., & Corno, L. (1988). Success and failure on classroom tasks: Adaptive learning and classroom teaching. *The Elementary School Journal, 88,* 297–312.

Scardamalia, M., & Bereiter, C. (1986). Fostering the development of self-regulation in children's knowledge processing. In S. S. Chipman, J. W. Segal, & R. Glaser (Eds.), *Thinking and learning skills: Current research and open questions,* (Vol. 2, pp. 563–577). Hillsdale, NJ: Lawrence Erlbaum Associates.

Schneider, W., & Bjorklund, D. F., (1997). Memory. In W. Damon (series Ed.), D. Kuhn, & R. S. Siegler (volume Eds.), *Handbook of Child Psychology: Volume 2. Cognition, Perception and Language* (pp. 467–521). New York: John Wiley & Sons.

Schunk, D. H. (1987). Peer models and children's behavioral change. *Review of Educational Research, 57,* 149–174.

Schunk, D. H., & Zimmerman, B. (1997). Social origins of self-regulatory competence. *Educational Psychologist, 32*(4), 195–208.

Simpson, S. M., Licht, B. G., Wagner, R. K., & Stader, S. P. (1996). Organization of children's academic ability-related self-perceptions. *Journal of Educational Psychology, 88*(3), 387–396.

Skinner, E. (1996). A guide to constructs of control. *Journal of Personality and Social Psychology, 71*(3), 549–570.

Skinner, E. A., Chapman, M., & Baltes, P. B. (1988). Control, means-ends, and agency beliefs: A new conceptualization and its measurement during childhood. *Journal of Personality and Social Psychology, 54,* 117–133.

Spencer, S. J., Steele, C. M., & Quinn, D. M. (1999). Stereotype threat and women's math performance. *Journal of Experimental Social Psychology, 35*(1), 4–28.

Steele, C. M. (1997). A threat in the air: How stereotypes shape intellectual identity and performance. *American Psychologist, 52*(6), 613–629.

Stipek, D. J., & Daniels, D. H. (1988). Declining perceptions of competence: A consequence of changes in the child or the educational environment? *Journal of Educational Psychology, 80,* 352–356.

Stipek, D., & Hoffman, J. (1980). Development of children's performance-related judgments. *Child Development, 51,* 912–914.

Stipek, D., & McIver, D. (1989). Developmental change in children's assessment of intellectual competence. *Child Development, 60,* 521–538.

Stipek, D., & Tannatt, L. (1984). Children's judgments of their own and their peers' academic competence. *Journal of Educational Psychology, 76,* 75–84.

Thompson, T., Davidson, J. A., & Barber, J. G. (1995). Self-worth protection in achievement motivation: Performance effects and attributional behavior. *Journal of Educational Psychology, 87*(4), 598–610.

Turner, J. C. (1995). The influence of classroom contexts on young children's motivation for literacy. *Reading Research Quarterly, 30,* 410–441.

Turner, J. C., Meyer, D. K., Cox, K. E., Logan, C., DiCintio, M., & Thomas, C. (1998). Creating contexts for involvement in mathematics. *Journal of Educational Psychology, 90,* 730–745.

VanLehn, K. (1990). *Mind bugs: The origins of procedural misconceptions.* Cambridge, MA: MIT Press/Bradford.

Vygotsky, L. (1986). *Thought and language.* Cambridge, MA: MIT Press.

Weinstein, C., & Mayer, R. (1986). The teaching of learning strategies. In M. Wittrock (Ed.), *Handbook of research on teaching* (pp. 315–327). New York: Macmillan.

Wellman, H. M. (1988). First steps in the child's theorizing about the mind. In J. Astington, P. Harris, & D. Olson (Eds.), *Developing theories of mind* (pp. 64–92). New York: Cambridge University Press.

Wellman, H. M., & Gelman, S. A. (1992). Cognitive development: Foundational theories of core domains. *Annual Review of Psychology, 43,* 337–375.

Wentzel, K. R. (1996). Social and academic motivation in middle school: Concurrent and long-term relations to academic effort. *Journal of Early Adolescence, 16,* 390–406.

Wigfield, A., Eccles, J. S., Yoon, K. S., Harold, R. D., Arbreton, A., Freedman-Doan, K., & Blumenfeld, P. C. (1996). Changes in children's competence beliefs and subjective task values across the elementary school years: A three year study. *Journal of Educational Psychology, 89*(3), 451–469.

Yussen, S. R., & Kane, P. T. (1985). Children's conception of intelligence. In S. Yussen (Ed.), *The growth of reflection in children* (pp. 207–241). Orlando, FL: Academic Press.

Zimmerman, B. J. (1989). A social-cognitive view of self-regulated academic learning. *Journal of Educational Psychology, 81,* 329–339.

Zimmerman, B. J., & Kitsantas, A. (1997). Developmental phases in self-regulation: Shifting from process to outcome goals. *Journal of Educational Psychology, 89,* 29–36.

Chapter 9

Reflections on Theories of Self-Regulated Learning and Academic Achievement

Barry J. Zimmerman
City University of New York

Dale H. Schunk
Purdue University

Formal investigations of students' self-regulation of their academic learning began less than two decades ago. Initially in the 1970s and early 1980s, researchers focused on the impact of separate self-regulatory processes, such as goal setting, self-efficacy, self-instruction, strategy learning, and self-management, with little consideration for their joint implications regarding students' development of academic learning skill. In the mid-1980s, interest in the topic of academic self-regulation began to coalesce with the publication of journal articles describing various types of self-regulated learning strategies, good strategy users, self-efficacious learners, and metacognitive engagement, among other topics (e.g., Corno & Mandinach, 1983; Pressley, Borkowski, & Schneider, 1987; Schunk, 1984; Simons & Beukhof, 1987; Weinstein & Mayor, 1986; Zimmerman, 1986). An early effort to capture the theoretical diversity in academic self-regulation approaches occurred in 1989 when many of the contributors to this book (Zimmerman & Schunk, 1989) described the historical as well as then contemporary features of major theoretical perspectives on self-regulation. In this volume, we have reassembled these authors to update their theories in light of a decade of research. Each theory has particular strengths in explaining certain aspects of the SRL process, and each theory has provoked controversy regarding some underlying issue. In this final chapter we discuss these theories in terms of their strengths and controversies, which are summarized in Table 9.1. We also consider

TABLE 9.1
Strengths and Controversies Associated With Major Theories of
Self-regulated Learning

Theories of SRL	Strengths	Controversies
Operant	Delay of gratification	Nature of self-reinforcement
Phenomenological	Role of self-identities	Defining, measuring and validating self-identities
Information Processing	Self-monitoring feedback loops	Negative versus positive feedback loops
Social Cognitive	Cognitive goals & expectancies Social modeling	Self-efficacy: redundant or limited in scope
Volitional	Persistence and attention	Separation of volition from motivation
Vygotskian	Self-verbalization and social dialogue	Self-verbalization versus co-constructivism
Constructivist	Personal theories and strategies	Role of cognitive conflict versus situational context

philosophical concerns about psychophysical dualism in contemporary theories of academic self-regulation.

OPERANT VIEWS

Strengths

Operant researchers emphasized that improvements in self-regulatory functioning require learners to forego existing modes of behavior to acquire new ones. Often rewards for making this shift are lacking in the current learning context and become available only after a learner acquires some degree of skill. For example, asking learners to highlight textbook passages is unlikely to produce instantaneous improvements in test performance, but once these learners can identify the type of information that will be tested and can highlight relevant passages, their test scores will increase. These conditions of insufficient initial rewards often undermine students' adoption and maintenance of self-regulatory techniques such as highlighting. Cognitively oriented theorists describe the capability of learners to defer immediate rewards for long term ones as *delay of gratification* (Mischel, 1983), and there is research (Bembenutty & Karabenick, 1998) showing that students' reports of their willingness to delay gratification is related to higher motivation and achievement.

From an operant perspective, learners are unable to delay gratification because of a disparity in reinforcement contingencies between short-term and long-term contexts. Typically, students must give up immediately pleasurable activities, such as television or phone conversations with friends, for delayed academic rewards. Thus, immediate outcomes of studying are inconsistent with long-term ones. The operant approach provides powerful tools for restructuring one's current environmental context to render it more consistent with long-term contexts. This can be accomplished by introducing (a) additional written cues or self-instructions to remind and guide the learner to the delayed rewards, (b) additional self-reinforcers, such as self-administered coffee breaks, for approximations of targeted behavior, and (c) self-recording devices and self-evaluation standards to link current behavioral attainments to the long term reinforcers. In addition, operant researchers can strengthen long-term outcomes if they are insufficiently reinforcing by introducing adjunctive rewards, such as activity privileges or material benefits.

Operant researchers view the introduction of reinforcers pragmatically rather than ideologically. Although natural reinforcers, such as praise for improved test grades, are preferred, subjectively chosen rewards, such as money, are used when necessary to induce students to pursue long-term outcomes. This flexibility in offering diverse reinforcers enables teachers to reach even academically disengaged students. Mace and colleagues (chapter 2, this volume) feel that operant approaches empower learners because they provide choices among alternative courses of action and among immediate and delayed reinforcers.

Controversy

A key dispute raised by operant theorists concerns whether self-reinforcement is a "true" reinforcement process. Essentially, operant theorists argue that because self-reinforcement is under control of the individual, it cannot be true reinforcement. They suggest that individuals must be completely free to self-reinforce in any way they wish. If students self-reinforce according to any external contingency, then the reward they give themselves is considered merely a form of "interresponse" control that is actually determined by external reinforcers.

The underlying point raised by the operant theorists is a good one: Learners do not self-reinforce or otherwise self-regulate in a social environmental vacuum. Self-regulation is not done because it is an inherently good thing to do. Indeed, learners will not use a known self-regulatory procedure unless the conditions and outcomes warrant it. For example, often successful students will not use a highlighting strategy with many forms of materials they read, such as newspapers or signs on the wall—unless, of course, they are graffiti artists! Efforts to self-regulate often demand additional time, planning, and effort, and those requirements differ on the basis of the learners' situational context. The operant approach directs practitioners to assess the impact of varying conditions on performance and to use adjunctive reinforcers, written cues, and other techniques when learners fail to self-regulate.

However, critics argue that self-administered reinforcers do enhance learning like external reinforcers and that learning progress feedback can sustain behavior over time by itself. There is also evidence that learners can come to value the self-regulatory process of learning as important in its own right. For example, students aspiring to become professional writers may find daily and weekly records of writing progress sufficiently reinforcing to sustain writing behavior, even when there are few prospects of eventually publishing the book. Writers such as Gertrude Stein had numerous rejections from publishers before their first work was published (White, 1982). Many aspiring writers have spurned monetary incentives for writing commercial articles to write instead on self-selected topics with little prospect of financial gain. Famous writers as well as other experts, such as composers and artists, often view their successful works not as ends but as mileposts along a path to higher levels of skill. The goal of task mastery can be a powerful motive to learn.

Mace and colleagues discuss self-reactions to self-recording as "reactivity" effects rather than as self-reinforcement or self-punishment. They point out that reactivity often varies due to the motivation of the subject, valence and nature of the target behavior, experimenter instructions or surveillance, timing and nature of self-recording, and self-evaluative goals. There is little disagreement with cognitive theorists that social contextual factors continue to affect learners' reactivity after learners achieve high levels of self-regulation. There also seems little discord about the need to ultimately shift learners from adjunctive reinforcers to natural ones to sustain long-term achievement. Mace and colleagues' emphasis on the role of self-evaluation bridges the historic gap between operant and cognitive views of self-reinforcement. Evaluative standards represent personal mastery criteria for self-reinforcement that are linked to important external contingencies. In our view, the controversy over the authenticity of self-reinforcement is less important than processes that enhance its effectiveness, such as the inclusion of self-evaluative criteria.

PHENOMENOLOGICAL VIEWS

Strengths

There is considerable agreement among theorists about the importance of including the self-perceived identities of the learners in self-regulation accounts. McCombs (chapter 3, this volume) describes self-identity as a key phenomenological component of learners' self-system. How a learner perceives a learning task is evaluated in terms of that learner's sense of identity, such as a scholar, athlete, or leader. Paris and colleagues (chapter 8, this volume) also include self-identity as a key element in their constructivist formulation to explain the long-term motivation of learners more effectively. The latter researchers describe the formation of self-identities developmentally, and they suggest that students' identities change radically during the course of schooling, especially during the elementary and middle school years. Both Paris et al. and McCombs describe how learners begin school in the first grade with highly optimistic views of their effectiveness, but experience a decline in perceived competence as a function of adverse feedback from teachers and social comparisons with classmates. This decline leads some students to reject an academic identity for themselves in favor of other often counterproductive identities, such as prankster, slacker, or jock. Once formed, these identities influence the goals that students set for themselves and methods of learning, and nonacademic identities often prompt students to disengage from academic learning (Steinberg, Dornbush, & Brown, 1996).

The importance of self-perceived identities has attracted other theorists besides phenomenologists and constructivists. Information processing theorists, such as Carver and Scheier (2000), envisioned ideal self goals as the highest goal in learners' hierarchical system. From Carver and Scheier's perspective, students' identities are linked to subordinate goal standards at three successive levels: "be goals," "do goals," and "motor control goals." For students with an academic self-identity, "be goals" refer to attributes of the self, such as "being prepared for class," and "do goals" refer to things that learners do to achieve a "be goal," such as reading assigned material. "Motor control goals" refer to methods of optimizing the "do goals," such as using highlighting to mark key passages that were read.

Academic self-identities are so widely perceived as important that theorists from diverse theoretical traditions now include them in revisions of their theory. Self-identities are seen as the ultimate goals that students use to self-regulate their learning, and experiences that are incompatible with students' identities are avoided. Older students with entrenched nonacademic identities constitute special problems for educators because they strongly resist adopting academic self-regulation techniques. McCombs (present volume) discussed some of the methods that phenomenological educators use to enhance regular students' as well as at-risk students' formation of academic identities.

Controversy

An important controversy centers on how self-identities are defined, measured, and validated. There are tremendous variations in definition of self-identities, with some theorists emphasizing current self-identities (e.g., Harter, 1999) and others emphasizing possible self-identities (Markus & Nurius, 1987). Certain theorists, such as Rogers (1951; 1969) and Maslow (1954) emphasized global definitions of self, whereas other theorists (Harter, 1999; Marsh, 1990) emphasized a hierarchical self-identity structure with increasingly domain-specific measures of self-identity nested within an academic self. Each of these definitions of self-identity leads to different methods of measurement, and the obtained results are often discrepant. In general, domain-specific quantitative measures of self-identities have provided better prediction of performance than global measures, although researchers continue to explore new methods including qualitative approaches. Although high correlations have emerged between domain-specific measures, such as math self-concepts, and achievement, an important validation issue remains: Are self-identity measures merely responsive to students' learning outcomes or are they predictive of future learning efforts? Advocates of self-identity measures usually emphasize the important causal role of self-identity beliefs, but there is more evidence of their reactive role to date.

INFORMATION PROCESSING VIEWS

Strengths

One of the most attractive features of information processing models of self-regulation is their description of self-monitoring processes in terms of feedback loops. Information processing theorists envisioned self-regulation in terms of self-evaluative standards, self-monitoring of performance outcomes relative to those standards, and adjustments or adaptations designed to rectify that performance. Negative discrepancies between feedback and self-evaluative standards compel learners to continue their efforts (i.e., recycling through the loop) until the discrepancies are resolved. This negative discrepancy analysis has provided much precision in explaining how learning efforts are self-adjusted, especially in the face of changing external conditions. The feedback control loop formulation was sufficiently generalizable that it could be used to explain the mechanistic performance of machines, such as thermostats, as well as human cognitive functioning. Because of the noncognitive utility of feedback loops, they can explain human self-regulation when it is automatized as well as when it involves conscious decision making (Vancouver, 2000). These feedback loops can be formed into hierarchies that allow self-evaluative standards of subordinate feedback loops to be controlled by superordinate loops. This hierarchical system of control loops sought to enable information processing theorists to explain how the self-regulatory system could improve itself.

Controversy

There is little debate that negative discrepancy models can explain important aspects of self-regulation, especially anticipated adjustments in performance in predictable environments. However, these models are pressed to explain variations in human reactions to negative feedback during learning in dynamic and unfamiliar environments (Bandura, 1991, in press). Some students develop better strategies and increase their efforts to meet their standards, whereas other students lower their standards and resign themselves to lesser outcomes. Still others may retain their standards but suffer from growing despondency. Finally, we note that the reduction of negative feedback discrepancies can not only confirm attainment of previously set goals but can also lead learners to set new challenging goals for themselves. This was labeled a positive control loop. Thus, the usefulness of feedback loops can be increased if they are expanded to include positive control reactions as well as negative control ones.

SOCIAL COGNITIVE VIEWS

Strengths

Although the importance of goals and expectancies was stressed in many theories of self-regulation, a social cognitive perspective on these two constructs is distinctive in two regards: the definition of goals and expectancies, and their linkage to modeling and other social experiences. Regarding the definition of *goals*, social cognitive theorists emphasized the importance of the situational task context of the learner, such as the completion of a particular homework assignment. Research (Bandura, 1986; Locke & Latham, 1990; Schunk, 1994; Zimmerman & Kitsantas, 1999) established the benefits of setting goals that are task-specific, proximal in their time of attainment, challenging to the individual (i.e., slightly above his or her current performance level), and linked hierarchically from process goals to outcome goals. By contrast, learners who set general goals, distal goals, absolute (unchanging) goals, or nonhierarchical goals are less motivated and successful. The latter properties of goals detract from efforts to self-regulate because (a) learners who lack a specific goal are often unsure about what to do next, (b) learners who set distal goals must wait long periods for corrective feedback, (c) learners who set absolute goals are often discouraged about their seemingly slow progress, and (d) learners who fail to discriminate strategy processes from performance outcomes hierarchically seldom develop high quality technique.

Regarding the formation of expectations, social cognitive theorists emphasized the importance of performance-based measures of expectation, such as self-efficacy. Unlike general expectancies, self-efficacy measures focus on learners' performance in specific contexts, such as solving fraction problems in arithmetic. The superior predictive power of self-efficacy judgments (Bandura, 1997; Schunk & Ertmer, 2000; Zimmerman, 2000b) compared to less task-specific measures of expectation has led to the inclusion of self-efficacy in many theoretical models in this volume. In addition, social cognitive researchers have demonstrated how social models can convey optimal forms of goal setting and can increase learners' sense of self-efficacy to undertake difficult learning tasks (Schunk, 1994).

Controversy

Some critics have charged that self-efficacy is merely a verbal index of a learner's subsequent behavioral performance (Eastman & Marzillier, 1984; Kirsch, 1982), and thus, its superior predictiveness compared to trait (i.e., transitional) measures of expectancy is an illusion. These critics argue that learners are merely describing what they will do behaviorally. In fact, self-efficacy judgments do not correlate perfectly with subsequent performances (Bandura, 1997). A wide range of individual differences in self-efficacy perceptions have emerged that are linked to learners' cognitive skills and social experiences. Learners' ability to accomplish a task requires expert appraisal of a task and a realistic evaluation of their level of skill. Thus, self-efficacy is an expectancy construct that is sensitive to cognitive, affective, and social judgment and is not a proxy for behavior.

A second criticism acknowledges the predictiveness of self-efficacy expectancy measures in a relevant performance context, but questions whether these measures can predict learning outcomes beyond that performance context. Factor analytic research (Bong, 1997) reported evidence that self-efficacy measures in an academic domain such as English do form a higher order *verbal* factor with self-efficacy measures from related academic domains such as Spanish and U.S. history. This verbal self-efficacy factor is, in turn, distinctive from a quantitative self-efficacy factor derived from algebra and geometry self-efficacy measures. Interestingly, the verbal and quantitative self-efficacy factors are also quite highly correlated ($r = .58$). Thus, the domain-related predictive validity of self-efficacy measures is not purchased at the expense of their construct validity with associated self-efficacy measures. Although academic task domains are conceptually distinctive to learners, these domains appear to tap common underlying sources of self-efficacy belief, such as verbal competence.

VOLITION VIEWS

Strengths

Interview and questionnaire studies of self-regulation reveal that students are often uncertain about their ability to resist distracting temptations despite their expressed intentions to study more diligently (e.g., Zimmerman & Martinez-Pons, 1986). At-risk students frequently express their willingness to alter poor study habits and to increase their amount of studying, but they are unable to implement these intentions in courses of action. Volition researchers have focused their theory on explaining this breakdown in persistence. Kuhl (2000) and his associates discussed learners' ability to resist distractions in terms of an action control volition orientation, and Corno (chapter 6, this volume) described a range of strategies that action control learners use to stay the course and remain engaged cognitively, such as restructuring their environment to remove distractions. College students can be encouraged to study in a quiet library rather than a noisy dormitory room and can be taught to control intrusive thoughts of past shortcomings. Volition researchers have compellingly pointed out the need to explain how students become able to resist distractions and ruminative thoughts or comments after undertaking a learning task.

Controversy

Although the need for learners to persist on tasks and to control their attention from various distractions is recognized by most theorists, there is reason to question whether volition is in fact a separate construct from traditional measures of motivation such as expectations or goals. Volitional theorists suggest that after learners commit themselves to a course of action, their initial sources of motivation are no longer operative. They emphasize that the results of learning efforts are being interpreted through a new volitional lens. To date, relatively little evidence has been offered to support this assumption, and there is considerable research to suggest that motivational measures, such as goals and self-efficacy beliefs, not only change during the course of learning, but these altered measures remain predictive of further attempts to learn. To our knowledge, volition measures such as action or state control indices have not proven more predictive of students' persistence during the course of learning than motivational measures, such as goal setting and self-efficacy beliefs.

On the other hand, volition theorists can legitimately argue that preintentional measures of goals or expectancies do not predict all aspects of the subsequent course of learning and that changes in these measures after engaging in learning represent new "volitional" phenomena. Kuhl (2000) sought to reconcile these complex relations using volitional control loops nested within a larger self-regulation network, but the advantages of a distinction between volition and motivation remain unclear.

VYGOTSKY'S VIEW

Strengths

The role of verbalization in the development and use of self-regulatory skill has been widely recognized as a result of Vygotsky's (1962) work. He provided a coherent account of how self-directed speech can guide and improve one's performance and also how students can systematically internalize self-verbalization skill and eventually use it as a conscious strategy. Vygotsky also noted that when children encounter difficult tasks or conditions, they often engage in self-directed speech, such as first graders' spelling aloud as they write each letter of their name. Similarly, adults often resort to overt self-verbalization when working under difficult conditions, such as verbally rehearsing an operator-provided phone number when written records were not available. There is evidence (Berk, 1992) that higher levels of self-directed speech during problem solving are associated with improved achievement, and that children rated by their teachers as high in self-direction engage in twice as much self-initiated task-regulatory speech as do students rated as low in self-direction (Meichenbaum & Beimiller, 1992). These findings support Vygotky's conclusion that bringing behavior under verbal control can significantly improve students' learning efforts.

Learners' verbal facility also enables them to participate as members of a community in coconstructive activities, as McCaslin and Hickey (chapter 7, this volume) described. Thus, the internalization of speech enhances both self-directed and group participatory learning opportunities. Finally, Vygotsky (1962, 1978) provided a compelling account of how self-directive speech is internalized progressively from verbal socialization experiences with adults. As a result of Vygotsky's theory and the research it sparked, most self-regulation researchers now include self-verbalization as a key learning strategy.

Controversy

Differing interpretations of Vygotsky's views of self-regulation led to contrasting academic interventions, with some researchers emphasizing self-verbalization as a cognitive behavioral regulatory technique and others emphasizing dialogue as coconstructive regulatory technique. Vygotsky (1978) discussed modeling as a powerful technique for assisting students to learn in the zone of proximal development, and Meichenbaum (1977) sought to improve students' academic functioning by systematically increasing their use of self-regulatory speech through modeling. He taught self-verbalization through the following multistep learning process. Initially, learners observe an adult model perform a task and articulate the underlying strategy. Then the learners are asked to perform under teacher verbal direction, followed by their performance under self-verbal guidance. Finally, students' self-verbalization is reduced to subvocal whisper level and then discontinued. This cognitive behavioral adaptation of Vygotsky's theory has enabled impulsive children to learn in a more reflective manner and increase their academic performance (Meichenbaum, 1992).

In contrast, other Vygotskian researchers (Diaz, Neal, & Amaya-Williams, 1990) decried self-verbalization training as too behavioral in focus and argued that modeling does not produce optimal levels of internalization and conscious control of learning. Some of these researchers focused instead on group learning processes, such as reciprocal teaching (Palincsar & Brown, 1984) and coconstructive learning (McCaslin & Hickey, this volume). Learners' dialogue with their classmates or teachers regarding new methods to regulate learning is hypothesized to increase the learners' sense of contribution and their commitment to persist in their learning efforts (Butler, 1998). The coconstructivist approach is especially attractive for students who have little initial self-regulatory motivation or skill and who are not current members of effective learning communities.

CONSTRUCTIVIST VIEWS

Strengths

A final quality of self-regulated learners that nearly all theories have embraced is the use of strategies in a metacognitively sophisticated manner. The literature on the effectiveness of learning strategies is well known (Pressley & McCormick, 1995), and there is extensive evidence that successful students use more effective learning strategies than unsuccessful students (Zimmerman & Martinez-Pons, 1986; 1988). Constructivist accounts emphasize the value of personal skill in developing strategies to learn or perform a task, such as using elaborative questioning or note-taking to improve reading comprehension of textbooks. To construct an effective strategy, learners must be able to decompose academic tasks into parts and to organize these parts in a hierarchical sequence, focusing first on the most elementary components. Although general strategies can be chosen from one's repertoire, they must be constructively adapted to a learning context to be effective, such as modifying a self-questioning strategy to better comprehend a particular text passage. Flavell (1979) coined the term *metacognition* to describe knowledge and thinking processes associated with the use of strategies, but Paris and colleagues (present volume) adopted a more encompassing construct— personal theories. They suggest that children appear to develop increasingly elaborate theories about themselves and the worlds around them as they age, and these highly personal theories are postulated to direct children's choice or construction of powerful learning strategies.

Controversy

As Zimmerman noted in his overview chapter to this volume, classic constructivist theories, such as Barlett's (1932) and Piaget's (1952), were cognitive in form. The primary source of a learner's motivation to construct a more developmentally advanced representation was cognitive conflict between an old representation and current experience. Constructivists' emphasis on conflict creation and resolution prompted teachers to use discovery learning and social conflict training methods. In contrast, Paris and colleagues (present volume) focused on the role of the situational context as a primary source of constructive activity rather than cognitive conflict. In their view, learners use their social and physical environment to construct coherent schemas, strategies, or theories.

Historically, situated cognition views (Brown, Collins, & Duguid, 1989) were associated with socially constructive theories, such as Vygotsky's (1978) account, and had very different educational implications than cognitively constructivist accounts. For example, situated cognition researchers advocated creation of social communities of learners who learn in authentic contexts. Collaboration in these contexts is usually structured to engender cooperation rather than conflict. However, it is possible that conflict between learners' existing conceptions of a task and their current experience could be expressed in contextual terms. This is what Paris and colleagues (present volume) sought to achieve in their expanded set of constructivist principles.

BEYOND PSYCHOPHYSICAL DUALISM

As theories of self-regulation attracted increasing international attention, some misconceptions arose regarding the philosophical foundations of contemporary theoretical models (e.g., Prawat, 1998). Each of the theories in this volume depicts self-regulation as an interactive process leading to personal goal attainment, rather than as an inner sensing and thinking mind triumphing over a reluctant outer body. *Psychophysical dualism* refers to theories that assume human nature is composed of two different and mutually irreducible elements: a mind and body (Misiak & Sexton, 1966). Early philosophies, such as Plato's and Descartes', were dualistic because they envisioned an inner person or soul that had to wrestle with a physical body that was unduly influenced by environments that produce boredom, fatigue, pleasure, and pain. Dualist theories assume that a soul or self gains bodily control through stringent training designed to internalize high standards of conduct along with the will to behave according to those standards. According to many dualist models, learners self-regulate in order to experience a sense of inner freedom or autonomy from external forces affecting the body.

There remain a few vestiges of dualism among current views of self-regulation, such as bipolar views of intrinsic and extrinsic motivation and some continuing use of the term *will* to refer to motivation. However, even these labels belie more complex interpretations of the underling phenomena, and the theories in the present volume have avoided describing self-regulation in terms of an inherent mind–body conflict. Because a dualistic perspective sees a fundamental division and conflict between internal and external forces (Dewey, 1988), it treats social and physical environment influences as forces to be overcome rather than as resources for self-attainment (Thoresen & Mahoney, 1974).

Contemporary accounts of self-regulation generally followed pragmatist philosophical traditions of Dewey (1913) and James (1890), which ascribed causality for human functioning to mental–behavioral activities used to adapt to changing environmental conditions. Self-regulatory activities, such as strategy use, self-monitoring, and self-evaluation, are not reducible to either a physical or mental level. Instead, these processes fuse human covert functioning, behavior, and environments in self-enhancing control loops (Zimmerman, 1989; 2000a). For example, students who seek to optimize their study environments must use their knowledge of those environments to develop a cognitive–behavioral strategy for restructuring them and must adapt that strategy to performance feedback that is at once mental, behavioral, and environmental. One's perceived efficacy in making these adaptations is viewed as a powerful motive to continue efforts to learn.

Unlike dualist models, which place causality for self-regulation in the mind of the learner, interactive models of self-regulation attribute causality to the adaptive activity of learners. This activity causally joins one's intended goals, strategic behavior, and environmental consequences in cyclical self-regulatory loops (see Fig. 9.1). Learning strategies are

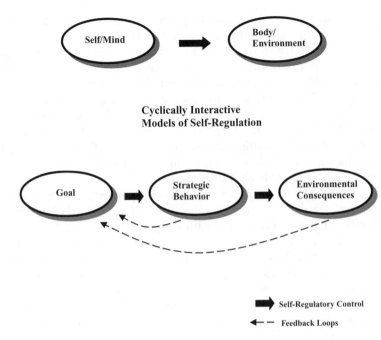

FIG. 9.1. Dualist and cyclically interactive models of self-regulation.

not presumed to be universally effective by self-regulation theorists but rather must be continually adjusted on the basis of their results, such as when a reader shifts the orientation and distance of a book to changing light conditions. From a cyclical perspective, learners self-regulate in order to attain personal goals, such as to read a text passage under lighting conditions that vary unpredictably (Powers, 1998). Cyclical theories define self-regulation in terms of the acquisition and use of specific processes, such as goal setting, strategy use, self-monitoring, and self-evaluative standards, rather than as a perceived state of autonomy.

Although most current self-regulation theorists avoid dualist assumptions, naïve learners do not (Zimmerman, 1998; 1999). As Paris and his colleagues (present volume) suggest, learners form personal theories of self-regulation, and developmentally immature or naïve learners often form dualistic formulations. These simplistic theories can jeopardize these learners' motivation when efforts to learn prove unsuccessful. For example, dualist assumptions lead naive learners to attribute their failures to insufficient will power, and as a result, they perceive little incentive to continue to try (Thoresen & Mahoney, 1974). By contrast, learners who see self-regulation as an acquired skill in orchestrating diverse regulatory processes cyclically will attribute failures to their strategies, which they can readily adjust during subsequent learning attempts. These cyclical learners view social and physical environments as potential resources for self-attainment. For example, there is extensive evidence that highly self-regulated learners seek help more frequently from classmates, teachers, or coaches than poorly regulated learners (Karabenick, 1998; Newman, 1994).

These help-seeking experiences enable learners to regulate better on their own, but there is evidence that even experts continue to rely on periodic social input and support to function at the highest levels of "self" regulation (Zimmerman, 2000a). For example, many of the top athletes, such as golfers and tennis players, retain the services of coaches who advise them regarding lapses in performance. To repeat a point made in the opening chapter of this book, the key issue defining academic learning as self-regulated is not whether it is socially isolated in a dualist sense but rather whether the learner displays personal initiative, perseverance, and cyclically adaptive skill in pursuing it.

CONCLUSION

As researchers became interested in describing and explaining how learners become self-regulatory of their academic learning in the mid-1980s, they drew on well known theories, ranging from operant to constructivist, to guide their hypothesizing. More than a decade of research on academic self-regulation has been conducted, and these theories have evolved due to new research findings and cross-fertilization of ideas. Initially, each theory tended to focus on distinctive aspects of self-regulation, depicted in Table 9.1. Collectively, these theories convey a profile of self-regulated learners who achieve academic success by delaying immediate gratification for later academic rewards and by forming an academic personal identity. Self-regulated students learn by monitoring their performance-related feedback and by setting goals and forming expectancies regarding specific academic contexts. Finally, these learners succeed by remaining attentive despite situational distractions and adverse outcomes, by self-verbalizing and coconstructing effective courses of academic learning, and by cognitively constructing strategies and theories to master academic tasks.

Inevitably, these differing theories produced controversies over key issues, such as whether external reinforcers are essential to intervention programs and how to measure and validate students' perceptions of self-identity. Other points of contention center on the need for positive as well as negative control loops related to self-monitoring and the need for task-specific goals and expectations, such as self-efficacy beliefs. Another contentious issue, the distinction between motivation and volition, remains unresolved, and the importance of cognitive conflict assumptions to constructivist accounts is less prominent than a decade ago. A final point of contention involved the relative effectiveness of self-verbalization and coconstructive dialogue.

Clearly, theoretical descriptions and understanding of how students become self-regulated have grown more detailed and elaborate during the last decade; however, many questions remain. As educators began to train students to use self-regulatory techniques (Schunk & Zimmerman, 1998), questions arose about the philosophical as well as pedagogical ramifications of research on students' self-regulation. Concern about possible psychophysical dualism was raised and whether contemporary models of self-regulation can avoid the philosophical pitfalls that entrapped earlier models, such as defining self-regulation as an autonomous inner state. Although some vestiges of dualist assumptions remain in contemporary accounts, the models described in this volume have depicted self-regulation instead in terms of skillfully orchestrating processes that are at once covert, behavioral, and environmental.

The pedagogical implications of self-regulation research have been explored through both experiments (Schunk & Zimmerman, 1994) and intervention studies (Schunk & Zimmerman, 1998), and researchers have reported compelling results in improving students' academic functioning throughout this volume. These academic achievements parallel gains from the use of self-regulation techniques in related fields, such as health, sports, business, music, and professional writing (Bandura, 1997; Zimmerman, 1998). High levels of excellence in almost any field require disciplined learning and practice, and experts report extensive use of self-regulatory techniques (Zimmerman, in press). As we enter the 21st century, impressive programs of research on self-regulation of academic learning have begun in Europe, North America, Australia, Africa, and Asia (Boekaerts, Pintrich, & Zeidner, 2000). The controversies we discussed will compel additional research and interventions, and we anticipate that the theories described in this volume will continue to evolve.

REFERENCES

Bandura, A. (1986). *Social foundations of thought and action: A social cognitive theory*. Englewood Cliffs, NJ: Prentice-Hall.

Bandura, A. (1991). Self-regulation of motivation through anticipatory and self-reactive mechanisms. In R. A. Dienstbier (Ed.), *Perspectives on motivation: Nebraska symposium on motivation* (Vol. 38, pp. 69–164). Lincoln: University of Nebraska Press.

Bandura, A. (1997). *Self-efficacy: The exercise of control.* New York: W. H. Freeman.

Bandura, A. (in press). Exploration of fortuitous determinants of life paths. *Psychological Inquiry.*

Bartlett, F. C. (1932). *Remembering.* London: Cambridge University Press.

Bembenutty, H., & Karabenick, S. A. (1998). Academic delay of gratification. *Learning and Individual Differences, 10,* 329–346.

Berk, L. E. (1992). Children's private speech: An overview of theory and the status of research. In L. E. Berk & R. Diaz (Eds.), *Private speech: From social interaction to self-regulation* (pp. 17–54). Hillsdale, NJ: Lawrence Erlbaum Associates.

Boekaerts, M., Pintrich, P. R., & Zeidner, M. (Eds.). (2000). *Self-regulation: Theory, research, and applications.* Orlando, FL: Academic Press.

Bong, M. (1997). Generality of academic self-efficacy judgments: Evidence of hierarchical relations. *Journal of Educational Psychology, 89,* 696–709.

Brown, J. S., Collins, A., & Duguid, P. (1989). Situated cognition and the culture of learning. *Educational Researcher, 18,* 32–42.

Butler, D. L. (1998). A strategic content learning approach to promoting self-regulated learning by students with learning disabilities. In D. H. Schunk & B. J. Zimmerman (Eds.), *Self-regulated learning: From teaching to self-reflective practice* (pp. 160–183). New York: Guilford Press.

Carver, C. S., & Scheier, M. F. (2000). On the structure of behavioral self-regulation. In M. Boekaerts, P. Pintrich, & M. Zeidner (Eds.), *Self-regulation: Theory, research, and applications* (pp. 42–84). Orlando, FL: Academic Press.

Corno, L., & Mandinach, E. (1983). The role of cognitive engagement in classroom learning and motivation. *Educational Psychologists, 18,* 88–108.

Dewey, J. (1913). *Interest and effort in education.* Boston: Riverside.

Dewey, J. (1988). Appendix. In J. A. Boydston (Ed.), *John Dewey: The later works (1925–1953, Vol. 14, pp. 379–410).* Carbondale, IL: Southern Illinois University Press. (Original work published 1940).

Diaz, R. M., Neal, C. J., & Amaya-Williams, M. (1990). The social origins of self-regulation. In L. C. Moll (Ed.), *Vygotsky and education: Instructional implications and applications of sociohistorical psychology* (pp. 127–154). New York: Cambridge University Press.

Eastman, C., & Marzillier, J. S. (1984). Theoretical and methodological difficulties in Bandura's self-efficacy theory. *Cognitive Therapy and Research, 8,* 231–230.

Flavell, J. H. (1979). Metacognition and cognitive monitoring: A new era of cognitive developmental inquiry. *American Psychologist, 34,* 906–911.

Harter, S. (1999). *The construction of self: A developmental perspective.* New York: Guilford Press.

James, W. (1890). *Principles of psychology.* New York: Holt.

Karabenick, S. A. (1998). *Strategic help-seeking: Implications for learning and teaching.* Mahwah, NJ: Lawrence Erlbaum Associates.

Kirsch, I. (1982). Efficacy expectations as response predictors: The meaning of efficacy ratings as a function of task characteristics. *Journal of Personality and Social Psychology, 42,* 132–136.

Kuhl, J. (2000). A functional-design approach to motivation and self-regulation: The dynamics of personality systems and interactions. In M. Boekaerts, P. Pintrich, & M. Zeidner (Eds.), *Self-regulation: Theory, research, and applications* (pp. 111–169). Orlando, FL: Academic Press.

Locke, E. A., & Latham, G. P. (1990). *A Theory of goal setting and task performance.* Englewood Cliffs, NJ: Prentice-Hall.

Markus, H., & Nurius, P. (1987). Possible selves: The interface between motivation and the self-concept. In K. Yardley & T. Honess (Eds.), *Self and identity: Psychosocial perspectives.* New York: Wiley.

Marsh, H. W. (1990). The structure of academic self-concept: The Marsh/Shavelson model. *Journal of Educational Psychology, 82,* 623–636.

Maslow, A. (1954). Motivation and personality. New York: Harper.

Meichenbaum, D. H. (1977). *Cognitive behavior modification*. New York: Plenum.

Meichenbaum, D. (1992). *Cognitive behavior modification: An integrative approach*. New York: Plenum Press.

Meichenbaum, D., & Biemiller, A. (1992). Task-regulatory speech of self-directed learners. In M. Pressley, K. Harris, & J. Guthrie (Eds.), *Promoting academic competence and literacy in school* (pp. 3–56). New York: Academic Press.

Mischel, W. (1983). Delay of gratification as a process and as person variable in development. In D. Magnusson & V. P. Allen (Eds.), *Human development: An interactional perspective* (pp. 149–165). New York: Academic Press.

Misiak, H., & Sexton, V. S. (1966). *The history of psychology: An overview*. New York: Grune & Stratton.

Newman, R. (1994). Academic help-seeking: A strategy of self-regulated learning. In D. H. Schunk & B. J. Zimmerman (Eds.), *Self-regulation of learning and Performance: Issues and educational applications* (pp. 283–301). Hillsdale, NJ: Lawrence Erlbaum Associates.

Palincsar, A. S., & Brown, A. (1984). Reciprocal teaching of comprehension-fostering and comprehension-monitoring activities. *Cognition and Instruction, 1,* 117–175.

Piaget, J. (1952). *The origins of intelligence in children*. New York: International Universities Press.

Powers, W. T. (1998). *Making sense of behavior: The meaning of control*. New Canaan, CT: Benchmark Press.

Prawat, R. (1998). Current self-regulation views of learning and motivation viewed through a Deweyan lens: The problems with dualism. *American Educational Research Journal, 35,* 199–224.

Pressley, M., Borkowski, J. G., & Schneider, W. (1987). Cognitive strategies: Good strategy users coordinate metacognition and knowledge. In R. Vasta & G. Whitehurst (Eds.), *Annals of child development* (Vol. 5, pp. 89–129). Greenwich, CT: JAI Press.

Pressley, M. J., & McCormick, C. (1995). *Advanced educational psychology for educators, researchers, and policymakers*. New York: HarperCollins.

Rogers, C. R. (1951). *Client-centered therapy: Its current practice, implications, and theory*. Boston: Houghton Mifflin.

Rogers, C. R. (1969). *Freedom to learn*. Columbus, OH: Merrill.

Schunk, D. H. (1984). The self-efficacy perspective on achievement behavior. *Educational Psychologist, 19,* 199–218.

Schunk, D. (1994). Self-regulation of self-efficacy and attributions in academic settings. In D. H. Schunk & B. J. Zimmerman (Eds.), *Self-Regulation of learning and performance: Issues and educational applications*. Hillsdale, NJ: Lawrence Erlbaum Associates.

Schunk, D. H., & Ertmer, P. (2000). Self-regulation and academic learning: self-efficacy enhancing interventions. In M. Boekaerts, P. Pintrich, & M. Zeidner (Eds.), *Self-regulation: Theory, research, and applications* (pp. 631–649). Orlando, FL: Academic Press.

Schunk, D. H., & Zimmerman, B. J. (Eds.) (1994). *Self-regulation of learning and performance: Issues and educational applications*. Hillsdale, NJ: Erlbaum, Inc.

Schunk, D. H., & Zimmerman, B. J. (Eds.) (1998). *Self-regulated learning: From teaching to self-reflective practice*. New York: Guilford Press.

Simons, R. P. J., & Beukhof, G. (1987). *Regulation of learning*. Gravenhage, Netherlands: S.V.O.

Steinberg, L., Dornbush, R., & Brown, B. (1996). *Beyond the classroom*. New York: Simon & Shuster.

Thoresen, C., & Mahoney, M. J. (1974). *Behavioral self-control*. New York: Holt, Rinehart & Winston.

Vancouver, J. B. (2000). Self-regulation in organizational settings: A tale of two paradigms. In M. Boekaerts, P. Pintrich, & M. Zeidner (Eds.), *Self-regulation: Theory, research, and applications* (pp. 303–341). Orlando, FL: Academic Press.

Vygotsky, L. S. (1962). *Thought and language* (E. Hanfman & G. Vakar, Eds.). Cambridge, MA: MIT Press.

Vygotsky, L. S. (1978). *Mind in society: The development of higher psychological processes.* Cambridge, MA: Harvard University Press.

Weinstein, C. E., & Mayor, R. E. (1986). The teaching of learning strategies. In M. C. Wittrock (Ed.), *Handbook of research on teaching.* (pp. 315–327). New York: Macmillan.

White, J. (1982). *Rejection.* Reading, MA: Addison-Wesley.

Zimmerman, B. J. (1986). Development of self-regulated learning: Which are the key sub-processes? *Contemporary Educational Psychology, 16,* 307–313.

Zimmerman, B. J. (1989). A social cognitive view of self-regulated academic learning. *Journal of Educational Psychology, 81,* 329–339.

Zimmerman, B. J. (1998). Academic studying and the development of personal skill: A self-regulatory perspective. *Educational Psychologist, 33,* 73–86.

Zimmerman, B. J. (1999). Commentary: Toward a cyclically interactive view of self-regulated learning. *International Journal of Educational Research,* in press.

Zimmerman, B. J. (2000a). Attainment of self-regulation: A social cognitive perspective. In M. Boekaerts, P. Pintrich, & M. Zeidner (Eds.), *Self-regulation: Theory, research, and applications* (pp. 13–39). Orlando, FL: Academic Press.

Zimmerman, B. J. (2000b). Self-efficacy: An essential motive to learn. *Contemporary Educational Psychology, 25,* 82–91.

Zimmerman B. J. (in press). Achieving academic excellence: A self-regulatory perspective. In M. Ferrari (Ed.) *Pursuit of excellence.* Mahwah, NJ, Lawrence Erlbaum Associates.

Zimmerman, B. J., & Kitsantas, A. (1999). Acquiring writing revision skill: Shifting from process to outcome self-regulatory goals. *Journal of Educational Psychology, 91,* 1–10.

Zimmerman, B. J., & Martinez-Pons, M. (1986). Development of a structured interview for assessing students' use of self-regulated learning strategies. *American Educational Research Journal, 23,* 614–628.

Zimmerman, B. J., & Martinez-Pons, M. (1988). Construct validation of a strategy model of student self-regulated learning. *Journal of Educational Psychology, 80,* 284–290.

Zimmerman, B. J., & Schunk, D. H. (Eds.). (1989). *Self-regulated learning and academic achievement: Theory, research, and practice.* New York: Springer.

Author Index

A

Abrahams, S., 100
Abramson, L. V., 266
Ach, N., 194
Ackerman, A., 46
Ackerman, P. L., 107, 172, 175, 185
Allen, E. M., 55
Alpert, G. P., 82
Altman, J., 47
Amaya–Williams, M., 27, 299
Ames, C., 100, 198, 243, 264, 269–270
Ames, R., 198
Anderson, J. R., 155–157, 159, 174, 255, 257–258
Anderson, S. M., 90
Andreassen, C., 201
APA Task Force on Psychology in Education, 112
APA Work Group of the Board of Educational Affairs, 112
Areglado, R. J., 106
Asher, S. R., 243

B

Baer, D. M., 10, 45, 47–48, 54, 57
Baird, J. R., 91
Baltes, P. B., 268
Bandura, A., 7, 19–20, 52, 90–91, 125–126, 128–130, 132–135, 144, 179–180, 196, 198, 209, 213, 234–235, 245, 267, 276, 295–296, 304
Barbaranelli, C., 91
Barber, B., 76
Barber, J. G., 266
Baron, A., 19
Baron, K. E., 270
Baron, J., 180–181
Bartlett, F. C., 29, 300

Bass, B. A., 54–55
Batstone, P., 56
Baumrind, D., 245
Beckmann, J., 194
Belansky, E., 76
Belfiore, P. J., 11, 43, 46, 49–51, 55, 131
Bembenutty, H., 206, 290
Benenson, J., 30
Bereiter, C., 208, 220, 269, 273
Berk, L. E., 298
Berliner, D. C., 220, 238, 244
Berlyne, D., 30
Bershon, B., 240, 247
Beukhof, G., 204, 289
Biddle, B., 238
Biemiller, A., 170, 298
Bijou, S. W., 10
Bjorklund, D. F., 273
Black, J. L., 46
Blakely, E., 39
Blom, D. E., 32
Bloom, B. S., 3
Blumenfeld, P. C., 13, 205, 263, 266, 271
Blyth, D. A., 30
Boehme, R., 39
Boekaerts, M., 96, 204, 277, 279, 304
Boggiano, A. K., 145
Bondy, E., 269
Bong, M., 296
Bonner, S., 140, 142
Boo, J., 97
Borkowski, J. G., 178, 289
Bossert, S. T., 271
Bowers, D. S., 54
Bowers, J., 255, 257
Boyd, C. M., 44
Boykin, A. R., 47
Boyle, R. A., 160, 178–179
Bozhovich, L. I., 233
Bracht, G. H., 3
Braden, J., 238

Subject Index

DATE DUE

6/24			
DEC 1 3 2014			
DEC 0 1 2014			